THE HOME REPORTER

A MANUAL FOR BUYERS AND HOMEOWNERS

Published by
Home Reporter Systems
Chester, Virginia
800-328-6775

Table of Contents

Table of Contents

Table of Contents

Table of Contents

Table of Contents

Table of Contents

Table of Contents

Table of Contents

Table of Contents

Table of Contents

Table of Contents

Table of Contents

Table of Contents

such as the original quality of the material, attic ventilation, sun angles, air pollution, the structure below, etc. The inspector is making the broadest of assumptions.

1.2.3 NUMBER OF LAYERS

The number of layers stated generally applies to asphalt shingles. All shingle roofs have several layers created by the shingling effect, but this is not the issue. Here the inspector is speaking of the number of different layers, applied at different times. This is important with asphalt shingle roofs because second layers, as a rule, do not last as long as the first. The preceding layer(s) tend to cause heat build up and may trap moisture, both of which may age the top layer prematurely. Second layers have their original life expectancy shortened by 10 to 50 percent. Third layers are usually prohibited by local codes. They add too much weight to the structure. If there are two layers, remove them before applying new roofing.

A second layer, called a nail over, may be applied if one layer is present. Removing the original layer, called a tear off, is a better job. Any uneven texture in the old roofing will show through the new roofing. Since a "nail over" can be 25% cheaper than a "tear off," most people opt for a second layer.

Occasionally, other types of roofing have more than one layer. (i.e. asphalt shingles over wood shingles, tin over asphalt etc.) These are unusual and should be discussed with an inspector or roofing expert.

1.2.4 ESTIMATED REMAINING LIFE

The inspector's opinion or estimation of remaining life in terms of years, assuming proper maintenance and repairs.

1.2.5 PRIOR LEAKS/CURED (YES OR NO)

It is impossible to prove or disprove whether a stain or similar evidence of a leak represents a current active leak or an old cured leak. If it has not rained in a day or two every leak appears

cured. The inspector may have to be "fortunate" to be there during or soon after a rain to detect an actual leak. Some leaks only leak under certain conditions, (rain and wind from the east at 30 MPH, etc.) and appear cured until the conditions reoccur. If it has leaked before, it may leak again. (See the Interior chapter for information on stains or other clues of cured or active leaks.)

1.2.5 a.
Pans in the attic may be a clue
and tell tale sign of active or prior
leaks in the roofing.

1.2.6 ACTIVE LEAKS (YES OR NO)

The inspector is reasonably sure the roofing is leaking now. They either saw or detected water below the roof covering. Cure active leaks immediately to protect the structure and contents.

1.1.2.3 a. Snow or Ice
The part of the roofing
covered by ice and snow
cannot be inspected.

1.1.2.4 MOISTURE OR FUNGUS

Moisture makes roofs slippery. Fungus, mold, and moss can block the inspector's view and make walking the roof hazardous. Fungus, mold, and moss may hide unsound roofing. (Also read 1.1.2 Restricted.)

1.1.2.5 HAZARDOUS

Hazardous to either the inspector or the roof. Slate roofs are never walked because loose slates could slip under the inspector. These roofs are generally steep, and the inspector could damage or break the slates causing leaks. Wooden roofs, clay tiles, asbestos cement, and cement tile roofs are similarly hazardous. Most of these roofs are unsafe to walk for owners as well. Leave repairs and maintenance to the professionals. Walking an asphalt roof in hot or cold weather could damage the roofing and cause it to leak. Walking on asphalt shingles exhibiting advanced cupping and curling can crush or break the shingles. (Also read 1.1.2 Restricted.)

1.1.2.6 BLANK SPACE

A space provided for the inspector to write. (Also read 1.1.2 Restricted.)

1.2 GENERAL ROOFING

A quick reference and overview of the inspector's opinions or impressions. This section is subjective and relies on the inspector's judgment and experience in estimating the age, whether clues are important and if toxins are present, etc. (Read the Roofing chapter fully before forming any final opinion.)

1.2.1 SYSTEM INSPECTED (YES, RESTRICTED, OR NO)

The inspector marks whether the system was inspected. No information will be given about a system that was not inspected. If the inspector writes in or circles "R" for restricted, the system was partially inspected. Check section 1.1 Limitations or discuss it with the inspector to learn the full extent of the restrictions. A severely limited inspection may not give you the information you need. You should do whatever is necessary to remove or overcome the restrictions and have the system fully inspected before you close on the house. (Read 1.1 Limitations.)

1.2.2 ESTIMATED AGE

The inspector's opinion of the apparent age of the upper or top layer of roofing. It is impossible to tell the actual age of the roofing material. Many things affect the aging process

1.3.1 d. Ground
Professional inspectors are trained to
spot apparent defects from the ground.

1.3.2 EAVES

The inspector stands on a deck rail, ladder or leans from a window to observe the roof. This inspection is visual and limited to what could be seen from the vantage point at the time of the inspection. (Read also section 1.3 Roof as Seen From:)

1.3.3 WALKED

The inspector mounted and walked on the roof. Walking a roof will only be done when the inspector thinks it is necessary and safe. Every attempt will be made to walk flat or built up roofs. (Read also sections 1.1 Limitations, 1.3 Roof as Seen From:)

1.3.4 BINOCULARS

Inspectors may use binoculars to improve their view of the roof. (Read also section 1.3 Roof As Seen From:)

1.3.5 NONE (NOT SEEN)

The inspector was unable to see the roof. Perhaps there was no roof scuttle, or the roof geometry or parapet walls made it invisible. This severely limits the inspection and inspectors can only comment on what they have seen. Make arrangements for access to the roof for a proper roof inspection before closing if you are buying. (Read also sections 1.1 Limitations and 1.3 Roof As Seen From:)

1.4 STYLES

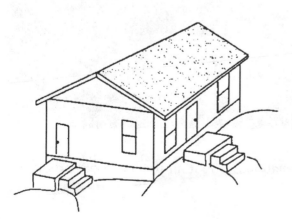

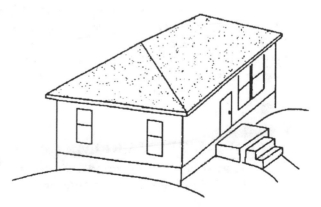

1.4.1 GABLE ROOF

1.4.2 HIP ROOF

1.2.7 FLASHING LEAKS (YES OR NO)

The inspector believes the flashing is leaking now. Flashing leaks are the most common of all roof leaks. Roofs tend to leak where a valley, dormer, plumbing stack, skylight, etc. interrupt the roofing. Flashing leaks can be very difficult and expensive to find and cure.

1.2.8 AMATEUR WORKMANSHIP (YES OR NO)

"YES" The inspector notes workmanship of less than professional quality. Poor workmanship may constitute a major defect. Major defects cost $500.00 or more to repair or may affect the habitability of the house. The work may not serve the purpose intended and will require repair or replacement.

"NO" No amateur workmanship was noted. Some amateurs produce workmanship of equal or better quality than professionals.

1.2.9 SUBJECTIVE RATING

The inspector's grade for the roofing system:

E   EXCELLENT, above average, new or like new. (e.g. a new roof on an older house.)

A   AVERAGE, in typical condition for its age, showing normal wear and tear. (e.g. five year old roof that looks 5 years old and a 5 year old house.)

C   BELOW AVERAGE, prematurely aged, showing heavy or excess wear and tear, or delayed maintenance. Perhaps showing minor (curable) defects. (e.g. A five year old roof that shows the wear and tear or age characteristics of a 10 year old roof.)

F   SUBSTANDARD, failed, or reaching the end of its life expectancy. Any further service, even with repairs, should be considered a gift.

1.2.9 a. Failing Asphalt Shingles.
Most people do not allow the roofing to deteriorate this badly before replacing. The risk of a leak is high. Notice the peeling paint on the trim and gutters. This house has 2.3.2.8 Cement Asbestos Shingle Siding.

1.3 ROOF AS SEEN FROM:

The inspector's location when they made their observations.   Not all roofs can or should be walked. (Read also section 1.1 Limitations.)

1.3.1 GROUND

Most roofs are inspected from the ground without the use of binoculars, etc.   A roof inspection is limited to items seen from that vantage point. (Read also section 1.3 Roof As Seen From:)

Keep the roofing, flashings, gutters, etc. in good repair. Read the sections applying to your house carefully for more information on maintaining your particular roofing system. Some types of roofing require frequent maintenance.

1.1 LIMITATIONS

This section describes the aspects which limit the inspection of the roof or roofing. Inspectors do the best inspection they can, but sometimes physical obstructions, weather conditions, or the condition of the roofing, prevents them from doing the whole job. In northern climates, there can be so much snow on the roof the inspector cannot identify the type of material or condition. Arrange for an inspection overcoming the limitations if possible (i.e. come back after the snow melts, even if it's in the spring). It is your responsibility to overcome the limitations. You should complete the inspection prior to closing even if you must hire others (roofers, flashing contractor's etc.) or pay an additional fee to the inspector or roofing industry specialist. Roofing repairs can be expensive and at some point replacement is the best alternative. An uninspected roof or one given a severely limited or restricted inspection could be a total unknown. The inspector cannot make representations about what was not inspected. If you purchase a house with a limited or restricted inspection you are accepting the responsibility for the unknown items about the system.

1.1.1 TYPICAL

The inspector feels they have seen as much of the roof as they normally see. The roof is inspected from the ground, while walking around the house, and from a distance ranging from several feet to perhaps the limits of the site. A typical inspection does not include pouring water on the roof or using a water hose to cause or induce leaks. (Also read section 1.1 Limitations.)

1.1.2 RESTRICTED

The inspector feels they have seen less of the roof than they typically see. (Also read section 1.1.1 Typical.) Some common restrictions are: no access to the roof either because the scuttle or hatch is sealed or doesn't exist; the roof is too steep; there is snow or ice restricting the inspectors view; moisture or fungus is present; or it is too hazardous. Read the following sections below for more detail on these restrictions.

1.1.2.1 NO ACCESS
(1)   No roof scuttle or access hatch found.
(2)   The roof scuttle or access hatch was sealed or locked.
(3)   The roof was too high for an inspector to reach with a 6 foot ladder.
        Inspectors carry one six foot ladder only. (Read section 1.1.2 Restricted.)

1.1.2.2 TOO STEEP

The roof is too steep to walk safely. This is a judgment call by the individual inspector. (Also read section 1.1.2 Restricted.)

1.1.2.3 SNOW OR ICE

Snow and ice prevent the inspector from walking the roof and from seeing it. The leaks may be frozen, also. Melting snow and ice can start leaks. Reinspect after the snow melts and before closing. It is not the responsibility of the inspector to remove ice, snow, leaves, etc. that prohibit observation of the roof. (Read 1.1.2 Restricted.)

CHAPTER ONE

ROOF

People have always concerned themselves with having a "roof over their head" because of climatic conditions such as rain, snow, wind, etc. Shelter is a basic need of man.

The type of roof has been dictated by the availability of materials. In warm climates a thatched roof was adequate to allow the water to run off. Wood shakes used during colonial days were of decay resistant cypress and oak that was readily available. Protection from the elements, durability, and fire resistance were concerns.

The roof's design and material are aspects of the architectural beauty of any structure. Today, technology has given us many types of materials such as asphalt roofing, clay tiles, asbestos cement, and a host of single ply membranes. Consider style, color, fire and wind resistance, economy, weight, and life expectancy when choosing roofing materials.

Roofing is measured in "squares." A square covers 100 square feet. Various types of roofing weigh different amounts per square. Some are so heavy the structure must be designed for them. Certain types are suitable for only particular pitches. Pitch or slope is the steepness of the roof stated as the amount of rise in 12 feet. (i.e. 4 in 12, 8 in 12, even 14 in 12, etc.)

Roofing materials and their suitable applications are discussed in this chapter. Read carefully each section that applies to your roof. If you have any questions, ask the inspector.

MAINTENANCE AND UPKEEP

The roof protects the structure from the weather. With a sound roof the structural components may last a long time. If the roof leaks, the structure begins to deteriorate rapidly.

Inspect the attic and roofing in the Spring. It is best to do this during a heavy rain looking for evidence of water infiltration, especially wherever something protrudes through the roof. Check for wet insulation, evidence of bird or rodent infestation, hornets, termites and/or woodborers, etc. in the attic. This gives you an opportunity to make repairs during the mild months.

Roofing starts aging the day it's installed. Weather wears the material slowly, but violent weather can destroy even a new roof. Sunlight destroys some types of roofing with heat and ultraviolet light. Water and cold are also harmful. Water in warm weather causes decay and in cold weather freezes in cracks and crevices enlarging them. Water also rusts iron and steel materials.

Chimney flashings leak at one time or another. Most chimneys are independent structures standing beside the house. Frame houses and masonry chimneys often respond (move) differently with changes in the weather and temperature. These different movements mean the flashing is constantly expanding and contracting and is prone to leak.

Therefore, if 1.5.1.2 Fiberglass Matrix Shingles is marked, read it and each of the preceding sections for more information on your roof. Also read any sections cross referenced in each section.

The checklist's organization is consistent from chapter to chapter. In the upper left corner is **Limitations**. The upper right is **General summary**. The left side of the page is **Identification** and the right side is **Observations**. At the bottom are **Comments, Estimated Annual Maintenance and Estimated Cost of Repairs.**

THE HOME REPORTER helps an inspector do a good inspection and prepare a useful report in a timely fashion. The owner benefits from the system because the book also serves as an owner's manual and provides suggestions for maintenance. It may help owners understand their homes better. The owner can use the book alone, but this is not a substitute for a professional inspection. There is no substitute for experience and training.

PREFACE

THE HOME REPORTER helps a professional inspect your home and report the results. It is also an owner's manual with maintenance and upkeep suggestions. The checklist with the book quickly summarizes the results of the inspection. Each of nine chapters describes a system or item in five sections:

Limitations describe the factors limiting the inspection. Homeowners and inspectors face the same limitations. e.g. Neither the homeowner nor the inspector can see an improperly concealed electrical splice. The inspector is not responsible for removing the limitations restricting the inspection. You should remove the limitations where possible and have every system fully inspected before closing. The responsibility is yours. Read further about limitations of inspectors in the **INTRODUCTION** section of this manual. Also each chapter discusses the limitations on each system.

General is a quick reference and overview of the inspection. Read the whole report before forming a final opinion.

Identification sections describe the equipment or materials giving the characteristics, life expectancy, maintenance, upkeep, etc..

Observations disclose conditions affecting the systems or materials. Some are part of normal aging and others require immediate repair.

Estimated Costs of Repairs are estimates from the inspector's judgment or a range of prices in the area. Get repair bids from reputable licensed contractors willing to do the work before making any decision. The cost ranges are an "order of magnitude" figure indicating the significance of the defect or problem observed by the inspector.

Estimated Annual Maintenance Costs gives an idea whether the cost of maintaining the system is low, high, or typical. Low is marked when the inspector anticipates the system may have below typical maintenance costs. Typical maintenance includes upkeep done on most houses and systems while aging. High is marked when the inspector anticipates maintenance costs will be higher than typical and indicates it would be wise to budget for replacement.

THE HOME REPORTER tells you what the inspector saw and its condition. The format is the same throughout the book and checklist. The number system ties it together. It looks complicated, but is simple. Every item checked has an unique number. The first digit is the chapter number. Other digits are section, subsections and items.

Example: 1.5.1.2 Fiberglass Matrix Shingles

Chapter	1	is ROOF
Section	1.5	is Roofing Materials
Subsection	1.5.1	is Asphalt
Item	1.5.1.2	is Fiberglass Matrix Shingles

house. The home inspector will never be able to predict every repair or maintenance item encountered while owning a house. An inspection does not constitute an insurance policy. It gives you an impression of the condition of the house and discloses necessary repairs. Insurance may pay for future repairs, but tells you nothing about the condition of the house.

Does an inspection predict future performance? Not really. Statistically, a one year old water heater should last at least 5 to 10 years. It may not. A 23 year old asphalt shingle roof probably will not last another year. It could last 5 years. Water use, heat settings, and maintenance differ from owner to owner.

Are there any other sources of information about this house? YES. Information can be obtained from realtors, county records, utility companies, appraisers, and mortgage companies, etc.. Do not forget the seller! No one source should be relied on when making the decision to purchase. You may have to find experts who perform more extensive tests. The inspection is not a recommendation of whether you should "buy" or "not buy" the property. Home inspections do not disclose the suitability of a building for a specific purpose or function. (e.g (1) A house appearing spacious occupied by a couple may feel crowded and cramped occupied by a family of six. The equipment may suffer from the additional wear and tear. (2) A residence converted into an office. The zoning, parking, and engineering required are outside the scope of the inspection.)

Is there anything a buyer should not expect a home inspector to do at an inspection. YES. Generally home inspections are visual and not technically exhaustive. Each major part of the house may have some limitations preventing the inspector from completing the inspection. It is your responsibility to see that steps are taken to remove those restrictions or to understand the ramifications of these restraints. Also read the contract for the inspection carefully for particular limitations of the company performing the inspection. There is no requirement for an inspector to use special instruments or testing devices like gas detectors, moisture meters, pressure gauges or amp meters. However, some inspectors may use gas detectors and moisture meters to determine hard to decipher gas or water leaks. A home inspection is visual and you should not expect the inspector to report on the interior of the flue of the fireplace. Until the chimney is cleaned by a chimney sweep, the condition is not visible.

If the inspector performs the inspection according to a national standard, it would be wise to ask for a copy. The more you understand the limitations and exclusions of any inspection the better you'll know what to expect when the inspector arrives to do your inspection. Inspectors do a valuable service but there is no way they are able to perform a totally comprehensive and exhaustive inspection in 2-3 hours and at a reasonable fee. A totally comprehensive and exhaustive inspection could run thousands of dollars and take many days to perform.

The inspector's report is an important aspect of the inspection. The report tells what was and was not inspected. It identifies the systems and items in the house and discloses their condition. It may give repair suggestions and life expectancies. Take this information, combined with the other things you know about the house, and draw your conclusions.

INTRODUCTION

What is a Home Inspection? The inspection is a reasonable effort to disclose the condition of the property on the day of the inspection—a look at your home with an experienced eye. The inspection should take 2-3 hours to perform. Some items such as windows and receptacles are checked by sampling. A representative number of light switches and receptacles are checked (one in each room). A representative number of windows are checked to see if they function. Other items such as shingles and siding are checked as a group, but not individually. Most people purchasing a home hire an inspector to check the roof, exterior, foundation/basement/structure, plumbing, electrical, heating, fireplace, air conditioning, insulation, and interior.

Is there anything an inspection does not cover? YES. The inspection does not reveal information on the concealed areas or items not inspected. e.g Insulation in the visible areas of the attic does not imply insulation under the attic floor. Prepurchase inspections do not cover asbestos, radon gas, lead paint, urea formaldehyde, toxic or inflammable chemicals, etc.. Some inspection companies offer additional services such as radon, well, septic inspections, etc. under separate agreements. Personal property such as washers, dryers, refrigerators, portable appliances, playground equipment, hot tubs, and fireplace inserts, etc. are not inspected. Cosmetics are not addressed. A home inspection does not cover soil conditions or defects caused by geological conditions. Inspectors will not endanger themselves or the property by going into wet crawlspaces or onto treacherous roofs. They will not purposefully damage the property. Inspectors cannot find things that have been intentionally concealed from them.

Does the inspection reveal code violations? NO. The inspector may have a general knowledge of local codes, but a prepurchase inspection is not designed to reveal specific code violations. The inspector could not be expected to know and keep up with all the codes that may have been in effect over the years in all the local jurisdictions. Be aware that you may not be required to upgrade your home to meet current codes until you remodel. Electrical improvements must usually be made to today's standards.

Who is an Inspector and what does he do? Home inspectors are generalists with broad knowledge on many topics. Some home inspectors are engineers and some are not. A good inspector must be well versed in all fields of residential construction and have good communication skills. They do not know or see everything. They are not experts on every item or system. The home inspector gives an overview of the condition of the property and discloses major defects.

What is a Major Defect? Major Defects are any items costing more than $500.00 to repair or items affecting the habitability of the house. One dripping faucet is not a major defect, but ten might be. Delayed maintenance may cost over $500.00. Defects are disclosed in a report.

Is a Home Inspection an Insurance policy or a warranty against future repairs? NO. Purchasing a home brings risk. An inspection cannot eliminate risk, but it discloses the condition of the

Table of Contents

Table of Contents

Table of Contents

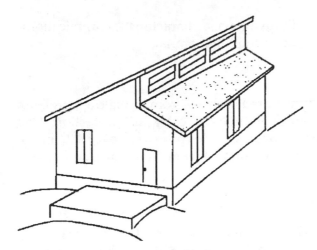

1.4.3 LEAN-TO OR SHED ROOF

1.4.4 GAMBREL

1.4.5 MANSARD

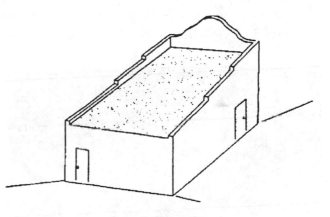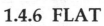

1.4.6 FLAT

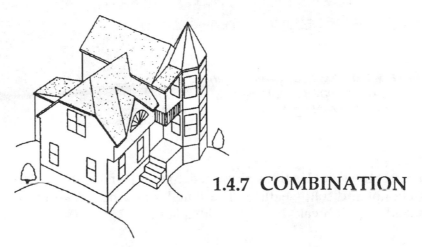

1.4.7 COMBINATION

1.5 ROOFING MATERIALS

The following sections give the advantages, disadvantages, characteristics, applications, estimated life expectancies, maintenance, etc. for each type of roofing material.

1.5.1 ASPHALT

Industry has given us asphalt roofing manufactured in sheets from asphalt, a petroleum product, a fiber matrix layer for strength, and a layer of granules for color and protection. The product is cut into many shapes, weights, and sizes. Asphalt shingles probably cover 80% of the new houses. These products offer economy, good color retention, low maintenance, and ease of application.

Some asphalt shingles are subject to wind damage and some are not very fire resistant. Shingles are recommended for roofs with at least a 4 in 12 pitch but can be installed on lower pitched roofs if you follow special application procedures available from the manufacturer. Life expectancies range from 10 years for roll roofing to 40 years for top quality shingles. Designer or multilayered shingles may not be technically superior. Their only advantage may be appearance. Woven and self sealing shingles offer the best wind resistance.

MAINTENANCE AND UPKEEP

Asphalt roofing shingles require little maintenance. Trees too close to the roof discourage proper drying and accelerate aging. Cut back overhanging tree limbs. In a wind storm even small twiggy limbs can tear shingles. Tree sap can stain or damage roofing. Large limbs can plunge through the roof and into the living space.

1.5.1 a.

1.5.1 b. Twigs or Overhanging Limbs.
Cut back limbs to promote proper drying
and protect the roofing from physical damage.

Protect the shingles from physical damage. Don't walk on them more than necessary. Be careful in hot and cold weather. The shingles may be soft and putty like when hot and brittle when cold. Don't break the edges with a ladder.

Painting an asphalt roof is not recommended. It doesn't seal the leaks and may loosen the granules. Tarring the roof or coating it with roof coating is only a temporary repair.

Improving the attic ventilation may extend the life of your roof. Asphalt roofs die from excess heat and moisture. Increasing the attic ventilation may allow heat and moisture to dissipate readily.

Soffit ventilation may be required by the roofing industry to maintain and enforce any warranty.

If you are buying a new house or a house with a new roof or having a new roof installed, be sure to get a written warranty from the manufacturer and the roofer. These often cover only the first owner, so be sure you are protected and double check the installation and ventilation to avoid losing the warranty.

1.5.1.1 FELT MATRIX SHINGLE

These asphalt shingles incorporate a felt or cellulose material or matrix paper for strength. Until the advent of the fiberglass material, felt was subject to water rot and ultraviolet (sunlight) damage. These shingles may last 15 to 20 years. Darker colored shingles generally have a lesser life expectancy than the lighter colored shingles because of the heat absorbing qualities of their color. Black shingles, for example, often last only 14 - 15 years; while white shingles may last as long as 23 - 27 years.

The advantages of this type of shingle are economy, beauty, adaptability, low maintenance and weather resistance. The disadvantages are trade-offs. Inexpensive shingles offer relatively lower fire resistance and life expectancy.

Life expectancies range from 15 years to 30 years for properly applied roofs. Weight ranges from 245 lbs. per square to 400 lbs. per square. (Read also 1.5.1 Asphalt.)

1.5.1.2 FIBERGLASS MATRIX SHINGLES

Fiberglass asphalt shingles are similar to felt shingles, but a fiberglass matrix replaces the paper. The fiberglass is nearly impervious to water and ultraviolet light allowing these shingles to last longer. They are thinner and slightly lighter in weight, ranging from 215 lbs. up to 400 lbs. per square. They have the same advantages as felt shingles, but last longer and are somewhat more fire resistant. They are slightly more expensive.

On the negative side, they are very supple and tend to "show through" any imperfections in the subroof. They may become soft and easily damaged by foot traffic in summer. Roofers and painters must be very careful not to scar them when it's hot. Fiberglass shingles have not been in use long enough to test fully their aging characteristics. (Read also 1.5.1 Asphalt and 1.5.1.1 Felt Matrix Shingle.)

The roofing industry strongly recommends excellent attic ventilation with fiberglass shingles and may require soffit ventilation. Poor or substandard ventilation may void your warranty and may ruin your roof.

1.5.1.3 ROLL ROOFING

Roll roofing is a roll or sheet of asphalt roofing manufactured similar to asphalt shingles but usually lighter in weight. The product is made in several styles (single ply application, two ply application, exposed nails, covered nails, etc.) and is suitable for low pitched roofs, down to about 1 in 12. The advantages are similar to those of asphalt shingles. This is not a very classy or permanent roof for a home because of the light weight and short life expectancy (roughly 10 years). Most roll roofing is used by the amateur or home handyman because it is economical and suitable for low sloped roofs. (Read also 1.5.1 Asphalt.)

1.5.2 WOODEN ROOFING

Wooden roofing has been in use for a long time. In colonial days, wood that was decay resistant and brittle was hand split and shaped into shakes and shingles. Today, western red cedar is commonly used, but some eastern cypress and white pine roofing is also available.

These products last a long time if applied over spaced 1X6 decking. The roofing can dry and may last 30 to 40 years. Most are now installed over plywood or solid decking with multiple layers of felt. These roofs may last only 15 to 20 years, because of rotting due to moisture and poor drying. Shakes (rough, hand split) come in a variety of lengths, thickness and grades. Shingles (smoother, machine sawn) come in many qualities and styles, including decorative shapes such as fish scales, round butts, scallops, etc.

Like asphalt shingles, they are recommended for roofs of 4 in 12 pitch or steeper. Wooden roofs offer the advantages of style, beauty, street appeal, durability, and wind resistance. Disadvantages are they require periodic maintenance and treatment with preservatives. They have little fire resistance unless specially treated. Shingles treated for fire resistance must be factory treated before application. This can be expensive and the success of the chemicals may dwindle over the life of the roof.

MAINTENANCE AND UPKEEP

Wooden roofs die from wet rot caused or aggravated by moss and fungus. Shading from over-hanging tree limbs and poor attic ventilation can retard drying and accelerate aging. If the roof has a greenish color (moss) when it is cool and damp, it is probably also rotting. It may turn brown or gray when the sun hits it, but if it's green early in the morning, damage is occurring.

The roof should be cleaned and treated with preservatives if you want it to last the full life expectancy. Remove any leaves, debris, and accumulated moss and fungus. This can range from simply sweeping the roof to chemical cleaning or high pressure washing. Then you may treat the roofing with a solution of 1/4 to 1/2 ounce of copper sulfate to ten gallons of water, or a solution of 3 pounds of zinc sulfate in 5 to 10 gallons of water per 600 square feet of roofing. These chemicals are very toxic (poisonous) to wood attacking bacteria, moss, and fungus and will protect the roof, but are equally poisonous to humans and ground plantings. The zinc solution is also corrosive to copper gutters and flashings and must be kept off of them. It may be wise to leave this work to professionals or at least contact your county Extension Agent, the manufacturer or the local poison control center for more information. Perhaps the Forest Products Laboratory or a local university could provide more information.

There is substantial danger of falling and exposing yourself to dangerous chemicals. This work should be left to professionals, unless you want to activate your life insurance and will. Keeping your wooden roof clean and treating it with preservatives every four or five years could double its useful life.

An alternative to chemicals may be to use copper, lead, or zinc flashings. Traces of the metal wash down the roofing each time it rains and retard the growth of fungus and bacteria. You can buy strips of "pure zinc" to run along the ridges of your roof. The metal may leave whitish streaks as it runs down the roof, but it does seem to protect the roofing from decay. This may be an easy and inexpensive way to extend the life of your roofing.

1.5.2 a. Wooden Roofing.
Individual shakes or shingles that curl or warp may have to be replaced to avoid leaks.

1.5.2.1 WOODEN SHINGLES

This is the machine cut or sawn type, often thin, (1/2 inch tapering to nothing) and sometimes shaped on the ends in decorative patterns. If knotty, they may be "under course" or "shim" shingles not intended for use as roofing. Clear, all heart, No. 1, or select grades last longer in the weather. They should be laid with cracks (1/4 inch) between them to allow for swelling when wet, and the cracks should not line up from layer to layer for 3 layers. Shingles may not last as long as shakes. They are thinner and fit tighter and may not dry as well. Moss, fungus, and rot attacks them. Unless specially treated, they burn readily. (Read also 1.5.2 Wooden Roofing Material.)

1.5.2.2 WOODEN SHAKES

Shakes are similar to shingles, but are the rougher, thicker "handsplit" version. They come in a variety of thicknesses and lengths and can be laid in many patterns. Several grades are available: clear, all heart, No. 1, select, etc. The better grades last longer. Generally, knotty shakes don't exist because knotty wood won't split well. Shakes may last longer than wooden shingles because they are thicker and the rough shape may dry better. Moss, fungus, and rot attacks them. Unless specially treated, they burn readily. They should be installed with cracks (1/4") between them to allow them to swell when wet. These cracks should not line up from layer to layer for 3 layers. Some modern shake roofs are little more than tar paper roofs and the shakes keep the wind from blowing it off. (Read also 1.5.2 Wooden Roofing Materials.)

1.5.2.2 a. Wooden Shakes.
Notice the dislodged shake near the ridge
and the peeling paint on the wood siding.

1.5.3 SLATE AND TILE ROOFING

Slate is a natural stone material that will easily split or cleave into thin layers. As used for roofing, it is usually 1/4 to 1/2 inch thick. The individual slates range in size from about 6" by 10" up. Manufacturers have tried to mimic the appearance and durability of natural slate, some with more success than others. In some parts of the world clay tiles are an ancient and classic form of roofing. Man made (terra-cotta) products are available in a wide variety of styles and colors. Cement tiles are a newer man made product and also available in a variety of shapes and styles. Asbestos cement shingles are thinner and lighter, and come in a variety of shapes and colors.

These types of roofing are very heavy, ranging from 800 to 2000 lbs. per square. Therefore, the structure below must be designed for them from the beginning. They do not blow off easily, but many of them are subject to infiltration by wind driven rain. This group is as fire resistant as roofing can be. They are recommended for roofs with a 6 in 12 or steeper pitch.

They offer the advantages of style, beauty, durability and fire and wind resistance. Their disadvantages are they are very heavy and require periodic maintenance. Life expectancies range from 30 to 75 years.

MAINTENANCE AND UPKEEP

These materials last a long time, but are only as good as their weakest "link." Often, the flashings do not last as long as the roofing. It seems strange, but many 50 year roofs had 20 or 30 year flashings. You may have to paint and repair flashings or replace them. Slate roofs and some of the others rely on tarred ridges. Nothing keeps the rain out but tar (black plastic roof cement) applied along the ridges. This occasionally cracks and must be repaired as often as annually.

These products crack and break because of their natural brittleness. They are subject to freeze/thaw damage. Sometimes low quality nails rust away or dissolve because of chemicals (acid) in the materials. Pieces, or whole tiles come loose and may slide off the roof. The older the roof gets, the more "normal" this type of damage becomes. Individual tiles or whole areas will require replacing periodically (perhaps every spring). This work demands skill and experience, and because the roofs are steep and treacherous repairs should be left to professionals. If you step on a loose slate, you could end up "surfing" into the bushes below. Walking on the roof could damage it. Professionals have proper equipment, materials, and insurance.

1.5.3 a. Slate and Tile Roofing.
Flashings must be kept in good condition.
Tar is not a quality repair on flashing.
(See 1.10.30 Tar on Flashing.)

1.5.3.1 VERMONT OR BUCKINGHAM SLATE

Quarried in Vermont, slate can be very colorful. Color ranges from black to brown, red to green, and purple to mottled. Quarried in Buckingham, Virginia the slate is blue-black and non fading. Both are very durable, lasting 50 to 75 years and are available in a wide variety of styles, shapes, and thicknesses. They can be laid in fanciful patterns. They range in weight from 800 pounds to 2000 pounds per square. These are some of the longest lived roofs available, are beautiful, stylish, and classy. They are very wind and fire resistant. Disadvantages are they are heavy, require professional maintenance as often as annually, and are subject to wind driven rain. They may be difficult to match for repairs, changes, or additions. (Read also 1.5.3 Slate and Tile Roofing.)

1.5.3.2 BANGOR SLATE

Bangor slate is quarried in Pennsylvania and originally blue-black in color, similar to Buckingham slate, but shorter lived, lasting only 30 to 50 years. It is subject to having a ribbon or band of discoloration visible on the surface. Veins in the rock may cause the slate to fail in as little as ten years. Bangor slate gives some clues to its deterioration.

When it has roughly 15 years of life left it may exhibit a whitish fringe or semicircular ring on individual slates similar to a water ring. Later, with 7 to 12 years left, slates may turn a brownish color. This may be difficult to distinguish from the brown Vermont slate but is a changing of color from black. Still later, the final stage is delamination and peeling, (exfoliation) where the slates are flaking and weathering away. They are becoming soft and thin and may have up to 7 years left.

As with other slates, these roofs are heavy (800 to 2000 pounds per square) and fire resistant. They require professional maintenance, and are subject to wind driven rain. Galvanized flashings and nails may be acceptable with this shorter lived material. (Read also 1.5.3 Slate and Tile Roofing.)

1.5.3.3 CLAY TILE

Clay tile roofs are common in some parts of the country. Commonly available in mission and Spanish styles, they are also available in a wide variety of colors and other shapes. For a price, you can have them custom made to fit your application. They are heavy (up to 2500 pounds per square). Their advantages are style, beauty, wind and fire resistance. Disadvantages are they are heavy, require professional maintenance periodically, subject to wind driven rain and may be difficult to match for repairs and additions.

The part of some clay tile roofs that keeps water from entering the structure below is the tar paper or base felt. The clay tiles are decorative and protect the tar paper from sun, wind, and fire. Here, the tiles are not nailed but are fastened with a dab of cement. (Read also 1.5.3 Slate and Tile Roofing.)

1.5.3.4 CEMENT TILE

Cement tiles differ from clay tiles in that they are cast in molds from a portland cement mix (concrete) that sets or cures at room temperature. Clay tiles must be fired in a kiln. Cement tiles are durable, lasting 30-50 years and fire resistant. They can be stylish and are available in many shapes. Advantages are style, durability, and wind and fire resistance. Disadvantages are they are heavy, (1000 to 2500 pounds per square), require professional maintenance, may be subject to wind driven rain, and difficult to match for repairs and additions.

The part of some cement tile roofs that keeps water from entering the structure below is the tar paper or base felt. The cement tiles are decorative and protect the tar paper from sun, wind, and fire. Here, the tiles are not nailed but are fastened with a dab of cement. (Read also 1.5.3 Slate and Tile Roofing.)

1.5.3.4 a. Cement Tiles.
Notice the dislodged ridge shingle that will leak.

1.5.3.5 ASBESTOS CEMENT SHINGLES

Now sometimes called "mineral fiber shingles" because asbestos is so controversial. The shingles were manufactured from asbestos fibers and portland cement combined in molds under high pressure. If they are still available, they are no longer made with asbestos in the USA. They are immune to rot and salt air but are very brittle. They were available in various colors but most have faded to a mottled brown and gray.

They sometimes appear rust stained. Moss occasionally attaches in the crevices on northern exposures or damp roofs. The moss should be removed.

Their advantages are relative light weight (600 to 800 pounds per square), long life (30 to 40 years), and wind and fire resistance. Disadvantages are they require professional maintenance and are subject damage from impact. Do not walk on them. Keep overhanging tree limbs properly pruned to avoid damage to the roof. As with slate, ridges are sometimes tarred to keep out water. They must be tarred from time to time and it is not unusual to be able to see daylight through the ridge from the attic when the tar cracks. They may also be difficult to match for repairs since the change away from asbestos. Cement asbestos shingles are sometimes available in Canada. (Read also 1.5.3 Slate and Tile Roofing.)

1.5.4 BUILT-UP ROOFS

Built-up roofs are normally applied to flat or low pitched roofs. Even "flat" roofs should be pitched or sloped enough to drain dry after a rain. This type of roof normally consists of 2 to 5 plies of roofing felt (tar paper) shingled or sandwiched together with bitumen. Bitumen is either asphalt or coal tar pitch and usually applied hot. One of the limitations on this type of roofing is it must be applied to a low sloped roof and the bitumen used must be selected for the slope. A 4 in 12 slope seems to be about the limit. These roofs are often topped with slag or gravel. On steeper roofs the bitumen and topping tends to sag and slide down the roof.

The topping protects the felt and bitumen from sunlight and impact and acts as ballast. It weighs the felt down preventing wind damage and promotes drying. Smooth surface roofs have no gravel. These roofs are lighter in weight but must be mechanically attached better than the gravel variety. They must use bitumens resistant to sunlight.

Advantages are style, and suitability to low pitched applications. Disadvantages are they are expensive, sensitive to poor attic ventilation, and may require professional maintenance. Life expectancy is 15 to 20 years. Flat roofs are difficult to inspect and trouble prone in the last 5 years. Since they usually cannot be seen from the ground they must be walked to be inspected.

Often there is little or no access to the attic space. This limits or eliminates the inspection of the structural parts of the roof.

MAINTENANCE AND UPKEEP

Built-up roofs require constant maintenance. Do not allow water to stand or pond. It seeps in and rots the felt or expands into vapor. When the sun hits the roof, trapped water may expand 1500 to 1800 times, causing blisters. Therefore, roof drains or gutters and downspouts must be kept functional.

Roofs surrounded by parapet walls have been known to collect water several feet deep when the drains were clogged. This extraordinary weight could cause the building to collapse. Any obstructions causing ponding should be eliminated. Sometimes it is necessary to remove portions of the roofing and build up under it, perhaps with tapered insulation, to promote proper drainage.

Flashings and copings (tops of parapet walls) and gravel stops (metal edges) must be kept in good repair. Leave this work to professionals. Repairs must be made with compatible materials.

Coal tar pitch is not compatible with asphalt. A small piece of coal tar pitch dropped into Varsol will turn yellow or yellow green. Asphalt turns brown or black. There are bitumens compatible with both coal tar and asphalt.

Adding roof penetrations (new plumbing stacks, TV antennas, etc.) should be avoided until you replace the roofing. It is difficult to seal new holes in old roofing. Pay special attention to properly ventilating the subroof space. Poor ventilation causes the early death of many roofs. Condensation and rot will damage the sheeting and roof structure.

Foot traffic tends to damage the roof. Paving or decking should be installed to protect any area receiving regular traffic. Do not step on blisters or bubbles. They may burst.

1.5.4.1 THREE OR FOUR PLY WITH GRAVEL

These roofs are composed of several plies of 15 pound roofing felt (tar paper) hot mopped with coal tar pitch or asphalt (bitumen). The top surface is flooded with bitumen and covered with slag or gravel. Rounded stones (river gravel) are preferable because they have less tendency to puncture the roofing. These roofs, widely used on commercial buildings, are rare on residences. They are expensive to install and are heavy (500-800 pounds per square). They last about 5 years per ply and should be sloped enough to drain dry. Standing or ponded water will cut the life of a roof in half. Their advantage is they are suitable for low pitched applications (up to 4 in 12). Disadvantages are the roofing is heavy, difficult to repair, short lived (15 to 20 years), and prone to be troublesome in the last five (5) years. (Read section 1.5.4 Built Up Roofing.)

1.5.4.2 THREE OR FOUR PLY SMOOTH BUILT-UP ROOFING

This roofing is similar to the gravel version (Section 1.5.4.1) without the gravel topping. Between two (2) and five (5) plies of 15 pound felt (tar paper) are hot mopped over a layer or layers of base felt. A topping or flood coat is applied and left smooth (no gravel). Without the gravel to protect it, this top coat must be "stabilized" chemically to withstand the sun's ultraviolet rays.

The advantages of this type of built-up roof are lighter weight than the gravel version (300 to 500 pounds per square) and suitability for low sloped applications. It is short lived (five years per ply up to about 20 years) and must be mechanically fastened (nailed) better than the gravel version to prevent blow off. Ponded or standing water will shorten its life by half. Do not walk on it more than essential for inspection and maintenance. (Read section 1.5.4 Built-Up Roofs.)

1.5.4.3 OTHER TYPES

There are other systems called built-up roofing. Cold applied systems are similar to the "hot mop" varieties. In these systems the bitumens are modified with solvents that liquefy them for application. As the solvents evaporate, the bitumens set or solidify the roofing into a solid mass.

There are also some Neoprene (TM) rubber based systems that rely on "painted" on layers of liquid Neoprene that cure into a waterproof coating. These systems are rare on residences and have not been in use long enough or in enough applications to establish a track record. A homeowner with little or no experience with roofing may attempt to use these systems. This use may suggest amateur workmanship. (Read section 1.5.4 Built-Up Roofs.)

1.5.5 METAL ROOFING

Metal has been used as a roof covering for thousands of years. Some of the structures in ancient Rome had bronze roofing. Castles in Europe sometimes had lead roofing. The metals commonly used in this country are galvanized iron (sheet iron coated with zinc), terne metal (sheet steel coated with a mixture of zinc and lead), copper, and aluminum.

Metal can be applied in many styles and shapes ranging from flat or standing seams to decorative stamped shapes mimicking Spanish tiles or wood shakes. Properly installed and maintained metal roofing lasts a long time and is fire and wind resistant. It can be suitable for almost any slope and can enhance the style of some homes. Galvanized and terne metal roofs must be kept painted and require periodic maintenance.

If allowed to rust and deteriorate, professional repairs may be required and can be costly. Installing and repairing metal roofs on residences seems to be a dying art. The difficulty and high cost of replacement makes homeowners consider alternative materials. Many are replaced with built-up roofing (section 1.5.4) and single membrane roofing (section 1.5.6) where they are applicable. On steeper slopes asphalt shingles (section 1.5.1) or wooden roofing (section 1.5.2) may be substituted. Don't substitute a heavier roofing without checking the structure's ability to support it.

MAINTENANCE AND UPKEEP

"Tin" or galvanized iron and terne metal will last indefinitely if kept properly painted. Maintenance consists of inspecting the roof annually, removing rust and failing paint, and properly repainting.

As with any paint job, proper preparation is essential. Rust and loose paint must be removed and areas of bare metal primed. Spot painting should be done on an as needed basis and repainting the whole roof will have to be done every 3 to 5 years. Use high quality paint to possibly stretch the time between applications.

Tarring a roof only delays the inevitable. Any tarred area of a metal roof is highly suspect. No one can judge the quality of the metal under the tar. All the water falling on the roof may leak in through a tarred valley. Be prepared to replace any tarred areas. Other maintenance involves repairing flashing and built-in gutters and pipe penetrations.

1.5.5.1 FLAT SEAM ROOFING

Often made of galvanized iron or terne metal and occasionally copper, this style of roofing has edges or seams folded flat, similar to the side seam on blue jeans. The seams are soldered to assure water tightness. The metal is often applied in long strips with the seams running up the roof. However, the seams can run in any direction. Sometimes, the metal is installed in squares turned diamond fashion. The metal may also be installed on roofs of fanciful shapes (spires, minarets, etc.). The advantages are style, beauty, flexibility of design, longevity, and fire and wind resistance. Disadvantages are most require regular painting (except copper) and occasional professional maintenance. (Read 1.5.5 Metal Roofing.)

1.5.5.2 STANDING SEAM METAL ROOFING

Standing seam metal roofing is similar to flat seam roofing except the seams are vertical (standing) and are not always soldered. The metals commonly used are tin, terne metal, and copper. The seams slightly limit the installation because they must be parallel to the path of the water flowing off the roof. The advantages of this type

of roofing are style, durability, beauty, and fire and wind resistance. Disadvantages are most require regular painting and occasional professional maintenance. (Read 1.5.5 Metal Roofing.)

1.5.2.2 a. Standing Seam Metal Roofing. Notice the 1.5.4.2 Smooth Built-up roofing on the rear addition. The metal roofing is 1.10.24 Painted.

1.5.5.3 CORRUGATED TIN

Corrugated tin roofing comes in different weights, lengths, and configurations, (wavy corrugations,"5-VEE," etc.). These products are not commonly used on the main roofs of houses (except perhaps in rural areas), but are seen on porches, shed roofs, detached garages, and outbuildings. If heavily galvanized, the roofing may last a long time without paint (20 to 30 years). Advantages are relatively low cost compared to flat or standing seam types and good fire resistance. Corrugated roofing may be installed over spaced sheeting.

Disadvantages are questionable appearance or stylishness and low wind resistance. Some varieties require painting and periodic maintenance. (Read 1.5.5 Metal Roofing.)

1.5.5.4 COPPER ROOFING

Copper roofing is a highly regarded and unusual material. It is usually installed as a standing seam roof (Section 1.5.5.2) or a flat seam roof (Section 1.5.5.1). A properly installed copper roof will last almost indefinitely unless attacked by a corrosive atmosphere. Copper does not require painting and weathers to a dark brown and then a copper oxide green. This and slate are the highest quality roofings available. Advantages are style, beauty, extreme longevity, and low periodic maintenance. Disadvantages are high cost and occasional professional attention required to flashings. (Read 1.5.5 Metal Roofing.)

1.5.5.5 ALUMINUM ROOFING

Aluminum is manufactured into many roofing products including ones like corrugated tin (Section 1.5.5.3). These sheet type products are seldom seen on residences in urban areas. They are seen on outbuildings.

Aluminum is also stamped into fanciful patterns resembling shakes and clay tiles. The red imitation shakes on Pizza Huts are aluminum panels. These products are also rare on residences. Aluminum's advantages are well known: light in weight and doesn't require paint. A disadvantage is high thermal expansion causing it to "wear out" its fasteners and become subject to wind damage and leaks. The panel systems are expensive. (Read 1.5.5 Metal Roofing.)

1.5.6 SINGLE MEMBRANE ROOFING

This catch all category for a wide variety of products developed in the last 10 to 20 years includes vinyl (PVC) and rubber or plastic sheets. Some of these products show promise, but have not withstood the test of time. They are vinyl-like sheets or wide rolls (2 meters or so) heat seamed or chemically bonded (glued) together.

They require professional installation and are coming into use on commercial buildings. Quality control during installation is critical. As these products prove themselves they will "filter down" to residential usage. Some of them are glued down (bonded) and some are mechanically attached (nailed) to the subroof. Some are merely laid in place and held down by a layer of gravel or slag. The lighter weight versions may prove to be acceptable replacements for some metal roofs. They are suitable for low pitched applications. Disadvantages are they are unproven, require professional installation by factory licensed installers, and may be expensive or difficult to obtain. Do not walk on them more than necessary for inspection and maintenance.

1.6 FLASHING AND JOINT MATERIAL

Flashings make areas where roofs intersect each other (valleys) or butt against walls or where pipes or chimneys protrude, watertight. Flashings are usually made of metal or plastic (rubber, vinyl, or Neoprene). Some are factory made (like pipe collars) and some are fabricated on the site. Flashings are critical, but often the first areas to leak. The flashing and roofing materials must be chemically compatible and have similar life expectancies.

MAINTENANCE AND UPKEEP

Maintaining the flashings on a roof is as important as maintaining the roofing. Expansion and contraction of the metal and movements within the structure may pull flashings away from chimneys and pipes. Occasionally the metal fatigues and splits or tears. Galvanized flashing can rust through. Maintenance includes periodically inspecting the flashings, painting rusted areas, resealing any that have pulled away, and replacing or repairing any that are split or torn. Some repairs may be within the capabilities of the homeowners, but some flashing details are intricate and you may need professional help.
Use extreme caution walking on any roof.

1.6 a. A Cricket or Saddle.
This type of flashing detail helps prevent debris and ice building up behind the chimney causing leaks.

1.6.1 GALVANIZED IRON OR TIN

A common flashing material with a life expectancy of 20 to 30 years. Lightly galvanized types may rust and require painting to last as long as the roofing. (Read section 1.6 Flashing and Joint Material.)

1.6.1 a. Galvanized Iron or Tin
Rusting flashings should
be replaced with roofing material. The tar is a
clue of leaks and only a temporary fix.

1.6.2 ALUMINUM

Manufacturers of continuous gutters and aluminum trim developed "coil stock." This sturdy aluminum has a baked on finish and makes excellent flashing. Avoid the thinner uncoated aluminum economy variety. Not only does it fatigue and tear easily but is also readily attacked by the caustic elements in masonry and mortar. The baked on finish and thicker type is more resistant and better looking. (Read section 1.6 Flashing and Joint Material.)

1.6.3 COPPER FLASHING

Just as with roofing, copper flashing is a premier product and tends to last as long as any roofing. Traces of the metal bleeding onto wooden roofing appear to protect the wood from decay. The greenish oxide can stain slate, but is a small price to pay compared to replacing lesser quality flashing. (Read section 1.6 Flashing and Joint Material.)

1.6.4 LEAD FLASHING

Lead, seldom seen except as pipe collars, lasts a long time, but is soft and subject to tearing. (Read section 1.6 Flashing and Joint Material.)

1.6.5 TAR FLASHING

Tar is not flashing material and requires replacement or repair with proper materials. The use of tar suggests amateur workmanship and leaks around the flashing. (Read section 1.6 Flashing and Joint Material.)

1.6.6 NEOPRENE (RUBBER)

Some pipe collars have a cuff or gasket of Neoprene (TM) that seals around a plumbing stack or pipe. The rest of the pipe collar can be plastic or galvanized metal. The Neoprene tends to split and fail at about 10 to 12 years. The split often occurs on the uphill side of the pipe which is difficult to see. The repair is to replace the roof collar. You may be able to install a new one over the old one until you re-roof. Pipe collars are inexpensive. (Read section 1.6 Flashing and Joint Material.)

1.6.7 ROOFING MATERIAL

Some roofing is "self flashing" such as metal roofs. Sometimes valleys are woven of asphalt shingles. Using the roofing material as flashing may be an acceptable practice.

Roofing materials improperly used as flashing, such as asphalt shingles turned up against an intersecting wall or chimney, suggest amateur workmanship and possible leaks. (Read section 1.6 Flashing and Joint Material.)

1.6.8 NONE

The absence of flashing requires the installation of appropriate flashing. (Read section 1.6 Flashing and Joint Material.)

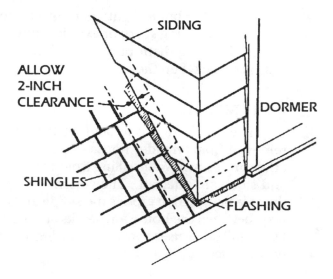

1.6.8 d. Flashing.
Diagram showing proper flashing at a dormer.
The flashing resists leaks better if the siding on
the dormer is parallel to the roof.

1.7 GUTTERS AND DOWNSPOUTS

Builders and homeowners universally dislike gutters and downspouts. A current trend is to omit them. They increase the cost of the construction and must be cleaned periodically. If you have them, keep them, if you don't, get them. They protect the house from splash damage and help to keep the basement or crawl space dry. They are hateful, but their importance to the house cannot be over stressed.

MAINTENANCE AND UPKEEP

The day to day required maintenance for gutters and downspouts is removing the leaves and debris. Cleaning is done on an "as needed" basis and frequency depends on the site and climate. Keep them clear of trash, etc. so water can flow freely.

Debris left in gutters turns into "potting soil" and can be corrosive. This will accelerate the deterioration of the gutters. Wet debris or water standing in gutters or downspouts can freeze, expand, and damage them severely. Galvanized gutters fail by rusting from the inside outward.

Be careful when working on attached gutters. Be sure they are securely and snugly attached against the house so water cannot run between the house and the gutter. Don't allow water to drain behind them. Be sure the spikes are driven level, not downward, punching a hole low in the back of the gutter. Narrow overhangs invite water to run directly into the interior of the house rather than dripping out through the soffit. If you have narrow overhangs, be sure to keep the gutters securely attached and do not allow them to overflow.

Be careful with the ladder. Do not touch overhead power lines with the ladder, your person, or tools. You could be electrocuted. Do not bang the ladder against the gutters or edge of the roofing. Aluminum and copper gutters are subject to "ladder damage" because they are soft. Always work safely and be sure of proper footing while on the ladder. Keep galvanized gutters and downspouts painted inside and out. Do not allow downspouts and draintiles to become or remain blocked. Blocked gutters overflow, often out the back, allowing water to cascade down the house or to leak into the house through the facia and soffit.

Internal or built-in gutters must be kept waterproof because they are part of the roof and are above the living space or exterior trim. Again, it is essential they be free flowing and clear of debris. Keeping them properly painted is important. Anything extending their useful life is wise because when they fail, repair or replacement is expensive and requires professional help.

1.7.1 NONE

There is evidence to suggest the absence of gutters may be a serious defect. Whether removed from an older house or never installed, the lack of gutters often causes or aggravates other problems. Water falling from the roof splashes onto the siding and damages it. Even brick and stone are affected. The splash damages garage doors, and pedestrian doors. Sometimes the splashing action erodes the siding and doors as they weather and decay. This water finds its way between the house and decks or leaks behind stoops or slabs and rots the siding or framing. Decks fall off houses because of rotting around the nails or bolts. Builders often omit flashing on new houses.

Newer Patio Doors and French Doors as well as smaller pedestrian doors often come assembled in a jamb or frame, complete with a sill and weatherstripping. The builder installs them in a hole left in the framing and basically sits them on top of the floor, often without flashing. Water leaks underneath them and rots the floor and framing below. Gutters may catch some of the water and reduce this splash damage.

Gutters give you an opportunity to catch the roof "run off" and direct it away from the foundation in either splashblocks or draintiles. The absence of gutters is a leading cause of wet basements and crawl spaces. As hateful as they are, gutters and downspouts are always a wise investment. (Read section 1.7 Gutters and Downspouts.)

1.7.2 ATTACHED GUTTERS

Commonly used, this type is nailed (spiked) or bracketed along the eaves, usually to a facia board. They should be attached securely to the facia so the water runs into them and not over or behind. They should be sloped to drain properly and not pond or hold water. (Read section 1.7 Gutters and Downspouts.)

1.7.2.1 PARTIAL

The house does not have a complete set of gutters. Examples: only above doors, front only, back only, etc. This also implies certain parts of the house do not have gutters. (Read sections 1.7 Gutters and Downspouts, 1.7.1 None, and 1.7.2 Attached.)

1.7.2.2 FULL

The gutters are extensive enough to intercept the water coming from the roof or the lack of gutters is minor. The inspector thinks the omission may not create a defect. (Read section 1.7.2 Attached Gutters.)

1.7.3 BUILT-IN GUTTERS

Built-in gutters were often used on low sloped metal roofs. A trough was framed into the lower edge of the roof and the roofing metal was extended as a liner to form a gutter. Downspouts were dropped out of these gutters, often through the soffit to the ground.

Built-in gutters were used differently on slate or tile roofs. A gutter or channel was framed into the edge of the roof and lined with metal. The downspouts were dropped out through the soffit below. In rare instances they are piped through the interior to the plumbing waste drainage system. The differences are the roof tends to be steeper and the gutters are not made of the same material as the roofing. There may be opportunities for water to leak around or under the gutters and through them. There is usually a strip of roofing below the gutter. This strip has no gutter of its own and may create a drip problem if it's too wide. These gutters must be maintained because they are above the exterior trim, framing, and the living space. A leak could do substantial damage. Keep the gutter cleaned, repaired, and painted as necessary.

Before cities had separate storm sewers, gutters were often piped into the sanitary sewer. Now cities are becoming more sensitive to storm water overloading sewage treatment plants. Many are improving their storm drainage systems and requiring downspouts to be piped into them.

Sometimes deep traps used on the downspout drains causes clogging with debris. They may be difficult to clean, but should be clear to protect the basement or crawl space from wetness and to protect the downspouts from freezing. (Read section 1.7 Gutters and Downspouts.)

1.7.4 GUTTER MATERIAL

The metal or material of which the gutters are made. (Read section 1.7 Gutters and Downspouts.)

1.7.4.1 ALUMINUM GUTTERS

Aluminum is light weight and corrosion resistant. Aluminum gutters come in two varieties: (1) preformed and (2) continuous. Preformed gutters, in factory made shapes and lengths, are assembled at the house. A machine at the site rolls out the desired length of continuous gutters. These are seamless gutters. Both are available with a baked on finish lasting from 10 to 20 years. They may be painted once the finish weathers, but it is not necessary. The disadvantage of aluminum gutters is they are soft and subject to physical damage from ladders, tree limbs, etc.

1.7.4.2 GALVANIZED IRON OR TIN GUTTERS

Galvanized gutters tend to be sturdier than aluminum, but are prone to rust unless they are painted inside and out. They are factory made in a variety of shapes and lengths and assembled at the site. The joints are often soldered, or sealed with caulking like sealants. They tend to last 15 to 20 years with proper maintenance.

1.7.4.3 COPPER GUTTERS

Copper gutter is a premium product and tends to last indefinitely unless physically damaged or stolen. Maintenance consists of keeping it clean and properly aligned. The soldered joints may need resoldering occasionally. If you replace copper gutters, the old ones may have scrap value.

1.7.4.4 VINYL OR PLASTIC GUTTERS

Several vinyl or plastic gutter systems are on the market, but are not widely accepted. They glue or snap together. They may be fragile or become brittle with age.

1.7.4.5 WOOD GUTTERS

Wood gutters are usually Douglas Fir in lengths of over 30 feet. Wood gutters of cedar, cypress, or redwood are rare in new construction. The butt joints and internal and external mitered corners are difficult to keep watertight. Gutter ends at gables should be closed off with galvanized metal, lead, or aluminum. Install wood gutters by nailing through the back top edge with galvanized nails. Paint the inside surface with two or three coats of asphalt paint before installing and repaint every five years afterwards.

1.7.5 SPLASH BLOCKS

None	No splash blocks
Partial	Some splash blocks seen
All	Splash blocks seen underneath all downspouts
Damaged	Splash blocks seen were damaged

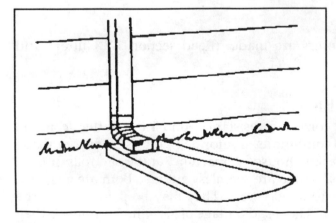

The splash blocks under the gutters and downspouts should be tilted to drain from the property. Splash blocks help control erosion under the downspouts and quickly direct water at least three feet from the foundation. Splash blocks do not carry 100% of the water away, but are better than nothing. They help to keep the basement or crawl space dry.

1.7.5 d. Splashblock

1.7.6 DRAINTILES

None	No draintiles connected to downspouts
Partial	Some downspouts were connected to draintiles
All	All downspouts were connected to draintiles
Damaged	Damage was seen to the draintiles

Any draintiles connected to downspouts should be free-flowing. A periodic flushing of these pipes would insure positive drainage of roof "run off" away from the structure. (Read section 1.7 Gutters and Downspouts.) Clogged draintiles may cause a wet or flooded basement or crawl space. Get professional help clearing or repairing blocked or damaged draintiles if necessary. Plumbers or "rooter" services may be able to help you.

1.8 VENTILATION

Attic ventilation is an important part of a house. Ventilation lets the heat out in summer and the moisture vapor out in winter. You can no longer rely on infiltration to protect the structure from condensation and the roofing from heat and moisture. Moisture vapor rising from below condenses in poorly ventilated attics and attacks the structure. In severe cases it can delaminate the plywood or waferboard sheeting. Heat "cooks" asphalt shingles accelerating their demise. Good ventilation may slightly lessen the effect of roof leaks by allowing moisture to evaporate and escape before rotting occurs. Rarely are attics over ventilated. The vents must keep rain, snow, insects, and vermin out, but allow air to pass freely.

Adequate ventilation is hard to define. Ventilation requirements are governed by the amount of moisture vapor and heat arriving in the attic. Houses on wet sites with dark roofing will need more. Houses over a dry crawl space may need less. It may be wise to reduce the amount of water vapor available by drying out the crawl space or basement, improving site drainage, and installing a vapor barrier in the crawl space.

As a guideline, you should have about one (1) square inch of vent opening for each square foot of attic. You must have two or more openings. A single vent can't let air in and out. If half the vent area is high (roof vents, turbines, or ridge vents) and half is low (soffit vents) and the vents are well distributed, you may need less total vent area.

Often small reductions in moisture vapor and small improvements in the ventilation will allow the attic to reach the "turning point." This may eliminate mold and mildew, reduce the risk to the structure, and extend the life of the roofing.

The best combination of vents is a ridge vent and soffit vents. The "chimney effect" allows hot air to rise out the ridge vent and cool air to draw in the soffit vents. They are not sensitive to wind direction. The roofing industry is beginning to require excellent ventilation including soffit ventilation for fiberglass matrix asphalt shingle in order to maintain the warranty in effect.

Power attic fans are not necessary. They appear to do little to cool the attic. The sun delivers more heat than they can remove. Be cautious of gable mounted fans. If they are blowing against the wind direction they can cancel the natural ventilation.

MAINTENANCE AND UPKEEP

Keep the screening in good condition to keep out birds, squirrels, bats, and insects. Paint and repair vents as necessary. Do not block attic vents in winter, moisture must escape.

1.8.1 GABLE VENTS

Louvered vents, either triangular or rectangular, mounted in the gables. Gable vents located in the ends of the attic space are the most common type of vents. (Read section 1.8 Ventilation.)

1.8.2 SOFFIT VENTS

These are under the soffit which is the roof overhang. They can be small round vents, rectangular, or a continuous strip vent about 2 inches wide. Some aluminum and vinyl trim systems have perforated soffit panels. (Read 1.8 Ventilation and 1.8.3 Ridge Vents.)

1.8.3 RIDGE VENTS

These are small continuous attachments installed along the roofs ridge allowing for a vent at the peak. This, combined with soffit vents is the best ventilation system available. It tends to vent all parts of the attic, is insensitive to wind direction, and takes advantage of the chimney effect. (i.e. The heat causes the air to rise out of the ridge pulling fresh air in at the soffits.) (Read section 1.8 Ventilation.)

1.8.4 TURBINES

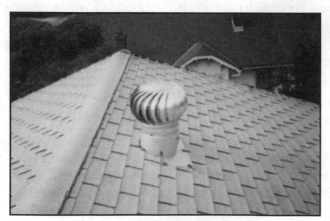

Turbines are spherical louvered wind driven vents that spin when the wind blows. The bearings may quickly wear out or rust and then stop spinning. Even stationary, these vents appear to increase the air movement in the attic by allowing hot air to rise and exit. (Read section 1.8 Ventilation and 1.8.5 Roof Vents.)

1.8.4 a. Turbine.
Notice the base flashing of the turbine "shingles" into the asphalt roofing to shed water. Beside the turbine is the ridge. Ridge shingles often split where they fold over the ridge. Also notice the faint lines or ridges in the tabs of the shingles. There may be another layer of shingles under these.

1.8.5 ROOF VENTS

Roof vents are aluminum or painted steel hoods that sit on the roof. Some are attached to bath and kitchen vent fans and some vent the attic. They seem to work as well as turbines, are cheaper, and not as noticeable. (Read section 1.8 Ventilation.)

1.8.6 WINDOWS OR FANS

Some attics have windows which don't provide any ventilation unless open. When open, they should be screened and protected from wind driven rain. (Read section 1.8 Ventilation.)

Power attic fans seldom move enough air to provide significant cooling. They do not usually operate in winter to help with removal of moisture. Gable fans sometimes blow against the wind, negating the natural ventilation. They are probably not worth the additional cost over passive vents. Passive vents such as soffit vents, ridge vents, and gable vents are more cost effective. (See 1.8.1 Gable Vents, 1.8.2 Soffit Vents, and 1.8.3 Ridge Vents.)

1.8.7 NONE

The absence of proper ventilation. Only slate or tile roofs, properly installed on board sheeting will stand being unventilated. The heat doesn't bother them and the moisture "breathes" out between the tiles.

1.9 MISCELLANEOUS

This section covers items normally inspected with the roofing.

1.9.1 SOFFITS AND FACIAS

While not necessarily an integral component of the roof, the facias, soffits and frieze can be influential on the roof structure. The facia is the vertical board immediately under the edge of the roof sheathing at the eaves where gutters may be attached. Behind and perpendicular to the facia is the soffit. This horizontal member can be used to provide inlet ventilation to the attic. The frieze is the vertical board nailed to the house under the soffit. Its prime function is trim, although in some instances, it helps hold up the soffit. (Read section 2.4 Exterior Trim.)

1.9.2 SKYLIGHTS

Skylights have been popular over the years. They have always been troublesome and prone to leak as any roof penetration. They have enjoyed a revival recently, but still tend to leak. The solar energy era in the 70's gave them a boost, but they are not a good solar feature. They lose more heat than they gain in winter and they gain more heat than they lose in summer. The main attraction is they let in additional light and make living areas seem spacious.

1.9.2.1 PLASTIC SKYLIGHTS

These range from aluminum framed double domed versions to single domed "one piece" models. Some are flush mounted (laid into the shingles) and some are curb mounted (raised on a wooden or aluminum curb). Single domed and skylights with uninsulated aluminum curbs tend to "sweat" in colder climates (north of Florida). This condensation can drool and stain the shaft, even drip to the floor. It is hard to see if the seal on a thermal (dome) skylight has failed. They are often frosted, bronzed, or dirty. (Read section 1.9.2 Skylights.)

1.9.2.2 GLASS SKYLIGHTS

Glass skylights range from old fashioned sky windows to modern factory built units similar to the plastic bubble type (section 1.9.2.1). The glass may break and should be wire reinforced or safety glass if there is living space below.

These are subject to leaking through any cracked panes, around the panes, and through the frame and curb. They may also "sweat" from condensation. Insulated glass units are less prone to sweat but often lose their seals and fog between the panes.

1.9.2.3 OPERABLE SKYLIGHTS

Operable means the skylights open. (Read section 1.9.2 Skylights.)

1.9.3 ROOF MOUNTED EQUIPMENT

Any equipment such as solar panels, antennas, satellite dishes, etc. will not be inspected or reported on as a part of the roof inspection. They are outside the scope of the home inspection and not included in the roofing section. If they damage the roofing or roof structure or are causing leaks, the inspector will report only the effect of the equipment on the roofing or structure.

1.10 ROOFING OBSERVATIONS

The inspector marks observations of conditions that may affect the roof. More than one item can be marked as the roof may exhibit more than one symptom or problem. Some items are part of the normal aging process and do not require correction. Other items require either maintenance or repair if the roof is to reach the full potential or life expectancy. Read carefully each section applying to the system inspected.

Maintenance is the on going care required if a system or item is to reach the full potential including lubricating, painting, etc. Do maintenance as required by the manufacturer of the equipment or item. Repairs put items or systems back in good condition after damage or decay, etc. Repairs are caused by delayed maintenance, aging, normal wear and tear, or abuse. The workmanship and materials of the repairs should be equal to the quality of the system and have the same life expectancy. e.g. A limb plunges through an asphalt shingle roof. If the roofing otherwise has a life expectancy of ten years, the repair should also have a life expectancy of at least ten years. If the roofing only has a life expectancy of one year, then the repair should be capable of lasting one year or more. It is not prudent to put a one year patch on a ten year roof or to waste a ten year repair on a one year roof. All repairs should be done by qualified competent professionals.

1.10.1 SOUND

The inspector thinks the item under inspection is functioning at the moment of the inspection. This does not imply perfection, absence of minor defects, or absence of wear and tear.

1.10.2 TYPICAL

The inspector thinks the item, material, or aspect of construction is characteristic or similar to comparable products in similar houses. The roof has normal wear and tear.

1.10.3 BLISTERS AND BUBBLES

Asphalt Shingles. Moisture trapped within the shingle expands creating a blister. It leaves a crater when the blister bursts. This may shorten the life of the shingles by exposing the felt or core. Little can be done until you replace the shingles. (Read section 1.5.1 Asphalt Materials.)

Built-Up Roofing. Trapped moisture expands forming bubbles several inches to several feet across. Do not step on the bubbles. In extreme cases they must be cut out and repaired (a professional job) and ventilation must be improved to allow the trapped moisture to escape. (Read section 1.5.4 Built-Up Roofs.)

1.10.4 CUPPING AND CURLING

Cupping and curling applies to asphalt shingles and indicates tabs of individual shingles are deforming. Their edges are turning or curling up or down. Excessive heat or poor ventilation aggravates cupping and curling. Little can be done until you replace the shingles. Increasing or improving attic ventilation may help. (Read section 1.5.1 Asphalt Materials.) Continued next page.

Flatten or remove deformed shingles before you install a new roof. Lighter shingle colors may reflect heat better. Advanced stages of cupping and curling dictate replacing the roofing soon if not immediately. They are susceptible to wind and hail damage and to damage from foot traffic.

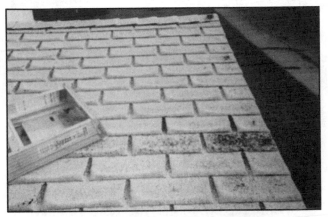

1.10.4 a. Cupping and Curling, 1.10.5 Erosion.
Tabs of individual shingles are deforming. Their edges are turning or curling up or down. Such shingles are subject to wind and hail damage and to crushing from foot traffic. Erosion or loss of granules exposes the asphalt and fabric of the shingle to sunlight.

1.10.5 EROSION

Erosion applies to asphalt shingles and indicates the granules are washing away. Unless this is happening at a rapid rate, it is normal aging. Losing the granules exposes asphalt in the shingle to more ultraviolet light from the sun. Eventually the shingles die from exposure. Little can be done except to replace the shingles when they reach the end of their useful life. (Read section 1.5.1 Asphalt Materials.)

1.10.6 SMALL FISSURES

These are small cracks forming in asphalt shingles from the loss of oils in the asphalt. This is normal aging for asphalt shingles. Little can be done except to replace the shingles when they reach the end of their useful life. Increasing attic ventilation to cool the attic may be wise. (Read section 1.5.1 Asphalt Materials.)

1.10.6 a. Small Fissures.
Small cracks indicate the shingles are "cooking" and losing the volatile part of the asphalt.

1.10.7 CRACKED RIDGE

Cracked ridge applies to asphalt shingles and indicates the ridge cap shingles are cracking or splitting where they fold over the peak. Replace them to avoid the possibility of a leak. (Read section 1.5.1 Asphalt Materials.)

1.10.8 PREMATURE AGING

The roofing is deteriorating at an unusually rapid rate. This may indicate the materials were defective or the installation or ventilation is poor. Defective materials will require replacement before the end of their life expectancy. Correct poor ventilation and installation defects.

1.10.8 a Premature Aging
The Tic-Tac-Toe appearance on the roof is a sign several bundles of defective shingles were installed.

1.10.9 PHYSICAL DAMAGE

Physical damage as applied to asphalt shingles, indicates broken or missing shingles caused by wind, foot traffic, hail, impact, tree limbs, ladder damage, etc. Physical damage happens to any type of roofing. Physical damage to roofing may require repair or replacement of the damaged material to prevent leaks or for appearance.

1.10.9 a. Physical Damage.
A large tree limb plunged through this roof. Watch for overhanging dead limbs. Such damage, if it is small can be repaired by patching the sheeting with metal and replacing the damaged shingles. If matching shingles are not available, consider using the starter shingles and replacing them with odd ones.

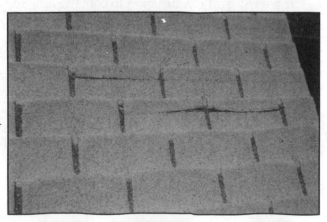

1.10.9 b. Split Shingle.
Occasionally shingles split or fail because of manufacturer's defects or abuse during installation.

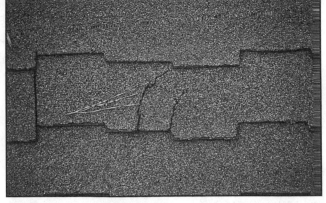

1.10.9 c. Split Shingle
Some shingles split from heat and age.

1.10.10 EXPOSED OR LIFTED NAILS

Nails not covered by the roofing. Some nails back out of the substructure and lift or penetrate the layer above. Exposed nails can be coated with tar. Nails that have moved and lifted or penetrated the layer above should be removed and the hole sealed or the shingle replaced. (Read section 1.5.1 Asphalt Materials.)

1.10.10 a. Exposed or Lifted Nails
in the center of the picture there are two
shingles lifted or held up by a nail below.
They have the appearance of "eyebrows."
Repair these properly to prevent "blow-off"
or the nail coming through like a stone
in your shoe.

1.10.11 MOSS OR MILDEW

Moss or mildew refers to plant life growing on wooden roofing. It may also affect other types of roof material including built-up roofs. Remove or chemically treat moss or mildew.

Moss and fungus can be a contributor to the early demise of the roof. A solution of three ounces of copper sulfate to a gallon of water will eliminate the problem, but it may also eliminate ground plantings. Another remedy is a 5% or 10% pentachlorophenol solution or a solution of phenyl-mercury-xoleate. These materials, marketed under various trade names, are highly toxic to wood attacking bacteria, ground plantings, and the applicator. Follow the instructions and use precautions.

Lead or copper flashing will lessen the ability of moss and fungus to form, and will do double duty for you. (Read 1.6.3 Copper Flashing and 1.5.2 Wooden Roofing Materials.)

1.10.12 WET ROT

Wet rot indicates damage to shakes or shingles from the long term effects of poor drying. Wood shingles installed over plywood or solid decking cannot dry from below as when installed over spaced sheeting. Cleaning and chemical treatments may arrest the rotting and extend the useful life of the roof. Tree limbing and improving attic ventilation may help. Replacement is the only answer if the rot is advanced. (Read section 1.5.2 Wooden Roofing Materials.)

1.10.13 IMPROPERLY INSTALLED ROOFING

This is a broad category affecting all roofing types. There are as many improper ways to install roofing as there are roofers, especially amateur roofers. Have the installation errors corrected. This may mean replacement.

1.10.13 a. Missing Ridge Cap.
The absence of the ridge is improper installation and will leak. Also shows 1.8.3 Ridge Vent.

1.10.14 TOO FLAT

The slope is too low for the type of roofing. This may mean replacement with a material suitable for the slope.

1.10.15 ICE DAMMING

Ice dams form when heat rising from the building, melts snow that refreezes on the overhangs, where there is no heat. Water then ponds and flows up under the shingles and leaks into the structure. In warmer climates, where this is rare, it may be feasible to increase attic insulation and ventilation and reduce the risk. In northern climates special eave details combat the problem. (See picture following.)

1.10.15 a. Ice Damming.

1.10.15 d. Flashing and Ventilation to prevent damage from ice dams.

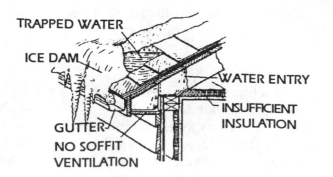

1.10.16 SLATES OR TILES MISSING

Slate and tile roofs are subject to losing whole tiles from breakage (physical damage) and from nails rusting or pulling loose. Have an experienced roofer, familiar with these materials, repair the defects. (Read section 1.5.3 Slate and Tile Roofing Materials.)

1.10.17 SLATES OR TILES BROKEN

Slates and tiles are brittle and subject to physical damage or cracking from freeze/thaw action. Replacing damaged tiles is part of periodic maintenance and should be done by an experienced roofer familiar with these materials. (Read sections 1.5.3 Slate and Tile Roofing Materials.)

1.10.17 a. Slates or Tiles Broken
Slates or tiles broken enough to expose the slot between the slates below should be replaced.

1.10.18 RIDGE SEAL LEAKING

On slate roofs this indicates the tar applied to the peaks and ridges is cracking or failing. Tarring ridges is part of the annual maintenance required on a slate roof. As applied to other types of roofing, this indicates the ridge is leaking. Repairs should be made by an experienced roofer familiar with the materials. (Read section 1.5.3 Slate and Tile Roofing Materials.)

1.10.19 POORLY PATCHED

Poorly patched indicates the roofing, regardless of type, is poorly or amateurishly patched. This patched area may fail again. Repairs should be made by an experienced professional roofer familiar with these materials.

1.10.20 EXPOSED FELT

Exposed felt applies to built-up roofing and indicates the felt is showing. The roof is either incomplete or for some reason weathered to the felt. Have an experienced roofer complete or repair the roofing. (Read section 1.5.4 Built-Up Roofs.)

Asphalt shingles so worn or defective the felt shows. Replace the affected area. (Read 1.5.1 Asphalt Roofing Materials.)

1.10.21 PONDING

Ponding indicates standing water on the roof. This accelerates the demise of the roofing and may turn a pin hole leak into a flood. Eliminate ponding by flooding the area with bitumen or by building a proper slope into the roof when replacing roofing. Keeping drains clear is essential. (Read section 1.5.4 Built-Up Roofs.)

1.10.22 ALLIGATORING

Built-up roofs sometimes exhibit cracking of the bitumen. This looks like alligator hide or a dried up mud-flat on a smaller scale. The cracks may permit water to infiltrate causing blisters (Section 1.10.3) or leaks. An experienced roofer may be able to repair this condition without replacing the roof, but it may lead to replacement. (Read section 1.5.4.2 Built-Up Roofs 3 or 4 Ply Smooth.)

1.10.23 BITUMEN (TAR) ON METAL ROOFING

Tar on metal roofing only avoids the inevitable. Replacement. Inspecting the metal is impossible because the tar conceals it. Expect to repair or replace the tarred areas soon. (Read 1.5.5 Metal Roofing.)

1.10.24 PAINTED

The metal roofing is painted, a good and proper sign. (Read section 1.5.5 Metal Roofing.)

Some asphalt shingle roofs are tarred or painted. This indicates the roof is dying and someone is struggling to extend the life a year or two. The only cure is replacement. (Read section 1.5.1 Asphalt Roofing.)

1.10.25 PAINT FAILING

Paint failing means it is time to repaint.

1.10.25 a. Paint Failing
This is a standing seam metal roof. (Section 1.5.5.2) It should be painted every 5 years. (See also 1.10.24 Painted and 1.10.26 Rusted)

1.10.26 RUSTED

Rusted means the metal is rusting. Immediate attention from a good painter, willing to do extensive preparation, may save the roof from further deterioration and eminent failure. (Read section 1.5.5 Metal Roofing.)

1.10.27 ROTTING GUTTERS

Wood gutters show evidence of decay. With proper maintenance they may last 30-40 years. When rot is found, replace sections. Carpenter ants may be found in damp or rotting gutters.

1.10.29 SPLIT OR SEPARATED

The metal fatigued, tore, or pulled away from the wall or chimney. Replace or repair to prevent or cure leaks. This may require professional help. Some flashing details are elaborate. Pipe collars also split and require replacement. (Read section 1.6.6 Neoprene Rubber.)

1.10.30 TAR ON FLASHING
Excessive or improper tarring indicates amateur repairs or attempts to extend the flashing beyond its useful life. Have the flashing professionally repaired or replaced.

1.10.31 LEAKING AT A VALLEY
Valleys are prone to leak for many reasons. They carry water and their slope is lower than the roof's slope. If the metal is too narrow and no diverter rib present, water may rush across and flow under the opposite shingles and cause a leak. Galvanized valleys rust because zinc galvanizing deteriorates over time. Sometimes the metal tears with thermal expansion and contraction. Woven valleys are difficult to diagnose. Cure the leak, probably with the help of a professional roofer.

1.10.31 a. Leaking at a valley
This is the "attic" view of a leaking valley.

1.10.32 LEAKING AT A DORMER
Similar to 1.10.31 Leaking at a Valley because many dormers also have valleys above them. The sides of dormers sometimes leak when their siding runs horizontally like clapboards or weatherboards. If the siding runs too close to the roofing, water may run along the upper edge of the siding toward the front and fall behind the flashing. There should be a 1 to 2 inch gap between the clapboard and the roofing material. An experienced roofer may be able to make repairs. However, a more prudent method of repair is reinstalling the siding parallel to the angle of the roof.

1.10.32 a. Leaking at a Dormer
There may be flashing behind the siding but it is not visible to the inspector. The staining is caused by water soaking in from the roof.
(See 1.6.d Flashing Diagram)

1.10.33 FLASHING OMITTED
There is no flashing or no functioning flashing. Have proper flashing installed. Without proper flashing a leak is inevitable. (Read 1.6 Flashing and Joint Material.)

1.10.33 a. Flashing Omitted.
There should have been flashing where the trim (rake board) touches the roofing. The leak was rotting the roof sheeting in the attic.

1.10.36 SAGGING

Sagging implies the gutters droop, or pull away from the house. Downspouts also drop occasionally. Realign and secure the gutters and downspouts to operate properly. (Read section 1.7 Gutters and Downspouts.)

1.10.37 DEBRIS

The gutters are full of debris limiting their function or creating an overflow problem. Clean the gutters.

Debris also accumulates on flat or low sloped roofs increasing the chances of a leak. Clean the roof. (Read section 1.7 Gutters and Downspouts.)

1.10.38 LEAKING

The gutters are leaking. Some leaks can be cured but leaks from general deterioration will require replacement.

1.10.39 OPEN JOINTS

The joint in the gutters is open or not properly sealed. Seal the joints with gutter sealant or solder them.

1.10.40 ROTTING OR DAMAGED WOOD GUTTERS

The wooden gutters are rotting or otherwise damaged.

1.10.42 ADEQUATE VENTILATION

Adequate implies the ventilation appeared to be functioning properly at the moment of the inspection. (Read section 1.8 Ventilation.)

1.10.43 MINIMAL VENTILATION

Minimal implies vents are present and functioning but they may be overwhelmed by severe weather, changes in occupancy, or changes in the roofing. Increase ventilation to adequate levels to protect the structure and extend the life of the roofing. (Read section 1.8 Ventilation.)

1.10.44 INADEQUATE VENTILATION

Inadequate ventilation implies not enough ventilation is present. The inspector saw few or no vents, evidence of condensation, mold, mildew, or frost in the attic, delamination of the plywood, rust stains on nails, etc. Increase ventilation to adequate levels to protect the structure and extend the life of the roofing. (Read section 1.8 Ventilation.)

1.10.45 CONDENSATION

The inspector saw drops of water on nails or metal surfaces, rust stains around nails, or delamination of plywood in the attic, but not from roof leaks. Increase attic ventilation to lower the moisture level. Often the moisture comes from a wet crawl space or basement. Curing the wetness problem in the crawl space may eliminate or decrease the condensation in the attic.

1.10.46 MOLD OR MILDEW

The inspector saw mildew in the attic. Under ventilation and condensation causes or aggravates mold and mildew. (See 1.10.45 Condensation.)   The source of the overwhelming moisture vapor is usually a wet crawl space or basement. Controlling the wetness in the underfloor area should reduce the moisture in the attic. If the moisture content is below 12 or 13 % in the lumber long enough, the mold and mildew will go dormant and eventually die. Some types of mold and mildew could take months or years to die.

1.10.47 RODENT OR BIRD DAMAGE OR INFESTATION

Rodents, especially squirrels, like to move into attics. Once in, they are hard to evict. They gnaw through vents and facia boards to get in. They get in the gutters and gnaw through above the gutter and under the shingles. Seal their entrances with heavy screen (hardware cloth) or sheet-metal. Do not block vents. Also seal out birds and bats. These animals are messy, noisy, destructive, and carry diseases.

Do not handle their droppings, as they can harbor disease and parasites. Leave the removal of animal droppings to professionals. Insects (bees) also occasionally infest attics. Bees can be deadly. Leave their removal and extermination to professionals also. Screen them out where feasible.

1.10.50 NARROW OR NO OVERHANG

Narrow or no overhang implies the roof has little or no overhang (No soffit). Overhangs are important and protect the house. This condition may make it difficult to improve attic ventilation. It is essential to keep gutters cleaned out and free flowing. If they overflow, water could quickly enter the house. The absence of overhangs makes gutters more important. Without them, roof water runs down the wall and falls close to the foundation. This invites a wet basement or crawl space.

1.10.51 FOGGED THERMAL SKYLIGHT

Indicates the seal between the two layers failed and the skylight fogged with condensation. The only cure is replacement. (Read section 1.9.2 Skylights.)

1.10.52 LEAKING SKYLIGHT

Indicates a leak around or through the skylight or its curb. This may be difficult to cure and may require professional expertise. (Read section 1.9.2 Skylights.)

1.10.53 CRACKED GLASS

The glass or plastic skylight cracked or failed and may leak. The only cure is replacement of the damaged pieces. (Read section 1.9.2 Skylights.)

1.10.54 LEAKING AT OTHER ROOF EQUIPMENT

The roof is leaking at the solar equipment, radio, TV, or dish antennae, etc. Have the leak cured properly. (Read section 1.9.3 Roof Mounted Equipment.)

CHAPTER TWO

EXTERIOR

The colonists built many types and styles of houses ranging from wood, thatched roof cottages to stone, brick and frame houses. Many home styles were copied from their homeland, while others developed into American styles.

The exterior design and materials are aspects of architectural beauty of any structure. The exterior of the house has been chosen for centuries because of style, color, fire and wind resistance, economy, weight, and life expectancy.

The exterior is the exterior skin of the structure and the outer surface keeping weather off the structural elements of the walls.

The factors affecting materials used on the exterior and their applications will be discussed in each section. The exterior inspection consists of siding material, trim, primary windows, exterior doors, porches and decks, and steps and rails. Read each section carefully. If you have questions, ask the inspector.

The use of "sand blasting" masonry and wood surfaces is not suggested as it shortens the life of materials. It is better to have a professional apply chemicals instead. Also periodic maintenance and upkeep of the exterior are essential to protecting the structure and are discussed in each section.

2.1 LIMITATIONS

This section describes the aspects which limit the inspection of the exterior. Inspectors do the best inspection they can, but sometimes physical obstructions, weather conditions, or the condition of the exterior, prevent them from doing the whole job. Arrange for an inspection overcoming the limitations, if possible (i.e. Prune vines or shrubs and have the exterior reinspected.) An uninspected exterior or a severely limited or restricted inspection could be a total unknown. It is your responsibility to overcome the limitations. You should complete the inspection prior to closing even if you must hire others (Painters, Engineers, Siding contractor's etc.) or pay an additional fee to the inspector or other industry specialist. Repairs can be expensive and at some point replacement is the best alternative. The inspector cannot make representations about what was not inspected. If you close on the house with a Limited or Restricted inspection you are accepting the responsibility for the unknown items about the system.

2.1.2 TYPICAL

The inspector feels they have seen as much of the exterior as they normally see. The exterior is inspected from the ground, while walking around the house, and from a distance ranging from several feet to perhaps the limits of the site. A typical inspection does not include noting or reporting on every minor defect in every board or brick. We do not remove siding or trim and do not use a water hose to induce leaks in windows or the exterior. (Read 2.1 Limitations.)

2.1.2 RESTRICTED

The inspector feels they have seen less of the exterior than they typically see. (Read 2.1.1 Typical.)

2.1.2.1 VEGETATION, VINES, OR SHRUBBERY

Vegetation, vines, or shrubs can obscure parts of the exterior and structure inhibiting the inspection. Vines growing on buildings are harmful and obstruct the inspector's view. Even display gardens can keep the inspector from approaching closely to make the inspection. (Read section 2.1.2 Restricted.)

2.1.2.2 TOPOGRAPHY OR SITE

The terrain makes it difficult or impossible for the inspector to get a vantage point to inspect the exterior. (Read 2.1.2 Restricted.)

2.1.2.3 ATTACHED OR LESS THAN THREE FEET

The structure is attached to another structure or separated from a nearby structure by less than three feet. (i.e. A row house or duplex beside a narrow alley or wall.) The inspector cannot enter the adjacent house to view the other side of the common wall. The narrowness of the alleyway restricts the inspector's view of the exterior. The inspector may be forced to look up at a wall instead of viewing it from a distance. (Read section 2.1.2 Restricted.)

2.1.2.4 PERSONAL PROPERTY

Personal property can block the inspector's view of the exterior. The inspector will not remove personal property. Boats, campers, or yard equipment parked close to the exterior block the inspector's view. (Read 2.1.2 Restricted.)

2.2 GENERAL

A quick reference and overview of the inspector's opinions or impressions. This section is subjective and relies on the inspector's judgment and experience in estimating the age, whether clues are important, and if toxins are present, etc. (Read the Exterior chapter fully before forming any final opinion.)

2.2.1 SYSTEM INSPECTED (YES, RESTRICTED, OR NO)

The inspector marks whether the system was inspected. No information will be given about a system that was not inspected. If the inspector writes in or circles "R" for restricted, the system was partially inspected. Check 2.1 LIMITATIONS or discuss it with the inspector to learn the full extent of the restrictions. A severely limited inspection may not give you the information you need. You should do whatever is necessary to remove or overcome the restrictions and have the system fully inspected before you close on the house. (Read 2.1 Limitations.)

2.2.2 CLUES OR TELL TALES (YES OR NO)

"YES" The inspector observes evidence suggesting an underlying problem. (i.e. rotted exterior trim may indicate failed and leaking built-in gutters.)

"NO" The inspector does not see evidence suggesting hidden defects.

2.2.3 ALERT TO TOXINS (YES OR NO)

"YES" The inspector sees material that may be asbestos, lead based paint, or urea formaldehyde foam, etc. (i.e. Most houses built before 1979 probably were painted with lead based paint.)

"NO" The inspector does not see a hazardous substance. A home inspection is a visual inspection not designed to reveal every possible hazard or dangerous chemical around the home. Experts can perform extensive tests to identify the presence of such matter or gas, if desired. (Read the contract and other sections in this report referring to toxic chemicals.)

2.2.4 MAJOR DEFECTS (YES OR NO)

"YES" The inspector sees a defect costing $500.00 or more to repair or affecting the habitability of the house. (e.g. Delayed maintenance can become a major defect if left uncured. Putting off exterior painting eventually may ruin the siding and windows.)

2.2.4 a. Major Defects
These masonry steps collapsed after 60 years of freeze thaw conditions and delayed maintenance. Repairs will cost over $500.00. Note the shrubbery blocks the view of any other major defects in the foundation.

"NO" The inspector does not see a major defect.

2.2.5 SITE

This is a space provided for the inspector to write whether the topography is level or sloping.

Level or gently sloping sites may have poor drainage. If the whole area is level, drainage problems may be difficult to solve without the help or cooperation of neighbors and the local government.

Sloping lots often have problems but may also have solutions. You may wish to read Foundations/Basements/Structures, Chapter 3 of this report for more information.

2.2.6 STYLE
The inspector may describe the building style such as colonial, contemporary, ranch, two story, etc.

2.2.7 WALLS PLUMB (YES OR NO)
"Yes" The exterior walls appear to be plumb (Vertical). This is desirable.

"NO" The walls are leaning or bulging (not plumb). Generally, walls are plumb and flat. If they are not plumb, it may be a clue or tell tale of an underlying problem, perhaps settlement, rot, insect damage, etc.

2.2.8 AMATEUR WORKMANSHIP (YES OR NO)
"Yes" The inspector notes workmanship of less than professional quality. Poor workmanship may constitute a major defect. Major defects cost $500.00 or more to repair or may affect the habitability or the house. The work may not serve the purpose intended and may require repair or replacement.

"NO" No amateur workmanship noted. Some amateurs produce workmanship better than professionals.

2.2.9 SUBJECTIVE RATING
The inspector's grade for the exterior:

E   EXCELLENT, above average, new or like new. (e.g. a new exterior on an older house.)

A   AVERAGE, in typical condition for its age, showing normal wear and tear and properly maintained. (e.g. five year old siding that looks five years old on a five year old house.)

C   BELOW AVERAGE, prematurely aged, showing heavy or excess wear and tear, or delayed maintenance. Perhaps showing minor defects.

F   SUBSTANDARD, failed or at the end of its life expectancy. Even with repairs, further service should be considered a gift.

2.3 EXTERIOR SIDING MATERIAL
Identification of the type of siding or cladding. An endless number of materials, types, and styles were used over the years for siding. Only the major types will be listed. Siding is the exterior skin of the structure and the outer surface keeping the weather off the structural elements of the walls. In masonry construction, there is an overlapping of functions. The masonry serves as both a structural element and a siding material. In this Exterior Section, the material is reported as siding material. (Structural problems will be reported under FOUNDATION/BASEMENTS/STRUCTURES,

Chapter 3. They also may be noted in section 2.2.2 Clues or Tell tales or section 2.2.7 Walls Plumb.)

The following sections give the advantages, disadvantages, characteristics, applications, estimated life expectancy, and maintenance, etc. for each type of exterior material.

Many houses suffer damage every day because of poor or delayed maintenance. Houses commonly appreciate, but they individually deteriorate (depreciate) from the forces of weather and time. Almost every house, regardless of age, style, materials of construction, or location needs regular periodic maintenance.

2.3.1 MASONRY

Houses built of masonry materials in which the brick, block, or stone, etc. form the structure of the walls are masonry houses. The walls are often 8 to 20 inches thick. Most often only the exterior walls are masonry and the interior partitions are frame with either plaster or drywall. In old houses, the inner side of the exterior walls will be plastered directly on the masonry. More recently, the walls were furred with 3/4" furring strips over felt paper and then plastered over the furring. (Read also 2.3.2.3 Brick Veneer.)

MAINTENANCE AND UPKEEP

Masonry houses require little maintenance until the mortar deteriorates. When the mortar softens, crumbles, and starts to slough out of the joints from weathering, it is time to point or tuckpoint the wall. Proper workmanship is difficult and should be done by professionals. It involves scraping or chiseling the joint to a depth several times its thickness, removing the loose debris, inserting (tucking) fresh mortar into the joints, properly compacting it, and tooling it (Pointing). The mortar should be compatible with the original in color, consistency, strength, texture, etc. Keeping the masonry clean and matching the old workmanship is tedious, expensive, and requires skill.

All masonry buildings need pointing eventually. What can you do to limit the work and perhaps delay the inevitable? Remove any vines growing on the exterior. Their grippers burrow into the masonry and mortar creating entry points for water. Gutters may be beneficial in protecting the walls from splash damage and wind driven water.

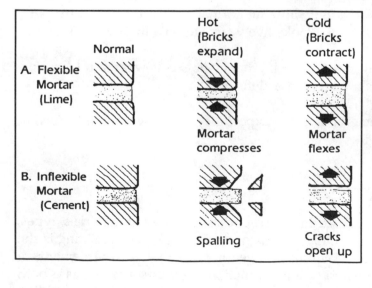

2.3.1 d. Masonry.
Repairs to masonry should be made with mortar as rich in lime as the original to avoid spalling and cracking.

Coating the masonry with a "breathing" or permeable clear sealer may also help. Do not use silicone because it does not breathe. Hydrozo is one brand of product that "breathes." (Write for more information to Hydrozo, 855 W. Street, Lincoln, Nebraska 68501.)

2.3.1.1 BRICK

Many older brick masonry buildings have two or more thickness of brick. Cured or fired exterior brick withstand exposure to the weather. Inner thicknesses were often raw or uncured brick.

These interior bricks were raw clay or lightly fired. They fail in less than five years if exposed to the weather. These are "Dead" or "Salmon" brick. They are occasionally seen in exterior walls of brick veneer houses of reused or salvaged brick. They may weather away to nothing in a few years, leaving a hole. Salmon brick should be discarded. On the interior, they may be crude and shed dust. If exposed on the exterior, they must be protected. Sealing them will not be sufficient. Siding or veneer will be necessary. Do not confuse the plainer "common" brick used on the sides and backs of many brick buildings with these unfired bricks.

Newer brick masonry homes tend to be a 4" layer of brick and a 4" or 8" layer of block and are characterized by brick "Header" Courses. Every seventh course of brick turned on its end (the narrow end showing) ties the brick and block together.

2.3.1.1 a. Brick Masonry.
Notice the 3.8.15 Fallen Arch above the window. This is a rather typical but inexpert repair. A good mason can remove and replace the material and leave little trace of the work.

2.3.1.2 STONE

Stone houses and the stone used vary. The stone ranges from uncut field or ruble stone to cut stone laid in fanciful patterns. As with brick, some buildings are solid stone, block and stone, or brick and stone. (Read Maintenance and Upkeep in section 2.3.1 Masonry.)

2.3.1.3 BLOCK

Block includes cinder, concrete, and light weight block. Once, the cinders from coal fired boilers were in abundant supply and used as aggregate in block. Unfortunately, the iron present in the cinders would rust and bleed down the walls. Cinder blocks soon fell into disfavor. Concrete blocks are strong and heavy, don't bleed, and have no rust residue. Substituting perlite or vermiculite for some of the aggregate makes blocks lighter. They are not as strong as cement block, but the lighter weight makes them more popular with masons, architects, and suppliers. Blocks are more porous than brick and most stone. Water flows through them freely. Block wicks water from the footing. Painting is necessary when using block as an exterior wall to retard the absorption of water. (Read Maintenance and Upkeep in section 2.3.1 Masonry.)

2.3.1.4 ADOBE

A Spanish name for sundried brick common in Mexico and the southwestern part of the United States. People like houses made of adobe because they are cooler than uninsulated homes made of wood or stone. Adobe is not suitable in damp climates. The bricks will crumble if exposed for a long time to rain and freeze/thaw.

2.3.2 FRAME

A skeleton of wooden structural members covered with an exterior skin of siding or cladding. In older and lower quality housing, the siding is applied directly to the studs (Vertical Members). In higher quality houses there is usually a subsiding or wall sheathing beneath the exterior siding. The wall sheathing often serves as a nailing base, a structural brace, and helps to cut infiltration and heat loss. The siding serves to keep the weather off the other components and to enhance the appearance of the house. In this section (Exterior) the inspector will check whether the siding protects the balance of the structure.

MAINTENANCE AND UPKEEP

Materials used for siding or cladding vary widely with climate, location, and culture, etc. Maintenance varies accordingly. General upkeep can affect the life expectancy of any siding. Keep vines from growing on, under and into the siding. Not only can certain vines (especially Ivy) penetrate the siding with their "grippers," they can grow under siding or trim and lift it off the house. Gutters are important to keep rain and splash off the siding. Splashing and wind driven water will work its way behind the siding and under sills rotting the framing. Trees and shrubbery should be pruned to prevent damage from wind and to allow for air circulation, drying, and inspection. All painted surfaces should be properly coated.

2.3.2.1 HARDBOARD OR COMPOSITION SIDING

Hardboard or composition sidings manufactured in a wide variety of styles, shapes, or textures range from simple smooth boards and panels to fanciful shapes imitating stone, stucco, shakes, etc. Hardboard is a wood fiber pulp, with a glue or bonding agent, molded under pressure into the desired shape. Many of these products are factory sealed with primer or clear sealer. Problems with the products range from shrinking, and swelling to decomposition. The wood fibers randomly oriented within the products cause it to shrink and swell more in length than natural wood. This can lead to cracks at joints when the siding dries and to buckling and bulging when the siding is wet. If the product becomes saturated, the glue may fail, and the siding may decompose or turn into pulp. Eventually it will rot.

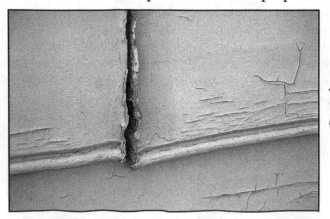

2.3.2.1 a. Hardboard Siding
Open joints can admit water to the structure behind.
(Note also 2.11.4 Paint failure.)

MAINTENANCE AND UPKEEP

Keep hardboard or composition siding painted, sealed, and protected from water. Today, paints appear to last only three to five years. Stretching a paint job a year or two may cost you the siding. Moisture migrating through the walls from within or under the house can enter the siding from the back and cause it to swell, buckle, and sometimes drool "tea" stains down the siding. Vapor barrier type interior paint, dehumidification, and a polyethylene vapor barrier on the grade of the crawl space might help. Once the siding has buckled or decomposed it will not return to its original shape. Hardboard or composition siding is an exterior "paper" product and must be properly protected. (Read also 2.3.2 Frame.)

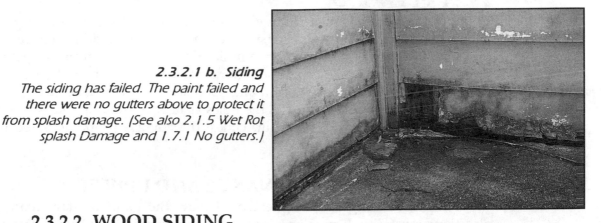

2.3.2.1 b. Siding
The siding has failed. The paint failed and there were no gutters above to protect it from splash damage. (See also 2.1.5 Wet Rot splash Damage and 1.7.1 No gutters.)

2.3.2.2 WOOD SIDING

Many species of wood are used as siding or cladding, some with more success than others. Redwood is the best. It is naturally decay resistant, takes paint, is strong and lightweight. Western Red Cedar, another decay resistant wood, is often knotty. The knots tend to fall out. Almost any wood that will stay straight and "lay" on the wall can be used as siding if it's painted or sealed. Wood expands and contracts with changes in moisture content. This expanding and contracting spurred the development of techniques allowing the siding to "Float" and remain weather tight. Nails in horizontal weather boards or lapped siding should penetrate the edge of only one board. This allows the other edge to move freely and not split the board. Problems range from splitting, warping, and decaying to loosing knots.

MAINTENANCE AND UPKEEP

Wood siding, unless it is a naturally decay resistant species, requires proper painting or sealing. Paint has two purposes: (1) to beautify, and (2) to preserve. A poorly applied coat of paint may prove harmful by trapping moisture and causing rot. Proper caulking is important.

At some point, the paint becomes so thick it must be removed. Once the paint stops acting like a flexible film, breaks, and cracks like a solid, or becomes too thick to "breath," it should be removed. Many older houses (Built before 1979) have lead based paint that can be hazardous to work and live around. Use proper precautions, clothes, masks, etc. and clean up. Contact a good paint supplier or the Health Department for advice.

2.3.2.3 SHINGLES AND SHAKES

Wooden shingles and shakes are popular as a siding material. This naturally decay resistant material can be painted, stained, or left to weather.

MAINTENANCE AND UPKEEP

Replace individual cracked or damaged pieces. Cleaning before painting can be a chore. Using a high pressure wash or scrubber can damage the siding. It is possible to "blast" a hole through the subsiding or any tar paper (felt) under the siding.

2.3.2.4 PLYWOOD

Plywood siding is manufactured from Redwood, Western Red Cedar, Southern Yellow Pine, Douglas Fir and other suitable woods. Plywood siding, properly installed, produces a strong house resistant to infiltration. Weather resistant putty used by some manufacturers fills knots and other surface defects. The putty does not "take" stain well and may "glare." Paint and solid stains may work better. Tiny interior voids may attract insects who use the holes as habitat. Woodpeckers may attack the siding to get the insects living within. Unless the siding is properly coated and sealed, it may delaminate.

MAINTENANCE AND UPKEEP

Keep the siding properly sealed. Follow the paint or stain manufacturer's directions carefully. It may be wise to seek out technical advice or literature. Stain literature reveals semi transparent stain's redo time is two to three years, solid stain may last three to four years and paint four to five years. Plywood needs sealing on its ends, edges and in the groves where water may soak into the interior plies.

2.3.2.5 BRICK VENEER

Veneer houses differ from masonry houses. The structure is wood and the brick is a thin (about 4") non structural siding. The veneer serves as siding to protect the rest of the structure from the elements but serves little or no structural purpose. Veneer must be braced by the structure it covers. Since the siding is somewhat independent of the actual structural elements, a crack in a veneer house may be less significant than a crack in a masonry house. Veneer houses do have some problems not common to masonry structures. If the veneer is not properly supported or if moisture penetrates the walls and destroys the metal straps (wall ties) used to anchor the brick to the structure, the veneer may crack, "bulge out," and pull away from the wall. In rare instances, in hurricanes and tornadoes, the weight of damaged and failing veneer has been known to cause the structure to fail.

MAINTENANCE AND UPKEEP

Water is the worst enemy of siding. It soaks in through the brick and rusts the wall ties and the lintels (Beams or angle irons) above openings. It may freeze and crack the brick, causing the faces to pop off or spall. Anything you can do to keep rain and splash off the walls will be beneficial. Gutters and downspouts are helpful. Keep vines, shrubs, and trees pruned to allow for drying and inspection. Mortar joints in veneer walls eventually suffer from aging and weathering. It softens and begins to crumble, soughs, or erodes out of the joints. At some point it must be repaired and pointed. (See Section 2.3.1 MASONRY for a description of "pointing.")

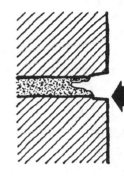

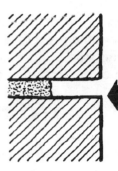

INCORRECT

Mortar not cleaned out to a sufficient uniform depth.

Edges of brick damaged by tool or grinder. Creates wider joint.

2.3.2.5 d. Brick Veneer.
This diagram details the proper cleaning of joints in masonry in preparation for repointing. The depth should be two or three times the thickness and uniform. The new mortar must match the original in color, texture, and strength.

CORRECT

Mortar cleaned out to a uniform depth - about 1" deep

Undamaged edges of brick.

2.3.2.6 VINYL OR ALUMINUM

Manufacturers have been working for years to perfect siding made of vinyl and aluminum. Aluminum siding has a factory finish of paint or a more permanent coating such as Teflon. Life expectancies quoted by manufacturers range from 20 to 40 years. The siding comes in many shapes and styles or profiles. There are also stock shapes used for corners and trim. Non stock shapes can be site fabricated from matching or contrasting materials to cover window trim, etc. Vinyl siding, made of solid vinyl, has the color throughout the material. Vinyl also comes in several stock shapes for corners, etc. Since vinyl cannot be fabricated on the site, aluminum is used for custom shapes. Most vinyl sided houses have some aluminum trim. Both products have some advantages and disadvantages. Aluminum dents easily and conducts electricity. Care must be taken not to "Electrify" the house with amateur or outmoded electrical work. Some people claim aluminum siding attracts lightning and interferes with television reception. Vinyl may crack or break in cold weather. Vinyl or aluminum siding must be installed so it "floats" allowing movement.

MAINTENANCE AND UPKEEP

Both vinyl and aluminum siding accumulate dirt, mold, and mildew. Occasionally you may wish to wash them. The siding can be cleaned with a sponge and a solution of 1/2 chlorine bleach and 1/2 water. The solution should be tried on a small area at first to determine its success. The washed area should be rinsed thoroughly to prevent damage to plants around the perimeter of the house. Professional house washing is available in many areas.

Once the finish on the aluminum weathers to the point the color is faded one may wish to replace or paint it. Once painted, you will have to redo every three to five years. Consult a good paint store, technical consultant of a paint company, or siding manufacturer before painting. You may not be able to paint vinyl successfully and some aluminum siding may not "take" paint.

2.3.2.7 STUCCO

Stucco siding is a sand cement exterior plaster ranging from 3/4" to 1 1/2" thickness applied over a mesh of metal reinforcing wire. Often the mesh was nailed directly to the studs and several coats of stucco were built-up to make a finished wall. Sometimes it will be applied over storm siding or a weather resistant membrane. Some block buildings are stuccoed. The finished wall can have many patterns ranging from smooth to a pebble texture with curlicues, to tooled stone or block shapes. The materials were inexpensive but the process was labor intensive. It is important to prevent cracks from forming in the stucco since water can seep into cracks, freeze, expand, and cause deterioration of the framing and further cracking of the stucco.

MAINTENANCE AND UPKEEP

When repainting a stucco house, a simple washdown with a garden hose may not remove all dirt, mildew, etc., because of the texture. A thorough steam-cleaning by a professional can clean the stucco, and show areas of loose paint, which should be removed. As with all siding, do not allow water to penetrate behind the stucco and rust its fasteners or the mesh. Gutters are beneficial. Keep limbs and vines pruned to promote drying. Keep wooden trim, especially window sills painted and caulked to shed water.

2.3.2.8 CEMENT ASBESTOS

Like cement asbestos roofing, this siding is manufactured from a mixture of asbestos fibers (for reinforcement) and cement molded under high pressure. Asbestos is no longer used in this type of siding. Cement asbestos siding does not present health problems to the occupant of the house. It is a hard brittle material needing no maintenance, unless it has been painted, in which case it will need periodic repainting. When installed properly, broken pieces can be removed and replaced easily. Cutting or drilling the material will generate asbestos dust. Use suitable respirator masks. There should be a 2" or so wide strip of tar paper under each butted edge of the siding to keep water from the sheathing. There should be no need for caulk in these areas, but caulk at all other joints as necessary.

MAINTENANCE AND UPKEEP

Protect the siding from physical damage. Since the change away from asbestos, it may be difficult to find matching pieces for repairs. Caulking and painting will be necessary to protect the underlying structure from water damage.

2.4 EXTERIOR TRIM

Exterior trim has two primary functions. It "completes" the siding or external skin and helps protect the structure from the weather. It makes the house more attractive. The facia serves as an anchor point for gutters. Shutters, once functional, now are primarily decorative. Trim exposed to climatic elements must be well maintained.

2.4.1 WOOD

Wood is a traditional trim material. In the past, naturally decay resistant species such as redwood, cedar, cypress, etc. were popular for trim. Recently, cost conscientious builders have started to use materials such as spruce, pine, etc. As a result, the trim on a newer home may not last as it did when using redwood, cedar, or cypress.

MAINTENANCE AND UPKEEP

Wood trim, like siding, should be painted, sealed, and dried thoroughly after wetting. It is wise to saturate trim with a wood preservative before painting. Caulk between the wood and masonry. This not only cuts air infiltration and heat loss, but protects the trim. Wood in contact with masonry or cement tends to absorb water and rot. Paint behind the gutters too. As mentioned in 2.3 Exterior Siding Material and 2.3.2.2 Wood, use extreme caution. Before 1979 lead based paint was widely used. Lead can be toxic (Poisonous) and its effects accumulate. Use proper masks and protective clothing. Get advice from a good paint store or manufacturer's representative. Local government may offer advice through the Health Department. Some wood preservatives are toxic and may cause blindness if splattered in your eyes. Wear eye protection.

2.4.1 a. Exterior Wood Trim
This soffit is suffering from rot damage caused by paint failure (See 2.1.4 Paint Failure and Leaks in Built-In Gutters 1.7.3)

2.4.2 VINYL AND ALUMINUM

Vinyl and aluminum are popular as trim materials because of the ease of application, consistency, cost, and low maintenance. Brick veneer and masonry houses sometimes have aluminum trim. People with brick houses and wooden trim sometimes use vinyl or aluminum to cover the wooden trim to avoid painting.

MAINTENANCE AND UPKEEP

Properly installed trim has relatively low maintenance. You may need to wash the trim occasionally as discussed in section 2.3.2.6 Vinyl or Aluminum. Protect it from physical damage and vines.

2.5 PRIMARY WINDOWS

The inspector will use this section to report on the largest number of the same type of window.

Many houses have more than one type of window, but the inspector will choose the most representative type. The others may be in better or worse condition. Windows are important to a house. They strongly affect its appearance, appeal, comfort, cost, etc. They gain and lose more heat and cold than any other element, affecting utility bills. Windows require maintenance periodically. In cold climates "sweating" on windows is common. Decreasing the interior humidity and improving the weather-stripping *may* help.

2.5.1 MATERIAL

The material can affect the character, quality, durability, and function of windows. Each material has particular strengths and weaknesses.

2.5.1.1 WOOD

Properly maintained wood is one of the finest materials for windows. It is durable, strong, insulates well, and handsome.

MAINTENANCE AND UPKEEP

Wood windows require periodic sealing and painting. Windows using glazing compound or putty to seal around the glass (the lights) will have to be reglazed occasionally. When repainting, check the window glazing for signs of cracking. Water seeping into these cracks will ultimately rot the window. Storm windows and storm sashes sometimes accelerate the drying and cracking of the glazing. Keep channels or holes open at the sill to allow wind driven rain to drain. Do not caulk storm windows across the sill. If windows fog up often, try to find the source of the water and eliminate it. Often, drying a wet crawl space or basement will help. Sometimes it's wise to drill small vent holes through the aluminum storm window, top and bottom, allowing the vapor to escape. Over a long period of time condensation will rot the sill or the sash. Consult a good painter or paint store.

2.5.1.2 ALUMINUM

Windows manufactured of aluminum range from shabby to good quality. Aluminum is light, rust resistant, stable, and easy to handle. The metal does not slide well on itself (High Friction), making it necessary to have nylon or plastic glides and weatherstripping of plastic or fiber brushes. It conducts heat rapidly making it a poor insulator. Thermal breaks, rubber or plastic insulator strips, limit heat loss. Many manufacturers choose to use plastic locks, latches, etc. They seem to deteriorate because of ultraviolet light and heat. Any steel parts (screws, rollers, etc.) rust.

MAINTENANCE AND UPKEEP

Keep the slides and tracks clean. Surfaces rubbing together may be lubricated with silicon. Grease attracts dirt and grit. Replacing hardware and plastic parts may cause a snag because some window manufacturers lack a supply of replacement parts. Some generic replacement parts are available but may not be an exact fit. In short, if you can find parts, buy spares. If you can't, you may eventually have to replace the windows.

2.5.1.3 STEEL

Steel windows have all the disadvantages of aluminum, plus they rust. Many casement or awning style windows open outward and present sharp edges to people working around the foundation. If well maintained they may operate reasonably well. Poor maintenance results in poor operation. (Read 2.5.1.2 Aluminum Windows.)

MAINTENANCE AND UPKEEP

Scrape, sand, and properly prepare before painting. Glazing or putty may be required. Keep them primed and properly painted. You may be able to weather-strip them with self adhesive foam or plastic. Be careful not to overdo the weather stripping. Avoid jamming or wedging, causing the glass to break.

2.5.1.4 PLASTIC OR VINYL

Windows made of plastic or vinyl have not been in use in the United States long enough to have withstood the test of time. Siding and windows are both exposed to the environment. Windows get man-handled more than siding. Recent plastics are tough and long lived as siding, but doubt remains about their performance as windows. In cold climates, problems are developing with the seals in the insulated glass of plastic windows making them fail early.

MAINTENANCE AND UPKEEP

Keeping direct sunlight off the windows might be good. Make sure the type oil or silicon used for lubrication is the manufacturer's suggested product. Don't dissolve them by mistake.

2.5.1.5 CLAD WINDOWS

Clad windows combine the best properties of several materials. Manufacturer's have been covering wooden windows with vinyl or aluminum since the 60's. Wood has strength and insulating qualities and covering it on the exterior imparts the durability of the cladding. Sometimes, the beauty of the wood is exposed on the interior. Some fine windows are made in this fashion. Most manufacturers use extrusions of vinyl cut to fit and heat sealed or chemically bonded at the corners. Others are attempting the same result with exotic paints applied and cured at the factory.

MAINTENANCE AND UPKEEP

Little maintenance is required except keeping them clean and lubricating the hardware. Check with the manufacturer and be careful not to apply lubricants that soften or damage the cladding, the finish, or attract dirt. If you paint these windows, you will have to repaint periodically. One drawback to these windows is many are "groove glazed," meaning the sash was assembled around the glass. Glass replacement is nearly impossible without replacing the sash.

2.5.2 TYPE

This section gives the inspector the opportunity to mark whether the primary windows slide up and down, horizontally, etc. Many houses have more than one type and each type has advantages and disadvantages.

2.5.2.1 DOUBLE HUNG

This is probably the most common type of window in the eastern United States. The sashes are one above the other and slide up and down. The upper sash is outside the lower sash, but in separate tracks. Since both sashes move, the window is "double hung." In some similar looking windows, the upper sash does not move and is fixed or fastened to the frame. Such windows are "single hung."

Double hung windows were popular before air conditioning because both sashes could be opened slightly to let hot air out at the top and pull cooler air in the bottom. Today, storm windows often cover the windows preventing this possibility.

Tall windows sometimes have three sashes and are "triple hung." If the window extends to the floor they are impromptu doors. Thomas Jefferson's Monticello in Charlottesville, Virginia has such a window.

Earlier versions of these windows had no counter weights or sash balances. The sashes were lifted and held open with sticks or small clamps, etc. For many years counter weights offset the weight of the sashes so the sash stayed "put." The weights were in a raceway in each side of the window, behind the facing or trim.

A cord from the weight extends over a pulley and down to the sash. As the sash rises the weight descends, and vice versa. The cords wear, rot, and break. This type of window was the standard thirty or forty years ago. So many are still in use, sash cord is commonly available. Replacing the cord is tedious, but within the ability of a good amateur handyman. Many home repair books have step by step pictorial instructions. With care and restoration, these fine old windows may outlast the replacement windows sold today.

Recent double hung windows are counter balanced by spring balances. Two types are commonly in use: (1) a coiled spring (like a screened door spring) usually in a tube on each side stretches when the sash lowers (2) a cord in a spring loaded pulley hidden in the top of the frame lifts the sash. Both types are subject to wear and replacement. "How to" books, the manufacturer, or a local supplier may be helpful.

All double hung windows are subject to air leakage and high rates of infiltration unless they are properly weatherstripped or covered with a good storm window or panel.

2.5.2.2 CASEMENT WINDOWS

Windows opening along a vertical axis (like a door) are casement windows. Some are hinged along one side and some pivot top and bottom. Some sashes slide toward the center as the window swings open. This feature allows both sides of the glass to be washed from inside the house, but may interfere with egress (escape) in an emergency.

Newer windows may have special hardware or latches, quickly freeing the window for emergencies. Examine the windows carefully. Get the manufacturer's literature if you can. You should open the windows occasionally to be sure they're not stuck, and lubricate the hardware as necessary. Do not leave casement windows open because they are susceptible to wind damage.

Casement windows often have good weatherstripping and locks pulling them tightly shut and then "kicking" the sashes open slightly when unlocked. These features make them resistant to infiltration and secure.

2.5.2.3 SLIDING WINDOWS
Windows rolling or sliding horizontally are sliding windows. This type has been popular with aluminum window manufacturers. They avoid the hardware problems of spring balances and pivots, etc. but are difficult to weatherstrip. Unless they are of exceptional quality infiltration will be high.

2.5.2.4 AWNING WINDOWS
Awning windows are hinged or pivoted along the top and open outward. Hopper windows are hinged along the bottom and generally open inward to avoid catching rain. Awning windows shed rain like an awning, hence the name. Both of these are like horizontal versions of casement windows and can offer the good weatherstripping and low infiltration. Awning windows have been particularly popular in bedrooms because they could be left open when raining and installed high to offer privacy. Building codes and the concern for emergency egress limit the use of this window. Climbing in and out of these windows can be difficult for firemen and homeowners alike. Emergency escape routes should be planned and practiced.

2.5.2.5 FIXED WINDOWS
Many types of fixed windows are in use and range from fixed sashes to solid glass walls. "Fixed" is any stationary non-opening window. Many "picture windows" are large sashes in a frame. Some eliminate the sash and install the glass directly in the frame. Since these windows never open they can be sealed tightly and securely. The frames are subject to rotting and present egress problems. You might be able to break the glass in an emergency, but some safety glass is tough and nearly impossible to break. Plan your escape routes.

2.5.2.6 JALOUSIE
These windows have narrow horizontal slat or strips of glass with no weatherstripping. They should be used as primary windows only in the mildest climates. They are seen on enclosed porches, sun spaces etc. If they are more than a few years old, they probably won't operate well. Replacement hardware may be available, but a constant problem. They also present egress problems. They don't open wide enough to allow escape in an emergency, so plan another route.

2.5.3 GLAZING

The most widely used meaning is "the clear part" of the window. This is usually glass, but is sometimes plastic. Sometimes the glazing is translucent - (Stained Glass, Frosted Glass, Cathedral Glass, etc.) but it is usually transparent (clear). We occasionally see bronze or gray glass used to block sunlight. Lately some exotic window coatings are showing up. Some of these coatings reflect damaging ultraviolet light and absorb heat. Some window glazing can reflect heat also.

Secondly, glazing applies to the putty or glazing compound used to seal the glass to the frame or sash. The glass should be held in place in a wooden frame by metal clips or glazer's points. Keep the putty painted to avoid drying. Putty is usually clay and oil. Scraping a window with a razor blade or sharp scraper often breaks the seal between the paint and glass. This allows the putty (glazing) to dry and crack, permitting water to seep into the frame.

2.5.3.1 SINGLE GLASS

Single glazing is a single layer of glass or plastic material. A single thin layer of any product is a poor insulator. A clear substance is worse because heat radiates through. Thus the glass in your windows accounts for significant heat loss and heat gain.

Single glass windows tend to "sweat" or have condensation. One "cure" is to install storm windows or storm panels. This increases the "R-Factor" so the interior glass warms, thus reducing condensation. It may also accelerate the drying of the putty.

2.5.3.2 INSULATED GLASS

Insulated glass is two layers of glass with an air space between. There are two versions or fundamental types.

(1) Two sheets of glass separated by a small aluminum spacer around the perimeter creating an air space from 1/4 to 3/4 of an inch. A sophisticated caulking compound seals the edges of the unit. Sometimes there is a desiccant or drying agent inside the spacer. These units can be made in 5 or 10 year versions. Eight to twelve years seems to be an optimistic life expectancy. Thermal stress, poor installation, vibration, settlement, etc. often cause them to fail early. The fogged or wet look between the panes suggests failure. When one pane fails all the others are subject to failure. If the fogging occurs for more than a few days, the water turns acidic and etches or frosts the glass making replacement the only acceptable cure. If caught soon enough, you may have the local glass company remove the glass unit, cut it apart, thoroughly clean it and remake it with new desiccant, sealant etc. Some windows will fog and clear with changes in the weather. If buying a house, inspect the windows carefully each time when viewing the house before closing. Repair and replacement are expensive and troublesome.

(2) This type is made by bending the edges of the glass sheets and welding them glass to glass, forming a flat thin "bottle." The space is filled with a dry gas through a small hole and then sealed. It may last twenty years, but is expensive. To the author's

knowledge, only one major manufacturer of windows (Andersen) uses this product regularly. They are moving away from true Thermopane (TM) or Twindow (TW) toward the insulated version mentioned above. This may be to allow for the exotic coating used between the panes of their "low-E" glass.

Pella uses a different approach. Their single pane clad windows have a skin of aluminum with a "baked" on finish. Independent sashes, "storm panels," are clipped on the inside. The interior panels are removable for cleaning. The air space between has vents to the exterior controlling condensation.

2.5.3.3 TRIPLE GLASS

Triple glass or glazing is insulated glass, except the "sandwich" includes three sheets of glass and two aluminum spacers to create two air spaces. (Read section 2.5.3.2 Insulated Glass.) Air is a good insulator and thus has the effect of warming the interior pane, reducing heat loss, and minimizing sweating or condensation. Triple pane windows are desirable in cold climates. They are subject to all the failings of insulated glass. In cold climates seals on the edges suffer causing early failure. To the author's knowledge no one makes a higher quality "glass on glass" version of triple pane.

2.5.4 SCREENS, STORM WINDOWS, STORM PANELS.

Window screens, storm windows, and storm panels are not inspected. As a courtesy to the client, a space will be included so the inspector may mark their presence or absence. They are not inventoried, checked for function, or considered major items.

2.5.4.1 STORM WINDOWS

Aluminum and vinyl storm windows have been a popular home "improvement" for years. They do not conserve energy unless they are reasonably tight and operated properly. Storm windows must be closed for them to be effective. Also, they must have drain holes at the bottom to allow wind driven water and condensation to escape. Water can pond and rot the sill and drool into the interior. They must "breath" to allow moisture vapor to escape. Storm windows are notorious for being difficult to open. For emergency egress storm windows must be easy to operate. Properly installed, they can protect the sashes from "weather" damage. If installed too tightly they can act as a solar collector and "cook" the inner window.

None	No storm windows
Partial	Some storm windows
All	Storm windows on all primary windows
Damaged	Dented, broken, missing parts, etc.

2.5.4.2 STORM PANELS

Storm panels are one piece storm windows installed in the fall, removed in the spring, and alternated with screens. The storm panels can be placed on the interior or exterior. A few houses, subject to violent storms, have heavy panels or operable shutters serving as true storm panels. (Read 2.5.4.1 Storm Windows.) If installed on the interior, the old leaky windows "breath" more than the new ones which limits condensation problems. The inside location of the new windows may lessen their architectural impact but make egress difficult.

None	No storm panels
Partial	Some storm panels
All	Storm panels on all primary windows
Damaged	Dented, broken, missing parts, etc.

2.5.4.3 SCREENS

Window screens keep bugs out and let in fresh air. Many versions exist and some reflect heat, create shade, and help cool the house.

None	No screens
Partial	Some screens
All	Screens on all primary windows
Damaged	Dented, broken, missing parts, etc.

2.6 EXTERIOR DOORS

The primary purpose of exterior doors is to allow for controlled entry to the house. The doors let people and air in when desirable and secure and exclude people and air when undesirable.

The primary purpose of the inspection of the exterior doors is to determine whether they are functional or damaged. The inspector does not specifically check the function of the locks or the weatherstripping. The level of security and the amount of weatherstripping desired on these doors are personal decisions. Examine the doors for security and weatherstripping.

2.6.1 ENTRY DOORS

Entry doors are pedestrian doors designed to let people in and out of the structure. The front and back doors are entry doors. In this particular category, entry doors are generally swinging doors as opposed to sliding glass or "French" type doors. Doors receive tremendous abuse. The opposite sides of the door are in different environments. Doors are sometimes abused by occupants in opening, closing, and slamming. Weather and physical wear and tear cause entry doors to require more maintenance than other aspects of the house.

2.6.1.1 WOODEN DOORS

Wood is a traditional material for exterior doors. Wood can shrink, swell, warp, crack, decay, etc. It is light in weight and sturdy.   It can be fabricated into many stylish types of doors. With proper maintenance wooden doors will withstand the use and abuse. Keep wooden doors painted. They should be treated or painted on sides, tops, bottoms, backs, fronts, edges, and so on. Doors not painted on all exposed edges invite water to enter and cause damage.

2.6.1.2 METAL DOORS

Metal entry doors used in residential construction are stamped from two face sheets of metal which clinch or seal onto a wooden frame. The core of the doors is often foam filled. These doors are complete with a door frame, sill, and weather-stripping. The ease of installation makes them popular with builders. The builder installs the door, frame, and weather-stripping at one time. Most models offer superior insulation and weather-stripping to a wooden door. The metal is galvanized or treated to resist rust and primed at the factory for painting at the site. Such doors are sturdy and durable. Do not allow the doors to become scratched, dented, or rusted, if possible. They are subject to a dog scratching the paint through to the galvanizing, allowing it to rust. The plastic inserts applied to the surface of the doors, such as decorative panels and window frames, are subject to heat damage. Many manufacturers of metal doors do not recommend the installation of storm doors over metal doors. Storm doors tend to turn metal doors into solar collectors. The temperature between the metal door and the storm door can rise dramatically and ruin both the storm door and any plastic appliques on the door.

2.6.2 SLIDING DOORS

Sliding glass doors have been popular in both traditional and contemporary homes. They offer a lot of glass at a low price. Sliding glass doors provide easy entry for burglars. Add locks, jimmy bars and other such safety features, if needed. One of the best patio door locks is a stick laying in the track.

2.6.2.1 WOODEN DOORS

Wooden patio doors have a reputation of high quality and are more elegant than their aluminum counterparts. Wooden doors are sensitive to splash damage from the roof run off if there are no gutters. Splashing water drives through the weather-stripping, erodes the paint, finds its way under the track, and eventually rots the framing of the house, the panels, and frame of the door. Replacement can be expensive.

2.6.2.2 ALUMINUM PATIO DOORS

Aluminum patio doors sell by the millions and range in quality from shabby to excellent. Good quality patio doors probably represent an excellent value and an inexpensive way to add glass area to a house. Aluminum doors are not subject to the splash and rot damage of wooden doors. Splash damage affects aluminum doors because water leaks through and under the sill rotting the wooden framing members of the house. Aluminum doors are subject to easy entry by burglars. Special locks or a wooden stick in the track can help secure aluminum patio doors.

The doors can be adjusted by a screw in the edge of the frame near the track. Raise or lower the roller by turning the screw. Often a simple adjustment can free the door to roll smoothly. At times the wheels wear out and replacement becomes necessary. If replacement parts can be found it is a simple process to remove the existing wheels and replace them. Manufacturers come and go and parts are often not available. This may require replacement of the door. Most patio doors recently have included insulated glass. This particular type of glass is two sheets of tempered safety glass caulked together with a special caulking compound sealing the space. When the seal fails the door fogs. The usual cure is to replace the glass. Most glass shops keep one or more pieces of patio door glass in stock and can replace the glass in minutes.

A handy homeowner might find it possible to replace the glass although it is tedious. A fogged pane may be saved if the glass is taken to a competent glass shop immediately after it fogs. They can cut it apart, clean it, put it back together, and reseal it for about half the price of a new paneled glass. If the glass remains fogged for more than a few days the water between the panes etches the glass and ruins it. (Read 2.5.3.2 Insulated Glass.)

2.6.3 FRENCH DOORS

The traditional ones are double wooden doors, one swinging left and one swinging right so they open a five or six foot wide opening. A newer version of the French door is the center folding type where one door folds back onto the other door. This variation offers the advantages of taking less wall space when open, being more secure, and easier to install screens. As with all exterior doors, French doors are subject to splash damage from the lack of gutters and improper flashing. The traditional French doors where both doors open are difficult to weather-strip, secure, require adjustment, and maintenance.

2.6.4 GARAGE DOORS

Garage doors come in many varieties ranging from swinging doors to overhead and bypass doors. They are made of wood, steel, fiberglass, etc. The overhead doors seem to be the most popular. Swinging doors are subject to wind damage and are difficult to operate when it is windy.

The design of garage doors makes it difficult to heat the garage. They provide security and keep out wind driven rain. Most are not weather-stripped and not insulated enough to allow for long term heating of the garage.

2.6.4.1 MATERIAL

The material of the garage door will affect its use, performance, and maintenance. Wood is a traditional material but will require staining or painting to prevent warping and decaying. Metal in the form of steel will require painting. Fiberglass doors made with aluminum parts may not require as much painting, but will require replacement because of the lightweight nature of the construction. They are subject to physical damage in terms of being punctured or dented.

2.6.4.1.1 WOOD

Wood is used for many types and styles of garage doors. Bypass doors, in which barn door style tracks allow one to roll to the left and another door to be rolled to the right were once common. Most garage doors installed now appear to be the overhead type doors with four or five horizontal panels hinged together rolling on a track up and over so the car can be driven in our out. Some of these doors have decorative or glass panels. All wooden doors require painting and upkeep of hardware.

2.6.4.1.2 METAL

Metal garage doors also come in several varieties. The metal used is either tin or steel and occasionally aluminum. Any door made of iron or steel products will require occasional priming and painting to avoid rust. Some of these doors are old and awkward. They are one piece and pivoted to rotate up over the car.

2.6.4.1.3 FIBERGLASS

Fiberglass doors are popular in some parts of the country. They are light in weight, come in a variety of styles, and have aluminum frames and fiberglass panels or inserts. They are the overhead type of door in which the panels roll up and over the car to allow for entry and exit of the garage. Often the fiberglass panels are translucent, allowing light to enter the garage while blocking the view of contents in the garage. Some of these panels are so light in weight, they are frail and subject to physical damage from day to day use and bumping by bicycles, etc.

2.6.4.2 TYPE

The "type" section is for the inspector to describe the operation of the doors.

2.6.4.2.1 OVERHEAD DOORS

Overhead doors have several sections horizontally hinged together, with rollers mounted on them, so they roll up and over the automobile to allow for entry and egress. One advantage to overhead doors is they easily adapt to automatic garage door openers. They are not particularly subject to wind damage. The doors, when open, are overhead inside the garage and when closed, are secure in the opening. There is a second type of hinged or pivoted overhead door which has lost popularity. This is a solid single piece door that has arms on it that swing it up and overhead.

2.6.4.2.2 HINGED

Occasionally, garage doors are hinged with two or more doors similar to double entry doors or French doors. These doors are large to allow for a car to enter the garage and usually open outward. One of the problems with hinged doors is on a windy day, they can be difficult to open and close. They are not easy to fit with automatic door openers. Often, they are homemade or owner built. Hinged doors are not popular for garage doors.

2.6.4.2.3 ROLLING DOORS

At one time, bypass or rolling doors were popular for garages. As discussed earlier, the doors hung from barn door type tracks, allowing one door to be rolled to the left and one door to be rolled to the right. For a single car garage, half of the door would roll each way. On a two car garage, you could only open one bay of the garage at a time. Both doors stood in front of the bay that was not open at the moment. These doors have fallen into disuse, although many of them are still seen on older inner city garages. If properly maintained and counter weighted for easy operation, an automatic garage opener can be installed.

2.6.4.3 OPERATION

The operation of the garage door will be marked to indicate whether the garage door is manually operated or an automatically operated door.

2.6.4.3.1 MANUAL

A manual door is a door that must be operated by the owner as opposed to a door that has an automatic device to open and close it. Most garage doors have been sprung or counterweighted and if they are properly adjusted, they are easy to open. Adjusting the springs or cables under tension can be dangerous. If the tension inadvertently releases, the springs and cables lash out violently. Do not attempt to adjust your garage doors unless you are completely and thoroughly familiar with their operation. Wear eye protection.

2.6.4.3.2 AUTOMATIC

"Automatic" refers to the motorized devices that open and close the doors. Door openers have become popular since the advent of radio control allowing the door to be opened from inside the car. Such devices should automatically lock the door in the closed position to prevent unauthorized entry. They should have a Auto-reverse or sensitivity feature that does not allow it to close on an object or person in its path. They should stop gently and return to the top position. This is a safety feature to protect your property and person in the event that the door closes at the wrong moment. Some doors may include an electric eye feature that stops the movement of the door if anything passes through the beam of the eye. If present, both features should work properly, if not present, you should consider adding them.

You should always double check to make sure that the automatic garage door opener did actually open the door for you. People have been known to push the button on the radio control, assume the door was open, and back the car through the unopened door. Be sure to acquire the radio controllers with the house when you buy it.

2.7 PORCHES AND DECKS

Porches, decks, and similar structures can add tremendously to the enjoyment and value of a home. Exposed to the weather, they may require more maintenance than some other parts of the house. Experience teaches us that stoops, decks, and patios without roofs tend to suffer from the weather worse than porches with roofs. Proper flashing, caulking, gutters, etc. must be maintained to keep water from entering the structure.

2.7.1 WOODEN PORCHES

The distinction between a stoop and a porch is the porch has a roof. A roof is highly desirable because it protects the wooden members from the weather. A roof may keep the weather off your guests while they wait to enter. Wooden porches built of redwood or cedar are usually decay resistant. Materials that are not decay resistant must be kept painted to extend their useful life. It is important for any structure exposed to the weather to dry quickly each time it rains or when moisture exists. Vines and shrubbery should be kept cut back from porches so that the structure and under floor area can dry rapidly. A pier foundation with brick trellis or wooden lattice screening may allow wooden porches to dry more rapidly than a solid perimeter wall.

2.7.1 a. Wooden Porches
Column bases allow the bottoms of posts and columns to dry quickly and avoid post or column damage (See 2.11.20 Post or Column Damage). They can be added if you don't have them.

2.7.2 MASONRY STOOPS

A stoop built of masonry offers a higher resistance to rot and weather damage than does a wooden stoop. Traditional masonry stoops built of brick and block had a concrete slab. The slab, stoop, and the upper surface of the stoop should slope away from the house so any rainwater falling on the stoop will drain away. There should be flashing between the house and the stoop to prevent water from leaking in under doors or behind the masonry. Flashing helps to stop water from deteriorating the wooden portions of the house.

In the past, stoops were often built hollow so that the concrete of the stoop rested on metal decking. This left an air space inside the stoop connected to the crawl space of the house by a vent. The vent was sometimes a block laid on its side. More recent stoops are filled with earth to avoid the trouble and expense of using metal decking. The earth filled stoops are not proving as successful as their older hollow counterparts. It appears that the earth not only absorbs water soaking in above, but also wicks water up from the ground below, sometimes transporting it up to the framing of the house.

This is also a favorite entry point for termites and other wood eating insects because construction debris and trash is often in the earth in the stoop. Modern day stoops will be found laid with the slab level. This method offers no clear path for the water to drain away from the house. Therefore, the material underneath doors and the floor joists, etc. have been known to decay when the house is still young.

2.7.3 DECKS

Decks are popular and are often of decay resistant material such as treated lumber, redwood, or cedar. Decks can range in size from a few square feet to as large as or larger than the house. Sometimes they serve as a yard substitute. If built of decay resistant materials, decks require little maintenance. They are subject to being discolored by mold, mildew, and dirt. Decks can be painted or stained and recently deck treatment programs have become available as a chemical wash that the homeowner can use. There are companies using high pressure washes, returning the wood to an almost new looking condition.

One problem often associated with decks is their installation against wooden houses or even masonry houses without the benefit of proper flashing between the house and the deck.

Water cascading off the roof, or driven by the wind, finds its way into the crack between the house and the deck, and rots the siding and material beneath the siding. The deck is usually undamaged, but the house rots.

2.7.4 SCREEN PORCHES

Screen porches offer the advantages of a deck with additional protection from the elements and insects. This may extend the useful time for the porch either earlier and later into the various seasons. They have the same problems that most other wooden structures have in the weather. The lower post and rail members accumulate moisture and rot wherever they contact the floor or slab. The screening is subject to being damaged and is sometimes expensive and difficult to replace. Replacement requires removing and replacing much of the lattice strip that holds the screen in place.

CAUTION. The screening does not serve as an adequate railing or barrier. Install an additional barrier or railing around the lower portion of the porch. This could avoid an injury to a child riding a tricycle or running through the lower portion of the screen.

Various types of screens are available depending on the local climate. Aluminum, galvanized, fiberglass, and bronze screening seem to be popular. The fiberglass screening does not rust, but can be tender and delicate to the touch. Several styles of shade screening and privacy screens are also available.

2.7.5 PATIO

Patios are traditionally slabs or other similar solid surfaces resting on the ground serving as an outdoor entertainment area. They can range from a simple slab on grade to elaborate brick, stone, or slate structures. Some include planters, fish ponds, etc. As with any paving surface exposed to the weather, they are subject to freeze\thaw damage, settlement, buckling caused by tree roots beneath the slab, etc.

2.8 STEPS AND RAILS

Exterior steps and rails allow for the safe and easy passage from the level of the yard to the level of the house. Rails and steps require upkeep and maintenance because of their safety aspects and exposure to the weather. Railings or pickets more than 3 1/2 inches apart are no longer considered safe.

2.8.1 MASONRY STEPS

Brick and other masonry materials are traditional for exterior steps as they are wear resistant and low in maintenance. On the other hand masonry steps are heavy, subject to settlement, and subject to freeze/thaw damage. Some builders dig a hole, poor a little mortar on the ground, and lay the steps on the mortar. Since the steps are most often a solid mass of masonry, they are heavy. If the dirt below is soft or is fill dirt, the steps are subject to settlement. Freeze/thaw damage affects the steps in terms of cracking and opening the mortar joints. This problem requires periodic pointing of the joints or damage will accelerate as water infiltrates.

2.8.2 WOODEN STEPS

Wooden steps are common even with masonry stoops. Wooden steps can be successful at resisting the weather provided they drain and dry quickly after a rain. The success of wooden steps can be attributed to the parts of the steps that contact the earth being of decay resistant materials. Often the material used for the stringer is not decay resistant and rots or decays where it touches the ground. Proper drainage and painting are important to wooden steps.

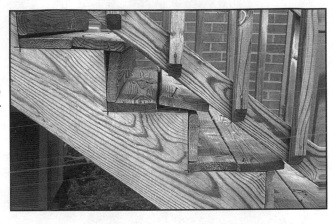

2.8.2 a. Wooden Steps-Maintenance and Upkeep
Keep steps securely nailed or replace nails with screws to avoid tripping and injury.

2.8.3 METAL RAILS

Metal rails are made in many forms from wrought iron, aluminum, and steel. Most metal rails require careful cleaning, preparation, and painting every two or three years to prevent them from rusting. Often rusted rails can be welded or repaired at the house without replacing the entire rail. Rails should be securely anchored and sturdy enough to support the weight of a person leaning on or falling against the rail. Pickets or rails should be less than 3 1/2 inches apart to prevent a small child slipping through and getting hung by the head.

2.8.4 WOODEN RAILS

Wooden rails are used extensively on decks and wooden porches. If made of decay resistant materials, they may last a long time. Rails made of non decay resistant material often rot where they contact the earth or where individual pieces join the rail. Water tends to soak through cracks in the paint and rots the wood where a rail contacts a post or where a picket contacts a rail. All such rails must be kept properly painted and maintained to reach their life expectancy. As with metal rails, they should be securely anchored and sturdy enough to support the weight of a person leaning or falling against the rail. Pickets or rails should be less than 3 1/2 inches apart to prevent a small child slipping through and getting hung by the head.

2.9 CARPORTS AND GARAGE

The inspector marks whether the carport or garage is attached to or detached from the main structure.

2.9.1 DETACHED GARAGE OR CARPORT

Detached garages are not inspected as a part of a pre-purchase inspection. If a client requests a detached garage or carport to be inspected it would be separate from the pre-purchase inspection and usually at an additional cost.

2.9.2 ATTACHED GARAGE OR CARPORT
Attached garages or carports are inspected as a part of the pre-purchase inspection and reported on as a part of the other sections in the book. The garage is not reported on separately.

2.9.3 DETACHED BUILDINGS
Detached buildings are not inspected under the scope of the inspection.

2.10 FIRE ESCAPE
The inspector marks the presence or absence of an exterior fire escape.

2.10.1 NONE
No fire escape seen.

2.10.2 EXTERIOR FIRE ESCAPE
There was a fire escape on the exterior.

2.11 EXTERIOR OBSERVATIONS
The inspector marks observations of conditions that may affect the exterior. More than one item can be marked as the exterior may exhibit more than one symptom or problem. Some items are part of the normal aging process and do not require correction. Other items require either maintenance or repair if the exterior is to reach the full potential or life expectancy. Read carefully each section that applies to the system inspected.

Maintenance is the on going care required if a system or item is to reach the full potential including lubricating, painting, etc. Do maintenance as required by the manufacturer of the equipment or item. Repairs put items or systems back in good condition after damage or decay, etc. Repairs are caused by delayed maintenance, aging, normal wear and tear, or abuse. The workmanship and materials of the repairs should be equal to the quality of the system and have the same life expectancy. e.g. A limb plunges through an asphalt shingle roof. If the roofing otherwise has a life expectancy of ten years, the repair should also have a life expectancy of at least ten years. If the roofing only has a life expectancy of one year, then the repair should be capable of lasting one year or more. It is not prudent to put a one year patch on a ten year roof or to waste a ten year repair on a one year roof. All repairs should be by qualified competent professionals.

2.11.1 SOUND
The inspector thinks the item under inspection is functioning at the moment of the inspection. This does not imply perfection, absence of minor defects, or absence of wear and tear.

2.11.2 TYPICAL
The inspector thinks the item, material, or aspect of construction is characteristic or similar to comparable products in similar houses. The exterior has normal wear and tear.

2.11.3 BUCKLING

Buckling is usually seen in hardboard type siding installed dry (with a very low moisture content) and too tight (no space left for expansion). Restrained by windows or corners, the siding swells length-wise and warps or buckles in a wavy fashion. Not usually a structural problem, buckling may indicate a slight misalignment of the studs (check the inner wall surface), or a wet crawl space. The "cure" is to replace the siding. Once warped, hardboard will not return to its original shape. Cure the wetness problem first, then properly install and paint the new siding.

2.11.4 PAINT FAILURE

The paint is too thin, peeling, blistering, chipping, flaking, or too thick. Exterior paint should be capable of protecting the structure from the weather and may improve its appearance. Paint fails for many reasons. It may die of old age, too many coats, or fail to "breath." It can lose its flexibility, crack, and flake off. Eventually, it must be properly removed and the surface prepared for new paint. Treat all paint as if it were "lead based" and poisonous unless you know better. Local paint stores or government authorities may be able to help. (See Figure 1.5.2.2 a. Wooden Shakes for an illustration of failing paint.)

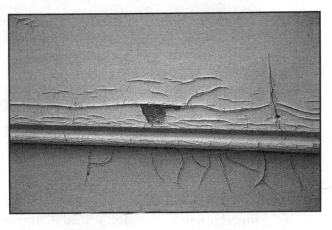

2.11.4 a. Paint Failure
The paint is cracking because it is not acting as a film to protect the siding. Water seeping in will damage the siding. Paint failure has many forms and appearances.

2.11.5 WET ROT OR SPLASH DAMAGE

Wood left damp or wet over a long period of time succumbs to fungus or bacteria and rots unless it is decay resistant or pressure treated. Rotted wood has no strength. Any structural or load bearing elements including beams, joists, sills, flooring, studs, columns, etc. should be repaired or replaced if damaged. Most rotting occurs when water leaks in where not intended. The source of the water should be found and eliminated to reduce the chance of a reoccurrence.

2.11.5 a. Wet Rot or Splash Damage.
The sill (2.4.1 Wooden Trim) under this 2.6.2.2 Aluminum Sliding Patio Door is suffering from splash damage aggravated by the lack of gutters.

2.11.5 b. Wet Rot or Splash Damage.
This picture shows the view from the crawl space of the band board under the door above. The lack of proper flashing and the absence of gutters combine to create a perfect environment for rot. If the deck is attached to the band it may collapse soon. This is seen often on houses less than 15 years old.

2.11.6 ATTACHMENT

Indicates that the connection between two items is failing or that an item is not properly or securely mounted or installed. (i.e. An iron rail that has lost a bolt or anchoring screw.) Properly secure the item.

2.11.7 VINES OR VEGETATION

Vines, especially ivy, can cause problems for houses. In houses with siding, vines may grow inside the walls and behind the siding. Avoid pulling the vines away from the wall since this may damage the brick or mortar. Carefully cut away a few square feet of vines in an inconspicuous area and see how much they have rooted into the brickwork. Also, inspect the exposed area for condition and appearance. Visualize the prospective appearance of the wall if all the vines are cut away. That should help you decide if removing the vines completely is necessary or feasible. In any event, trim vines away from around windows, gutters, woodwork and other decorations.

Other vegetation may damage the building also. Shrubs too close to the building may be blocking ventilation through foundation vents increasing wetness in the crawl space. Plantings should be cut back or moved far enough to allow free air circulation around the building to promote drying and to allow for inspection and maintenance. Trees should be far enough from the building to avoid roots damaging the foundation or roof. (See also 2.1.2.1 Vegetation, Vines, or Shrubbery, and 3.7.2.9 Vegetation.)

2.11.7 a. Vines
This vine has grown 4-5 feet behind the aluminum siding and come out at the window sill. Left undisturbed it will push the siding off the house.

2.11.8 DELAMINATION

Delamination means that two or more layers are separating. It usually refers to the layers of plywood siding coming apart. The only "cure" may be replacement. Partially delaminated plywood may still be suitable as a nailing base for other types of siding, but this will dramatically change the appearance of the house. Other plywood and hardboard siding occasionally delaminate.

2.11.9 LOOSE

The inspector has seen attached items that may be subject to wind damage or may cause personal injury. Examples might be aluminum siding that has slipped its attachment and is dangling or railings poorly anchored. Safety items should be repaired immediately.

2.11.10 WICKING

Wicking is the process of water soaking upward or in any direction through a material. Also called capillary action or rising damp. Clay soil and brick along with many other building products are subject to wicking. This may be a major source of dampness in some basements and crawl spaces and may cause rotted sills and joist ends.

2.11.11 TOO LOW

The inspector feels that some portion of the structure is subject to decay or is too close to the grade. An example would be when wood siding and the sill or band behind it is within six inches of the ground. This is also an invitation to termites. Correct the grading.

2.11.12 CRACKED

An observation usually regarding masonry or masonry veneer parts of the structure and potentially a clue or tell tail sign of a structural or settlement problem. Cracks are a cause of concern for all homeowners. When we look at a crack, we are looking at one frame of a motion picture that may be 10, 20, 30, or more years long. Based on the physical evidence presented at the inspection, the structural significance of the crack (if any) will be addressed in the Foundation, Basement, Structure section (Chapter 3).

2.11.12 a. Cracked
The block wall has cracked near the end of the lintel.
Cracks may be a sign of structural distress.

2.11.13 SPALLING

A defect of masonry or concrete. The face is chipping or sloughing off. The material is crumbling away in thin layers often caused by water migrating through the product freezing just under the surface. (Read section 2.11.10.) Salts or other chemicals carried by the water and left behind under the surface as the water evaporates can also cause the face to peel off.

2.11.14 MOVEMENT
Some part of the structure has apparently moved from its original or "as built" position.

2.11.14 a. Movement
The front wall and steps or this 2.7.2 Masonry Stoop settled because it was founded on poor or disturbed soil. If left unrepaired, this could be a tripping hazard.

2.11.15 MORTAR DAMAGE
The inspector has seen open, damaged, or eroding mortar joints. Older masonry buildings were often built with mortar rich in lime and low in cement. Such mortar allows the wicking, moisture migration, and resulting damage to occur mainly in the mortar where it can be repaired (repointed) from time to time. Modern cement mortar may be causing damage to the brick by not allowing free passage of moisture. One of the responsibilities of owning a masonry home is repointing the mortar joints occasionally. Walls and vertical surfaces should be repaired with mortar as rich in lime as the original. Steps and horizontal surfaces may require mortar rich in cement.

2.11.15 a. Mortar Damage
It is time to repair these eroding mortar joints.

2.11.16 EFFLORESCENCE
The inspector has noted the white powdery substance that is sometimes left behind by water migrating through masonry. Usually a harmless metallic salt. Suggests a damp or wet basement. Mild cases are usually harmless to the masonry. Severe cases can destroy the mortar and cause spalling. (Read section 2.11.13 Spalling.)

2.11.17 MILDEW
Mold and mildew will grow on any surface and can survive on little more than moisture. Modern paints (without lead) are only mildew resistant, not mildew proof. It must be removed before repainting. Before repainting composition (hardboard, e.g. Masonite, etc.) siding, professionals recommend that the siding be washed with an anti-mildew detergent or a solution of 1/2 chlorine bleach and 1/2 water. The chlorine vapor is harmful if breathed in quantity, and the spillage could be harmful to plants and shrubs. Appropriate care should be taken.

Aluminum and vinyl siding can accumulate moisture and mildew and the gray film can be unsightly. The siding can be cleaned with a sponge and the solution mentioned above. The solution should be tried on a small area at first to determine its success. The washed area should be rinsed thoroughly to prevent damage to plants around perimeter of the house. The washing should not be done during either too hot or too cold weather.

2.11.20 POST OR COLUMN DAMAGE

Post or column damage will be marked when posts that enter the ground or wooden columns that rest on floors exhibit rot damage. Usually the posts must be replaced, but sometimes can be repaired. On small columns that are not severely damaged, one to two inches of the base can be cut off and an aluminum column base (like a trivet) can be added. This allows for drying and helps prevent further rot. Bigger more elaborate columns may require splicing or more elaborate bases.

2.11.20 a. Post or Column Damage
The damage caused by point failure and water can be expensive. Repairing this column in a historically accurate fashion will require custom

millwork and an experienced craftsman.

2.11.20 b.
Simpler columns are easier to repair if caught soon enough. It may be possible to cut away the bottom and install a metal column base.

2.11.21 FLASHING OMITTED

The lack of proper flashing has the potential to allow damage to occur. Flashing is the metal or plastic sheet material keeping water from entering between the house and a chimney, or above a window or door, etc. Experience has taught us the lack of flashing between the house and a deck is a serious omission, especially if there are no gutters to catch the roof run off and rainwater. Often, after only two or three years the framing of the house will rot to the point that the deck will pull away and possibly collapse. (See 2.11.5 b. Wet Rot or Splash Damage for a picture of the result of leaving the flashing out between the house and deck.)

2.11.24 BROKEN OR MISSING GLASS

The inspector observes damaged, cracked or missing glass. Missing glass allows rain and snow to enter and heat to escape. Cracked glass may allow water to seep in and rot the frame. Repair immediately.

2.11.25 LOST SEAL

The seal around the edge of the insulated glass has failed. Moisture vapor infiltrates the air space, condenses, and is acidic enough to etch and "frost" the glass if the unit remains fogged more than a few days. Replacing the glass or sash is the cure.

2.11.26 GLAZING FAILURE

The inspector observes cracked or crumbling glazing (putty) around the glass (lights) in

windows or doors. Checking the window glazing for signs of cracking when repainting is important. Water seeping into these cracks will ultimately rot the window. Repair when repainting.

2.11.26 d. Glazing Failure.
The illustration shows one step in replacing the putty around a window pane. If cracked putty is not replaced and kept properly painted, the sash or wooden part of the window will rot.

2.11.27 DELAYED MAINTENANCE

Maintenance is a necessary part of home ownership. Delaying maintenance and repairs may allow ordinary wear and tear to become a serious problem. The inspector feels that ordinary maintenance chores were put off. An example would be windows with cracked and failing putty allowing the sashes to rot.

2.11.28 RUSTED

Applies to any iron or steel product, (i.e. windows, railings, etc.) or any products which must be properly primed, painted, or lubricated to avoid rust damage.

2.11.29 PHYSICAL DAMAGE

The inspector notes any type of damage that may affect the performance or life expectancy of the product. Examples range from broken and missing hardware to holes in doors, etc.

2.11.30 FUNCTIONAL

Implies only that the windows or doors operate (open and close). It does not imply easy, safe, or perfect operation and does not address energy efficiency, security, or durability.

2.11.33 MISALIGNMENT

The doors or windows have sagged, shifted or settled enough that they or their hardware is out of alignment and perhaps not functional. Misalignment indicates wear and tear of the individual unit or may be a clue or tell tail of settling or sagging of the structure.

2.11.34 NONE OR DAMAGED WEATHERSTRIPPING

The weatherstripping interferes with the operation of the window or door or appears dangerous to passers by.

2.11.35 OPENER FAILURE

The automatic garage door opener fails to cycle properly or at all. This section is also used to indicate the auto-reverse feature fails to function or functions improperly. The door and the opener should be repaired to operate properly. On doors including an electric eye, both reverse features should be repaired to operate properly.

2.11.36 NO SAFETY REVERSE FEATURE

This section may be marked when the opener fails to have a safety reverse designed to protect passers by or property from being damaged by the operation of the door. Newer doors may have both a contact feature reversing or halting the door when it touches something in its path and an electric eye feature stopping the door if anything passes through the path of the eye. It may be possible to add the electric eye feature to an older door opener.

2.11.38 SETTLEMENT OR ROTATION

Applies to stoops or steps. Masonry stoops placed on poorly compacted fill, particularly on houses with basements, may show signs of settlement. The fill consolidates or settles allowing the stoop or steps to settle or rotate. Some settlement occurs on original soil because of undersized footings (or no footing) or from erosion or undermining of the footings. If the stoop is sloped toward the house it may funnel rainwater into the structure contributing to wetness and rot. If the stoop or steps pond water, they may become treacherous in freezing weather.

2.11.38 a. Settlement or Rotation
This stoop has settled.

2.11.41 NO RAILS
The inspector notes the absence of hand rails or safety rails. Opinions on railings vary but they are wise when there are three or more risers in the steps or when the deck or floor surface is more than 24 inches above the surrounding surface.

2.11.44 NO FIRE WALL
Recent codes have started to require some fire protection between the house and garage. (Often a 1/2 inch of fire rated drywall and a solid core, steel, or "labeled" door will suffice for local codes in new construction. Check with the local building official or fire marshal for more information.) This item may be marked if the inspector observes that the firewall is damaged or has been removed.

2.11.44 a. No Fire Wall
The pull down stair or attic access hatch may provide a route for fire to spread into the house. The thin plywood cover is not adequate.

2.11.45 NOT INSPECTED
The item is outside the scope and intent of the inspection and not examined. Do not rely on the report for any information on this item.

2.11.46 NONE PRESENT
The item was not present or inspected.

CHAPTER THREE

FOUNDATIONS, BASEMENTS, & STRUCTURES

3.1 LIMITATIONS

This section describes the aspects which limit the inspection of the foundation, basement, or structure. Inspectors do the best inspection they can, but sometimes physical obstructions, weather conditions, or the condition of the foundation, basement, or structure, prevent them from doing the whole job. Arrange for an inspection overcoming the limitations, if possible. Realize every inspection is limited in some fashion. The inspector is a generalist with broad knowledge on many topics and does not represent he knows or can see everything about every system. It is your responsibility to overcome the limitations. You should complete the inspection prior to closing even if you must hire others (Engineers, contractor's etc.) or pay an additional fee to the inspector or industry specialist. Repairs can be expensive and at some point replacement of components is the best alternative. An uninspected structural system or one given a severely limited or restricted inspection could be a total unknown. The inspector cannot make representations about what was not inspected. If you close on the house with a Limited or Restricted inspection you are accepting the responsibility for the unknown items about the system. The inspector cannot make representations about what was not inspected.

3.1.1 TYPICAL

The inspector feels they have seen as much of the foundation, basement, or structure as they normally see. The inspection of every system is limited in some fashion. Some parts of every system are hidden from view and can only be inspected indirectly or not at all. The footings and the structure behind the wall covering are examples. Often less than 10% can be seen. We can't report on the 90% we can't see. Inspectors cannot find structural problems concealed by finishes such as wall and floor coverings or insulation. (Also read section 3.1 Limitations.)

3.1.2 RESTRICTED

The inspector feels they have seen less of the foundation, basement, or structure than they typically see. It would be wise to have the crawl space or attic properly inspected before buying the house. There may be concealed defects. (Also read section 3.1.1 Typical.)

3.1.2.1 ACCESS TOO SMALL

The inspector was unable to enter the crawl space because the crawl space or attic access was too small. You should arrange to have the access enlarged for proper access for inspection and for maintenance and repairs. Only a small percentage of the area can usually be seen from the hatch. (Also read section 3.1.2 Restricted.)

3.1.2.2 TOO LOW

The inspector was unable to enter or inspect all areas in the crawl space because the floor system was too low to the ground (Less than two feet high). The inspector may write in a percentage or area that was restricted. (Also read section 3.1.2 Restricted.)

3.1.2.3 WET OR HAZARDOUS, INACCESSIBLE

The inspector found the crawl space wet or unsafe. It may be unsafe because of hazardous chemicals or possible electrocution. (Also read section 3.1.2 Restricted.)

3.1.2.4 VERMIN OR INSECTS

The inspector saw vermin or insects (i.e. snakes, bees, etc.) making the crawl space unsafe. (Also read section 3.1.2 Restricted.)

3.1.2.5 PERSONAL POSSESSIONS OR DEBRIS

Personal property (purposely or accidentally) blocks the inspector's view of part of the structure. The inspector will not move personal property or debris in order to inspect. (Also read section 3.1.2 Restricted.)

3.1.2.5 a. Personal Possessions
No one should enter a crawl space with personal possessions blocking the way. Have this limitation removed by the seller to allow access and inspection of the crawl space.

3.1.2.6 LOWER LEVEL (_____%)FINISHED

The structural elements of the basement or lower level are partially concealed or covered by finished surfaces. The inspection does not include concealed items. (Also read section 3.1.2. Restricted.)

3.2 GENERAL

A quick reference and overview of the inspector's opinions or impressions. This section is subjective and relies on the inspector's judgment and experience in estimating the age, whether clues are important and if toxins are present, etc. (Read the *FOUNDATIONS/BASEMENTS/STRUCTURES* chapter fully before forming any final opinion.)

3.2.1 SYSTEM INSPECTED (YES, RESTRICTED, OR NO)

The inspector marks whether the system was inspected. No information will be given about a system that was not inspected. If the inspector writes in or circles "R" for restricted, the system was partially inspected. Check 3.1 **LIMITATIONS** or discuss it with the inspector to learn the full extent of the restrictions. A severely limited inspection may not give you the information you need. You should do whatever is necessary to remove or overcome the restrictions and have the system fully inspected before you close on the house. (Read 3.1 Limitations.)

3.2.2 EVIDENCE OF PRIOR WATER (YES OR NO)

"YES" The inspector noted evidence of water either in the crawl space or in the basement of the structure. The water or wetness may be present during the inspection or there may be evidence water has been present in the past. If the inspection occurs during a dry period or repairs and improvements to the grading and drainage and water proofing have been less than adequate, the water may return.

Wet basements and crawl spaces contribute to many problems: mold and mildew in the crawl space and on interior surfaces, rotting of the structure, rusting of metal parts, condensation or sweating on windows, premature failing and aging of paint, deteriorating R-values of the insulation, sweating or condensation in the attic and on pipes, etc.

"NO" The inspector sees no evidence of water in the crawl space or basement.

3.2.3 EVIDENCE OF WOOD EATING INSECTS (YES OR NO)

Many home inspection companies do not provide a specific termite or wood eating insect inspection. Monitor for insect activity carefully. Some chemicals in use today do not remain effective over a year. It may be wise to keep your house under a warranty from a reputable Pest Control Operator.

"YES" The inspector sees evidence of damage apparently caused by wood destroying insects. Contact others, such as termite companies, for specific advice about curing the infestation and identifying the particular type of insect. Cure insect infestations to limit further damage to the structure.

"NO" The inspector does not see damage caused by wood destroying insects.

3.2.3 a. Wood Eating Insect Damage.
Be sure the infestation is cured. Sometimes the
damage is so slight no structural repair is required.
If the activity goes undetected long enough,
repairs will be necessary in addition to getting rid
of the insects.

3.2.4 EVIDENCE OF STRUCTURAL DISTRESS (YES OR NO)

"YES" The inspector sees evidence of structural distress in the form of settlement, sagging, or other failure of structural members.

"NO" The inspector sees little or no evidence of structural distress.

3.2.5 AMATEUR WORKMANSHIP (YES OR NO)

"YES" The inspector notes workmanship of less than professional quality. Poor workmanship may constitute a major defect. Major defects cost $500.00 or more to repair or may affect the habitability of the house. The work may not serve the purpose intended and may require repair or replacement.

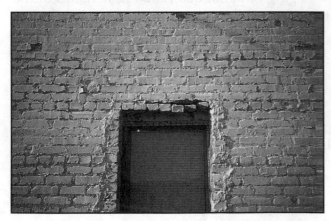

3.2.5 a. Amateur Workmanship
Cutting a hole in the wall and installing a window is
not enough. Install a proper lintel or beam to support
the brick above.

"NO" No amateur workmanship noted. Some amateurs produce workmanship of equal or better quality than professionals.

3.2.6 SUBJECTIVE RATING

The inspector's grade for the foundation, basement, or structural system:

E   **EXCELLENT**, above average, new or like new, (e.g. new, good quality, structural renovations on an older house).

A   **AVERAGE**, in typical condition for its age, showing normal wear and tear. (e.g. a five year old dry basement looks five years old.)

C   **BELOW AVERAGE**, prematurely aged, showing heavy or excess wear and tear, or delayed maintenance. Perhaps showing minor (curable) defects. (e.g. a five year old floor system decayed by minor plumbing leaks shows the wear and tear or age characteristics of an older house.)

F   **SUBSTANDARD**, failed, or reaching the end of its life expectancy. Any further service, even with repairs, should be considered a gift.

3.3 FOUNDATION

The foundation is the part of the house resting on the earth and ending at the first floor level. The footing is the part of the house transmitting the weight of the house to the earth. The footing is normally buried and not seen by the inspector. The footing is often indirectly inspected by drawing information from visible portions of the structure. (e.g. A cracked or failing foundation wall may indicate a settled or cracked footing.) These subjective opinions cannot be verified without excavating and exposing the footing.

The foundation transmits the weight of the structure to the footing. The inspector inspects only the visible part of the structure rising from the footing to the first floor. This includes the perimeter wall of the basement and the center line wall or other interior support structure, such as piers or columns, carrying the building's weight.

Often there is little distinction between the footing and foundation. Older houses were often founded on spread footings. Trenches were dug with reasonably level bottoms and stone or brick placed directly on the earth. The bottom courses or layers were somewhat wider than the upper layers. The mason might start off three or four bricks wide and gradually step back until reaching the two brick thickness of the foundation wall. Spread footings were common until ready mixed concrete became available. Concrete replaced indigenous or native materials for footings. Many people are startled to learn their older home has no concrete footing. Should a concrete footing be put underneath it? If the building has withstood the test of time, do not disturb it by installing a concrete footing.

Footings must be founded below the frost line on stable soil with enough bearing capacity to support the weight of the structure. If the soil beneath the footing freezes it may expand (frost heave) lifting the structure, damaging, or destroying it.

Styles of foundations are affected by the topography of the site. Hillside lots lend themselves to basement foundations out of the ground on one side (walk out or English basements), and split foyer style basements shallow in the ground. Lots sloping left to right appear ideal for tri-level houses. Siting is important in architecture and foundation design. If the topography is ignored, appearance and function suffer.

Tradition is a factor in foundation style in a locality. In some parts of the country, it is almost unacceptable to build anything but a basement because, "they always have been built that way." Slabs are often unacceptable because they are thought to be damp and cold, but in certain parts of the country slabs are popular. Often tradition dictates the style of foundations.

MAINTENANCE AND UPKEEP

The foundation and the structure are important aspects of the house. More water damage occurs than the combined total of termite damage, fire damage, lightning damage, wind damage, etc. A homeowner's primary responsibility to a home is to control the flow of moisture into the house and to be sure the moisture is properly contained (i.e. inside the plumbing system). Maintain proper grading and drainage, and be sure settlement has not occurred, allowing water to accumulate around the foundation and leak into the basement or crawl space. Keep shrubbery and trees pruned so the house can dry properly and not suffer from rot, mold, and mildew. Keep the roof properly water-tight and leak free to prevent water damage to the structure. This responsibility continues to all the other systems in the house having any potential affect on the structural system. Plumbing systems have been known to leak and rot important structural elements of the house.

Part of maintenance is a periodic inspection program looking for changes in the materials indicating minor water damage, wood destroying insect damage, water leaks, etc. In individual sections of this report maintenance of the various facets of the Foundation, Basements, or Structures is discussed.

3.3.1 TYPE

The type of foundation is classified as a crawl space, basement, slab, piers, etc. As mentioned earlier, the type is often a response to the site. (i. e. A basement may work on a hill side site.) Siting determines whether the house fits the location.

3.3.1.1 CRAWL SPACE

The open space between the underside of the floor joists and the ground. The crawl space offers access to the systems under the floor by crawling, hence the name. This is an advantage over slab construction. Any piping or services installed below the level of the slab are inaccessible without removing part of the floor. There was a time when there was no ductwork or plumbing. Crawl spaces are often low and some are nearly or completely inaccessible. Crowded ductwork, wiring, and plumbing make maintenance and upkeep a difficult task.

MAINTENANCE AND UPKEEP

Get into the crawl space, once or twice a year, in cold and hot weather, no matter how inhospitable. Look for damage or evidence of wildlife infestation, leaky pipes, condensation, cracked foundations, etc. A damp or wet crawl space can contribute moisture to the house. It is important to keep the crawl space dry. Suggestions for maintaining a dry crawl space include properly opening and closing the foundation vents. Usually the foundation vents should be closed only in the coldest weather. They can be open in spring, summer, and fall. Another suggestion is to cover the ground's surface in the crawl space with four or six mil polyethylene, with a minimum of joints. The polyethylene should cover 100% of the area as nearly as possible and touch or lap onto the perimeter walls. When installing the polyethylene do not damage the plumbing or other systems in the crawl space. Crawl spaces may contain exposed wires or junctions, etc., so use extreme caution. Shut off your main breaker or other main power disconnect device to be sure you are not electrocuted while in the crawl space. Cure any plumbing leaks discovered.

Condensation on the plumbing pipes or ductwork indicates the crawl space is damp and humid. The humidity will cause mold and mildew and prevent the evaporation of water leaking in behind decks, underneath doors, etc. This water, having no opportunity to evaporate in a damp crawl space, will rot the framing. If the crawl space is dry the water may evaporate.

Another reason to discourage dampness or wetness in the crawl space and throughout the structure is many wood destroying insects get the moisture they need from the lumber they eat. Dry lumber discourages insect infestation.

Moisture from the wet crawl space can rise through the house and condense on windows and walls behind pieces of furniture or in closets causing mold and mildew. It can rise into the attic and condense on the underside of the roof sheathing or drip from the metal surfaces, such as nails. It may cause plywood roof sheathing to delaminate. Read Sections 3.6 Interior and 3.7 Exterior Drainage for more information on establishing and maintaining a dry crawl space.

3.3.1.2 BASEMENT

The lowest story of a building or the one below the main floor, usually wholly or partially lower than the surface of the ground. Basements are popular in some parts of the country. One of the most common defects found in basements is wetness. Evidence of wetness in a basement could be a musty smell, efflorescence on the outside walls, staining or visual evidence of dampness or rot, evidence of water running across the floor, and so on. Efflorescence is a white powder forming on masonry as water migrates through it. A metallic salt dissolves and leaves deposits on the surface as the water evaporates. The efflorescence is harmless but messy. However, under the right conditions the water evaporates under the surface, leaving the salts behind and causing the face of the brick to pop off or spall.

Other problems exist in basement walls. The pressure of the earth and water attempts to overturn them or cause them to buckle or fall into the basement. Paneling or other wall coverings prevent the inspector from directly inspecting the walls for evidence of buckling, settling, or wetness.

MAINTENANCE AND UPKEEP

Properly maintain the drainage systems keeping the basement dry. The drainage systems include the general site drainage, the system controlling the roof run off, and the subslab system. Read the sections 3.6 Interior and 3.7 Exterior Drainage for more information. Also read the section 1.7 Gutters and Downspouts for more information on controlling roof run off.

Do not allow the topography of the site to change so surface or roof water soaks into the soil around the foundation. The importance of controlling roof and surface water in maintaining a dry basement cannot be over stressed.

It may be necessary to reestablish site grading if settlement has occurred around the foundation. Grade the site to drain away from the basement at a rate or a slope of two inches or more per foot for a horizontal distance greater than the vertical depth of the basement. In other words, if the basement is six feet deep the site should slope twelve or more inches in six feet. If surface and roof water runs quickly away from the foundation, it probably will not migrate into the basement.

Any holes/cracks admitting water directly to the basement should be dug up and sealed from the outside. Seal around pipes and other penetrations with a flexible sealant such as tar, silicone rubber, or other basement sealing compound. If the house or soil settles or moves, the pipes may have an opportunity to move rather than to break. Sealing holes or cracks on the inside of the walls and/or floors may help prevent moisture, insect, and/or radon entry.

Beyond the site grading, sealing holes, and controlling roof and surface water, the next step is to install an interior sump pump if one is not already present. Chop a hole through the basement floor slab, dig a pit or a sump, line it with gravel and a sump crock or a sump liner and install a sump pump. The sump pump should be discharged into the storm drainage system if possible or on the downhill side. Do not discharge the sump pump on the uphill side because the water runs down the hill and into the basement. Do not discharge the sump pump into the septic tank and drainfield because the water will flood and ruin the drainfield. In many localities it is not acceptable or legal to discharge a sump pump into the city sewer.

If site drainage and roof run off are controlled, it is seldom necessary to do more to assure a reasonably dry basement. In those cases a sump pump is usually the answer. Infrequently it may be necessary to install an interior perimeter drain to lead water into the sump.

3.3.1.3 SLAB

Slab construction is popular in some parts of the country. There are two types of slabs. A slab and footing poured simultaneously in one piece is a monolithic slab. Often these slabs are reinforced with pre-stressed or post tensioned cables. The second type of slab construction uses a footing and a masonry perimeter or foundation wall. The interior of the foundation is filled and the slab poured inside the foundation wall. There should be several inches of gravel below the slab, the perimeter insulated with foam, and a layer of plastic or polyethylene over the gravel. The purpose of the gravel is to provide for drainage and a "capillary cut off" or boundary layer. Water will soak up underneath the slab until it reaches the gravel. If there is drainage from the gravel the water will drain away. Water can still rise as a vapor and condense on the bottom of the slab. The vapor rises, touches the plastic, drips back into the gravel, and drains away. A properly built slab floor should be reasonably warm, dry, and solid.

In many older houses the basement or cellar floor slabs were not built by today's standards. Often the slabs were poured over a thin layer of cinders and the slab ranged from less than one inch to three inches thick. They were often uneven and unleveled and were little more than a walking or sweeping surface. Do not attempt to use this slab (or any other slab) for a structural load bearing member. The column or screw jack may punch a hole through the slab and into the dirt if you attempt to lift the house. The proper technique is to cut through the slab, dig down to solid undisturbed earth, install a proper pier or pad for the column, install the column, and repair the slab.

MAINTENANCE AND UPKEEP

A slab requires little maintenance from a homeowner. If your slab is wearing away and creating powdery dust, sealing compounds are available to spray or roll onto the floor. These compounds appear to be similar to varnish, but are porous enough to breath and allow moisture from the slab to migrate through without ruining the finish.

Maintain the sump pump in working order if there is one. If there is a subfloor drainage system that drains to daylight, (i.e. Down the hill until it comes out on top of the ground) it should be kept clean and free flowing to prevent the possibility of water backing up beneath the slab.

3.3.1.4 COMBINATION

Many houses have a combination of the various types of foundation systems. Read the various sections for information on those systems.

3.3.1.5 PIERS

Piers are short columns bearing on pads resting on the earth. Pier foundations support the house with rows of individual piers carrying the weight of the structure. In moderate climates pier foundations are common because they are inexpensive and allow air to circulate freely keeping the crawl space dry.

Demands to vermin proof the house have lead to pier foundations being skirted with everything from brick to wood. Almost any material imaginable has been used as skirting. Brick skirting is little more than a brick curtain wall of one thickness resting on the dirt. The weight of the structure should not be bearing upon the skirting. Often the piers have wicked or soaked moisture from the ground causing framing members to rot. Here some or all the weight of the structure may be bearing on the curtain wall.

MAINTENANCE AND UPKEEP

Site drainage should be positive, (i.e. Away from the foundation). It may be necessary to build up around the foundation, preventing water running against the skirting or piers and into the crawl space. If the framing is rotted above the piers, only contractors experienced in making these repairs should be considered.

3.3.2 MATERIAL

Many different materials have been used to build foundations. To be suitable, a material must be durable and capable of bearing the weight imposed on it. Foundations are usually built of masonry materials, but wood has been used. Many houses were built with stone foundations because the stone was locally available. Northeastern farmers say it rains rocks. They go into their fields, remove rocks, and make fences and foundations. The art of stone masonry has fallen by the wayside and now we think of stone as a premium material. There was a time when stone was used in the footing below grade where it could be covered and brick was used where it showed.

Brick foundations are common in parts of the country where clay is available for making brick. In other parts of the country block foundations are popular. Block is made from sand and cement and a light weight gravel material similar to vermiculite. Many foundations are combinations of materials such as brick and block or block and stone.

Poured concrete foundations are popular. Concrete is a mixture of stone, sand, and cement. Wooden foundations are not as unusual as people may think. In modern wooden foundations pressure treated pine and plywood resist decay and insect attack. Redwood, bald cypress, eastern red cedar, and several other species are naturally decay resistant. These materials have long been used as foundations for barns, yard buildings, and some homes. Terra cotta is a fired clay material laid like brick to form foundations.

MAINTENANCE AND UPKEEP

Each particular material has its own maintenance and upkeep requirements. Properly maintain the foundation because it bears the weight of the structure. Prune any brush or shrubbery that retards drying to reduce freeze/thaw damage or rot. Prevent vines from growing on the masonry materials. Their grippers or roots work into the surface and allow water to soak in, freeze, and damage the masonry. Repoint mortar joints as necessary keeping the foundation resistant to the weather. For more information read each section that applies to your foundation.

3.3.2.1 BRICK

In the east, brick is a traditional material for foundations. Made by mixing various additives to clay, brick are fired for durability. Bricks come in various sizes, thickness, lengths, and widths. Some are solid and some have holes in them. Some are fired to be hard and some are lightly fired to be soft.

Avoid unfired brick, known as a salmon brick, on the exterior. The unfired salmon brick were used for the interior courses of masonry walls. When old masonry buildings are torn down and the brick are salvaged for reuse, only the fired brick should be reused. The salmon or unfired brick should be thrown away. (Read section 2.3.1.1 Brick and 2.3.1 Masonry.)

MAINTENANCE AND UPKEEP

Brick lasts a long time if it is properly manufactured and maintained. The homeowner's maintenance consists primarily of keeping running or splashing water off the brick. i.e. Keep gutters in good condition and downspouts properly aligned so roof water does not cascade down the face of the walls or splash onto the brick. Mortar joints have to be repointed from time to time. (Read section 2.3.1 Masonry, Upkeep and Maintenance for more information on the repair of brick.)

3.3.2.2 BLOCK

Block is manufactured of many materials including cement, sand cement, cinders, and light weight aggregate material such as vermiculite or perlite. The two most common block types still available are the sand cement block and the light weight blocks. Cinder blocks have fallen from favor because the cinders used in their manufacture contained iron particles which rusted and bled, ruining their appearance.

Block is porous or sponge like. Water or air can pass through the block material. The exterior of a block basement should be properly parged and waterproofed to help keep the basement dry. Parging is the practice of coating the exterior of the block with a sand cement plaster. The plaster is less porous to both air and water than block. Proper parging and waterproofing are also a good defense against radon infiltration. Waterproofing and parging are done below grade and the inspector will not be able to inspect them directly and will only be able to judge their success by the dryness of the basement.

Block is unfired and cure slowly as the cement sets. There are characteristic cracking patterns associated with block because they tend to shrink after installation. If they are laid when they are "green" or not fully cured or if laid wet and allowed to dry in place, the cracking may be exaggerated.

MAINTENANCE AND UPKEEP

The maintenance and upkeep of the block wall is similar to the maintenance and upkeep of any other masonry structure. Keep them pointed and allow them to dry properly, etc. Site drainage is important in avoiding water running against the block. (Read section 2.3.1 Masonry, Upkeep and Maintenance.)

3.3.2.3 BRICK AND BLOCK

One of the most common combinations of foundation materials is the use of block on the inside of the wall and brick on the outside. Several combinations exist. Thicker block may be used below grade to create a basement with thinner block and brick above grade. Some masonry houses are built of solid brick, but many were built with a layer of brick and a layer of block.

In rare instances, the blocks shrink after they are laid and brick expand or grow, creating problems. Generally, these problems are not noticeable in buildings as small as residences.

MAINTENANCE AND UPKEEP

The maintenance and upkeep of the brick and block wall is similar to the maintenance and upkeep of any other masonry structure. Keep the joints pointed and allow the masonry to dry properly, etc. Site drainage is also important in avoiding water running against the foundation. (Read section 2.3.1 Masonry, Upkeep and Maintenance.)

3.3.2.4 STONE

As mentioned previously stone was once a common building material, particularly in areas where stone was abundant or indigenous. The structures built of stone masonry may be as strong and durable as stone. If the stone is sturdy and durable, structures tend to last indefinitely. There are soft types subject to weathering. Stone laid of random size pieces just as it was found is rubble stone. Stone may be cut square and neat and laid in courses or an ashlar pattern. There are hundreds of combinations of patterns. The strength of the wall is affected by the pattern.

MAINTENANCE AND UPKEEP

The maintenance and upkeep of the stone wall is similar to the maintenance and upkeep of any other masonry structure. Keep the joints pointed and allow the masonry to dry properly, etc. Site drainage is important in avoiding water running against the stone. (Read section 2.3.1 Masonry, Upkeep and Maintenance.)

3.3.2.5 CONCRETE

Concrete is a mixture of gravel, sand, and cement. Foundations and basements are commonly poured of concrete in the Northeast. The concrete in foundations and basements is often unreinforced. i.e. The concrete is not reinforced with steel rods. Such concrete may crack from shrinkage and these foundations and basements often have one or more sizable cracks. Some of these cracks are largely cosmetic and do little or no harm to the structure. A crack can cause a basement to leak severely.

MAINTENANCE AND UPKEEP

The maintenance and upkeep of a concrete basement or foundation wall is similar to other masonry structures. Keep the wall dry through proper site drainage and the control of roof run off and splashing water. Concrete is not impervious to water and is porous. Consider sealing or painting the concrete if dampness is a problem. Any open cracks may be sealed with high quality (swimming pool) caulk. The cracks should be monitored for movement. If they are stable, they can be pressure grouted with epoxy by commercial grouting contractors. (Read section 2.3.1 Masonry, Maintenance and Upkeep.)

3.3.2.6 WOOD

Wood has been used in foundations throughout history. Some of the castles in Europe were built on Cedars of Lebanon flattened on two sides and laid in ditches. The stone was then laid on top of the timbers and the trenches refilled. Some of these castles are now four or five hundred years old and the timbers are beginning to rot. The modern version of the wooden foundation uses pressure treated materials to create both crawl spaces and basements. Some wooden foundations are sheeted on the outside with treated plywood and rest on footings of gravel.

These foundations offer several advantages over traditional masonry foundations and concrete footings. One, the gravel footing is an excellent drainage system below the basement floor level or level of the crawl space. If a daylight drain or sump pump is provided from the gravel, the basement will probably be drier than a masonry basement. Second, the plywood and the wood offers great resistance to bending and more resilient than the masonry. They are capable of resisting the pressure without loosing their strength. One of the problems with a masonry wall is once the masonry moves, it cracks. Once it cracks it looses all the strength. Wood is flexible and retains most of its strength even if it is deformed or bent.

Sometimes inappropriate pieces of wood are used in foundations. These materials are not treated or naturally decay resistant. Such woods as redwood, bald Cyprus, eastern aromatic cedar, and several others are naturally decay resistant and have been used as the legs of decks and piers under houses. On the west coast it was common to use vertical grain fir as a foundation material.

MAINTENANCE AND UPKEEP

Wood foundations benefit from proper site drainage and control the roof water as do masonry foundations. Keep the shrubbery, trees, etc. pruned so the materials can dry properly. Even the decay resistant materials may eventually decay if the conditions are conducive.

3.3.2.7 TERRA COTTA

Terra cotta is a clay material in which the wet clay is formed into shapes and fired. Clay tiles roughly four inches by four inches by eight inches long are laid like brick. They are square or rectangular and hollow from end to end. Some tiles were turned inward through the wall to create small square holes to serve as vents.

Houses have been built of terra cotta tiles formed in twelve by twelve by four inch pieces. These were both an exterior finish and structure. They could be covered with other materials and often were plastered on the inside.

MAINTENANCE AND UPKEEP

Maintenance and upkeep of a clay tile or terra cotta foundation is the same as with any other masonry foundation. The control of surface water and roof run off is important to keep the water from eroding the tiles and the mortar joints. (Read section 2.3.1 Masonry, Maintenance and Upkeep.)

3.3.2.7 a. Terra Cotta
Shows the inside of a tile foundation from the crawl space. Notice the "vents" through the pillar are closed with newspaper. When open these holes provide ventilation but allow vermin to enter unless screened.

3.4 STRUCTURE AND MATERIALS

Houses in this country have been built of almost any material conceivable. The materials had to be durable and locally available. Only recently have we had the luxury of being able to ship materials from one end of the country to the other. This was part of the reason for regional architecture. The local climate and indigenous materials were strong factors in the style and design of houses. As shipping costs lowered houses lost their regionalism and their local appearance. Now you see Texas ranchers on the east cost, colonial houses in California and California contemporaries in the east.

Masonry materials have appeal as building material because of their durability, availability, strength, and resistance to decay, fire and vermin, etc. Masonry materials are heavy, brittle, and difficult to use. Masonry does not make superior beams, joists, rafters, and so on. Masons attempted to overcome these limitations through the fabrication of arches, but in modern residences arches on this scale are seldom seen. Other materials that span well, such as wood or steel, are substituted for masonry.

Wood is a traditional material and has many advantages. In many places it was locally available. Pioneers built log cabins because they had the logs and because they were sturdy, offered protection from attack, and were easy to build with crude tools. Wood is relatively lightweight and will span long distances producing reasonably solid floors. It works well as rafters, ceiling joists, and studs. It also has some disadvantages. Except for a few naturally decay resistant species and treated materials, it decays or rots readily when wet. It will burn and may be attacked by insects.

Masonry materials are relatively unaffected by changes in moisture content, but change dramatically with response to temperature. Wooden materials are relatively unaffected by changes in temperature, but change dramatically (particularly across the grain), with moisture content. Many structures are built with a combination of materials. Builders and craftsmen have to compensate for the characteristics of various materials.

An example is a three story masonry row house with wooden interior framing. The masonry exterior of the house remains the same size. If built of brick it may expand slightly. The interior wooden members shrink as they age. The wood shrinks about ten times as much in width as in length. The shrinkage is slight, but may amount to an 1/8 inch in 100 inches of length and an 1/8 inch in 10 inches of width. The floor joists are about 10 inches wide and the studs are about 100 inches tall. For each floor they shrink about 1/4 inch or more. Rising through the structure, you accumulate 1/4 to 1/2 inch of shrinkage per floor. The first floor may seem level, the second floor may sag slightly, and the third floor sags dramatically. The third floor sagging as much as 1 1/2 inches is not a defect, but characteristic of the type of construction.

MAINTENANCE AND UPKEEP

The owner's responsibility to maintain the structural aspects of the foundation, basement, and structure of their house is obvious. This is the shell or skeleton of the house. One of the primary aspects of maintenance is to protect the structure from the elements. Maintenance of site drainage is of key importance as is the proper maintenance of the roofing system. Properly maintain the plumbing and other systems having the potential to leak and or damage the structure.

The structural materials of the house must be protected from excessive exposure to the weather. The exterior shell of masonry houses is the external structure of the house. In frame structures, the frame is the skeleton of the house and is protected by an external skin of siding. In both cases the roof is an essential element in protecting the structure from the weather. Houses with wide roof overhangs, proper gutters and proper site drainage last longer and endure the weather better than houses that do not have wide overhangs and proper drainage.

For masonry houses with parapet walls (walls extending above the level of the roof), it cannot be over stressed how important it is to maintain the masonry above the roof level, including the chimneys. A leak occurring above the roofing, circumvents the roof and flashing, and may find its way into the structure. Leaks have the potential to damage the masonry and rot the wooden elements.

3.4.1 MASONRY

One of the advantages of masonry is its durability. Some of the oldest surviving man made structures are built of masonry. The masonry materials used in construction have been selected for use because of their durability and proven performance. Masonry is also resistant to fire, insects, rot, and vermin. Masonry materials, because of their longevity, have a reputation of being maintenance free. This is not true. Masonry does require maintenance, but perhaps at a less frequent interval than some other materials. Masonry materials exposed to the weather must be kept weather resistant and weather tight.

MAINTENANCE AND UPKEEP

One of the primary responsibilities in maintaining a masonry structure is to maintain its ability to resist the infiltration of water. Caulk around windows and doors to keep water from blowing or leaking in beside the windows, etc. Point mortar joints as necessary. The mortar joints must be scraped out to depth of about twice their thickness and replaced with mortar similar to the original mortar. It may be 30 to 50 years before a substantial pointing is necessary. As structures age the necessity to point occurs more often.

3.4.1 a. Point
A more skillful craftsman could keep the brick cleaner reducing the necessity to acid wash the wall.

The people building older masonry structures knew water migrated through the masonry. The mortar they used was rich in lime and considered a soft mortar. Modern mortar, rich in cement, is a hard mortar. The soft mortar allows water to migrate easily around the brick or stone. If damage occurs, it is in the mortar and can be repaired by pointing. If the water migrates through the stone or brick, the damage is to the masonry. Repair is best left to professionals. Use mortar as rich in lime as the original so the path for water migrating through the masonry is not sealed.

Parapet walls will require repair and pointing two or three times as often as the general masonry of the structure. Parapet walls are the walls rising above the level of the roof. Since they are exposed to the weather on both sides and do not receive any heat from the building, they may freeze. Any water leaking down through parapet walls may leak into the house or rot the ends of floor joists. Some parapet walls may be coped or capped with other materials such as terra cotta, clay tiles, or metal. Keep chimneys and parapet walls in sound condition. Individual loose bricks or whole sections have been known to collapse and damage the roof or fall on passers by. A brick falling from the third story can be a deadly missile.

A technique used to protect masonry from the action of migrating water is a sacrificial coating of mortar. In basements water migrates through the brick and evaporates from just beneath the surface, leaving metallic salts. The salts accumulate beneath the surface and eventually develop enough pressure to cause the face of the brick to pop or slough off. A thin coating of soft lime mortar, like plaster, over the inside of the masonry, allows the salts to accumulate in the mortar or plaster. Eventually the plaster pops or sloughs off, exposing the brick. The mortar is purposely being allowed to deteriorate, protecting the brick behind it. Repair or replace the sacrificial coating as necessary. Similar coatings may be applied along the exterior base of foundations, one to two feet above the ground. The purpose is the same. Water wicking from the ground migrates out and pops the faces off the brick. On the exterior, this can be particularly damaging because of freezing. If the sacrificial coating is present, the freezing or salt deposition occurs in the mortar rather than in the brick. If you have sacrificial mortar, it is often a mistake to paint it. Paint slows the drying process, causing the brick behind the mortar to be damaged. The most important chore the homeowner has in maintaining the masonry of the home is to protect it from the effects of water and weather. Water has done more harm than all other forces of nature combined. (Read section 2.3.1 Masonry.)

3.4.1.1 BRICK

Brick has been used as a construction material since early colonial times in America. Many of the buildings in Williamsburg were built from brick manufactured on the site. One of the stories about the interesting brick pattern used in the Bruton Parish Church in Williamsburg is they accidentally burned some of the brick. This was a tremendous mistake. All these bricks were hand made and there was no time to make another batch. They decided to lay these particular brick endwise in the wall and thus created a striking and beautiful pattern. This error has been mimicked many times and has become a highly desirable brick pattern.

Brick can be laid in many bond patterns including running bond, Flemish bond, English bond, etc. Brick masonry residences are laid with walls at least 8 inches thick and sometimes 12 or 16 inches thick. There was a time when the inner thicknesses or withes of brick were made of a brick called a salmon brick. These bricks were either not fired at all or only lightly fired. Salmon brick occasionally are recovered when buildings are demolished and the brick is reused. Any salmon brick should be disposed of because they will not withstand exposure to the weather. Modern bricks are fired in kilns under carefully controlled conditions. These products are better and more consistent than they were. Masonry has fallen into disfavor in the construction of homes because of the expense. It is an excellent material and many masonry homes exist.

MAINTENANCE AND UPKEEP

As mentioned in section 3.4.1 Masonry, one of the responsibilities of owning a brick home is to repoint the mortar joints as they erode and weather. Sometimes the joints were designed to allow water to migrate through the wall. Point failing joints as necessary. This chore is required fairly often on steps, perhaps annually, but on other parts of the structure may require repointing only every twenty years.

One characteristic problem of older masonry structures has been noted with masonry arches above windows. These arches are flat and have a tendency to settle and to rest on the window. There may be a floor joist bearing in the wall above the window and the floor joist settles with the arch. A skillful mason can remove the brick arch, support the floor joist, rebuild the arch, and leave little evidence of his work. (Read sections 3.4.1 Masonry, 2.3.1 Masonry, and 2.3.2.5 Brick Veneer.)

3.4.1.2 BLOCK

Block has been made of many materials including cement and cinders. Cinder blocks fell into disuse because the cinders contained iron particles which rust and bleed down the face of the blocks. Modern blocks are often made with a light weight aggregate such as vermiculite and perlite in order to reduce the weight of the block. Most blocks manufactured today are of either sand cement or the lightweight variety.

Block has a tendency to shrink slightly, particularly if laid when still "green" or uncured or if laid while wet. This cracking usually does not create structural problems. The material used in block is so course and porous, wind will blow through a block wall. Water will soak or leak through the wall until the exterior is sealed or painted. The exterior may be parged or plastered with a sand cement plaster. Parging is more impervious to the infiltration of water and air than the block. This forms a suitable exterior coating, but is subject to the infiltration of water and moisture from the interior.

MAINTENANCE AND UPKEEP

As with all masonry structures block structures tend to be durable provided they are properly maintained. These are low maintenance structures, but don't neglect required maintenance until the structure has suffered. Do not allow water to migrate into the block wall from the parapet walls or from within the structure. The water passing through the block from the inside may freeze in the wall and cause any exterior coating of paint, parging, stucco etc. to pop off the wall. (Read sections 3.4.1 Masonry, 2.3.1 Masonry, and 2.3.2.5 Brick Veneer.)

3.4.1.3 BRICK AND BLOCK

Masonry houses were once built several thicknesses of brick or stone. In the last 50 years it has become popular to build with composite materials such as a combination of block on the inside and brick on the outside. Often these structures can be recognized by the characteristic header courses every 16 inches. The brick and block work together and six courses of bricks are the same thickness as two courses of blocks. Every seventh course of brick, turned inward, expose their ends on the exterior. This ties the brick and block together as a solid structure.

This technique works well in small structures the size of residences. In large structures it has been known to create some problems because bricks sometimes grow or swell slightly after installation and blocks may shrink slightly. The shrinking and swelling phenomenon occurs in hundredths of an inch per linear foot of brick and block and is absorbed in small structures. In large structures it can become a problem.

MAINTENANCE AND UPKEEP

The maintenance and upkeep of the brick and block structure is similar to the maintenance and upkeep of any other masonry structure. The homeowner's primary responsibility is to protect the structure from the effects of weather. Repoint mortar joints as necessary and keep the roof and parapet walls in good repair. (Read sections 3.4 and 3.4.1 Masonry, 2.3.1 Masonry and 2.3.1.1 Brick Veneer for more on maintaining masonry.)

3.4.1.4 STONE

Stone has been used throughout history for construction and was the original masonry material. Man made materials such as brick and concrete mimic the characteristics of stone and make the work of a mason easier. Bricks are usually regular shapes, and easier to fabricate into walls, etc. Stone comes in a wide variety of shapes. When laid up in irregular shapes it is known as rubble stone. When cut square or quarried in rectangular pieces and laid in patterns, the patterns are known as ashlar or random ashlar. Stone may also be a veneer over block or frame, but in most traditional stone structures, it is both the exterior facing and the structural element. The durability of the stone determines the durability of the wall. The mortar used should be softer than the stone not only to provide a cushion between the stones, but a path for moisture migration from within the walls. The mortar is repairable.

MAINTENANCE AND UPKEEP

Stone, as with every other masonry product requires a certain amount of maintenance. Prevent water leaking into the stone causing freeze/thaw damage to parapet walls. Repoint or replace the mortar joints as necessary. It may not be necessary to repoint more than once every twenty years. If the wall is subject to splash damage the part of the wall getting splashed will require repointing more often than the rest. (Read sections 3.4 and 3.4.1 Masonry, 2.3.1 Masonry and 2.3.1.2 Stone Veneer for more on maintaining masonry structures.)

3.4.2 FRAME

Frame structures have been in use in this country since colonial times. In a frame structure the structural load or the weight is borne by a skeleton or a frame of wooden members. Other materials, such as steel, serve as framing elements in structures, but in residences "frame" means wood. The vertical members in the walls are studs. The horizontal members in the floor and ceiling are joists. The sloping members in the roof similar to joists are rafters. Joists in floors are floor joists and joists in ceilings are ceiling joists. Often joists are of dual purpose. Ceiling joists of the first floor are the floor joists of the second floor.

In frame structures, many of the structural elements are hidden from view. The siding and the interior wall covering are not structural elements and the frame (studs) is hidden from view. These elements are only inspected indirectly. The inspector looks for clues or tell tale signs of underlining structural elements, but cannot remove the wall covering to inspect the structural members directly.

Wood is the dominant material in residential framing and the species of wood used locally is chosen for its strength, availability, durability, etc. Only recently have we developed the ability to ship materials long distances and therefore use materials not indigenous or locally available. In the south, a common framing material is yellow pine or southern yellow pine. In the west, fir, larch, and redwood have been common framing materials. In the north other species of pine, fir, and spruce are common. In the deep south there were large forests of magnolia trees and they were harvested and used for timber. The framing material must be strong enough to bear the loads imposed on it and resistant to decay and insect attack. Some native woods are resistant to decay and insect attack. Such materials as redwood, bald cypress, western red cedar, eastern aromatic cedar, are durable in contact with the ground or when left exposed to the elements. Such materials are rare or expensive and only used in locations where the builders think the risks are high.

Industry has developed a method of pressure treating lumber. The material is put into a large tank, a vacuum is drawn, and the tank flooded with a liquid containing a chemical such as chromated copper arsenate under high pressure. The preservative material is all the way through the wood in a concentration sufficient to protect the wood from decay and insect attack. Southern yellow pine has proven to be a receptive material for treatment. Other lumber species have not been shown to be successfully treatable. This material can be used in locations subject to moisture and insect attack. There is controversy surrounding the use of treated lumber. Environmentalists feel chemicals may be leaching into the environment and they may be harmful to workmen who work with it constantly. As far as the author knows there is little or no risk for the homeowner.

MAINTENANCE AND UPKEEP

The maintenance and upkeep of the frame of the structure consists primarily keeping that portion of the house dry and free from the attack of insects. The materials, if properly used and dry, have a long life expectancy. Keep the roof and roof drainage system, gutters, etc. in good working order. Properly maintain the paint, caulking, siding, and exterior trim to protect the framing members from the infiltration of water. The crawl space or basement must be kept as dry as possible to reduce the affects of dampness rising from underneath the house. Keep plumbing and mechanical systems in good working order so those systems do not damage the structural elements of the house. Plumbing leaks have been known to destroy major structural elements by causing them to rot.

Consider the structural aspect of the various parts of the house as you make repairs and renovations. Plumbers have done more damage to houses than termites ever have. This may be an exaggeration, but plumbers bore large holes through joists and beams and have been known to cut joists entirely to run a pipe. This is also true of other tradesman. Be sure to maintain the structural integrity.

3.4.2.1 WOOD

Wood is the dominant framing material used in this country and probably world wide. Wood has many characteristics making it desirable as a framing material. It has a good ratio of strength to weight. It makes sturdy beams and joists capable of forming solid floors. Wood is commonly available and if kept dry and free from insect attack it is durable. There are wooden structures hundreds of years old.

Wood goes through several stages in its life. Originally, it comes from the sawmill and is selected for straightness, freedom from serious defects, etc. At some point in its life, thirty five to fifty years after installation, wood appears to go through a slight change in the shape of its cells. The wood may sag or relax slightly causing sagging floors. This appears to have little effect on the strength of the wood. It acquires a new shape and then continues to perform as it did before.

Wood has some undesirable characteristics. It is subject to fire, rot, insect attack and is an inconsistent material. It has knots and splits. It shrinks and swells with changes in moisture content. Natural wood shrinks and swells as much as 10 times in the width as it does in the length. Over a long period of time it shrinks gradually. This was mentioned in 3.4 Structure and Materials section. Most of the characteristics of wood have been taken into account in the design of structures. The framers of wooden structures were aware of the problems wood exhibits and have compensated for them in the style and design of the frame.

MAINTENANCE AND UPKEEP

Keep the wooden elements of a house dry. They should be protected from moisture from roof leaks, wet crawl spaces or basements, and from plumbing leaks. The fungus causing rot is not particular where the moisture comes from. Some wood eating insects find lumber with a high moisture content more desirable than dry lumber. This is another reason wood framed structures should be kept dry as possible.   Dry lumber discourages rot, mold, mildew, and the activity of wood eating insects. (Read sections 1 Roof, 3.7 Exterior Drainage, 3.6 Interior, and Chapter 2 Exterior for more information on how to protect the frame elements of the structure from the weather.)

3.4.2.1 a. Wood
The floor joist and girder rotted because of a wet crawl space. Some of the joist have been doubled or sistered with new pressure treated joist of the same size. Part of the girder has been replaced. Maintaining a crawl space in a dry condition will prevent the need for these repairs. (See 3.8.2.2 Repaired Rot Damage.)

3.4.2.1.1 SILL

A sill is a wooden member resting on top of the masonry foundation. It helps distribute the weight of the structure from the wooden frame to the masonry. The sill is anchored to the foundation to help counter the forces of wind, hurricanes, tornadoes and earthquakes. The sill in direct contact with the masonry is subject to rising dampness or water wicking. It is desirable to have a metal shield between the sill and the masonry or the sill should be made of decay resistant material.

3.4.2.1.2 BAND

The band board is also known as the ribbon board. The band forms the perimeter around the floor framing system. It is the first and last floor joist and is the joist turned perpendicular to the ends of the other floor joists. The band is immediately behind the siding and one of the framing elements most attacked by weather.

One problem often associated with the band board is poor flashing details or omitted flashing. Water leaks under doors or between the house and the deck (or stoop) and rots the band board. Often the band board is difficult to repair because it is inaccessible.

3.4.2.1.3 JOISTS

As mentioned earlier, joists are horizontal framing members supporting the weight of the floor or ceiling. Joists are beams used in multiples, in rows, and usually on regular centers. There will be many joists, side by side, on perhaps 16 inch centers supporting the floor. These joists may all rest on a single large beam or girder.

3.4.2.1.3 a. Joists
A manufactured floor joist shaped similar to an I-Beam can provide an excellent floor. However, this one has been cut. (See Trades Damage 3.8.25.)

3.4.2.1.4 GIRDERS

Girders in residential construction are also called beams. They are large framing members usually of wood (sometimes of steel). Each girder supports substantial weight, such as the ends of all the floor joists, or the load of a bearing wall. Girders differ from joists. They are used as singular members, but joists are used as multiples.

Girders often form one of the central and important framing elements. If a single floor joist is cut, little harm usually results. The structure is purposely redundant as possible to allow for the occasional cutting of a stud or a joist. Cutting a beam may have disastrous results because it is a singular element.

3.4.2.1.5 RAFTERS

Rafters are similar to floor joists. The difference is rafters run at a slope and are the structural element supporting the roof. Rafters are used in multiples and on perhaps 16 or 24 inch centers.

3.4.2.1.6 COLUMNS

Columns are vertical framing members and usually substantial in size. Steel pipe columns may be 3 1/2 or 4 inches in diameter and may be filled with concrete. Wood and masonry are as large as 8 inches by 8 inches and up. Columns most often support the weight of a girder and the structure above. They are not used repetitiously the way studs and joists are, so use extreme caution cutting, drilling, removing, or any way affecting the strength of a column.

3.4.2.1.7 TRUSSES

Industry has given us trusses. They are manufactured off site and trucked in. Often trusses are used to form the structure of the roof system and are vaguely triangular in shape. The bottom chord of the truss forms a ceiling joist and the top chord takes the place of a rafter. There are usually diagonal members in the truss transmitting the stresses and loads from one member to the other throughout the truss. Trusses are engineered and built to perform as a unit or as a large single piece and should not be cut or modified at the site.

Before trusses were manufactured in factories and shipped to the site they were built or fabricated on the site. It will have to be the inspector's subjective opinion whether site built trusses (and manufactured trusses) are performing as they should and supporting the loads imposed on them. Do not store personal items in a truss "attic". Most trusses are not designed for storage loads.

There is a problem associated with trusses known as truss uplift. Trusses tend to react to changes in the weather. The upper chords of the trusses, the rafter part, and the webs of the trusses are exposed to the air in the attic. The lower chord, the ceiling joist part, is buried in the insulation. The parts are in somewhat different environments. Trusses have been known to arch their backs or rise in the center in winter and come back down on the walls in the summer. This phenomenon occurs rarely, but when it does it can be aggravating and frustrating because little can be done. The trusses are very strong and when they operate in this fashion they have a will of their own. People have tried to bolt the trusses down to the wall or even bolt them to the center of the floor below. The forces causing them to arch are so strong they will either lift the structure below or destroy themselves trying. Truss uplift is somewhat rare and not clearly understood. No one is sure why it occurs.

One remedy has been to attach crown molding around the rooms so it is attached to the ceiling and slides up and down as the trusses move. In other words, the trusses are free to move and the crown molding is installed to telescope up and down with them and disguise the problem. (Read also 9.10.29 Truss Lift.)

3.4.2.2 STEEL

Steel is an excellent material for some framing members such as girders, columns, lintels, and other spanning members. Steel framing is common in commercial buildings, but because of the expense of fabrication it has not been generally adopted for residential building. There are efforts to introduce products such as light weight steel studs to take the place of non load bearing members. These may catch on as wood becomes scarce. The forest industry advertises wood as a renewable resource and steel is not. We can grow more wood but we can't grow more steel. Steel does not rot and is not attacked by insects. It will rust and in a fire the steel loses its strength rapidly as it heats up. Steel structural elements must be protected from the heat of a fire.

3.4.2.2.1 GIRDERS

Girders or beams are often one of the main load bearing interior supports to a house. Where it is desirable to have a beam or girder spanning a long distance without intermediate columns or other supports, steel replaces wood girders. Building codes have become more and more restrictive and the span of wood girders has been limited. Steel girders can be bought strong enough to support residential loads over almost any distance. As the girders become longer they become springy.

3.4.2.2.2 COLUMNS

The use of steel in columns is common in residences, particularly in basements for pipe columns. They can be small and can be run through a concrete floor onto a pad below with little danger of the column rotting. They may rust.

3.4.2.2.3 LINTELS

Lintels are beams supporting the weight of the masonry above openings. Lintels used in exterior walls must be protected from rusting. Steel expands five or six times to one as it rusts and lintels have been known to swell at their ends if water infiltrates the wall and rusts the steel. The swelling steel can lift the wall or masonry above, crack it creating problems. Removing a rusted lintel is a difficult process. The masonry must be removed, the lintel repaired or replaced, properly waterproofed, and the masonry reinstalled. It takes a skillful mason to do this and not leave the structure scared.

3.5 VENTILATION

The main purpose of ventilation in the structure is to allow unwanted moisture or heat to escape. Ventilation includes foundation ventilation for crawl spaces and attic ventilation. (Read section 1.8 Ventilation.) Maintaining the crawl space in a proper dry condition is important to the structure. As with all ventilation you should look to the source of the moisture. It is better to prevent the moisture from entering the structure than to try to ventilate it out after it is in.

Some model building codes require foundation vents equal to one square foot of net free ventilating area for each one hundred and fifty square feet in the crawl space. Those vents should be

Foundation/Basement/Structure

distributed evenly around the structure and one should be located within three feet of each corner of the crawl space. Most houses do not have this much ventilation. If the crawl space has a tendency to be wet, problems result from under ventilation. The dampness problems can be subtle and it may take years for the homeowner to recognize their existence. By this time the damage is done.

Homeowners who repair structures and reduce air leaks sometimes aggravate damp crawl spaces or moisture problems. Such things as installing storm windows, new siding, caulking, and other efforts to seal the structure may change what had been a slightly damp crawl space into wet crawl space. Adding decks or planting shrubbery around the foundation may reduce the amount of natural ventilation flowing through the crawl space vents.

MAINTENANCE AND UPKEEP

Keep foundation vents securely in place with screens to keep insects and vermin out. In colder climates, closures or flaps sealed in winter, conserve energy and prevent frozen pipes. It is important the crawl space remain dry. Wetness encourages mold, mildew, and rot. It also decreases the effectiveness of the insulation. It is attractive to termites and may dilute the effectiveness of any soil poisoning used to prevent termites. Get into the crawl space, regardless of how inhospitable, twice a year (cold and hot seasons) to look for damage, wildlife infestation, leaky pipes, condensation, cracked foundations, etc.

3.5.1 FOUNDATION VENTS

Foundation vents come in many shapes and sizes. The standard version is an 8x16 inch vent which conveniently replaces five or six bricks or one block in the foundation. Many of these vents are aluminum or other corrosion resistant metal and include proper screening and closures. Black plastic vents, probably polypropylene, are tough and corrosion resistant. The plastic vents also include closures and screening. Many of the plastic vents exhibit much less net free ventilating area than do the corresponding metal vents. Some of the metal vents open more than 70 square inches of the vent area. The plastic vents open as little as twenty four square inches. At 24 square inches or less, it would take six vents to equal one square foot of net free ventilating area.

In the past the foundation vents were manufactured in other sizes with and without closures and screens. Builders have used other techniques such as laying a block on a side, exposing the holes, or leaving part of a brick out of the foundation. Sometimes clay tiles were turned so the tubular opening through the center of the tile opened into the foundation.

There is some controversy over when foundation vents should be closed because of air transported moisture. If the air outside is warmer and more humid than air in the crawl space, ventilating would transport moisture into the crawl space. It may be wise to install plastic (polyethylene) on the ground and close the foundation vents and leave them closed.

Automatic vents open and close according to the temperature. These vents include a thermostatically controlled operating mechanism that opens the vents when the weather is warm and closes the vents in cool weather. Where the hole is not the correct shape for the vents, the automatic action may be blocked. If you have automatic vents check them occasionally to be sure they are responding to changes in temperature.

MAINTENANCE AND UPKEEP

Maintain the foundation vent devices in proper working condition, complete with screens and closures. The screening should be repaired or replaced to prevent vermin entering the crawl space. Where the vents are within five feet of pipes, check the closure of the vents to be sure they can be closed to prevent the pipes from freezing. Ventilating and keeping the crawl space dry is sometimes more important than energy conservation. It may be necessary to insulate the pipes and leave the vents open.

For air transported moisture, it is likely winter air will be colder and drier than the air inside the crawl space and therefore ventilation in the winter may dry the crawl space. In summer the outside air is warmer and more moist than the air in the crawl space and ventilation may be harmful.

Close the vents in winter and leave them open in the spring, summer, and fall. This advice is designed to protect the pipes from freezing. It is not necessarily the best advice for ventilating the crawl space of moisture.

Do not close attic vents. Leave them open year round. Attic vents tend to let heat out in summer and moisture vapor out in winter. Closing off the vents may induce condensation on the framing or roof sheeting. A cold, dry attic is better than a wet one.

3.5.2 WINDOWS

Many basements include windows for ventilation. These windows are often little more than fixed sashes or sashes hinged to open either as hopper windows or awning windows. Basement windows suffer from splash damage and rot from rising dampness because of their proximity to grade. Basement windows will require more maintenance than the primary windows. Basement windows are often neglected.

MAINTENANCE AND UPKEEP

Keep these windows properly painted to protect them from rot, rust and decay. Basement windows may be particularly difficult to protect because of their proximity to grade and the close humid environment in window wells. Keep window wells dry and free of debris.

3.5.3 DOOR(S)

Many basements include exterior doors. In a walk out basement, doors may exit at ground level. In other cases there may be an areaway or exterior stairwell leading to the basement door.

MAINTENANCE AND UPKEEP

Keep all exterior doors properly painted to protect them from rot, rust and decay. Basement doors may be difficult to protect because of their proximity to grade and the humid environment. Keep areaways dry and their drainage functioning properly.

3.6 INTERIOR DRAINAGE

Drainage systems located inside the foundation drain water from the interior. Interior drainage systems may be an important part of keeping crawl spaces and basements dry. They collect and discharge water rising from below the foundation. These systems allow the water to flow away harmlessly. Unfortunately, they may invite the water to flow into the structure. It may be better to control the water outside the structure as opposed to letting it in and then letting it back out. Interior drainage systems, open sumps, open floor drains, etc. have been sources for pollution, notably radon and sewer gas in houses.

MAINTENANCE AND UPKEEP

Keep any interior drainage system functioning properly and flowing freely. It may be an essential part of keeping the crawl space or basement dry and the reduction of moisture may be important to the structure. Open sumps in basements should be sealed to prevent radon entry and personal injury.

3.6.1 SUMP PUMP

The sump is the hole below the earth or slab level into which water from beneath the building flows. Most sumps have a crock, but some are unlined. The sump pump discharges water outside the building or into the sewer or storm drainage system.

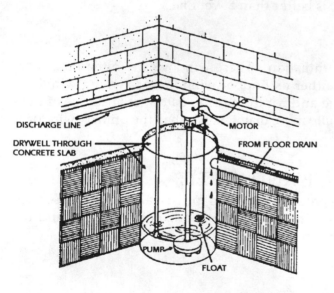

DISCHARGE LINE

DRYWELL THROUGH CONCRETE SLAB

MOTOR

FROM FLOOR DRAIN

PUMP

FLOAT

3.6.1 d. Sump and Sump Pump.
The pump should not lower the water level in the surrounding soil far enough below the level of footings to invite infiltration or undermining. In extreme cases desiccation or shrinking of the soil may be a problem.

One disadvantage of a sump pump is, as mechanical device, it will eventually fail. Repair and maintenance are required to keep it operational. It may be critical in maintaining a dry basement or crawl space. Another disadvantage is the interior drainage system may allow water to flow into the building. If the sump is open any pollutants in the water such as radon gas may be exhausted into the interior of the building.

Most sump pumps operate on a float switch. When the level of water rises, the pump comes on and the water is discharged. The float switch falls with the level of the water and turns the pump off. The switch must be maintained in proper working order.

MAINTENANCE AND UPKEEP

Keep pump, switch, wiring, and piping in proper working order. Investigate the type and style of the pump and follow the manufacture's directions for proper maintenance. It may have internal washers or diaphragms requiring replacement from time to time. If the pump runs frequently, install a backup or secondary pump. In extreme cases, install a battery backup system for potential power failures. Power failures most often occur in severe weather, when it would be most difficult to get the pump repaired, and when the pump would be most needed. When the first pump fails, the second pump will assume the duties until the first pump can be repaired or power returns.

Often sump pumps discharge into the city sewer. Some localities are sensitive about processing storm water and other drainage water through the sewage treatment plants. Some require redesign of roof drains and other drainage systems to discharge to storm sewers or other locations not processed by the sewage treatment plant. When remodeling you may be required to discharge storm water somewhere other than the city sewers.

If your sump pump operates often, reconsider the drainage on your property and look for other, nonmechanical solutions. It may be possible to drain the foundation drains and the sump to daylight, i.e. down the hill by gravity, if the site has enough slope. Try improving the grading and other drainage systems such as the downspouts, perimeter drains, etc. to the point the sump pump becomes either unnecessary or only operates occasionally. (Read section 1.7 Gutters and Downspouts and 3.7 Exterior Drainage.)

Keep sumps, particularly in basements, properly covered and sealed to prevent people stepping or falling into the sump and radon and other pollutants entering the house.

3.6.2 FLOOR DRAINS

Many buildings with concrete slabs have floor drains to drain water from above the slabs. The traps beneath them must be kept wet to avoid sewer gases backing up into the house. Some people have forgotten these traps and many are dry. Floor drains can be an important part of the drainage system in an emergency.

MAINTENANCE AND UPKEEP

Keep floor drains free flowing. Promptly remove trash or debris. Check them from time to time by pouring water down the drain. This will also serve the function of keeping the trap wet so sewer gases do not enter. In obscure drains, difficult to keep wet, pour a liquid into the trap that does not evaporate, such as mineral oil or baby oil. It does not gel, harden, or evaporate, but floats and allows an in-rush of water to drain away. The drain remains functional.

Floor drains can work backwards. If the city sewer stops up, sewage may flow into the house. Find out if "check valves" are permissible in your location. You could install a check valve to prevent it from happening.

3.6.3 DRAIN TILES

Drain tile traditionally consisted of terra cotta or clay tiles about 4 inches in diameter and 12 to 16 inches long. Some tiles were cast of cement. Tiles end to end, about 1/2 inch apart, allow water to enter. The tops of the tiles are covered with tar paper to keep out dirt. They are in a bed of gravel and covered with gravel to keep soil from soaking into the tiles and filling them up.

Recently, technology has brought us PVC and polyethylene pipe either perforated with holes or slotted with saw cuts to serve the same function. This pipe is lighter and comes in 10 foot sections or long coils. It is also laid in a gravel bed to prevent silting. More recently, technology has brought us filter fabrics similar to felt, but rot proof. It can be laid over the gravel to keep fine material from washing in and silting the pipe full. The drain tile is not visible for inspection. Clay or concrete tiles have been known to crush, crack or fail, and stop functioning. The inspector has no way of knowing the condition of the buried parts of the system.

MAINTENANCE AND UPKEEP

Clean or flush out the drain tile system once or twice a year. Rooter services can cut roots and flush the pipe. This can be essential for foundation drains or the drains connected to downspouts.

3.6.4 VAPOR BARRIER

No material is a perfect vapor barrier. A better description of the function is a vapor retarder. Moisture rises into the crawl space through capillary action. A vapor barrier retards or slows the evaporating moisture from rising into the structure.

Droplets of water hanging on the bottom of the sheeting indicate the vapor barrier is functioning. Water condensed on the cooler plastic sheeting hangs there dripping back to the ground. This moisture is underneath the plastic and no longer rising and wetting the structure.

The most common vapor barrier is polyethylene sheeting either four or six mils (.004" or .006") thick. Technically, this may not be a part of the drainage system, but improves its effectiveness. Polyethylene is inexpensive, easy to install, and commonly available. However, it does tend to deteriorate with age.

MAINTENANCE AND UPKEEP

A plastic vapor barrier should cover 100 % of the crawl space grade. It should be lapped and turned up onto the perimeter wall. Remove any wood or debris before installing a plastic vapor barrier. Moist wood is attractive to termites and other wood eating pests. Any holes in the vapor barrier will hamper its' function. Do not disturb or puncture the vapor barrier.

3.6.5 NONE

No interior drainage system seen. This does not imply a system is needed. A dry site with good drainage may not require interior drainage.

3.7 EXTERIOR DRAINAGE

The importance of exterior drainage to the life expectancy of the structure cannot be over stressed. It is second only to the roof. Poor site grading and drainage contribute to wet basements and crawl spaces. Good grading and drainage can often cure water problems. Exterior drainage systems enhance the flow of rainwater away from the property. The system functions without pumps. Ditches, swales, contouring, and grading are preferred to piping, French or blind drains, pumps, etc. Surface drainage systems are more reliable and easier to maintain.

A few hundred dollars spent on landscaping and improved drainage may cure a chronically wet crawl space or basement. Sometimes the site and surrounding topography make exterior drainage difficult.

MAINTENANCE AND UPKEEP

It is essential the homeowner keep these systems functioning properly and freely. Any drain tile or underground piping systems should be monitored, making sure they flow properly. It may be necessary from time to time to root out drain lines and clear them of tree roots, etc. If subsurface drainage systems or the drain tiles leading from downspouts clog, water may flow into the basement or crawl space.

Observe surface drainage systems, such as ditches and swales, making sure they have not silted or eroded, stopping the flow of water. Silted or eroded ditches could create a negative flow toward the house. Positive drainage can keep the structure dry.

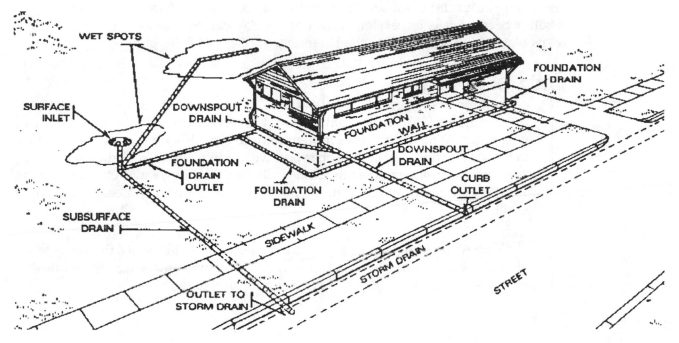

3.7 d. Exterior Drainage.
You can install subsurface drainage systems to remove excess water if the topography permits. Such systems can be effective but are more expensive and difficult to maintain than surface systems.

3.7.1 SITE

The site is the land or property purchased with the structure. Examine the neighborhood topography before making a decision to buy. It is better to be at the top of a hill than in a valley, natural swale, or at the bottom. Rain running off hundreds of acres sometimes drains across individual lots making it difficult to maintain a dry basement or crawl space. If the drainage problem is large in scope, it can be nearly impossible to change the drainage on the lot without the cooperation of your neighbors. The grading necessary to improve the drainage problem on one lot may require the cooperation of all landowners in the area.

3.7.1.1 LEVEL

Building lots are seldom absolutely level. Many people desire flat or nearly level lots thinking they require less care and are easier to mow, etc. Level or flat lots can present difficult drainage problems if the house is in a depression. Positive drainage can be difficult to accomplish. Do not select the lowest lot in the neighborhood. On flat lots water may pond for days after a heavy rain. Look at a lot after a rain or during the wet season before you buy.

MAINTENANCE AND UPKEEP

The upkeep on a properly established level lot may be easier than the maintenance on a sloping lot. Level lots have less erosion. Inspect the drainage flow at least twice a year, checking for negative drainage.

Clean out ditches and swales often. Use the soil from the swales to counteract the settling around the house. Technically, clay soil installed around the foundation is better because it is impervious to water. A clay cap installed over the softer soil keeps water from soaking into the basement.

3.7.1.2 SLOPING

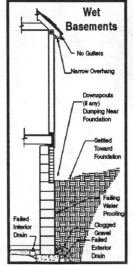

Sloping lots range from gentle lots to steep hill sides. Sloping lots present both problems and opportunities for builders, landscape designers, and homeowners. The water comes from uphill and runs downhill whether the house is in the way or not. Establish proper positive grading (away from the foundation) using such techniques as berms, swales, ditches, retaining walls, etc. Be sure the water flows away from the foundation, around the house, and continues down the hill.

Some water also flows underground. It flows downhill, seeks the water table, and soaks from wetter to drier. It may follow water and sewer lines into the house despite the appearance of good surface drainage.

3.7.1.2 d
Water problems usually start outside the structure. Most of them
can be corrected, if you understand how the water gets into the structure.

MAINTENANCE AND UPKEEP

Inspect the drainage systems often, particularly during rain. Clean out silted and eroded ditches and swales, reestablish berms and banks, and replace soil settled around the foundation. It may be necessary to install a clay cap around a basement to prevent water from soaking into the soil disturbed during construction. Impervious soil on top of the ground may prevent water from soaking into the basement. (Read section 1.7 Gutters and Downspouts and 3.7.2 Improvements.)

3.7.2 IMPROVEMENTS

Any reshaping of the grading or natural topography of the lot could be an improvement. Many techniques improve on nature's drainage. Drainage should be positive, so water flows away from the foundation. The techniques range from swales, ditches, retaining walls, underground drainage systems, etc. Each individual lot must be analyzed and the landscape or grading contractor involved in the construction must use the systems necessary to maintain a dry basement or crawl space.

MAINTENANCE AND UPKEEP

All drainage systems require maintenance and upkeep from time to time. Protect the system from freeze/thaw damage, erosion and the other forces of nature destroying their usefulness. Inspect the drainage frequently while it's raining and remove silt or debris hampering it.

3.7.2.1 SWALES

Grass and other ground plantings establish easily in these shallow wide ditches. They can be useful for accumulating water to flow away and off the lot. They are gentle and unobtrusive and easily maintained. They can be mowed and observed by the homeowner. If they fill with silt, it is easy to remove.

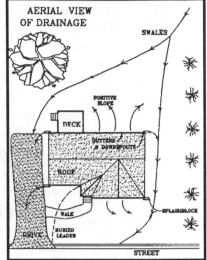

3.7.2.1 d Swales
A view of the structure looking down.
Good drainage may be a simple solution,
but often isn't easy to create.

MAINTENANCE AND UPKEEP

Protect them from erosion and silting. Inspect periodically, particularly during a heavy rain, to be sure they are an adequate size and shape to accumulate the water and carry it away.

3.7.2.2 DITCHES

Ditches are similar to swales but deeper and narrower. Ditches are sometimes lined with grass or other natural material and on occasion paved or lined with concrete, asphalt, stone, brick, etc. Ditches are more unsightly than swales but often necessary.

MAINTENANCE AND UPKEEP

Inspect them from time to time, particularly when it is raining, for adequate size, silting, or erosion. Remove any siltation and debris from the ditches and repair erosion. Line ditches showing constant erosion with protective material.

3.7.2.3 TERRACES

Terraces are the opposite of ditches. Terraces are small ridges or banks created to shift the flow of water so it flows down in stair step fashion. If there is a ditch or a swale located behind the terrace, it may form the lip or outer bank of the ditch. It may capture and divert the water to the left or right, so it flows around the house not against it. These terraces are banked or perched swales.

MAINTENANCE AND UPKEEP

Proper flow of the water must be maintained and the effects of the water controlled or offset. Remove any siltation preventing the proper flow of water.

3.7.2.4 RETAINING WALL

Retaining walls come in all sizes and shapes. Homeowners use everything from railroad ties to concrete in building retaining walls. The materials must be durable and resist the forces of the earth pressing against the wall. Retaining walls are difficult to build properly. Water can dramatically increase the pressure against the wall. The walls suffer from freeze/thaw damage. Often retaining walls are built without giving enough consideration to the destructiveness of the environment. Retaining walls should have weep holes through them for drainage behind the wall to reduce the pressure. If the soil above the wall is as high as or higher than the wall, the water can flow down and cascade over the wall. Often retaining walls are higher than the soil is behind them. The water is blocked and soaks in behind the wall. It may exert hydrostatic pressure or freeze and push the wall.

MAINTENANCE AND UPKEEP

Maintenance and upkeep of retaining walls varies as the nature and style of the walls. Keep drainage systems, including draintiles and holes through the walls functioning properly. Repair the wall according to the nature of the material. Masonry walls may require the repointing of joints from time to time. (Read section 3.4.1 Masonry.) Wooden walls may eventually decay and require replacement.

3.7.2.5 DRAINTILES

Draintiles are underground and not visible for direct inspection. Usually the inspector has no way of knowing whether the draintiles are functioning properly at the moment of the inspection. Clay tile draintiles or the cast concrete ones are often crushed or blocked by roots or vermin. Draintiles do not last forever and may be destined to fail. Surface drainage may be better.

MAINTENANCE AND UPKEEP

Properly maintain the draintile system. Companies can rod or root the draintiles and remove roots and other blockages. If your draintiles are connected to downspouts, you should check the discharge from them occasionally to be sure they are flowing properly. This can be done either with a hose or during a rain.

3.7.2.6 WINDOW WELLS

Protect basement windows or foundation vents with window wells. The drainage around window wells keeps out water. Window wells work better if covered or protected from the rain by a wide roof overhang. Often it is necessary to install a drain from the bottom of the window well to allow accumulated moisture to escape.

MAINTENANCE AND UPKEEP

Keep window wells clean and free of debris. Keep their drains clean and free flowing. The window well should be repaired or replaced as necessary. It may be necessary to caulk or seal the window well to the wall to prevent water from entering. Install covers or plastic bubbles if necessary.

3.7.2.7 DRIVEWAYS

Driveways are inspected only as to how they affect the house. Driveways can be a major source of runoff from snow and rain. Paved drives in particular can cause increased run-off and adversely affect the crawl space or basement. Nearly 100% of the rain runs off paving and a large percentage, perhaps 80%, runs off tightly compacted gravel. A much larger percentage is absorbed by grass and woodlands. If the drive slopes toward the foundation, it can flood the crawl space or basement. As with all surfaces around the foundation, drives should slope away from the building.

MAINTENANCE AND UPKEEP

Keep asphalt drives sealed to avoid water soaking through. Seal cracks in concrete drives also. Follow the manufacturer's instructions on the coating. Keep salt off concrete drives. It may damage the surface. Salty water running off the drive may kill surrounding plant life. Water soaking in under the paving is its worst enemy. Once underneath, it may freeze and heave the pavement or soften the soil allowing the traffic to destroy the paving.

You must also keep the paving sloped away from the foundation. If any of it settles and slopes toward the foundation, or was sloped incorrectly to begin with, it may have to be removed and reinstalled sloping properly. To avoid puddles that may freeze and form tripping hazards, paving must be sloped to drain properly dry. Unless very well done, concrete must have at least 1/4" per foot (5" in 20 feet) and asphalt must have even more slope.

Well established gravel drives may be easier and less expensive to maintain than paving. The best gravel for drives has sharply angular broken stones with a combination of sizes ranging from sand-like dust to stones of an inch to an inch and a half. Rounded river stones or pebbles do not work well because they will not compact and "lock" together unless they are run through a crusher to crack them into angular pieces. Gravel drives may require a little raking or occasional scraping with a tractor and road-blade, but this work is less expensive than sealing asphalt drives annually and the eventual repair and replacement of paving.

3.7.2.8 WALKWAYS

Walks are inspected as to their impact on the house.

Walks sloping toward the foundation may drain water into the basement or crawl space (3.8.64 Negative Drainage). Walks immediately beside the foundation often tilt or settle with the soil around the foundation as it consolidates. (See 2.1.38 Settlement or Rotation.) Any surface sloped toward the house should be corrected to drain the water away. These surfaces act like funnels and can dump large amounts of rain into the foundation.

Another hazard to the house associated with the walk is ponding. A concrete walk may extend from the steps to the paved drive, creating a pond between the walk, drive, and foundation. Unless there is good positive drainage away from the house and water flows freely over or under the walk, the area may become soggy, killing the plantings and causing water to soak into the foundation.

Evaluate the walk for yourself for tripping hazards and usefulness. The inspector does not inspect these aspects or the suitability of various materials used for walks.

MAINTENANCE AND UPKEEP

Maintain walks so they drain away from the foundation and do not contribute to wet basements and crawl spaces. Pay particular attention to walks adjacent to the foundation. If such walks settle and tip toward the foundation, they may act as a funnel and deliver water into the foundation. Keep walks clear of debris and irregularities forming tripping hazards. Steps of less than two inches are often not considered tripping hazards, but larger ones may be. If your walk has several steps, you may need handrails. If your walk is along the top of a retaining wall or areaway, you may need guardrails.

It may be necessary to remove and replace sections if tree roots or freeze thaw action lifts sections to the point the walk becomes dangerous or unserviceable. Steep walks or those with stairs in them may require handrails. Be certain walks drain dry after rains (away from the house) and do not pond water. In colder climates the water on the walk may freeze and become a hazard. If the walk tilts toward the foundation you should replace it or repair it to slope positively away. Caulking between the foundation and a paved walk generally will not keep the water out if it tends to slope toward the foundation. Maintain positive drainage from the space between the walk and the house. If there are no gutters and roof water floods this space, there can be substantial water to drain away.

3.7.2.9 VEGETATION

Vegetation is inspected only as to its impact on the structure. The inspector is not a horticulturalist and will not identify the various plants on the site. If you are allergic to any plants, you will need to inspect the area for these particular plants yourself. The inspector will not identify any illegal or illicit plants that may be growing in the area. (See 2.1.2.1 Vegetation, Vines, Shrubbery and 2.1.7 Vines for more information on how vegetation may affect the house.)

In general, plantings should be far enough from the foundation to permit inspection and maintenance. Plants close to the house tend to obstruct the view of the house and making it difficult to paint and do other maintenance. They also tend to cause water to splash onto the house and to retard drying. This will cause the early failure of the paint and contribute to rot damage to the siding. Even long lived materials such as masonry last longer and accumulate less moss and mildew with out vegetation retarding drying.

Trees close to the house have overhanging limbs that may plunge through the roof and may retard drying there also. Roots from the trees and shrubs may pass under or through foundations and damage them.

Shrubs close to the foundation may prevent the inspector from seeing and therefore they won't be able to report on any defects in those concealed areas.

MAINTENANCE AND UPKEEP

Keep vegetation cut back from the building. Do not allow vines to grow on the building. Keep trees back far enough the roots will not penetrate the foundation. Their roots generally extend as far as their limbs. You should be able to walk between any plantings and the building. This allows for "air drainage" or circulation to dry the building, and for maintenance and inspection and also reducing the splash onto the house. Drying is promoted. Shrubbery should not be in front of or blocking foundation vents or blocking ventilation to the crawl space. Vines should not be allowed to grow on the house. (See also the Maintenance and Upkeep sections under Roofing and 2.11.7 Vines and Vegetation and Maintenance and Upkeep under Roof.) Get advice from an Arborist or tree expert on keeping tree roots out of your foundation and from under walks. There are some trees so invasive it may be wise to remove them.

3.8 OBSERVATIONS

The inspector marks observations of conditions affecting the foundation, basement, or structure. More than one item may be marked as the foundation, basement, or structure may exhibit more than one symptom or problem. Some items are part of the normal aging process and do not require correction. Other items require either maintenance or repair if the house is to reach its full potential or life expectancy. Read carefully each section applying to the system inspected.

Maintenance is the on going care required if a system or item is to reach the full potential including lubricating, painting, etc. Do maintenance as required by the manufacturer of the equipment or item. Repairs put items or systems back in good condition after damage or decay, etc. Repairs are caused by delayed maintenance, aging, normal wear and tear, or abuse. The workmanship and materials of the repairs should be equal to the quality of the system and have the same life expectancy. e.g. A limb plunges through an asphalt shingle roof. If the roofing otherwise has a life expectancy of ten years, the repair should also have a life expectancy of at least ten years. If the roofing only has a life expectancy of one year, then the repair should be capable of lasting one year or more. It is not prudent to put a one year patch on a ten year roof or to waste a ten year repair on a one year roof. All repairs should be by qualified competent professionals.

3.8.1 SOUND

The inspector thinks the item is functioning at the moment of the inspection. This does not imply perfection, absence of minor defects, or absence of wear and tear.

3.8.2 TYPICAL

The inspector thinks the item, material, or aspect of construction is characteristic or similar to comparable products in similar houses. The item has normal wear and tear.

3.8.3 EXTERIOR CRACKED

The masonry material is cracked either in the mortar joints or through the individual units. The cracking of the masonry may be a symptom of some underlying problem such as settlement or

freeze\thaw damage. Sometimes the settlement has stabilized and is unlikely to cause further problems. Individual cracks will be analyzed on a case by case basis.

3.8.3 a. Exterior Cracked.
This crack in a parged block foundation wall (3.3.2.2 Block) opens and closes with seasonal changes in the moisture content of the soil. In such a case the solution must address the soil problem as well as repairing the crack.

It is important to know the history of the crack. How long the structure has been cracked and whether the crack moves or changes. Does it change with moisture or temperature? It is nearly impossible for the inspector to analyze a crack during a single visit. It may be necessary to monitor the crack over a long period to determine the cause and its importance.

Cracks should not be repaired or filled with mortar or other hard materials before consulting with an expert. If they open and close annually or seasonally, filling the cracks may do more harm than good. Clear silicon rubber often works. It is unobtrusive, flexible, and durable. It seals cracks against the infiltration of wind and water until they can be monitored.

3.8.3 b. Exterior Cracked.
The masonry beside the window may carry the weight of the structure above. This dislodged piece of masonry may shift under the weight, crush the window and allow the wall above to settle.

3.8.4 EVIDENCE OF SETTLEMENT
Some portion of the structure has apparently shifted or settled. Almost all buildings settle. If they settle slightly and evenly the settlement may go unnoticed. If they settle differentially (i.e. one part settles more than another part), buildings often crack and sometimes require repairs. It is necessary to know the history of the problem to make a diagnosis of whether repairs are necessary. More investigation and monitoring may be necessary.

3.8.4 a. Evidence of Settlement.
The wall of the basement settled because the soil under the footing eroded away in a heavy rain. Proper exterior drainage would have prevented the problem.

3.8.5 NO SETTLEMENT NOTED

No evidence of settlement seen. The structure may be cracked or damaged, but apparently has not settled.

3.8.6 UNSTABLE SOIL

Certain soil types are unstable and unsuitable for construction. Shrink/swell clays shrink when they dry causing the building to settle. When wet, the soil swells and may lift the building. These soils may cycle seasonally or annually, opening and closing cracks.

Other unstable soils consolidate or compress under the footings allowing the building to settle or subside. Some soil types or formations slip or move laterally and translate part or all the building from its original position. Inspectors are not soils mechanics experts, nor do they have the training to recognize one soil type from another. This is an area of science for soil scientists and engineers with specific training. If the inspector suspects unstable soil, further investigation by experts is wise. This may include test borings and a laboratory analysis of the soil.

3.8.6 a. Unstable Soil
Soil that cracks, forms the dried mud flat look or separates from the curb or foundation in dry weather. This may be a clue of unstable soil.

3.8.6 b. Mud Flat Look

3.8.7 BASEMENT WALL CRACKED

The basement wall has cracked indicating movement or failure. It is often difficult to determine the exact cause of the crack in the wall without knowing the history of the crack and observing it over a period of time. Monitor the crack and get further information from previous owners, etc. Improve on the drainage around the basement, extend downspouts, slope the soil away from the foundation, etc.   Anything reducing the weight of the soil and exterior water pressure against the wall is desirable. Minor stable cracks may have little or no structural significance. The wall can be repaired and sealed by companies specializing in the grouting of cement block walls or the injection of epoxy into cement walls. In minor cases, it may be possible to repair the cracks by caulking or pointing with mortar.

3.8.8 BASEMENT WALL BUCKLING

The basement wall is buckling or heaving (usually inward). Buckling walls must be treated with extreme caution. It may be impossible for the inspector to determine the exact cause of the problem without knowing the history of the building and the crack or phenomenon. Make repairs before the wall collapses. If the property is occupied and any movement seen in the wall, evacuate for safety.

Many homeowner's immediate response is to install temporary support under the floor above to take the weight off the wall. Do not do it. The compression or weight of the structure may be helping the walls resist the overturning forces. Removing the weight may cause the wall to collapse immediately with disastrous results. Only professionals who fully understand the work involved and have appropriate insurance should attempt to repair buckling walls.

3.8.9 PIER OR COLUMN DAMAGE

A pier or column supporting part of the structure is rusted or physically damaged. The piers and columns are main structural elements in the building and any damaged members should be properly repaired or reinforced.

3.8.10 UNDERMINING

Running water causes undermining. Running water flowing beneath the footings or piers of a building erodes the soil below and allows the structure to subside or settle. The repair of undermining starts with finding the source of the flowing water and eliminating it. For a burst pipe or water main, shut off the water until repairs are made. After the source of the water is found, stopped, or diverted, repair the undermined area by underpinning the existing footings with concrete or pressure grouting. The nature of the extent of the repairs will be determined by the nature and extent of the damage. Leave the repairs to professionals.

3.8.11 SITE SLIPPAGE OR DRAINAGE

Site Slippage. An unusual phenomenon in most parts of the country. A dramatic example is the mud slides occurring in California. The entire lot or even an entire section of lots, slides or translates down the hill. Leave the repairs of site slippage to engineers and professionals who understand the phenomenon.

Site Drainage. The particular lot is subject to an unusually large amount of drainage from off site. Occasionally houses are seen in the middle of a large natural drainage course. It is difficult to have proper site drainage when the problem involved represents dozens or even hundreds of lots. You may need community or subdivision help.

3.8.14 RUSTED OR DAMAGED LINTEL

Iron or steel lintels above windows and other openings in the masonry walls are subject to damage from rusting. Iron expands five or six times its original volume as it rusts. The rusting action expands the lintel in the mortar joints and lifts the masonry. When lintels expand and the weight of the masonry is sufficient, the rusting action causes the lintel to deflect downward. Stopping the infiltration of water causing the lintel to rust and expand is part of the repair. In some cases it is necessary to remove masonry above the lintel, replace the lintel, properly waterproof, and reinstall the masonry.

3.8.14 a. Rusted or Damaged Lintel
The lintels shown 3.8.14 a. and close up 3.8.14 b.
swelled enough in thickness to lift the masonry of the
house about 1/4". The lintel in 3.8.14 c. has cracked
from possible freeze thaw damage (See 3.8.17 Freeze/
Thaw Damage).

3.8.14 b.

3.8.14 c.

3.8.15 FALLING ARCHES

Many older masonry buildings had shallow or flat arches. They rose only a few inches at their center or were flat or jack arches. The openings have spread or bulged open from the thrust of the arches, or the mortar joints have eroded, allowing the arches to settle and rest on the windows. Sometimes the masonry supports a floor joist above the window openings and the joist settles with the arch. Cracks may let water leak in. If the arches settle, have an experienced mason remove and reinstall the arch in the proper position. A skillful mason will leave little evidence of the repair. (See Page 42, 2.3.1.1 a. figure.)

3.8.16 DAMAGED PARAPET WALL

The parapet wall on a masonry building is the part of the wall extending above the level of the roof. Freeze/thaw action often damages parapet walls. They erode or crack in the mortar joints. Water infiltrating through cracked joints or failed copings or caps can bypass the roof flashing and leak into the structure and damage the structural elements below.

3.8.16 a. Damaged Parapet Wall.

3.8.16 b. Damaged Parapet Wall
The unprofessional repairs are unattractive and may not
function as long and as well as they should.

Parapet walls exhibiting loose brick or other material should be repaired because the loose material can be hazardous to passers by if it is blown or falls from the wall. Have an experienced mason repoint or tear down and rebuild the wall. Properly cope or cap the wall.

3.8.17 FREEZE/THAW DAMAGE

Freeze/thaw damage is characteristic damage in masonry. Water infiltrates minor cracks or the surface of masonry and freezes. The ice expands opening the crack. When the ice thaws, more water infiltrates the crack. It freezes again, opening the crack wider. Repairing freeze/thaw damage ranges from caulking or pointing the affected joints to the taking down and rebuilding damaged sections.

3.8.18 BULGING OR UNPLUMB

Masonry walls are sagging or budging out of the plane of the wall. Often caused by water infiltrating the interior spaces between the bricks and freezing. The freezing action causes the exterior faces of the wall to bulge outward. In stucco, water infiltrates and rusts its connections, causing it to fail or bulge outward.

Walls not plumb or leaning can be hazardous because they may fall. Repairs depend on the nature and extent of the damage but often sections of the walls require removal and replacement by experienced masons.

3.8.19 FAILING MORTAR

Like every component of the building, mortar has a life expectancy. Eventually, the effects of weather and time cause it to fail. It often fails through freeze/thaw action or the erosion caused by water.

Older masonry buildings were laid with mortar rich in lime and the mortar was soft. Repairs should be made with similar mortar so the moisture flow patterns through the wall will not be altered. Do not cover the older, soft, permeable, mortar with harder, less permeable cement mortar.

The repair for failing mortar is usually repointing. Mortar is scraped from the joints to a depth of about twice the joint's thickness. Fresh mortar is tuck pointed or packed into the joint and properly tooled. In extreme cases it may be necessary to dismantle the wall and relay it completely with fresh mortar.

3.8.20 CRACKED OR FAILING SLAB

Many concrete slabs exhibit minor cracks because of shrinkage in the concrete as it cures. The inspector looks for evidence the slab has cracked, shifted, settled, or failed in some serious way. Without knowing the history of the crack or failure, it may be necessary to monitor the slab over time. There are companies that can repair slabs or jack them back into position, but often costs are prohibitive. It may be more reasonable to replace the slab.

3.8.21 UNREPAIRED ROT GIRDER, SILL, BAND, JOISTS

Unrepaired rot noted will be marked according to the damaged location (girder, sill, band, or joist). Rot damage may occur in two or more areas.

3.8.21 a. Unrepaired Rotted Joists. Also shows 3.8.52 Mold and Mildew and 5.9.7 Unsupported Wire. Notice the 8.5.3 Falling Insulation. The mold, rot, and falling insulation all indicate a wet crawl space.

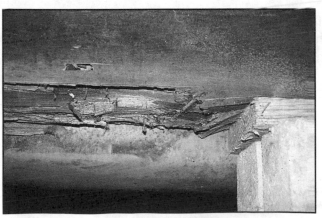

3.8.21 b. Unrepaired Rotted Girder

The source of the water causing the rot must be found and eliminated or the problem will continue or reappear. Properly repair any damaged structural members. Leave repairs to experienced craftsman. Damaged girders represent a major structural element and should be replaced, laminated, or reinforced to return adequate strength to them. The same is true of all other structural elements. In advanced or complex cases consult with a Professional Engineer or other expert.

3.8.22 REPAIRED ROT DAMAGE

There is rot damage in the structure, but the water source causing the problem is cured and the structural aspect repaired. The repairs appear adequate.

3.8.22 a. Repaired Rot Damage.
Notice the fresh new blocking between the floor joists and the new patches of plywood subfloor. The bath tub above had leaked and rotted the floor. The primary cause was the failure to caulk around the tile and beside the floor. The picture also shows a 4.5.3.2 Trap and 4.4.3.2 Copper Waste Piping.

3.8.23 UNREPAIRED TERMITE DAMAGE

As with rot damage there are two problems associated with termite damage. Be certain the termite infestation has been cured or eliminated so the problem will not continue or reassert itself. Repair the structural aspect if the damage is extensive enough. Any substantially damaged structural elements should be properly laminated, reinforced, repaired, underpinned, replaced, etc. Leave repairs to experienced craftsman. (See page 73, 3.2.3 a. Wood Eating Insects.)

3.8.24 REPAIRED TERMITE

There was damage, apparently caused by wood destroying organisms, but repairs appear adequate. Consult with a termite company or other expert to be sure there is no current insect activity.

3.8.25 TRADES DAMAGE

Trades damage is a broad category and reflects any damage done to structural elements by craftsmen such as plumbers, electricians, or heating contractors. Any such damage to the integrity of the building should be properly repaired. Leave repairs to craftsmen with experience.

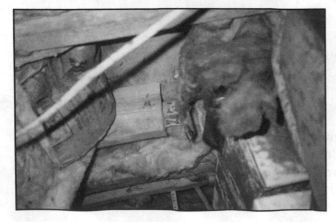

3.8.25 a. Trades Damage.
Notice the floor joist cut to make room for the ductwork. There should be a header or beam supporting the cut end. The floor above was sagging. This is also a 3.8.29 Cut and Unrepaired Element.

3.8.26 UNDERSIZED OR SAGGING GIRDER

The main girder or girders are undersized or sagging. Often the sagging of the girder is misinterpreted as settlement. Settlement is the sinking of the structure into the earth. The beam or girder has sagged between the supports because it is too weak to support the imposed loads in its original straight condition. Leave repairs, if necessary, to experienced professionals.

Often, sagging beams and girders are only slightly deformed and have become part of the "charm" of older buildings. Care should be taken in attempting to correct the condition. Harm may be done in correcting minor sagging problems. Beams or girders with significant sag adversely affecting the structure should be reinforced, repaired, or additionally underpinned to eliminate as much of the sagging as desired. This work should be done carefully and slowly to avoid any more damage to the structure than is necessary.

3.8.26 a. Sagging Girder.
This girder was sagging about 2 inches and the floor above was too. There should have been an additional pier in the middle. The 3.8.52 Mold and Mildew and falling insulation indicate a chronically 3.8.45 Wet Crawl space. All of this plus other observations added up to 3.2.28 Amateur Workmanship.

3.8.27 UNDERSIZED/SAGGING JOISTS

Undersized floor joists were used or the loads in the structure have increased and joists have sagged, creating unleveled floors.

Straighten sagging joists by underpinning them at their mid point with an additional beam and piers. In other cases, it is necessary to reinforce or laminate additional joists next to each sagging joist and jack them into position. Leave this work to experienced professionals.

3.8.28 AMATEUR WORKMANSHIP

The inspector notes workmanship of less than professional quality. Poor workmanship may constitute a major defect. Major defects cost $500.00 or more to repair or may affect the habitability of the house. The work may not serve the purpose intended and may require repair or replacement. The cure is usually to have professionals repair or replace the work.

3.8.29 CUT OR UNREPAIRED ELEMENT

Elements, such as beams or joists were cut but left unrepaired. Such damage may affect the structural integrity of the building. Repairs usually consist of replacing or splicing the cut element. It is possible to "sister" the element by putting an identical member immediately adjacent to the cut element. Leave this work to professionals.

3.8.30 CUT or DAMAGED TRUSSES

Trusses operate as a unit or as a whole. Every element of the truss, including the top and bottom chords and the web members running from chord to chord, are important to the strength. Individual pieces or elements of trusses should not be cut or removed. Often little or no harm results from the cutting of a single element of a single truss, but it is a questionable practice. Significantly damaged trusses should be repaired under the auspices of a truss manufacturer or an engineer familiar with truss design. Leave repairs to experienced professionals.

3.8.31 ROT DAMAGED ROOF SUBSTRUCTURE

The rafters or trusses supporting the weight of the roof are damaged by rot. Substantial rot damage to the roof substructure should be repaired to return adequate strength to the structural elements. Leave repairs to experienced professionals. For trusses, make the repairs under the auspices of a truss manufacturing company or an engineer familiar with the design and repair of trusses. Cure the leak causing the damage or it will reoccur.

3.8.32 ROT DAMAGED ROOF SHEETING

Rot damage to the roof sheeting is most likely caused by the roof leaking. As with most rotting problems the repair breaks down into two parts. One, the leak causing the damage must be repaired to assure the problem does not continue or reoccur. Second, it may be necessary to replace or repair the damaged roof sheeting. Sometimes all or part of the roofing must be removed to repair the damaged sheeting. Leave repairs to experienced professionals.

Some rotting roof systems are not leaking. They are damaged by water rising from within or below the structure. (Read sections 3.6 Interior and 3.7 Exterior Drainage and 1.8 Ventilation.)

3.8.33 DELAMINATING SHEETING

The individual layers or plies of the plywood sheathing are coming apart or delaminating. The condition is usually caused by water saturating the plywood over a long period of time.

Often the moisture saturating the plywood is rising from a damp crawl space or basement below, or from excessive moisture inside the structure. Moisture rises in the form of vapor or warm moist air into the attic. The vapor will penetrate the ceiling and condense on the cold underside of the roof sheeting. Such moisture may delaminate the plywood and in extreme instances will rot the sheathing.

Repairs involving water damage break down into two parts. Find and cure the original source of moisture or the problem will reoccur. Repair or replace the delaminated plywood. Often all or part of the roofing material must be removed when making the repair. Leave the repairs to professionals.

3.8.34 MARGINAL or UNDERSIZED FRAMING

Framing elements were marginal or undersized. Such framing has a tendency to create springy floors and weaken the structure. Repair, reinforce, or underpin the undersized elements. Leave repairs to experienced professionals.

3.8.35 FIRE DAMAGE

The structure has been damaged by fire. Often repairs to fire damaged structures do not include removing every structural element slightly damaged by the fire. It is not unusual to find damaged or charred beams, girders, rafters, etc. Many localities use the rule of thumb; if not more than twenty five percent of the framing element has been weakened or burned by the fire, the element may remain in service.

One aspect of fire repairs proving to be most difficult is the elimination of "burned" odor from the building. This is often attempted by scraping away all the char and ash possible and painting the damaged areas with enamel paint.

3.8.36 RUSTED COLUMNS

Excessive rust damage to either pipe or sectional columns. Columns rust where they contact or penetrate the slab. Repair or replace substantially rusted columns. They are major structural elements. Leave repairs to experienced professionals.

3.8.37 TEMPORARY SUPPORTS

Repairs were made to floors underpinned or supported with temporary materials. Except for decay and termite resistant species, wood in contact with the ground is temporary. It forms an avenue of entrance for termites and other wood destroying pests and is subject to decay. Repair or replace temporary supports with proper decay and rust resistant materials founded on adequate bearing. Leave repairs to experienced professionals.

3.8.37 a. Temporary Support.
This aging and failing floor system was supported on temporary supports. If this was intended to be permanent it would be 3.8.28 Amateur Workmanship.

3.8.38 a. Poor Bearing.
The beam should have about 4 inches of bearing and this one has about 2 inches. Sometimes they are found with little or no support. If they crush or slip off the bearing surface the structure may shift, settle, or collapse.

3.8.38 POOR BEARING

Beams or joists appear to have inadequate bearing or the bearing surface seems to be decaying or failing. Horizontal elements of the framing must rest or bear upon beams, columns, or walls. They must have sufficient bearing to support the load. Repair or rebuild bearing surfaces or extend or reinforce beams or joists for adequate support. Leave repairs to experienced professionals.

3.8.41 FOUNDATION UNVENTILATED

The foundation is unventilated and the inspector feels ventilation is necessary. Ventilation can be installed in most foundations as 8 X 16 foundation vents with screens and closures. The screening keeps insects and vermin from the crawl space. The closures seal the vents in winter to prevent frozen pipes.

3.8.42 UNDER VENTILATED

The foundation or attic is under ventilated and a problem is manifesting. Sometimes it is necessary to increase the amount of ventilation for the foundation or attic. It is more important to find the source of the moisture creating the problem. It is often possible to reduce the need for ventilation by reducing the amount of moisture entering the space. Improving drainage and grading and installing a vapor barrier or vapor retarder in the crawl space will reduce the necessity for foundation ventilation. If attics are overheating, improve attic ventilation. (Read section 1.8 Ventilation.)

3.8.43 VENTS DAMAGED

Vents are physically damaged, screens missing, or closures not functional or missing. Repair or replace vents to allow them to operate properly and serve their function.

3.8.44 BASEMENT WINDOWS BROKEN/DAMAGED/INOPERABLE

Basement windows are damaged. These windows are often neglected and allowed to go unrepaired. Repair them to operate properly for security and ventilation.

3.8.45 CRAWL SPACE WET OR DAMP

The crawl space is wet or damp. It is important the crawl space remains dry. The wetness encourages mold, mildew, and rot. It also decreases the R-Value of the insulation. It is attractive to termites and may dilute the effectiveness of any soil poisoning used to prevent them. Improve exterior drainage, drain gutters and downspouts into splashblocks or draintiles, seal holes through the foundation wall, and install plastic on the surface of the crawl space grade. Positive drainage is important.

3.8.45 a. Crawl space Wet.
Mushrooms growing in crawl space is a sign it is too wet. The same wetness encourages rot and decay.

3.8.46 STANDING WATER

There is ponded or standing water in the crawl space or basement. This wetness can be hazardous. Water rises into the structure as a vapor and passes through most materials. The water encourages mold, mildew, and rot. A dry crawl space or basement encourages water infiltrating under doors, behind decks, and from plumbing leaks to evaporate. If the crawl space is wet the damage from other leaks will be enhanced. (Read section 3.8.45 Crawl space Wet or Damp.)

3.8.46 a. Standing Water.
Read sections 3.6 Interior Drainage and 3.7 Exterior Drainage. 3.5 Ventilation may help also.

3.8.47 BASEMENT WET OR DAMP

The basement is either wet or damp. Most wet or damp basements can be improved or the problem reduced with exterior drainage techniques.

The grading and drainage around the perimeter of the basement should be improved so it is positive (i.e. away from the foundation) at a slope of two inches per foot or more for a distance greater than the depth of the basement. Clay soil can be compacted into an impervious layer and will not permit water to soak into the soil around the basement. This is clay capping.

3.8.47 a. Water Marks.
Staining and water marks around the perimeter may indicate a wet basement. In this case water was soaking or wicking up from the foundation. The problem was aggravated by poor (negative) exterior drainage. After the drainage was improved slightly and the downspouts were extended, the problem diminished further.

3.8.48 EFFLORESCENCE

Efflorescence is a white, powdery substance (a metallic salt) deposited or left behind on the surface by water migrating through masonry. This indicates the basement is damp and water is soaking through the walls. The efflorescence is somewhat messy but is not poisonous or harmful to the occupants. It can be swept off the wall, but the only cure for efflorescence is to reduce the amount of water flowing through it. In extreme or long term cases, the leaching action may damage the mortar or masonry.

3.8.49 CONDENSATION OR SWEATING

Condensation or sweating on pipes or other cold surfaces indicates the humidity in the space is too high. If condensation or sweating is occurring, a moisture problem exists. You should look to the source of the moisture and attempt to eliminate it. Uninsulated air conditioning ducts will sweat in an unconditioned space. They should be insulated and should have a proper vapor barrier.

3.8.50 MUSTY ODOR

Musty odor in a basement or crawl space is a tell tale sign or clue the area is or has been damp. Try to eliminate the moisture at the source.

3.8.51 DEHUMIDIFIER

A dehumidifier may indicate the basement is or has been damp. The drying action of the dehumidifier draws moisture through the walls and may aggravate the process of efflorescence. (Read section 3.8.48 Efflorescence.) Try eliminating the moisture before it enters the building rather than extracting it from the air and returning it to the outside. Improve the grading and drainage and extend the downspouts away from the perimeter. In some climates dehumidifiers are almost standard equipment.

3.8.52 MOLD/MILDEW

Mold and mildew flourishes at a temperature above 50 degrees and in a moist environment. Mold and mildew can create an odor problem in severe cases and some people are allergic to them. It is a warning the moisture content of the space is higher than it should be. If the space remains damp, rot may set in. (See 3.8.21 a. Unrepaired Rot Damage and 3.8.26 a. Sagging Girder.)

The cure for mold and mildew is to reduce the moisture content below the minimum 12 or 13 percent in lumber necessary to sustain it. Lumber appears to acquire a moisture content roughly 1/5 of the relative humidity of the surrounding air. In other words, it is possible to have the desirable 30 to 50% relative humidity indoors and have framing lumber at the 12% for the elimination of mold and mildew. Look for the source of the moisture and eliminate it. Often plastic vapor barriers are effective in reducing the viability of mold and mildew in the crawl space.

3.8.52 a. Mold/Mildew
Various molds growing on a girder and floor joist in a wet crawl space, left unattended can cause substantial rot damage.

3.8.55 FUNCTIONAL

The sump pump is functional at the moment of the inspection. The inspector inspected the pump and it is operational.

3.8.56 FLOOR DRAIN BLOCKED OR DAMAGED

Blocked or damaged floor drains should be repaired and cleared to operate properly. The inverted cup under the grill of some floor drains is part of the trap preventing sewer gases entering the property. The cup is inverted into a ring of water and serves as a cap over the drain. The cup allows water to exit but blocks sewer gases. Proper maintenance of floor drains and their traps may block radon. Keep drains clean and free flowing and traps wet.

3.8.57 SUMP PUMP INOPERABLE

The sump pump fails to respond properly. Promptly repair the sump pump. It may be an essential part of maintaining a dry basement or crawl space. Leave the repairs to an experienced plumber.

3.8.58 SUMP PUMP DAMAGED OR IMPROPERLY INSTALLED

The sump pump is operational, but shows evidence of damage, wear and tear, or eminent failure. Repair damaged sump pumps to insure a reasonable life expectancy. Sump pumps may be essential in maintaining a dry basement or crawl space. Correct improper installations to allow the pump to operate properly. Leave repairs to an experienced plumber. (See 3.6.1 d. Sump pump.)

3.8.59 SUMP DRY

The sump was dry at the beginning of the inspection. Some sump pumps pump the laundry water from the basement into the city sewer. If the laundry was not used before the inspection the sump may be dry. Other sumps may be dry in the dry season. Keep sumps properly capped and sealed to prevent radon or other gases entering the property. Proper lids also reduce personal injury and block vermin.

3.8.60 WATER ON TOP VAPOR BARRIER

A plastic vapor barrier or vapor retarder in the crawl space helps prevent ground water from rising as a vapor and attacking the structure. Water vapor rises, condenses on the bottom of the vapor barrier, drips off, and soaks away. Water below the vapor barrier is unlikely to harm the structure. Water on top of the vapor barrier may be detrimental and may indicate plumbing or roof leaks.

Find the source of the water and eliminate it. If the crawl space is flooding, improve drainage to the point the crawl space no longer floods. If the water is coming from plumbing leaks, cure the leaks. If the water is condensation, it may be air transported moisture. On a warm moist day outside, air carried into the crawl space cools and deposits moisture. In effect, it is raining inside the crawl space. For this phenomenon it may be necessary to reduce the ventilation into the crawl space or to stop it completely.

3.8.63 NEGATIVE DRAINAGE

It appears water will flow toward the building. Fill any areas of negative or neutral drainage with soil to slope away from the property at a rate of at least one inch per foot for a distance of

at least four to five feet or a distance greater than the depth of the basement. Clay or impervious soil is best but top soil may work for minor problems. The soil should not come within 6" of decay prone wooden siding. You may have to lower the surrounding grading to achieve positive drainage.

3.8.63 a. Negative Drainage
Negative drainage may funnel water into the basement.

3.8.64 NEUTRAL DRAINAGE

The area is more level than is desirable and water may not flow in any particular direction. Neutral drainage allows water to soak in deeply and wet the foundation or the basement. It causes standing or ponded water. It is best to have good, clear, positive drainage away from the foundation and off the lot. (Read section 3.8.63 Negative Drainage.)

3.8.64 a. Neutral Drainage

Neutral drainage causes standing or ponded water.

3.8.64 b. Neutral Drainage
The area bound by the walk and drive will pond water when it rains.

3.8.65 MIXED DRAINAGE
Indicates some of the drainage is positive (away from the foundation) and some is either neutral or toward the building. The drainage should be studied and modified to create positive drainage away from the building. (Read section 3.8.63 Negative Drainage.)

3.8.66 NEEDS SWALE(S)
Install a gentle ditch or swale to divert the water around the house and away. The soil from the swale(s) can be used to fill in the areas of negative or neutral drainage around the foundation.

3.8.67 FREEZE/THAW DAMAGE
Freeze/thaw damage often happens to retaining and parapet walls. Retaining walls suffer more freeze/thaw damage than the exterior of the house because they receive no heat from the house. Parapet walls, exposed to the cold air on both sides, may be more subject to freeze/thaw damage than retaining walls.

Freeze/thaw damage should be repaired by either repointing or caulking the masonry to prevent water from entering and accelerating the process. Drainage for retaining walls is important and it may be necessary to drill holes through the base of the wall to allow moisture to escape from behind the wall. In severe cases the walls may have to be rebuilt. (Read section 3.8.17 above also Freeze/thaw Damage.)

3.8.68 LEANING OR OVER TURNING RETAINING WALLS
Retaining walls often lean or begin to turn over from the pressure of soil and water behind them. The water may freeze and push against the wall, accelerating the process. Sometimes leaning walls can be buttressed with masonry or anchored with cables to blocks of concrete buried, known as "dead men." It may be necessary to tear the walls down and rebuild them, or to remove the earth behind the walls, return them to an upright position, anchor them properly, and return the soil.

3.8.68 a. Leaning or Over
Turning Retaining Walls
If this belongs to your neighbor, it could
one day collapse onto your yard.

3.8.69 RETAINING WALLS LACK FOOTING OR RELIEF DRAINS

There should be proper drainage from behind the walls. Many retaining walls require holes or penetrations near their base to allow water to escape. It may not be possible for the inspector to tell if a drain system exists. Buried footings or relief drains are not visible for inspection.

3.8.70 ADEQUATE

The site drainage appears to be functioning properly, carrying away roof and surface water, protecting the foundation and the structure. Drainage changes with the seasons and with erosion and siltation. Monitor and maintain the site drainage in proper working order.

3.8.71 INSTALL PROPER VAPOR BARRIER

A plastic vapor barrier should be placed on the grade of the crawl space covering 100% of the area as nearly as possible. The plastic should be lapped 12 inches at any seams and should turn up on the perimeter wall. Six mil polyethylene works well. Remove any debris attracting wood eating insects before installing the vapor barrier.

CHAPTER FOUR

PLUMBING

One of the most welcomed advancements was "indoor plumbing." To have a bathroom on the interior was a luxury. Not until after World War II were most houses built with running water for cooking, bathing, and washing. Today, plumbing fixtures have been modernized. Many fixtures used in pre-war houses are antiques. The ball claw bathtub is an example. Reproductions are now available.

Plumbing materials and their suitable applications will be discussed. Carefully read each section about your plumbing system. If you have any questions, ask the inspector. The plumbing inspection consists of the visible interior plumbing lines, drainage flow, fixtures and faucets, and hot water source.

4.1 LIMITATIONS

This section describes the aspects limiting the inspection of the plumbing system. Inspectors do the best inspection they can, but sometimes physical obstructions, weather conditions, or the condition of the plumbing, prevent them from doing the whole job. e.g. If the water is off, arrange for the inspector to come back after you have the water turned on. It is your responsibility to overcome the limitations. You should complete the inspection prior to closing even if you must hire others (plumbing contractor's etc.) or pay an additional fee to the inspector or industry specialist. Repairs can be expensive and at some point replacement is the best alternative. An uninspected plumbing system or one given a severely limited or restricted inspection could be a total unknown. The inspector cannot make representations about what was not inspected. If you close on the house with a Limited or Restricted inspection you are accepting the responsibility for the unknown items about the system.

4.1.1 TYPICAL

The inspector feels they have seen as much of the plumbing system as they normally see. It does not mean he has seen or inspected the entire system. Portions of the plumbing system are concealed from inspection. Fresh interior painting, wallpapering, etc. obscures evidence of prior plumbing leaks. A typical inspection does not include cutting holes, damaging the house or inducing leaks. (Read section 4.1 Limitations.)

4.1.2 RESTRICTED

The inspector feels they have seen less of the plumbing than they typically see. Every inspection is limited in some fashion. Major parts of the plumbing system are concealed by the structure. Pipes are run in floors, walls, and other inaccessible locations. Often, valves and fittings are enclosed and are inaccessible for inspection. This is particularly true in slab houses or houses with inaccessible crawl spaces.

The inspector cannot do an inspection of the system with the water off. Unpressurized plumbing pipes may look perfectly adequate and yet leak badly when the water is turned on. The water must have been on for at least 24 hours before the inspection so any minor leaks will have time to show. You should make arrangements to clear the restriction if possible. For example, if the crawl space or attic is blocked by personal possessions, remove them to allow for an inspection before closing. (Read 4.1.1 Typical.)

4.1.2.1 CRAWL SPACE INACCESSIBLE

The crawl space was not entered. It is less than two feet high, the access hole was too small, or it is too wet to enter safely. This leaves much of the plumbing system uninspected and a total unknown. (Read section 4.1.2 Restricted.)

4.1.2.2 ATTIC INACCESSIBLE

Personal possessions, lack of an access hole, or the size of the attic can make access to the attic impossible. The inspector will not remove personal possessions or do damage to gain access to the attic. There may be portions of the plumbing system in the attic left uninspected. Eliminate this restriction, so the attic can be inspected. (Read section 4.1.2 Restricted.)

4.1.2.3 HOUSE UNOCCUPIED

If the house has been unoccupied for more than a few days before the inspection, it may be impossible to judge whether stains are from active or cured leaks. e.g. A stain under a toilet not flushed in weeks will appear dry, even if the wax ring is leaking. The leak may be too slight to show up during the inspection. Assume all stains indicate active leaks. Monitor the plumbing carefully after you start using the system. (Read 4.1.2 Restricted.)

4.2 GENERAL PLUMBING

A quick reference and overview of the inspector's opinions or impressions. This section is subjective and relies on the inspector's judgment and experience in estimating the age, whether clues are important and if toxins are present, etc. (Read the Plumbing chapter fully before forming any final opinion.)

4.2.1 SYSTEM INSPECTED (YES, RESTRICTED, OR NO)

The inspector marks whether the system was inspected. No information will be given about a system that was not inspected. If the inspector writes in or circles "R" for restricted, the system was partially inspected. Check 4.1 LIMITATIONS or discuss it with the inspector to learn the full extent of the restrictions. A severely limited inspection may not give you the information you need. You should do whatever is necessary to remove or overcome the restrictions and have the system fully inspected before you close on the house. (Read 4.1 Limitations.)

4.2.2 WATER (ON OR OFF)

"ON" The water was on and the system pressurized at the beginning of the inspection. Experience teaches us the plumbing system must be pressurized for at least 24 hours before the inspection to get valid results. Twenty four hours are usually enough for the system to "present" leaks. Minor leaks may not show up for hours or days after pressurizing the system.

"OFF"   The water was off at the beginning of the inspection. Any system inspected with the water off has been given a severely restricted inspection. Plumbing may appear sound and leak badly or prove to be in poor condition when pressurized.

4.2.3 AMATEUR WORKMANSHIP (YES OR NO)

"YES"   The inspector notes workmanship of less than professional quality. Poor workmanship may constitute a major defect. Major defects cost $500.00 or more to repair or may affect the habitability of the house. The work may not serve the purpose intended and may require repair or replacement.

4.2.3 a. Amateur Workmanship.
This shows an automobile water hose connected to the hot water heater. This is a 4.9.4 Temporary Repair at best. Notice the wiring is not protected by conduit or flexible armored cable as required in some areas. The pressure relief valve is not piped to or through the floor but at least it is aimed at the wall.

"NO"   No amateur workmanship was noted. Some amateurs produce workmanship of equal or better quality than professionals.

4.2.4 SUPPLY (PRIVATE OR OTHER)

"PRIVATE"   The water supply comes from a private source such as a spring, well or central community well. Well water is often acidic or corrosive and piping systems last 1/4 to 1/2 as long as they do on public water systems. Private water sources are subject to many forms of contamination. Test the water before closing and annually.

"OTHER"   The water in most public water systems is treated and balanced to be noncorrosive. This extends the life expectancy of pipes and reduces the leaching of lead from any lead bearing pipes and joints in the system. Some neighborhoods or subdivisions have central well systems. Some such systems treat the water and some do not. Water quality is a serious concern. Check the quality of yours.

4.2.5 WASTE (PRIVATE OR OTHER)

"PRIVATE"   The waste disposal system appears to be private disposal system such as a septic tank or cess pool. Many private systems work, but some require high maintenance or replacement. Replacement may be impossible in some types of soil. The underground part of the system is outside the scope of a home inspection. Contact experts or the local government or health department for advice and help.

"OTHER"   The system appears to empty into a public or community sewer system.

4.2.5 a. Gray Water Discharge.
This is not a proper waste disposal method. Gray water is what comes from bathing and laundry as opposed to sewage coming from toilets.

4.2.6 SHUT OFF VALVE LOCATION

This is a "fill in the blank space" so the inspector can write in the location of the main water shut off valve. "None" will be written in this space when one is not present. Know where the main water shut off valve is so you can turn off the water rapidly. Turning the water off may lessen the damage from a leak. Install a valve or use a water meter key if there is no valve in the system.

4.2.7 ESTIMATED AGE OF THE WATER HEATER

The inspector's opinion of the estimated age of the water heater.   It is often impossible to tell the actual age of the water heater. Many things affect the aging process such as the quality of the water, number of gallons used daily, and the quality of the tank when new.   The inspector is making the broadest of assumptions. Turn the power or fuel and water off to leaking water heaters to avoid damage and injury. Life expectancies of various heaters are discussed in 4.7.1 Type.

4.2.8 ACTIVE LEAKS (YES OR NO)

"YES"   The plumbing system leaks. Cure active leaks immediately to protect the structure and its contents.

"NO"   No active plumbing leaks noted.

4.2.8 a. Active Leak.
This shows a leaking bathtub drain. If you look closely, you may see drops falling and water splashed up on the wall. Leaks may wet the crawl space causing rot, mold, and mildew.

4.2.9 SUBJECTIVE RATING

The inspector's grade for the plumbing system:

E **Excellent,** above average, new or like new. An example would be an older home with a new or upgraded system.

A **Average,** in typical condition for its age, showing the normal wear and tear and properly maintained. e.g. A ten year old plumbing system in a ten year old house looking and acting its age.

C **Below Average,** prematurely aged, showing an excessive wear and tear, or signs of delayed maintenance. Perhaps showing minor curable defects and leaks.

F **Substandard** or failed, reaching the end of its normal life expectancy and any further service even with repairs should be considered a gift.

4.3 MAIN SUPPLY LINE AND SHUT OFF VALVE

The material of the incoming water supply line and the location of the main water shut off valve. "None" indicates no valve is present. The material is important for several reasons. Various materials have different life expectancies and impart different tastes and trace elements into the water. One concern is lead. Lead water lines were used for many years before the danger of lead poisoning was recognized.

Most copper water piping systems have lead in the solder joints. Sometimes these solder joints are poorly made and excess lead is exposed inside the piping. Solder, often 50% lead and 50% tin, ran inside the pipe during the soldering process. Municipal water systems often balance the chemical content of the water to limit leaching from lead piping or lead in solder joints. Lead poisoning has become such a concern recent code changes have required the elimination of most of the lead in solder joints. Solder used today should be 95% tin and 5% lead. In extreme cases plastic piping replaces systems containing lead.

Metal incoming water lines can provide a ground for the electrical system. If you change the incoming water line to a plastic line, drive a ground rod and properly ground the electrical system according to local codes.

MAINTENANCE AND UPKEEP

Protect the incoming line from freezing and physical damage. Do not allow erosion or construction to expose the line. Don't drive or park heavy vehicles on it. In very cold weather, if there is a danger of freezing, leave a trickle of water running. Drain outside faucets in winter.

To reduce your exposure to lead and other contaminates in the system, flush the system every morning and each time water stands in the system for more than a few hours. Run the faucet two or three minutes with a strong stream before using the water. This may flush away accumulated lead and other contaminates. Never drink or cook with the water from the hot water heater. It has been stagnant in the system too long.

4.3.1 MATERIAL

Identifies the material of the incoming supply line. Many materials have been used over the years. Only the major types are listed here. The following sections give the advantages, disadvantages, characteristics, applications, estimated life expectancy and maintenance, etc. for each type of plumbing material. The material of the incoming water line influences its performance and longevity.

4.3.1.1 COPPER

Many incoming water lines are copper. Copper pipe will last as long as sixty years on municipal water where the water is balanced or treated for corrosiveness. On well water, copper piping often lasts 15 years or less. Copper is also affected by the corrosiveness of the soil. Lead in solder joints may leach into the water. (Read section 4.3 Main Supply Line and Shut Off Value.)

4.3.1.2 LEAD PIPING

Lead piping was popular until the danger of lead poisoning was recognized. Lead piping is so durable many homes are still supplied with water through lead incoming water lines. The fact lead pipe is still in service may indicate little lead is leaching into the water. White lead oxide which prevents further leaching sometimes coats the inside of pipes. Contact a reputable testing laboratory for recommendations on testing the water. (Read section 4.3 Main Supply Line and Shut Off Valve.)

4.3.1.2 a. Lead Incoming Water Line.
Notice the small bulge at the valve on the curved gray pipe.
The bulge, gray color, and curve all indicate lead piping.
The lead is soft and scratches easily, revealing silvery
untarnished metal. The valve is 4.3.2.2 Main Shut Off Valve
In Basement.

4.3.1.3 PLASTIC

Plastic piping is popular for incoming water lines. Various forms of plastic have been used ranging from polyethylene to polybutylene. Properly installed, of high quality materials, plastic piping is durable. It has not been in use long enough to give an accurate life expectancy. Plastic piping seems less affected by corrosiveness or acidity of the water and soil than metal pipe. Polybutylene pipe has been controversial and subject to failure. (Read section 5.5.5 Grounding and Bonding, also read section 4.4.1.5.3 Polybutylene.)

4.3.1.4 IRON PIPE

Iron or galvanized iron. This is one of the least acceptable applications for iron pipe. It is attacked by both the soil and the water. The pipe tends to rust quickly, particularly where it enters the grade. The life expectancy may be less than twenty years. (Read section 4.3 Main Supply Line and Shut Off Valve.)

4.3.2 SHUT OFF VALVE

You will want to be able to shut off the water rapidly and limit the damage from a leak. A shut off valve seized from disuse or in an inaccessible location, such as in the far corner of the crawl space, may be no valve at all. Make arrangements to have a suitable shut off valve installed. This is particularly true for an aging and fragile plumbing system.

The inspector will not test the main water shut off valve. Most valves have not been "exercised" for years and often leak if tested. Check the function periodically.

4.3.2.1 CRAWL SPACE

The main water shut off valve is in the crawl space. The accessibility of the crawl space and the shut off valve varies from house to house. If the valve is near the crawl space access door, it may be convenient. A valve in an inaccessible corner of the crawl space is impractical.

4.3.2.2 BASEMENT

The main water shut off valve is in the basement. It is common for such valves to be near the entry point of the incoming water line.

4.3.2.3 OUTSIDE

The main water shut off valve is outside. It is often three or four feet from the foundation, and accessible through a pipe or small box. Make sure the enclosure is free of debris and the valve is accessible, operable, and protected from freezing.

4.3.2.4 METER

When no main water shut off valve is located, use the shut off valve located at the meter. Often this requires a meter wrench or meter key. Keep the key handy for emergencies.

4.4 INTERIOR PLUMBING LINE MATERIAL

The material of the interior plumbing lines influences the taste of the water, their ability to resist freezing, longevity, and the amount of noise the system makes when water is running. Plumbing systems are grounded or bonded to the electrical system to maintain what is known as a zero potential between the two systems. When repairing or replacing the plumbing with plastic pipe, the grounding of the electrical system may be affected. A qualified electrician should check and repair the system including a proper ground rod, if necessary.

4.4.1 SUPPLY PIPING

The material of water supply lines influences the quality of the water and the success of the system. Copper piping sometimes imparts a coppery taste to the water. Lead piping has been known to leach lead into the water. Each type of piping has its strengths and weaknesses. (Read section 4.3 Main Supply Line and Shut Off Valve.)

4.4.1.1 COPPER PIPING

Copper piping has been popular for thirty or forty years. It is often installed as hard copper tubing with soldered joints. The joints are coming under scrutiny. Many contain 50% lead and 50% tin. There is concern the lead may be leaching into the water. The only way to know if your drinking water has lead in it is to have the water tested. (Read section 4.3.1.2 Lead.)

Copper piping comes in several thicknesses and alloys and may last as long as 60 years if used with municipal water balanced to avoid corrosiveness. Well water may shorten the life of copper piping to as little as 15 years. (Read section 4.3 Main Supply Line and Shut off Valve.)

4.4.1.2 GALVANIZED

Galvanized iron water pipes rust from the inside out and may require replacement within 20-30 years. This is usually done in two stages: horizontal piping in the crawl space or basement first and vertical pipes throughout the house later as needed.

Any time pipes of dissimilar metals, such as iron and copper, join without proper precautions, galvanic corrosion will result. Often, older galvanized systems have been repaired by replacing parts of the system with copper piping. This almost always results in corrosion at the joints where the two metals join. This accelerates the demise of the galvanized pipe. (Read section 4.3 Main Supply Line and Shut Off Valve.)

4.4.1.3 BRASS

There are yellow brasses and red brasses. The same corrosiveness in water shortening the life of copper and iron pipe dissolves the various alloys in brass. Brass pipe is most often installed with threaded joints. Some chrome plated fittings on fixtures are a brass that dissolves from the inside outward. (Read section 4.3 Main Supply Line and Shut off Valve.)

4.4.1.4 LEAD PIPING

Forty to fifty years ago lead piping for supply lines was common. Most lead piping has been replaced. The most common continuing application for lead supply piping is for the incoming water line. The danger of lead poisoning is addressed in water pollution studies. An in-depth analysis of possible toxins in your water supply can be obtained from your local hospital, the state Water Control Board or a commercial water tester. (See 4.3.1.2 a. Lead Incoming Water Line.)

4.4.1.5 PLASTIC PIPING

The plumbing industry is proving the durability and longevity of plastic piping. Not all plastics have been approved for residential use. Ridged plastic piping such as PVC (polyvinyl chloride), ABS (acrylonitrile butadiene styrenes), PB (polybutylene), and CPVC (chlorinated polyvinyl chloride) are acceptable for cold water piping inside finished walls. The PB piping resists freezing. It may expand rather than rupture. Only the CPVC and the PB piping have shown satisfactory results in hot water service. Plastic piping may be improved to the point it will replace most metal pipe. Better grades of polyethylene pipe are successful as an incoming water line in cold water service only. (Read section 5.5.5 Grounding and Bonding.)

4.4.1.5.1 PVC

Polyvinyl chloride pipe is a semi-ridged plastic pipe, white or cream in color and when correctly joined with correct cement forms a watertight system for cold water applications. (Read section 5.5.5 Grounding and Bonding.)

4.4.1.5.2 CPVC PIPE

Chlorinated polyvinyl chloride is successful in residences for both hot and cold water applications when correctly joined with correct cement or bonding agent, or proper mechanical fasteners. (Read section 5.5.5 Grounding and Bonding.)

4.4.1.5.3 POLYBUTYLENE (PB)

Polybutylene pipe and fittings are a new development. This special blend of plastics is designed to allow limited freezing, but is virtually "break-free." The fittings adapt readily to the existing plumbing for easy repairs and additions. Polybutylene pipe is manufactured in several systems. One sells under the trade name of Quest (TM) piping. There are copper or aluminum clinch rings inside the fittings which are tightened by the compression nuts at the end of each fitting. The copper rings appear more successful.

An early version of the system used plastic fittings that slipped inside the pipe. Some of the fittings were of defective manufacture and became brittle with age and exposure to chlorine or other chemicals commonly in drinking water. The fittings burst and houses were damaged. The system has been the subject of numerous individual lawsuits and class action suits.

Another version system uses special copper fittings inserted inside the pipe and copper clinch rings around pipe. The rings are squeezed or compressed around the pipe and copper fitting. This appears to be a more successful system, but is in its infancy. One problem with this system is the copper of the fittings. It is subjected to the same corrosive elements as copper pipe. Well water that destroys a copper piping system in fifteen years will probably destroy the copper fittings in a PB piping system in less time. Another problem with PB pipe may be "creep" in the joints. Poorly made connections may slip apart eventually and burst.

On October 25, 1994 the Washington Post ran a front page article by Maryann Haggerty and Ann Mariano titled "Plastic Pipe Settlement Reached." The article reports the previous day three big chemical companies reached a tentative settlement in the controversy over polybutylene pipe. To paraphrase, they are offering to establish a seven hundred and fifty million dollar trust fund to be used to find those homeowners damaged by leaks in polybutylene piping systems and pay for repair and replacement of the systems.

The District of Columbia based Trial Lawyers for Public Justice, a public interest law firm that handled the class action suit against the three firms, has announced that if the settlement is approved by the Texas judge in the case, it will be the largest property damage settlement in U.S. history. As always, certain restrictions apply. If approved, within in a few months, advertising will start seeking those with damage.

According to the article, if you have had two leaks in the past and you follow the rules of notification, or you have a single leak in the future, you may qualify for full reimbursement. There will be differing rules for mobile homes and variations in the pipe and fittings. Some will qualify for thirteen years and some for sixteen years from the date the plumbing was installed. Whether or not you are a participant in any of the many suits involving the pipe, and the nature of your settlement, if any, will affect your standing under this settlement offer. Millions of houses are affected and some localities have banned the pipe in new installations, but others have not, and it is still being installed. The article does not address how the pipe being installed currently is affected by the settlement offer.

The settlement offer covers the gray indoor piping and the blue or blue/green pipe often used as an incoming water supply line. It also addresses the plastic fittings and the metal insert type fittings. According to the article the piping was installed after 1981. The three chemical companies listed in the article are Shell Oil Co., DuPont Co., and Hoechst Celanese. As this is written the details continue to unfold and there may be changes and further restrictions. Contact the principles involved for more details.

According to U.S. News & World Report's "Newswatch" of November 1994, you can file complaints through a joint Plumbing Claims Group (PCG) at (800) 356-3496. This group represents the three companies in the settlement. Save your repair receipts and damaged pipe.

4.4.1.6 OTHER

Other materials for supply piping include wrought iron, steel, and stainless steel piping. Many systems have been less than successful. One version of stainless steel piping was manufactured as a substitute for copper and sometimes used copper fittings sweated to the pipe. The alloy of the stainless was so low the piping corroded or dissolved into the water like brass or copper piping. This particular stainless steel system does not represent a large number of houses or a very successful system.

4.4.2 WASTE LINES

The waste piping must withstand the corrosiveness of the waste water, but little internal pressure. The system must be internally smooth and free of snags to avoid blockages. The lines should all slope properly to drain freely and not leave solids behind.

4.4.2.1 CAST IRON

Cast iron is a traditional material for waste piping. The older cast iron pipe had bells or hubs on one end to receive the next pipe. The joint is packed, often with oakum, and molten lead poured in and tamped. This system is successful. The joints will flex slightly with the structure, but the pipe is ridged and brittle.

A later system was known as No-Hub pipe. The pipes were cast with a slightly raised ring around the end. It could be cut and joined at any point with a patented hose clamp and Neoprene gasket system.

Cast iron pipe has been largely displaced in residential construction by plastic piping, but much is still in use. It is quieter in operation than a plastic piping system.

Cast iron pipe cracks or breaks under stress because it's brittle. It eventually rusts from the interior through pitting. The pits will show on the exterior as rust cancers or scabs. When the pipe reaches this condition it is necessary to replace it. It will soon rust through and leak. "Repairs" include tape, patches, bandages, wooden plugs, or strap on clamps. Any repairs should be as permanent as the pipe. Properly installed cast iron pipe may last 50 to 75 years.

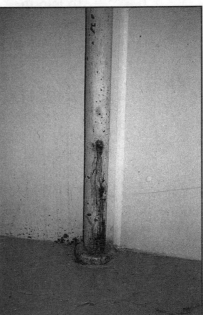

4.4.2.1 a. Cast Iron Pipe
After more than 60 years of service
the cast iron pipe rusted through.

4.4.2.2 GALVANIZED PIPE
Galvanized pipe is used with cast iron pipe for waste lines and vent stacks. Often smaller galvanized piping is included with a cast iron system of main stacks and larger pipes. Galvanized piping is successful as drainage piping although it rusts from the inside. It may last 30 to 40 years in waste service if properly installed.

4.4.2.3 COPPER PIPING
Copper domestic waste piping in residences is seen in diameters of up to four inches. The system uses the same sweated joints as in the supply piping systems. The piping seems to be durable and has an indefinite life expectancy.

4.4.2.4 PLASTIC PIPING
As previously mentioned, plastic piping is replacing metal piping in residential plumbing. Plastic piping is less expensive, easier to install, and slick or smooth on the interior. It resists blockages. Plastic waste piping may be noisy from water flowing through the system.

Plastic piping is attractive to amateur plumbers. (Read Section 4.2.3 Amateur Workmanship.) Amateurs often mix different types of plastic and join PVC pipe with ABS fittings or vice-versa. When plastic is glued it forms a solvent weld between the pipe and the fitting. The pipe and the fitting must be the same material to weld. The glue will stick the fittings together, however, the bond is not strong. Mixed materials probably should not be concealed above finished spaces.

4.4.2.4.1 ABS PIPE (ACRYLONITRILE BUTADIENE STYRENES)

ABS is black plastic pipe seen as domestic waste piping. When correctly joined with correct adhesive, the pipe appears to be durable and successful. Plastic piping has only been in use for 25 or 30 years and does not have as long a track record as metal piping.

4.4.2.4.2 PVC (POLYVINYL CHLORIDE)

PVC is the white plastic pipe often seen in use as domestic waste piping. To join the piping correctly to the fittings, requires a two part system for PVC pipe. A cleaner must be used on the pipe before the adhesive. (ABS uses a one part glue.) The PVC pipe is also proving itself successful as a plumbing material in waste piping.

4.4.2.5 LEAD

The softness, flexibility, and ease of installation made lead popular as waste piping and supply piping. One application for lead piping still seen is the lead closet flange used to join the toilet to the piping system. The lead is soft enough it can be a molded, bent, or contorted to make alignment between the toilet and the piping easy. The lead absorbed slight changes in alignment caused by shrinking, swelling and warping of framing members. Lead has fallen into disuse and its reputation has been injured by the concern over lead poisoning. Many jurisdictions require the replacement or removal of lead piping from the systems.

4.4.2.6 TERRA-COTTA OR CLAY PIPING

Clay or terra-cotta piping, in its glazed form was used as the main sewer from the house to the street. In some communities, clay piping has been used for municipal sewer lines. Clay piping has fallen into disuse because it was subject to mechanical damage and penetration of tree roots.

4.4.2.7 OTHER

Many other materials have been used for domestic waste piping, including asphalt impregnated fiber piping, used underground for non-pressure service, waste lines, etc. Rubber and "rubber-like" piping was used both as supply and waste piping. Hard rubber piping was once used in some laboratory applications. Cement asbestos or transite piping is used by utility companies for water mains and in residences for waste lines and gas vent piping. Concrete piping serves as culverts but has found little other use in residences. Glass piping is seldom seen except perhaps as view glasses on boilers, etc.

4.4.3 INSULATED OR UNINSULATED

Only hot water pipes and any sections that may freeze are usually insulated. Some pipe insulation contained asbestos. Asbestos, wherever it's found, is of concern to all homeowners. If it breaks down into small fibers (becomes friable) and is inhaled or ingested, it can have serious and far reaching health effects. Only proper laboratory tests can confirm or deny its presence and only then can an appropriate response be suggested. The treatment and removal of asbestos is dangerous and expensive. Leave it to experts.

4.5 WATER PRESSURE AND DRAINAGE FLOW

Both the volume and pressure to operate the fixtures and fulfill the needs of the owner should be present. Proper drainage flow is necessary to carry waste products away from the property.

4.5.1 SUPPLY

The supply piping must be capable of delivering adequate water to the fixtures. The flow of water is a relationship between the volume and the pressure. Some faucets are capable of delivering a large volume of water at low pressure. Other fixtures require high pressure, but operate properly at small volume. An example is a shower head capable of producing a stimulating shower with two gallons of water a minute is better than the one requiring four gallons a minute to produce the same sensation. The judgment of pressure and volume are often subjective.

4.5.1.1 FUNCTIONAL FLOW

Functional flow is enough water volume and pressure to wash a fixture down. In other words, enough water comes out of the spigot with enough force to wash or clean the fixture.

4.5.1.2 ADEQUATE FLOW

Adequate flow is "the flow from a fixture remains functional when two or more fixtures are operating." (Read Section 4.5.1.1 Functional Flow.) The piping system is capable of providing functional flow to two or more fixtures simultaneously.

4.5.2 WASTE

Drainage flow disposes of waste from the domestic plumbing system to the sewer or other disposal method.

4.5.2.1 FUNCTIONAL

Functional drainage is "the fixture drain has the capacity to discharge the entire supply of water from the fixture." The drain for the sink or the bathtub is capable of draining the water away as fast as the faucets deliver it.

4.5.2.2 NON-FUNCTIONAL

Non-functional drainage; "the drainage from a fixture is not capable of carrying away the water as rapidly as the faucets deliver it." A fixture draining slowly and subject to overflowing does not have functional drainage.

4.5.3 VENTING

Plumbing drainage systems connect from the sewer through the house and into the atmosphere with a venting system. When a toilet is flushed or water drains from a fixture, it should flow smoothly through the piping. It must draw air into the system as the water flows. Without proper venting, it bubbles, gurgles, and leaves deposits behind. Water sucks air through fixtures and traps if there is inadequate venting.

The traps in the system are the U shaped bends located under fixtures. The toilet trap is part of the toilet and is filled with water remaining in the bowl after flushing. Water in the trap forms a liquid stopper preventing sewer gases entering the building. Sewer gases may be noxious, poisonous, or even explosive.

4.5.3.1 VENTED TO THE ATMOSPHERE

The plumbing system must be vented to the atmosphere so water released from a fixture may draw in air to allow for a smooth and even drainage flow. The system will attempt to draw air through other fixtures and siphon the water from their traps if not properly vented. The vents are pipes extending through the roof or up an exterior wall. Vents should be above the roof or ten feet or more from any window or door so sewer gases will not be drawn into the house.

In cold climates, vents must be oversized to prevent the moisture in the air condensing, freezing, and blocking the vent. Some jurisdictions require metal vent pipes through the roof with plastic waste systems to prevent ultraviolet degradation of the plastic pipe.

As roof penetrations, vents are often the source of roof leaks. Keep the plumbing collar, roof jack, or flashing around the pipe in good condition to avoid leaks. Keep the venting system watertight so condensation, rainwater, etc. will be carried into the plumbing system and drained into the sewer.

4.5.3.2 TRAPS

The traps are the U shaped bends located under most plumbing fixtures. The trap forms a liquid stopper preventing the sewer gases and fumes entering the house. All interior plumbing fixtures include traps. The trap in the toilet is filled with water remaining in the bowl after flushing.

Do not allow traps to dry out. Most plumbing fixtures receive enough water in daily use to remain properly sealed. Some fixtures, such as floor drains, receive water so rarely they will dry out and may allow sewer gases to enter the house. Pour water into seldom used drains occasionally. An alternative is to pour mineral oil or baby oil into unused traps. The oil will not evaporate readily and yet remain liquid. In an emergency, the oil flushes down the drain. Do not use an oil that will age, coagulate, or solidify. Sewer gases may be poisonous and explosive.

4.6 FIXTURES AND FAUCETS

These are the fixtures and faucets of the plumbing system most of us see daily. Maintain in a safe, clean, and sanitary condition.

Older bathtubs and ceramic showers have smooth slick bottoms and may cause accidents. Use safety mats or nonskid "stick-ons." Damaged and chipped fixtures, broken handles on faucets, etc. not only present sharp edges that scratch or cut, they also provide locations for bacteria and germs to grow. Sharp edges and rough surfaces should be eliminated or replaced.

Maintain faucets so they do not leak or drip at the washer or stem. Leaks may damage the structure and also waste water, a valuable resource. Hot water leaks waste energy. Leaks deplete the well and flood the drain field or add to sewer and water bills.

4.6.1 FIXTURE MATERIAL

The materials must be sturdy, durable, and provide a finish or surface that can be kept clean and sanitary.

4.6.1.1 CAST IRON

Cast iron has been a popular material for bathtubs and sinks because it's durable. The finish is porcelain or a glass-like coating. This finish endures the day to day wear and must be kept clean and smooth. Sometimes the finish has either been chipped or warn away and the cast iron exposed. Do not drop heavy or hard objects onto cast iron fixtures. They may chip or break.

4.6.1.2 STEEL

Steel bathtubs arc lighter and cheaper than cast iron. Steel fixtures are stamped of thin metal and may dent. The overflow drains on steel sinks are not lined or protected from rust and leak quickly. The steel is coated with a porcelain or glass-like on the interior. The porcelain finish chips or cracks more easily than on cast iron products. Do not drop heavy or hard objects into steel fixtures. They may chip the finish or dent the fixture.

4.6.1.3 PLASTIC

Plastic is molded into plumbing fixtures, notably sinks and recently toilets or commodes. When new, plastic has a slick, smooth surface. Abrasive cleansers can ruin the finish on a plastic fixture. Do not rest burning cigarettes, etc. on plastic fixtures because they burn. Do not use abrasive cleansers.

4.6.1.4 FIBERGLASS

Fiberglass is used for many plumbing fixtures, most notably bathtubs and showers. Molded one piece fiberglass tub and showers are popular. These fixtures are relatively low cost and come in a variety of styles, shapes, and colors. The one piece construction makes them impervious to water splashing and finding its way through the cracks traditional with ceramic tile surrounds. Keep fiberglass fixtures clean without the use of abrasive cleansers. Any abrasive cleanser will cut through the finish on the fixtures.

4.6.1.5 CHINA

Most toilets (water closets) and many sinks are molded vitreous china similar to the china used for dinner plates. Some bathtubs are a similar material. The glazed surface of the china forms a slick and impervious surface easy to clean and keep sanitary. The fixtures are brittle and break from impact loads, freezing, and even the settlement of the structure.

4.6.1.6 MARBLE

Natural marble plumbing fixtures are rare. Cultured or man made marble fixtures are popular. They are made of pulverized marble powder combined with a resin or plastic binder, molded into the form of the fixture. The surface is coated with a slick polymer finish. The fixtures are available in a wide variety of styles, shapes, and colors.

Similar to plastic and fiberglass fixtures, they should be kept clean without the use of abrasive cleansers. They are subject to cigarette burns, cracking, or crazing of the surface. The fixtures are repairable if chipped. Local marble fixture manufacturers have repairmen who repair chipped or damaged surfaces.

4.6.1.7 STAINLESS STEEL

The most common application for stainless steel is the kitchen sink. Stainless steel is an excellent material to use in this application because it is tough, durable, and easy to clean and maintain in a sanitary condition.

4.6.2 FAUCETS

The faucets control the flow of water into the fixtures. Faucets have evolved from single faucets for hot and cold to washerless combined faucets.

MAINTENANCE AND UPKEEP

Almost all faucets have internal parts that wear and require replacement. Preventing drips and leaks saves water and energy and protects the structure. Leaking faucets deplete wells and flood drainfields. Many "how to" books are available explaining maintenance in detail.

4.6.2.1 MATERIAL

The faucet material must be durable, resistant to corrosion, and attractive. Brass is the traditional material. Plastic is replacing the more expensive brass.

4.6.2.1.1 BRASS

Brass is the traditional faucet material. It is cast and then machined, polished, and usually chrome plated. Occasionally it is plated with other materials such as gold. Sometimes the brass is left exposed and coated with a clear finish. Brass fixtures are durable and repairable. Many faucet sets have replaceable internal parts allowing them to be repaired or rebuilt.

4.6.2.1.2 PLASTIC

Plastic faucet sets are available. They may not prove to be as durable as brass faucet sets, but initially are less expensive.

4.6.2.2 TYPE

Faucet sets come in various styles such as single lever, double lever, individual faucets, and so on. Here they are divided into faucets containing washers and the washerless types.

4.6.2.2.1 WASHER

Faucets containing washers are the traditional type. The stem or shaft attached to the knob, screws up and down and applies pressure against the seat. A washer forms a stopper over the seat and prevents the water from flowing.

Replacing a washer is a simple maintenance job and can be accomplished by a handy homeowner. Besides washers, there is a fibrous material (stem packing) preventing water from leaking around the stem. This material must be changed or adjusted occasionally to prevent a stem leak. Water leaking around the stem can sometimes be stopped by slightly tightening the packing nut or bonnet nut. The packing must be tight enough to prevent the water from leaking out, but not tight enough to prevent the stem from being turned and the faucet operated. Stem leaks can be treacherous. The water can leak behind the ceramic tile or tub enclosure and damage the floor or structure under a bathroom.

4.6.2.2.2 WASHERLESS FAUCETS

The faucets do not contain washers. This is somewhat misleading. Many people assume washerless faucets have no internal parts requiring repair or replacement. Most washerless faucets contain o-rings, seats, or other internal parts serving the same function as washers. They wear and must be replaced occasionally. Kits containing these parts are available at hardware and plumbing supply stores for most faucets.

4.6.3 TUBS

Bathtubs come in a variety of sizes, shapes, materials, and styles. Keep the finish smooth and free of defects that may harbor germs and bacteria. Many bathtubs do not have the modern non-skid interior surface. These tubs become slippery with water and soap. Use a non-skid mat or appliques in the bottom of the tub to prevent personal injury.

Bathroom tile installed in a mortar bed is excellent. Keep the joint between the tile and the tub/shower caulked or sealed to prevent water spillage leaking through and damaging the floor or structure. Ceramic tile is often installed in mastic. It is important to keep the tile caulked or water seeps behind it causing deterioration. Carefully seal around faucets and other tile penetrations.

4.6.4 SINKS

Sinks are manufactured of almost every material ever used for plumbing fixtures. Keep them clean, safe, and sanitary. Chipped or damaged finishes may provide opportunities for bacteria and disease.

4.6.5 TOILETS

Traditionally toilets were manufactured of vitreous china and in many styles, varieties, and flushing techniques. The toilet should flush completely and thoroughly. It is desirable for them to flush quietly and refill quickly for frequent use. The water in the bowl of the toilet is there by design to create a trap so sewer gases do not enter through the toilet.

Toilets connect to the waste piping through a flange (funnel) with a wax ring. The ring is bee's wax and is molded around the connection between the toilet and plumbing flange. It prevents water leaking into the floor system when the toilet flushes. These rings are not elastic. They are soft and when the toilet wiggles or moves the ring becomes deformed, causing a leak. Any toilet showing evidence of leak, or easy to move, should be remounted to prevent wax ring failure. A leak will eventually damage the floor system and the structure. Replacing a wax ring is an inexpensive maintenance chore opposed to replacing a bathroom floor.

4.6.5 a. Toilets
The toilet above has leaked enough to stain the floor. If the leak is active the area will rot soon, monitor the stain closely or reinstall the toilet with a new wax ring. (See 4.9.51 Toilet Loose or Wetness On The Floor.)

A common problem with commodes is overfilling. If the float is not properly adjusted, water constantly runs down the overfill pipe. Sometimes bending the arm of the float so the valve shuts the water off earlier will help. You may find it necessary to replace the filler valve, ball cock, or flapper valve. Toilet parts are available in generic forms fitting almost any toilet. Replacement is often easier than repairing valves. Toilets can be repaired until the china breaks.

4.6.6 SHOWERS

Many showers are ceramic tile. Under the ceramic tile floor is a pan. Thin lead sheeting is a traditional material for the pan. More recently vinyl and even some fiber materials substitute for the lead. The life expectancy of the pan appears to be between 20 and 30 years.

Once the pan fails, or begins to leak, the only cure may be to remove the floor from the shower, remove and replace the pan, and reinstall the floor and the shower. If the pan leaks, it is not possible to cure the leak by caulking the surface of the ceramic tile.

Fiberglass showers are single piece units and do not include a separate pan. The drain from a fiberglass shower is tightened directly to the fiberglass.

Bathroom tile installed in a mortar bed is excellent. Keep the joint between the tile and the tub/shower caulked or sealed to prevent water spillage leaking through and damaging the floor or structure. Ceramic tile is often installed in mastic. It is important to keep the tile caulked or water seeps behind it causing deterioration. Carefully seal around faucets and other tile penetrations.

4.6.7 WHIRLPOOL TYPE TUBS

Whirlpool tubs are popular as part of luxury bathrooms. Maintain the tub properly because electricity and water do not mix and often result in accidents. These tubs often have flat decks that are less waterproof than they appear. Spilling water around the tub usually results in damage. Take extreme care not to touch parts of the electrical system while in the water. Some of the tubs retain water within the pump system when the tub drains. Run the tub once or twice, flush it thoroughly, and use chlorine bleach in the tub to sterilize it. Whirlpool tubs in vacant houses should be cleaned before using.

4.6.8 STEAM AND SAUNA

Steam and sauna baths should be properly maintained according to the manufacturers directions and local codes to avoid injury or electrocution. Heat and humidity can stress your heart. Check with your Physician.

4.7 HOT WATER SOURCE

A reliable, economical source of hot water is the accepted norm. Electric and gas fired water heaters are common. Oil fired water heaters are rare. Traditional heaters have a tank of heated water and wait for demand. The size of the tank is governed by the anticipated demand and the size of the heating element or firing unit. As the size of the heating element or burner increases, it may be possible to reduce the size of the tank. A variation is to eliminate the tank and use an "on demand" water heater. It has a large heating element and heats the water as needed. The tankless water heater eliminates the tank reducing or eliminating "stand by" or tank losses. This saves energy. Tankless water heaters are not as popular as the traditional water heaters. They cost more initially and do not always heat rapidly enough to maintain a constant supply of hot water.

It is impossible to predict the life expectancy of any water heater because the useful life is related to the type of water and the demands made on the heater. It is impossible to judge the remaining life expectancy of a water heater by its external appearance. The corrosion causing the tank to leak is in the interior and therefore is not visible. A water heater with one day of remaining life may have the same appearance as one with ten years of remaining life. Fortunately, water heaters do not generally fail catastrophically. People have been known to wipe up the water for two or three days before they realize the water heater is leaking. If the tank leaks replace the heater.

MAINTENANCE AND UPKEEP

A proper temperature and pressure relief valve is an essential part of any water heating system. This valve will open and exhaust water if the system's pressure or temperature goes too high. A pressure and temperature relief valve constantly opening or dribbling water suggests a problem with the system. Have a qualified plumber correct the problem or replace the valve. The exhaust or vent from the valve should be extended down safely near the floor through a full sized pipe.

Set the heater at the lowest practical setting. Water above 150 degrees Fahrenheit can cause third degree burns in two seconds. Water at 140 degrees Fahrenheit can cause third degree burns in six seconds. Water at 130 degrees Fahrenheit can cause third degree burns in twenty seconds.

Heater manufacturers recommend flushing sediment from the tank once or twice a year. Connect a hose to the drain valve and run the water until it turns clear. Be careful. The water may be scalding hot. Tip: If there is no sediment in your toilet tanks, you may not need to do this often. If the toilet tanks are discolored or you use well water, flush the tank to protect the elements.

Water Heaters usually have a rod of magnesium or aluminum protecting the tank from corrosion. The rod is a sacrificial anode. Its metal is slowly destroyed protecting the tank from galvanic corrosion. If the water remains in the tank more than a few days, algae or bacteria may thrive on the decomposition by-products. If your hot water smells funny or is cloudy and your cold water is good, flush the tank thoroughly by running several tankfuls down the drain. If the problem persists contact a reputable plumber or the manufacturer of the heater to chlorinate the tank. If chlorinating does not work you may have to change the anode rod. Never drink or cook with water from the hot water heater.

4.7.1 TYPE
Water heaters are classified by the fuel heating the water. Traditional water heaters heat the water in large tanks, but there are tankless varieties. There are also domestic coil systems either submerged within or attached to the boiler. Domestic hot water is the water you use for showers, bathing, and washing.

4.7.1.1 ELECTRIC
Electric water heaters have one of the most frequent replacement schedules of any appliance in the house. Most heaters are glass lined and have lifetimes of between 8 and 12 years. Well water may shorten the life expectancy of the tank as much as 50 percent. The size of the tank is dictated by the energy used to heat it and the number of occupants in the house. Usually, one estimates the size of the tank at 10 gallons per occupant, with a minimum of 30 gallons. Electric water heaters have slow recovery rates, therefore 15 gallons per person may be a better estimate with a minimum size of 40 gallons. Temperatures should be set between 120 degrees and 140 degrees Fahrenheit, using the upper end of the range if there is a dishwasher. (Read section 4.7 Hot Water Source.)

4.7.1.2 GAS
Water heaters have one of the most frequent replacement schedules of any appliance in the house. Most heaters are glass lined and have lifetimes of between 12 and 20 years. Well water may shorten the life expectancy of the tank as much as 50 percent. The size of the tank is dictated by the energy used to heat it and the number of occupants in the house. Usually, one estimates the size of the tank at 10 gallons per occupant, with a minimum of 30 gallons. Gas heaters are available with recovery rates of 100% capacity per hour. Temperatures should be set between 120 degrees and 140 degrees Fahrenheit, using the upper end of the range if there is a dishwasher. Keep the unit clean around the burner and replace the thermocouple as required. Keep the flue sound, clean and properly connected. See section 6.3.1 Gas for more information on maintaining gas fired equipment. (Read section 4.7 Hot Water Source.)

4.7.1.3 OIL

Oil fired water heaters are rare, but have high recovery rates. Usually, one estimates the size of the tank at 10 gallons per occupant, with a minimum of 30 gallons. Temperatures should be set between 120 degrees and 140 degrees F, using the upper end of the range if there is a dishwasher. As with any oil fired appliance, annual service is recommended. See the section 6.3.2 Oil for more information on maintaining oil fired equipment. (Read section 4.7 Hot Water Source.)

4.7.1.4 DOMESTIC COIL

A domestic coil is an attachment or insert for a boiler allowing it to heat domestic hot water besides heating the house. The coil picks up heat, but assures you domestic water does not mix with the water in the boiler. The life expectancy of a domestic coil water heater is estimated from the age of the boiler and circulator pump. There is quick recovery and problem-free usage as long as the heating unit is properly maintained. If the coil within the boiler becomes coated with deposits such as lime, calcium, or slime on the interior or exterior of the coil, its efficiency will be reduced. Some older domestic coils produce endless warm water rather than endless hot water.

Domestic coils may require operating the boiler at a lower temperature. Home heating systems can operate between 180 to 200 degrees Fahrenheit, but it is safer to provide domestic hot water between 120 and 140 degrees. Therefore, some heating systems are set back in temperature to prevent scalding but operate at reduced efficiency. One possibility is to install a tempering valve which automatically introduces cold water and mixes it with the hot water to cool it to the desired and safer temperature.

The boiler must be fired year round in order to maintain a supply of hot water. In summer you may be firing a 150,000 BTU boiler to produce domestic hot water. Heat loss from the boiler may add to air conditioning costs. Some owners install an electric water heater in line with the domestic coil to boost the temperature if it is not hot enough in the winter. This also allows shutting off the boiler in mild seasons. The electric water heater heats the water. This may save wear and tear on the boiler and reduce air conditioning costs in summer. (Read section 4.7 Hot Water Source.)

4.7.1.5 OTHER

There are many other types of water heating systems such as tankless heaters, and solar systems. These systems are somewhat unusual and rare. Solar systems were popular recently, but are falling into disuse. Solar systems are not in the scope of the inspection. Obtain literature or instruction from the previous owner, manufacturer, or seller of the solar equipment. (Read section 4.7 Hot Water Source.)

4.8 PRIVATE WATER SYSTEMS

Private systems are usually wells and their associated pumps. Occasionally springs or cisterns are in use. Private waste disposal systems are usually septic systems. Occasionally cess pools and private mechanical sewer systems are seen. Any private system, whether it's a well or other supply system or waste disposal system will require maintenance and upkeep. Advice is available from suppliers, government officials, health officials, etc. The pre-purchase inspection does not cover a well, private water system, septic inspection, or private waste disposal system.

4.8.1 SUPPLY EQUIPMENT

Supply equipment is the pump used to pump water from a well or water system. Often these pumps are submersible or installed in the well or in the water supply itself, therefore making it invisible to the inspector. The pump, when visible, will be inspected. The inspector will test the system's water supply flow and pressure, thus testing the pump. No attempt is made to test the total output of the pump, its general performance or to estimate the remaining life. The quantity and quality of the water available from the well is not within the scope of this inspection.

4.8.2 WASTE DISPOSAL

Private waste disposal systems are often septic tanks and drainfields. The sewage is flushed into a large underground tank. The solid material remains in the tank where it is broken down and digested by bacteria and other decomposition processes. The liquid from the system passes through into a drainfield or leach field, (a series of underground trenches filled with stone). The water peculates or soaks into the ground. Some of the moisture transpires into the atmosphere.

Drainfields occupy a large area of the yard. They are subject to damage from tree roots, chemicals, and heavy traffic. Learn where your septic tank is and do not drive on it. Do not allow heavy trucks such as cement trucks and moving vans to drive on top of the septic tank. It may collapse. Driving on the drainfield could compact the soil and cut the efficiency of the percolation and transpiration of moisture. Occasionally the septic tank will fill up with solids and will have to be pumped or emptied. The bacterial decomposition of the material in the tank is subject to damage from household chemicals and laundry detergents containing phosphates. Contact local health authorities for advice on maintaining your septic tank and drainfield.

The drainfield is given only a cursory examination by the inspector since this system is largely underground. Only the surface area above the drainfield will be inspected for signs of effluent (liquid) coming to the surface. Have the tank emptied (pumped) every 5 years maximum. Have it pumped when you take possession to be sure you start properly.

4.9 OBSERVATIONS

The inspector marks observations of conditions affecting the plumbing. More than one item can be marked as the plumbing may exhibit more than one symptom or problem. Some items are part of the normal aging process and do not require correction. Other items require either maintenance or repair if the plumbing is to reach the full potential or life expectancy. Read carefully each section applying to the system inspected.

Maintenance is the on going care required if a system or item is to reach the full potential including lubricating, painting, etc. Do maintenance as required by the manufacturer of the equipment or item. Repairs put items or systems back in good condition after damage or decay, etc. Repairs are caused by delayed maintenance, aging, normal wear and tear, or abuse. The workmanship and materials of the repairs should be equal to the quality of the system and have the same life expectancy. e.g. A limb plunges through an asphalt shingle roof. If the roofing otherwise has a life expectancy of ten years, the repair should also have a life expectancy of at least ten years. If the roofing only has a life expectancy of one year, then the repair should be capable of lasting one year or more. It is not prudent to put a one year patch on a ten year roof or to waste a ten year repair on a one year roof. All repairs should be by qualified competent professionals.

4.9.1 SOUND

The inspector thinks the item inspected is functioning at the moment of the inspection. This does not imply perfection, absence of minor defects, or absence of wear and tear.

4.9.2 TYPICAL

The inspector thinks the item, material, or aspect of construction is characteristic or similar to comparable products in similar houses. The plumbing has normal wear and tear.

4.9.3 MECHANICAL OR PHYSICAL DAMAGE

The inspector sees mechanical or physical damage to a part of the system. Examples range from broken or cracked pipes, dented water heaters, to intentional damage such as the partial removal or abandonment of systems. Have a qualified plumber repair the damage.

4.9.4 TEMPORARY REPAIRS

The inspector notes repairs of a temporary or substandard nature. Includes taped leaks, use of straps, rubber gasket type patches, and wooden plugs driven into leaks, etc. Repairs should be of the same quality and have the same life expectancy as the system.

4.9.4 a. Temporary Repair.
The gasket material strapped around this 4.4.2.1 Cast Iron waste line is either a temporary repair or 4.2.3 Amateur Workmanship. If this indicates the piping has rusted from the inside out in general, this could be a systemic problem. It may mean large parts of the system must be replaced.

4.9.4 b. Temporary Repair.
The use of duct tape is a temporary repair and will not last as long as the pipe. The pipe in the picture is not of a type intended for waste disposal. It is thin wall pipe used for storm drainage such as extending downspouts. Definitely 4.2.3 Amateur Workmanship.

4.9.5 CORROSION

The inspector notes the characteristic evidence of corrosion. Iron pipes rust, often at the joints, but sometimes have pinhole leaks which form rust cancers and heal themselves temporarily. Copper pipes sometimes exhibit a characteristic turquoise or blue green color indicating slow long term leaks or even the thinning of the pipe walls to the point the plumbing system has reached the end of its useful life. Have a qualified plumber make proper repairs. This may require replacing part or all of the system.
(Read section 4.4.1 Supply Piping and 4.4.2 Waste Piping.)

4.9.5 a. Corrosion
This galvanized iron drainline has rusted through from the interior and is leaking. (See 4.9.6 Drips and Leaks.)

4.9.6 DRIPS AND LEAKS

The inspector notes the presence of active leaks in the system. (i.e. water leaking, dripping, spraying, or escaping from the system.) Have a qualified plumber make proper repairs.

4.9.7 NO VALVE OR INACCESSIBLE

There is no main water shut off valve or the valve is inaccessible. The valve is useless in an emergency. Consider having a proper valve installed in an accessible location. (Read 4.3.2 Shut Off Valve.)

4.9.8 PRESSURE REDUCING VALVE

There is a pressure reducing valve probably at the connection between the incoming water line and the interior plumbing system. Pressure reducing valves are required in localities where water pressure in municipal lines is excessive and may cause wear and tear on plumbing fixtures. Such valves fail in either of two fashions: 1. They shut the water off. 2. They stop reducing the pressure of the water. If you experience loss of water or a sudden increase in water pressure, it may mean the pressure reducing valve has failed.

4.9.11 UNSUPPORTED

Piping runs are not completely supported or left unsupported. Piping should be properly supported to reduce the mechanical stress and strain on the system reducing the probability of a leak.

4.9.11 a. Unsupported.
The copper pipe is unsupported and may be putting a strain on its connections. Notice the 8.5.5 Falling or Collapsed Insulation and 3.8.45 Wet or Damp Crawl space

4.9.12 POSSIBLE ASBESTOS

Certain pipe insulations have been known to contain asbestos. Asbestos was used as the insulation on some older water heaters and boilers. Possible asbestos will be marked if the inspector notes a product possibly containing asbestos. Asbestos, wherever it's found, is of concern to all homeowners. If it breaks down into small fibers (becomes friable) and is inhaled or ingested, it can have serious and far reaching health effects. Only proper laboratory tests can confirm or deny its presence. The treatment and removal of asbestos is dangerous, expensive and should be left to experts.

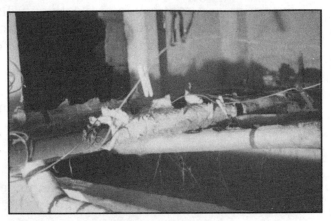

4.9.12 a. Possible Asbestos.
The pipe insulation is one of many products possibly containing asbestos. Treat it as asbestos until you have it tested.

4.9.13 HOT AND COLD PIPING TOO CLOSE TOGETHER

The hot and cold water lines are run too close to one another. The cold water line may cause a chilling of the hot water line. It may be possible to alleviate the problem by insulating the hot water line.

4.9.14 RUNS OFF

Portions of the system were off and not tested. This is sometimes done in anticipation of future expansion. If the shut down "runs" are part of the system that should be active, find out why they are shut off. The inspector does not turn on deactivated sections. There is too much risk of a leak. (Read section 4.1.2 Restricted.)

4.9.15 ABANDONED PIPING

Abandoned piping is often found in renovated houses. Good practice demands removing abandoned piping to avoid confusion and a possible reuse of defective plumbing systems. If not properly abandoned or removed, such piping may leak or vent sewer gases into the house.

4.9.15 a. Abandoned Piping.
The 4.4.2.2 Galvanized Iron waste pipe has been abandoned in place and replaced with 4.4.2.4.1 ABS waste piping. Notice that the connection between the new ABS and the older galvanized piping lacks a proper adapter fitting and will probably leak.

4.9.16 FAILED OR LEAKING PRESSURE TANK OR BOOSTER PUMP

The pressure tank or booster pump has failed or is leaking. Repairs should be made by a qualified plumber.

4.9.17 HANGER DAMAGE

Plumbing pipe is often supported in hangers. The hangers allow for movement from expansion and contraction of the pipes as they heat and cool, and vibration from turning the water on and off. Improper hangers or improperly installed hangers may abrade, wear, dent, or damage piping. Have the hangers repaired or replaced and the system repaired as necessary.

4.9.18 IMPROPER PITCH

The waste system is not sloped to drain properly. Repairs should be made by a qualified plumber.

4.9.19 IMPROPER TRAPS

Traps in the waste system from improper sloping of the pipes or S traps are in use. Repairs should be made by a qualified plumber. (Read section 4.5.3.2 Traps.)

4.9.20 LACK OF VACUUM BREAKERS

Recent codes require outside faucets have anti-siphon devices or vacuum breakers. They prevent gray water or waste water being siphoned into the municipal water system. Vacuum breakers or anti-siphon devices are available at hardware and plumbing supply stores.

4.9.21 SEALED OR DAMAGED CLEAN OUTS

Plumbing waste systems require cleanout plugs or fittings where piping turns or at the ends of runs. This enables someone to snake or clean out the system. Occasionally the access plugs are glued or sealed to prevent leaking. They can break. Open or damaged clean outs permit sewer gases to enter. They may permit sewage to spill. Repairs should be made by a qualified plumber.

4.9.22 UNVENTED

The plumbing system is not properly vented. (Read section 4.5.3 Venting.)

4.9.23 RAIN LEADER CONNECTED TO CITY SEWER

It was common to connect the rain leaders or downspouts to the city sewer through the interior plumbing system. Many cities now have separate storm water drainage systems. Storm water increases the work load on sewage treatment plants. Many municipalities are requiring roof water drained to the surface or into the storm water drainage systems. Check with local authorities for the conditions prevailing in your area.

4.9.24 WET VENTING

Many vents in plumbing systems are dry. (i.e. Carry away sewer gases and allow air into the system.) Often when houses are remodeled, a dry vent is converted into a wet vent. Waste water from above drains through the vent stack. This occasionally has disastrous results in terms of blockages. A qualified plumber should properly repair or vent the system. (Read section 4.5.3 Venting.)

4.9.25 SEWER EJECTOR

A sewer ejector pump or grinder pump lifts sewage into the sewer or septic tank. These are high maintenance items and should have an alarm switch so when they fail you can have them repaired quickly before an overflow occurs.

4.9.26 FIXTURE BELOW THE OUTLET

A fixture is below the main sewer outlet. Usually an ejector pump is required to lift the effluent from the fixture into the sewer.

4.9.27 MIXED METALS OR MIXED PLASTICS

Corrosion will result where dissimilar metals join without proper precautions. The two metals attack one another through a process known as galvanic corrosion. The iron piping will corrode, rapidly accelerating its demise. Special dielectric couplings are available, but seldom used.

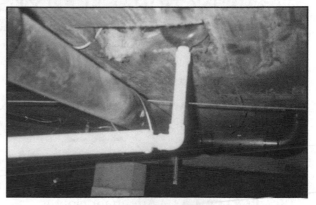

4.9.27 a. Mixed Plastics.
This is a PVC Pipe screwed into an ABS bath tub trap. (Actually it is acceptable to screw the two together, but not to glue them.) This drains the trap causing a 4.9.19 Open or Improper Trap. The piping is 4.9.11 Unsupported unless you count the wires and they may cause 4.9.17 Hanger damage. Definitely 4.2.3 Amateur Workmanship.

The prohibition against using mixed plastics comes from the fact plastic piping is solvent welded. The glue melts the surface of the plastic and the pipe and fitting solvent weld or fuse directly into one another. The same glue is suitable for use with different types of plastic, but it will not glue mixed types of plastic to each other because the solvent weld will not form properly.

Mixed plastics are also an indication of amateur workmanship or repairs. Any location where mixed plastics will be concealed above or within finished walls or floors are highly suspect and consideration should be given to eliminating the potential problem.

4.9.28 FREEZE DAMAGE OR DANGER

The system has frozen or there is danger the system may freeze. Protect pipes from freezing. Pipe insulation is available at hardware stores and plumbing supply houses. Locate pipes on the warm side of the building's insulation. Close vents in winter.

4.9.28 a. Freeze Damage or Danger
The pipe concealed in the wall froze, burst, and water running out through the siding froze outside the house. Don't turn off heating while away for long periods of time.

4.9.31 ADEQUATE SUPPLY FLOW

The water supply is sufficient to create a functional flow when two or more fixtures operate simultaneously. (Read section 4.5.1.2 Adequate Flow.)

4.9.32 FUNCTIONAL SUPPLY FLOW

The flow of supply water, pressure and volume, are sufficient to qualify as a functional supply. (Read section 4.5.1.1 Functional Flow.)

4.9.33 NON-FUNCTIONAL SUPPLY

The flow of water is not adequate to meet the definition of a functional flow. (Read section 4.5.1.1 Functional Flow.)

4.9.34 INADEQUATE SUPPLY FLOW

The water supply is incapable of providing a functional flow at two fixtures simultaneously. (Read section 4.5.1.2 Adequate Flow.)

4.9.35 NON-FUNCTIONAL DRAINAGE

There are fixtures not capable of draining as rapidly as water runs in.   i.e. Slow or blocked drains. (Read section 4.5.2.2 Non Functional.) Drain cleaners may help. Repairs should be made by an experienced plumber.

4.9.36 NOISY

Excessive noise either in the supply or drain lines. An experienced plumber may be able to help.

4.9.37 WATER HAMMER

Water hammer is a characteristic noise in the plumbing systems when the water shuts off suddenly. It is also caused by rapidly closing solenoid valves in devices like washing machines and dishwashers. Water hammer is often associated with poorly supported pipes. The problem can sometimes be solved by the installation of air chambers or hammer chambers in the lines. An experienced plumber may be able to help.

4.9.38 SOUND OF WATER RUNNING

The inspector hears running water and cannot find a specific cause for the sound. This often indicates a leaking water supply line under a slab or a leak in the incoming water line that has not surfaced. This problem should be found and cured to prevent the loss of water, possible undermining, and damage to the structure. An experienced plumber may be able to help.

4.9.39 SWEATING

Condensation or sweating on cold parts of the plumbing system. This is not a plumbing problem, but an indication the space is humid. Solving the dampness problem may eliminate the sweating. (Read section 3.8.49 Condensation or Sweating.)

4.9.40 SEWAGE ODOR

The characteristic dank or sweet smell of sewage or sewer gases. This indicates a cracked or broken sewer line or open vent. Perhaps a trap is dry allowing sewer gases to enter the property. The source of the odor should be found and corrected. An experienced plumber may be able to help.

4.9.41 OPEN OR IMPROPER VENTS

Vents terminating within the property or close to an opening in the exterior wall. Such vents should be extended so they exit the property properly and allow for the venting of sewer gases. An experienced plumber may be able to help. (Read section 4.5.3 Venting.)

4.9.44 DAMAGE TO THE FINISH

Slight scratching to the finish of plumbing fixtures may be a part of normal wear and tear. Chipping extending through the glaze coat exposes the vitreous china, cast iron, or the substrate of fiberglass. This may offer a place for bacteria and other disease causing organisms to thrive. These problems make it difficult to sanitize the fixtures and may require repair or replacement.

4.9.44 a. Damaged Finish
The steel sink may rust through quickly
if not protected from corrosion.

4.9.45 SINKS LOOSE

Wall hung sinks must be securely mounted to prevent dislodging or falling, and damaging the plumbing or the sink. Countertop mounted sinks must be secured with mechanical fasteners or adhesive caulking. This prevents damage to the sink and the plumbing. Have the fixtures properly installed.

4.9.46 SPRAY HOSE

Spray hoses are used on the kitchen sink and on the bathroom shower or tub faucet set. The hoses and attached fittings leak and are subject to wear and tear. An experienced plumber may be able to repair or replace them.

4.9.47 FAUCETS LOOSE

Faucets should be securely mounted to the deck or surface of the sink. Faucets moving may cause mechanical stress to the plumbing system and induce leaks or other failures. An experienced plumber may be able to help.

4.9.48 FAUCETS DRIP OR LEAK

Faucets dripping from the washer or leaking at the stems waste water and hot water leaks also waste energy. Any leaks deplete wells and flood drainfields or add to sewer and water bills. They also have the potential to cause damage to the structure and to finished surfaces. Such leaks should be repaired and cured as a part of normal maintenance. (Read section 4.6.2 Faucets.)

4.9.49 PHYSICAL DAMAGE TO FAUCETS

Missing or broken   handles, stoppers, or operating hardware can be noted under this section. Porcelain or china handles sometimes break exposing sharp edges. Missing handles on tub fixtures leave the stem exposed presenting a sharp object and a possible source of personal injury in a fall in the bathtub. Damaged faucets should be repaired promptly for safety and proper operation. (Read section 4.6.2 Faucets.)

4.9.50 TRAP LEAK

The chrome plated traps suffer from interior erosion and dissolve in the acidity of the water and waste sitting in the traps. There are numerous connections (possible leaks) made between the sink or fixture and the entry into the waste system. Leaks have the potential to damage the floor structure and cabinets and should be properly repaired promptly. (Read section 4.5 3.2 Traps.)

4.9.51 TOILET LOOSE OR WETNESS ON FLOOR

A loose toilet rocking or moving easily indicates a leak at the wax ring (the connection to the waste system). If it's not leaking now, it will be soon. Wetness on the floor or seen from below indicates the toilet is leaking. Replacing wax rings and reinstalling toilets are a part of maintenance to avoid damage to the floor system and structure. It is far less expensive to cure this type leak promptly than to replace the floor. Have loose or leaking toilets properly reinstalled. (Read section 4.6.5 Toilets.)

4.9.51 a. Wax Ring Leak.
A loose toilet or leaking wax ring allows water to seep into the subfloor and framing each time the toilet is flushed or continuously if the toilet leaks internally. This is seen from the crawl space. The damage concealed by the toilet may be more extensive than it appears. The piping is 4.4.2.3 Copper Waste Line.

4.9.52 TOILET DAMAGED

The toilet is physically damaged. Cracks occurring in the base of the toilet where it is mounted, within the bowl, or in the tank may cause leaks. Any time the china of the commode cracks replacement is indicated. (Read section 4.6.5 Toilets.)

4.9.53 TOILET ABANDONED OR UNUSED

Keep toilets filled with water to avoid the trap drying out and sewer gases or radon entering the house. If the toilet is going to be permanently abandoned it should be removed and the drain permanently plugged. (Read section 4.5.2 Toilets.)

4.9.54 FAILS TO FLUSH

The toilet fails to properly flush. Either it fails to carry away the waste products or the flush mechanism is damaged or deteriorated so the toilet will not flush properly. Repair or replace it to assure proper operation. Toilets flushing sluggishly or overflowing may indicate blocked pipes or a flooded septic tank and drainfield. An experienced plumber may be able to help. (Read section 4.5.2 Toilets.)

4.9.55 SHOWER PAN LEAK

From the crawl space or from the ceiling below the inspector has seen an indication the lead or vinyl pan under the shower is leaking. (Read section 4.6.6 Shower.) If the pan is leaking, the cure is to replace it.

4.9.55 a.
The white "stalactites" are clues the shower pan above may be leaking. If the pan is leaking the repairs are expensive and may require carpentry to replace rotting floor parts, a plumber to reinstall the pan, and new ceramic tile. Ceramic tile may be difficult or impossible to match.

4.9.56 S TRAPS

S traps were common under wall hung sinks. The waste pipe comes vertically from the bottom of the sink and goes down through an S (on its side) or circular loop and exits vertically through the floor. S traps are subject to siphoning. The water is drawn through the trap and goes down the drain, leaving the trap dry, permitting sewer gases to enter the house. S traps have fallen into disuse and should be replaced wherever feasible with P traps. (Read section 4.5.3.2 Traps.)

4.9.59 NO PRESSURE AND TEMPERATURE RELIEF VALVE

There is no proper temperature and pressure relief valve on the system. (Read section 4.7 Hot Water Source, including appropriate subchapters.) Have a proper valve installed promptly for safety. It is wise to extend the outlet down to within 4 inches of the floor through a full size pipe.

4.9.60 POWER OR FUEL OFF

The water heater is not heating water because the power or fuel is turned off to the system. This represents a severe limitation on the inspection and gives no indication whether the system will operate properly when there is fuel. Remove this limitation by arranging to have the fuel or power turned on, the water heater lit, and a reinspection before closing.

4.9.61 GAS OR FUEL LEAKS OR IMPROPER WIRING

There are fuel or gas leaks associated with the water heater, or improper wiring to an electric heater. Such defects should be properly repaired promptly for safety. It may be wise to turn off the fuel or power until repaired. Leave this work to competent professionals.

4.9.62 ELEMENT FAILED

An element in the water heater failed to respond and properly heat the water. A competent plumber or electrician should be able to pinpoint and repair the problem.

4.9.63 DAMAGED BURNER OR CONTROLS

The burner assembly or controls on the water heater appear damaged or are not functioning properly. A competent plumber, heating contractor, or local gas utility should be able to pinpoint the problem and properly repair or adjust the unit. Repairs should be made promptly to assure safe operation.

CHAPTER FIVE

ELECTRICAL

Since prehistoric times, torches, candles, oil lamps, and burning logs have given light. Thomas Edison's light bulb and filament changed the world. The development of electrical lines allowing most people to have electricity made a difference in every day life. Electricity operates appliances, warms us, cools us, preserves food, directs traffic, powers computers, and dispels the darkness.

MAINTENANCE AND UPKEEP

Electricity, unlike other systems in the house presents a unique danger, electrocution. Not only is the electrical system a potential source for fires destroying the structure, the electricity may kill or injure you if you come into contact with it. For both reasons you should properly maintain the system and keep it updated. Have repairs made promptly and well. Do not do the work yourself unless you are sure you are qualified and work safely. Always turn the power off before you work on the system.

Devices such as smoke detectors and Ground Fault Interrupter breakers and outlets are now required by Code and commonplace in newer houses, but many older homes still don't have them. They are inexpensive and could save your life. You would be wise to install them. Carbon monoxide detectors are available similar to smoke detectors and would certainly be a good idea in any house with any source of carbon monoxide such as gas or oil fired heat or a fireplace.

5.1 LIMITATIONS

This section describes the aspects limiting the inspection of the electrical system. Inspectors do the best inspection they can, but sometimes are prevented from doing the whole job by physical obstructions or the lack of power, etc. Most of the electrical system is not visible for inspection and only a representative number of outlets, switches, and built-in devices are tested for operation. The inspector normally inspects one outlet per room, one light switch per room, etc. The inspector does not attempt to inspect and test every single electrical device where there are dozens or scores. They remove the panel cover. Arrange for an inspection overcoming the limitations, if possible. (i.e. Come back after the power is on or repairs completed.) An uninspected electrical system or a severely limited or restricted inspection could be a total unknown. It is your responsibility to overcome the limitations. You should complete the inspection prior to closing even if you must hire others (Electricians, etc.) or pay an additional fee to the inspector or electrical industry specialist. Repairs can be expensive and at some point replacement is the best alternative. An uninspected electrical system or one given a severely limited or restricted inspection could be a total unknown. The inspector cannot make representations about what was not inspected. If you close on the house with a Limited or Restricted inspection you are accepting the responsibility for the unknown items about the system.

5.1.1 TYPICAL

The inspector feels they have seen as much of the electrical system as they normally see. Typically, they remove the panel box cover and inspect the contents and other exposed elements of the system. (Read section 5.1 Limitations.) Components and wiring concealed in the walls and other building cavities are not inspected. Some outlets are tested with devices determining whether they operate properly. The inspection is primarily a visual inspection. Some items are inspected on a sample basis such as one per room or perhaps one per wall. Junctions and junction boxes hidden during construction are undetectable. A typical inspection does not include supplying fuses or light bulbs, overriding safety devices, or damaging the building to gain access. (Read 5.1 Limitations.)

5.1.2 RESTRICTED

The inspector feels they have seen less of the electrical system than they typically see. (Read 5.1.1 Typical and 5.1 Limitations.) Make arrangements before closing to have the system fully inspected. A restricted inspection may be a total unknown and the inspector cannot make representations about what was not inspected. (Read 5.1.1 Typical.)

5.1.2.1 CRAWL SPACE INACCESSIBLE

The crawl space is too low (less than two feet), too wet, or too dangerous. Dangling and potentially dangerous electrical connections make the crawl space inaccessible. The system and other systems in the crawl space will not be inspected. (Read 5.1.2 Restricted.)

5.1.2.2 ATTIC INACCESSIBLE

(1) There is no attic access, or (2) the attic is too small to enter or (3) the attic is less than three feet high above the access. The inspector will not enter the attic or parts of the attic not accessible. Therefore, this system and other systems in the inaccessible part of the attic are not inspected. (Read section 5.1.2 Restricted.)

5.1.2.3 EQUIPMENT INACCESSIBLE

Parts of the electrical system are inaccessible. An example is an electrical panel covered over by paneling or blocked by other equipment. An inspector will not remove covers painted or wallpapered to the wall. The inspector cannot remove the cover to inspect the interior of the panel. Personal possessions piled in front of the equipment make it inaccessible. It is not the inspector's responsibility to remove personal belongings to gain access to the equipment. (Read 5.1.2 Restricted.)

5.2 GENERAL

A quick reference and overview of the inspector's opinions or impressions. This section is subjective and relies on the inspector's judgment and experience in estimating the age, whether clues are important and if toxins are present, etc. (Read the electrical chapter fully before forming any final opinion.)

5.2.1 SYSTEM INSPECTED (YES, RESTRICTED, OR NO)

The inspector marks whether the system was inspected. No information will be given about a system that was not inspected. If the inspector writes in or circles "R" for restricted, the system was partially inspected. Check 5.1 LIMITATIONS or discuss it with the inspector to learn the full extent of the restrictions. A severely limited inspection may not give you the information you need. You should do whatever is necessary to remove or overcome the restrictions and have the system fully inspected before you close on the house. (Read 5.1 Limitations.)

5.2.2 POWER (ON OR OFF)

"ON" The power was on. The power must be on for the inspector to do an inspection of the electrical system.

"OFF" The power is off. If the power is off the inspector can only judge the general condition of the visible parts of the system and cannot determine whether the system can operate properly once energized. "OFF" is a severe limitation on the inspection. Have the system energized and reinspected before closing. Power OFF also restricts or limits the inspection of other systems or devices such as heat, water heaters, appliances, smoke detectors, etc.

5.2.3 AMATEUR WORKMANSHIP (YES OR NO)

"YES" The inspector notes workmanship of less than professional quality. Poor workmanship may constitute a major defect. Major defects cost $500.00 or more to repair or may affect the habitability of the house. The work may not serve the purpose intended and may require repair or replacement. (Read section 2.2.4 Major Defect.) Have a qualified electrician make repairs to the electrical system.

"NO" No amateur workmanship noted. Some amateurs produce workmanship of equal or better quality than professionals.

5.2.4 MAIN PANEL RATING AND LOCATION

The **Number** of Main Panels, the total **Amperage** of the incoming service, the **Voltage** of the service and the **Location** of the Main Panel are noted. (Read Section 5.4 Main and Subpanels.)

5.2.6 ALUMINUM WIRE IN GENERAL USAGE (YES OR NO)

"YES" There is aluminum wire in the 120 volt branch circuits. It is controversial because fires have been traced to the improper use of aluminum. Aluminum wiring was common in the late 60's and early 70's. Homes still have aluminum wire in the branch circuits. There appears to be little or no controversy about the use of stranded aluminum conductors in the incoming service or in the larger 240 volt circuits. (Read also 5.5.3.2 Aluminum and 5.5.4.3 Compatibility.)

"NO" The inspector saw no evidence of aluminum wire in the 120 Volt branch circuits.

5.2.7 SHOCK HAZARD (YES OR NO)

"YES" There are conditions presenting the possibility of electrical shock. i.e. Bare and unprotected wires or connections not properly enclosed in boxes, metal parts of the system have become energized, etc.

"NO" No shock hazard noted.

5.2.8 ROOM FOR FUTURE EXPANSION (YES OR NO)
"YES" There is space and ampacity for moderate future expansion.

"NO" The system is fully expanded or has little or no room for future expansion or additions to the service. Such systems may be safe and compatible with the existing use but do not allow for major expansions to the system such as central air conditioning, hot tubs, etc. These systems may be a candidate for upgrading or up sizing of the service.

5.2.9 SUBJECTIVE RATING
The inspector's grade for the electrical system:

E   **EXCELLENT**, above average, new or like new. (e.g. An upgraded and replaced electrical system in a house originally wired with knob and tubing wiring.)

A   **AVERAGE**, in typical condition for its age, showing normal wear and tear. (e.g. Five year old electrical system that looks 5 years old and a 5 year old house.)

C   **BELOW AVERAGE**, prematurely aged, showing heavy or excess wear and tear, or delayed maintenance. Perhaps showing minor (curable) defects. (e.g. A five year old electrical system that shows the wear and tear or age characteristics of a 10 year old system.)

F   **SUBSTANDARD**, failed, or reaching the end of its life expectancy, probably exhibiting extensive wear and tear, and the need for repairs or upgrading. (Potentially hazardous) Any further safe service from this system should be considered a gift.

5.3 EXTERIOR SERVICE AND METER
In most localities, the exterior service from the power company to the meter, including the meter, belong to and are the responsibility of the local power company. This part of the service is inspected only as a courtesy to the client and to point out the potential hazards involved in the service. This part of the system will be maintained by the power company. If problems exist, you should contact them to see if they are willing to repair, replace, cut tree limbs, etc.

5.3.1 OVERHEAD SERVICE AND NUMBER OF CONDUCTORS
Most modern overhead services have three or more conductors in order to deliver 240 volts of current to the property. In a few cases, older two conductor services provide the property with 120 volt service only. 120 volt service is adequate only for small loads such as lighting, general outlets, etc. Most heavier devices such as water heaters, air conditioners, dryers, ranges, etc. require 240 volt service. If your property has a 120 volt service do not expect to expand or upgrade the service without converting.

Overhead service lines should be a minimum of 10 feet above the ground, away from windows, garage roofs, and other areas where people might be able to reach or touch the power lines. Above driveways and traffic areas the restrictions are higher, a minimum of 12 feet.

MAINTENANCE AND UPKEEP

The homeowner should inspect his overhead power lines several times a year for weather damage, lines pulled loose, or physical damage to the house. Tree limbs growing too close to the power lines should be trimmed. The maintenance on this portion of the system is usually done by the local power company at your request. Some power companies provide free up sizing of their portion of the service.

5.3.2 UNDERGROUND SERVICE

Underground service from the power company equipment to the residence is popular and is the norm in some parts of the country. Underground lines are concealed from direct inspection.

MAINTENANCE AND UPKEEP

The homeowner should inspect the area of the underground service and look for potential damage or the exposure of cables etc. This portion of the system should be maintained by your local utility company at your request.

In many localities, the law requires you notify the power company, to give them the opportunity to mark the location of the service, before you dig in the yard. This is for your safety; to avoid the possibility you will injure yourself by contacting underground power lines, and to avoid the interruption of service. In Virginia the number to call is 1-800- 552-7001. In other localities, the front of your phone book may have the number to call or call your local utility company.

5.3.3 METER AND METER BASE

The meter and meter base usually are the property of the local power company and maintained by them. The inspector will give them a cursory inspection to be sure no dangerous condition is apparent. The meter base should be anchored securely. It should be intact and weather resistant and should not have obvious holes and defects.

MAINTENANCE AND UPKEEP

Inspect the meter base and associated equipment occasionally to see if this portion of the system is intact or has sustained weather or physical damage. The power company will maintain this part of the system at your request.

5.4 MAIN PANEL AND SUB-PANELS

A wide variety of equipment serves as panels and subpanels. They are metal boxes or cabinets enclosing the fuses, breakers, or switch gear. Wiring should pass through holes in the box and be secured with cable clamps. The cable clamp serves two purposes: (1) it clamps the wire safely, avoiding abrasion or damaged insulation causing an electrical hazard, (2) it fills the hole and seals the cabinet so an arc or short circuit flash will be contained and not expose the rest of the structure to a fire hazard. Keep the cabinet in good condition and physically undamaged. Water entering the panel is undesirable because water and electricity together are hazardous. Water can rust or damage the switch gear and the cabinet and cause electrocution.

MAINTENANCE AND UPKEEP

Inspect the main panel occasionally. Be sure the cover is securely in place, there are no open holes in the cabinet, and the cabinet has not been invaded by mice, bees, or other vermin. Make sure the cabinet is in a dry, safe location, and water has not leaked in. Necessary repairs should be made by a qualified electrician. Do not remove the panel cover unless you are sure you know what you are doing. There is enough electricity in there to activate your life insurance.

5.4.1 FUSE PANELS

For many years fuses were the dominant type of safety device used to protect the user from overcurrent or excess current. Fuse panels came in many varieties and are still commonly in use. Fuses fall into two or three categories. Fuse blocks or pullers normally control 240 volt current. When pulled from the panel, they contain two cartridge type fuses. 120 volt current is provided through screw-in type fuses which come in two varieties. One is the older Edison type fuse threaded like a light bulb's base. The second is a National Electrical Code (NEC) or safety (type S) fuse having a smaller, finer threaded base.

The NEC fuse and its associated adapter screws into the fuse panel and is not interchangeable with any other size fuse. This prevents the possibility of overfusing. Any size fuse can be screwed into any location in the Edison base fuse panel. There is a tendency for people to use a larger fuse than required, thus overfusing the wiring. Overfusing is dangerous because it allows excess current to flow into the wiring, causing a fire or shock hazard.

Fuse panels are still widely used and if properly maintained will provide adequate protection, but they are falling into disfavor. The preference has shifted to breakers. People like breakers better because they do not have to maintain a stock of spare fuses. It is simpler and easier to reset a breaker than it is to find and replace a blown fuse.

MAINTENANCE AND UPKEEP

A properly maintained fuse panel should provide adequate protection to the owner and the structure. Keep the panel intact, unmodified, and in sound condition. Changes or additions should be made by knowledgeable persons or qualified electricians. Maintain a stock of fuses

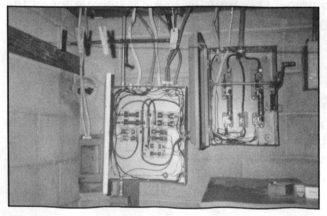

including replacement fuses for all the various sizes and types of fuses in the panel. Keep a flashlight near the panel. Get a fuse tester so you can determine which fuses are sound.

5.4.1 a. Fuse Panel.
These cartridge fuses are somewhat difficult to change and you must have a fuse tester to know which ones are bad. Fuse pullers that look like plastic pliers are available to make removing and replacing them safer and easier. There are 5.4.3.1 Fuse Subpanels also.

There are a variety of fuse types available within each group. One common type is a "time delay fuse" often used on motor circuits having a surge demand. This particular type of fuse allows the motor to pull an extreme amount of current briefly, and not trip. As the motor reaches full operating speed the demand for current drops and levels off. This is characteristic of motors, therefore time delay type fuses accommodate the motor's demand.

Since fuse panels have fallen into disuse, replacement parts are almost impossible to get. Use care when removing pullers, inserting fuses, etc. If you break a critical part of your panel you will be forced to replace the entire panel.

5.4.2 BREAKER PANEL

Breaker panels come in two styles. One includes a main breaker disconnecting the service to all the other breakers in the panel. An earlier version was the split buss breaker panel. There were up to six breakers in a separate section of the panel called service disconnects. One or two of these breakers controlled the lower breakers in the panel and the other four or five breakers were independent.

Circuit breakers are popular and have almost replaced fuses in new work. It is much simpler and easier to reset a tripped circuit breaker than to find and replace a blown fuse. Breakers should not trip often. If they do, you have an overloaded circuit. An electrician should find the problem and cure it. They may separate it into two circuits making the system safer and more convenient to use.

MAINTENANCE AND UPKEEP

All breaker panels require care and maintenance. It is a good idea to trip or exercise the circuit breakers occasionally. Turn off and reset your circuit breakers, including the main, once or twice a year. If you have a GFCI or Ground Fault Current Interrupter breaker, (with the test button), press the button once a month to exercise the breaker. Be sure the breakers have not stiffened or seized with age and no longer function.

This is not done on the inspection because of the possibility the breakers will not reset for the inspector. You may want to do this prior to closing. If you have any service done on the electrical system, have the electrician test and reset all the breakers in the property. If any fail to reset properly, the electrician is equipped to replace them.

5.4.2.1 MAIN BREAKER

Main breaker panels have a single breaker shutting off the service to the other breakers in the panel. This breaker serves as a main disconnect and establishes the ampacity of the panel. A 200 amp panel will have a 200 amp main breaker. Turning off the main breaker only turns off the power from a breaker through the panel and to the rest of the house. It does not turn off the power in the service entrance cable (the wire from the meter base to the panel). Often this wire runs 20 feet or more through the house and carries electricity.

5.4.2.2 SPLIT BUSS

Split buss breaker panels were an adaptation from fuse panels. It was acceptable to have up to six devices to turn off the power in the residence. This carryover gave us split buss panels with as many as six breakers in the upper section of the panel, labeled service disconnects. You must turn off all six in order to shut off all the power in the house. One or two of these breakers usually control the branch circuit breakers below them in the panel.

If you choose to work on your electrical system, be very cautious to be sure the device is off. Often air conditioners, water heaters, ranges, etc. connect to one of the service disconnects and are not controlled by the branch circuit breakers. People have been injured because they turned off what they thought was the main breaker, turning off the lights and the electrical outlets, but had not turned off the water heater or the range. Use caution and a circuit tester for checking the power to the device. For this reason split buss breaker panels have fallen into disuse, in favor of main breaker panels. Only qualified electricians should make repairs to an electrical system.

5.4.3 SUBPANELS

Subpanels get their power through or from the main panel. They may be installed near the main panel or located remotely in the structure, or near the equipment they power. Subpanels are sometimes used to extend or expand the size of the system or the number of circuits available. They must be treated with the same respect and given the same care and maintenance as main panels.

5.4.3.1 FUSE SUBPANELS

Fuse subpanels can be used in conjunction with fuse main panels or with breaker main panels. (Read 5.4.1 Fuse Panels for more information on fuses, etc.)

5.4.3.2 BREAKER SUBPANELS

Breaker subpanels can be used in conjunction with fused main panels or with breaker main panels. They must be given the same maintenance and care as any other breaker panel. (Read Section 5.4.2 Breaker panels.)

5.4.4 OVERFUSING

Overfusing is installing fuses or breakers larger than or with greater ampacity than the wire connected to them. Overfusing is a dangerous practice allowing excess current to pass into the branch circuit. This increases the probability of a fire or shock hazard.

The main breaker in the panel, the main fuse, and the ampacity of the panel must be checked against the ampacity of the incoming wire. An oversized panel on a smaller incoming service cable may be dangerous. This allows the system to pull excessive current through the service entrance cable increasing the probability of overheating and fire.

MAINTENANCE AND UPKEEP

Eliminate overfusing. Often it is as simple as replacing the fuses or breakers with ones of the correct size. Sometimes the wiring must be replaced in order to provide appropriate amperage to the device. The service entrance cable may have to be replaced to provide adequate service to the system. A qualified electrician can help you with eliminating overfusing for safety.

5.5 WIRING

Only the visible portion of the wiring portion will be inspected. The wiring concealed within the walls and other cavities cannot be inspected. It is possible devices and connections within the system are within those same walls and cavities. Most standards do not permit the total concealment of such splices. They should be in junction or fixture boxes openable for service. If such improper splices exist, the inspector has no way of knowing.

Copper, and to a lesser extent, aluminum are the standard materials. Aluminum wire was used to wire about two million homes in the late 60's and early 70's. It is controversial because of what appears to be an increased risk of fire associated with the aluminum wiring. It has fallen into disuse in 120 volt branch circuits. Aluminum wire is still in some homes. Opinion over the severity of the problem and what should be done to correct it varies throughout the industry. (For more information see 5.4.3.2 Aluminum Wiring.)

One of the earliest successful wiring systems in the country was knob and tubing wiring. The "knobs," porcelain knobs or carriers, were similar to the porcelain spools farmers used for electric fences. The "tubes" were porcelain tubes inserted through holes drilled in framing members. The wires were strung through the house as individual conductors about 10 or 12 inches apart. The system is archaic although it is "legal." It has been "grandfathered" into the National Electric Code. Wiring systems including knob and tubing wiring may be safe to use provided they are properly maintained, but repair parts are impossible to get and repairs are not up to standards. Replace and upgrade any undersized and archaic wiring system. Knob and tubing wiring was a two conductor system and did not contain a ground wire and grounding facility common in modern wiring.

MAINTENANCE AND UPKEEP

Inspect the wiring system periodically for physical damage to be sure wires are not becoming frayed, damaged, or conductors exposed. Protect this system from abuse. Properly support any dangling wires. Avoid the danger of shock or electrocution when working around the wiring system. This includes the overhead portions of the service such as the service drop. Use extreme care when painting or working around the outside of the house with ladders, poles, pool hooks, etc. They might come into contact with exterior wiring and conduct electricity. If you have any doubt about the safety of your wiring system, contact your local power company, a qualified electrician, or a home inspector.

5.5.1 SERVICE DROP OR LATERAL

The wiring coming from the power company to your house or to your meter is known as the service drop (overhead) or service lateral (underground). The service drop and service lateral are usually owned and maintained by the local power company.

MAINTENANCE AND UPKEEP

Inspect the service drop or service lateral occasionally to be sure they are not damaged and do not show excessive weathering, frayed wires, exposed conductors, etc. Often the wire is physically supported by a cable. The cable is usually anchored to the house with an eye bolt. There is a device called a weatherhead with a hood and the conductors are looped downward and then upward into the weatherhead. The purpose of this loop is to form a "drip" so water will drip off rather than follow the service drop and leak into the house or meter base.

Do not hit the lines with vehicles. Take particular care with oversized vehicles such as campers, boats, trucks, etc.

Do not allow vines, tree limbs, or vegetation of any type to grow on or near the power line. A service lateral wiring is underground. Take care not to dig up the lateral or allow it to become exposed through erosion, tree planting, gardening, etc. If you see damage to the weatherhead, eye bolt, mast, cable, exterior wiring, etc., contact the local power company or reputable electrician for repairs. Only the power company can turn off the electricity in this part of the service. It remains live (energized), even when the main breaker or fuse is off.

5.5.2 SERVICE ENTRANCE

The service entrance is the cable running from the meter base to your main panel. The cable (wire) is either copper or aluminum, most often aluminum. It is sometimes encased in a conduit. The ampacity of the cable must be equal to or greater than the main panel's ampacity.

In many older homes the service entrance runs a distance of 10 feet or more before it reaches the main panel. Sometimes the service entrance runs the entire length of the house. Turning off the main breaker or pulling the main fuse pullers, shutting off service inside the house, does not "kill" or de-energize the service entrance cable.

Recent changes in the National Electric Code require the service entrance cable be less than five feet long if unfused. If you change your service, you may have to install a switch or device on the outside of the house in a weather-proof cabinet to turn off the power in the service entrance cable. This introduces several changes in the wiring system including the use of four conductor cable from the exterior service disconnect to the main panel inside the house. You pay for the extra complexity of the service entrance cable and the outside service disconnect. Sometimes this doubles the cost of upsizing the service. You will not be required to make these changes until you upgrade the service.

MAINTENANCE AND UPKEEP

Care of the service entrance is the same as any other part of the wiring system. Do not damage the service entrance cable and do not allow it to become frayed or the conductors exposed. Protect it from physical damage and wetness.

The homeowner usually does not have the ability to de-energize this wire. Often it is necessary to remove the electric meter. Removing the meter is dangerous and illegal for the homeowner. Before attempting to repair, move, or work on this cable, contact your local power company or a reputable electrician for help and advice.

5.5.3 MATERIAL

The material most cables are made of is either copper or aluminum. Rarely, aluminum conductors are clad or coated with a thin coating of copper. The copper wiring has more capacity or ampacity for a given size. Copper is considerably more expensive than aluminum and so in service entrance cables, aluminum is the material of choice. Aluminum wiring must be somewhat larger than copper wiring to do the same task, but this has not been a problem and the switch gear and devices have been designed to accept the larger size. Aluminum wire is larger, but less expensive than copper.

Service entrance cables are of several types. Sometimes individual conductors run through conduit. Often they are cables. Insulated 120 volt conductors are bundled together and wrapped with the strands of the neutral wire and insulated on the exterior with a fabric, rubber, or vinyl coating. The neutral conductors around the hot wires provide physical protection to the more dangerous part of the cable.

There is little or no controversy associated with aluminum in this size conductor. The connections are made with an anti-oxide coating to protect the aluminum from oxidation, in proper connectors properly clamping the aluminum and conducting the current.

5.5.3.1 COPPER

Copper is an excellent material for wiring. The metal has high current carrying ability making relatively small wires possible. Copper is also ductile and malleable. i.e. It can be drawn into long thin wires and will withstand the bending and twisting necessary in an electrical system without fracturing, cracking, or breaking. It is more expensive than its aluminum counterpart and therefore is not often used as residential service entrance cables.

5.5.3.2 ALUMINUM

Aluminum wiring has a relatively high current carrying capacity, but not as great as copper. Aluminum service entrance cables and aluminum wiring in general must be larger than their copper counterparts. Aluminum wiring has been troublesome in 120 volt branch circuits as single stranded conductors. This problem has not exhibited itself in 240 volt circuits where multi-stranded conductors have been installed with proper connecting devices. There has been little or no controversy associated with aluminum wiring as service entrance cables.

5.5.3.3 COPPER CLAD

In an effort to overcome some of the problems associated with the oxidation of aluminum wiring, industry developed a method for copper cladding the aluminum conductors. A thin plating of copper is applied over the outer surface of the aluminum conductors and individual strands are wound together to form copper clad aluminum cables. Copper clad aluminum wiring is somewhat rare and is difficult to recognize. The inspector has to look directly at the end of an individual conductor in order to tell if it is aluminum in the center and copper plated or clad on the outside. As far as the author knows there has been no controversy associated with copper clad aluminum wiring.

5.5.4 AMPACITY

Ampacity is the capacity of a wire or device to carry current (amperes) safely. Homeowners must be concerned with the ampacity of the system in several respects. The total ampacity of the system is related to the size of the incoming service drop or lateral, the service entrance, and the size of the main panel.

The ampacity of the system is determined by whichever is lower. In other words, a system with a 60 amp service entrance cable leading to a 100 amp main breaker panel is still a 60 amp service. Such a service may also be unsafe. The 100 amp breaker is capable of asking for or allowing more current to pass than the 60 amp cable is capable of delivering safely. This may produce overheating and is a fire hazard.

Cases are found where homeowners or unscrupulous electricians have upsized the panel from perhaps 60 amps to as much as 150 amps without bothering to upsize the entrance cable. This has the potential to cause the incoming wire to overheat and start a fire.

5.5.4.1 OVERCURRENT DEVICE

The overcurrent device may be either the main fuse or the main breaker. There may not be a single overcurrent device. Often there is a main fuse and a range (kitchen stove) fuse. There may be six service disconnects in fuse panels. Earlier breaker panels sometimes had up to six service disconnect breakers.

Theoretically the amperage of the service disconnects should add up to less than the ampacity of the service entrance cable. Often they add up to more, but because of load distribution, this does not always create a problem. Some things never run simultaneously (e.g. heat and air conditioning). The smaller of these loads can be ignored when adding up possible simultaneous demand.

It is unlikely all electrical devices are on at one time. This is the reason the smaller breakers in the panel often add up to 1 1/2 to 2 1/2 times the capacity of the service disconnect controlling them. This usually does not create a problem.

MAINTENANCE AND UPKEEP

If the overcurrent device is a breaker, trip and reset manually once or twice a year to check the function. When modifications are made to the system do not circumvent the protection built-in and demand more current than the service entrance cable is capable of delivering.

If the system is improperly upsized and the panel substantially larger than the ampacity of the service entrance cable, contact your local power company or a qualified reputable electrician. Most electric utilities will upsize their portion of the cable at little or no charge.

5.5.4.2 WIRING

The capacity of the wiring in the system is difficult to judge. A given size of wire does not have an exact and specific ampacity. The capacity or ampacity of the wire is determined from the load on the wire. A wire handling 30 amps continuously might be capable of handling fifty or sixty amps instantaneously or over a short period of time. Therefore it is difficult for an inspector to look at a particular wire and state its specific capacity or ampacity.

Also, the location of the wire has a bearing on its capacity. Wires in open space, such as service entrance drops, have a larger capacity than wires installed within cavities or conduits. Wires in free air have the opportunity to radiate and dissipate heat readily and carry more current safely. Wires in enclosed locations carry a smaller current before they generate excessive heat and become a fire hazard.

It is important the wiring be protected by a proper overcurrent device. The main disconnect protects the service entrance cable by not allowing the system to ask for more current than the cable is capable of supplying. The individual branch circuit breakers protect the wiring after the breaker by not allowing more current to pass than the wire is capable of handling.

MAINTENANCE AND UPKEEP
Inspect the visible portions of the system occasionally, looking for frayed, damaged wires, and evidence of heat. Scorching, discoloration, evidence of arcing, overheating, or damage, are all reasons to call a qualified electrician for repairs. Slight overheating over a long period of time can cause copper wiring to crystallize. The wire will become brittle and may shatter.

5.5.4.3 COMPATIBILITY
The overcurrent device and the wire must be compatible with one another. The breaker or fuse must be capable of passing only the amount of current the wire is capable of handling.

Aluminum wire must be used with switches and devices with connectors compatible with aluminum. Many of the problems with aluminum wiring were caused by devices designed for copper wire only. Aluminum wire is larger than copper wire. Aluminum oxidizes, forming a coating not readily passing current. The screw heads were not sized to accommodate the larger wire. As a wire oxidized, heat developed, causing the wires to expand and contract and squirm from under the screws. Fires resulted.

Later devices were developed labeled CU-AL or CO/ALR. These devices had larger head screws of alloys compatible with aluminum and tended to solve the problems associated with aluminum wiring.

MAINTENANCE AND UPKEEP
Maintain compatibility as discussed above. Avoid overfusing (installing a breaker or fuse too large for the associated wire). It is dangerous.

Use devices labeled for use with aluminum wiring when making repairs.

5.5.5 GROUNDING AND BONDING
Grounding and bonding are important safety features in any electrical system. The neutral wire is part of the operating electrical system. It is used in 120 volt services as the second wire and provides for the operation of the light, motor, etc. The neutral wire returns current to the system. If a short circuit occurs and electricity is passed to the metal parts of a device, the ground wire carries current away to the ground. A bond wire is similar to a ground wire. It ties together various parts of the system or

systems. In other words the metal parts of the plumbing system may be bonded to the ground of the electrical system. If electricity is applied to the plumbing system, it will be carried to ground.

There was a time when most incoming water lines were metal and buried in the earth making an excellent ground. The plumbing and electrical systems tied together through the bond wire. The plumbing system provides the ground for the electrical system. Now many plumbing systems use plastic pipe, including a plastic incoming water line, and therefore the plumbing system is not "naturally" grounded. This requires one or more ground rods be driven and the electrical system connected to the ground rod through a ground wire. A second wire is installed from the electrical system as a bond to the plumbing system. The electrical system now grounds the plumbing system.

MAINTENANCE AND UPKEEP

Inspect the grounding system occasionally and be sure the ground wire has not been disconnected from the ground rod, etc. They are subject to lawn mower or rototiller damage. The plumbing system must remain bonded to the electrical system. If you install a new plastic incoming water line, you have "lost" the system ground. Have an electrician install a proper ground rod and properly ground the systems.

Properly grounding a system serves an additional function in allowing static charges to bleed away. If you are a lover of fine music and you want the ultimate in quiet operation of your stereo system you will find it necessary to have the system plugged into a properly grounded outlet. Also if you have a home computer you may find the system requires proper grounding and a "clean" circuit free from power surges etc. Some of these devices will not operate properly when plugged into a two wire system. They must have the ground.

A three prong grounded outlet requires a third wire in the system. One substitution allowing the use of three prong outlets in a two wire system is to use a GFCI or Ground Fault Current Interrupter outlet. This substitution does not provide actual grounding of the outlet but does provide a measure of safety for the occupants.

5.5.5.1 GROUNDING

The grounding system in most houses consists of one or more metal rods or pipes driven approximately 8 feet into the earth. In some locations grounding is provided by a metal rod or conductor installed in the footings or by the incoming metal water line. They connect to the electrical system with a ground conductor. Most of the grounding system is underground and not open for inspection. A system can and will operate on a day to day basis, but an ungrounded system has a potential to become dangerous if a short circuit applies electricity to parts of the system not normally energized. e.g. The metal cabinet of a refrigerator, range, motor, or the plumbing system.

MAINTENANCE AND UPKEEP

Inspect the grounding system occasionally to be sure it has not become detached or damaged. It should be maintained in proper working order for safety. Properly grounded systems may suffer less damage from a lightning strike than systems not properly grounded.

5.5.5.2 BONDING

Bonding is the practice of electrically tying together parts of a system or systems. The bond is usually a wire connecting the grounded portion of the electrical system to the plumbing system to maintain a "zero potential" between the two systems. The purpose is to provide a safe path for electricity to return to ground if some part of the plumbing system becomes energized.

MAINTENANCE AND UPKEEP

Do not allow the bond between the plumbing and electrical systems to become disconnected or damaged. The potential for electrocution exists if the system is not properly bonded.

5.5.6 TYPE

Wire types are classified here by the type of insulation used on the wire. In Romex cables, wires are bundled together and sheathed in an outer covering of plastic or vinyl. BX cable is metal sheathed and looks like a spiral or spring. An older system was knob and tubing wiring in which individual conductors were strung from porcelain "fence" insulators. Individual conductors run in conduit of either metal or plastic are common in commercial buildings but are somewhat rare in residences.

5.5.6.1 ROMEX

"Romex" is individually insulated conductors sheathed together in a fabric, rubber, vinyl, or plastic flexible coating. The fabric coatings have given way to a vinyl or plastic outer sheath and these wires now come in several varieties. Some are for direct burial. Others are for interior use in dry, protected locations.

MAINTENANCE AND UPKEEP

Inspect the visible portions of the wiring occasionally for evidence of fraying, wear and tear, heat damage, and rodent damage, etc. The wiring should be protected from abrasion and physical abuse. Any dangling wires should be properly supported. Any evidence the wiring system has deteriorated is cause to call a qualified competent electrician to repair the system.

5.5.6.2 METALLIC CABLE

Metallic Cable is the cable looking like a spiral or coil spring and commonly known as BX cable. BX cable offers the advantage of being tough and resistant to abrasion, abuse, rodent damage, etc. It is not waterproof and should not be exposed to the weather, directly buried, or submerged in water.

MAINTENANCE AND UPKEEP

Metallic sheathed wiring is subject to rusting and pulling loose from the connectors exposing sharp edges which may in turn cut the inner conductors. Inspect the system occasionally. Any evidence of damage to the system warrants calling a qualified competent electrician for repairs.

5.5.6.3 KNOB AND TUBING WIRING

Knob and tubing wiring is the oldest commercially successful wiring system in this country. The wiring was strung throughout the house on small insulators, similar to the white porcelain insulators on electric fences. Those were the knobs. The tubes were porcelain straws or tubes were inserted through holes in framing members to avoid abrasion on the wiring. The wires were single conductors and the hot and neutral wires were run ten or twelve inches apart.

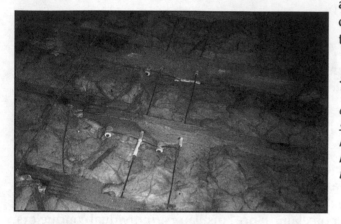

5.5.6.3 a. Knob and Tubing Wiring
The system has several drawbacks: One, the conductors, even though they appear large, are small by today's standards. Two, the system does not include a ground wire, therefore, unless protected by a GFCI or Ground Fault Current Interrupter device, the system cannot use three prong outlets.

This system is archaic and antiquated, but is still "legal." It has been grandfathered into the electrical codes, under the condition it is properly maintained. Maintenance is a problem because parts are difficult to get, and the current generation of electricians seems to have lost or forgotten the requirements and techniques for working with knob and tubing wiring. The system is aging and may be suffering from concealed damage such as dry rot or vermin damage to the insulation. Sometimes the individual conductors have been used for hangers, to hang up coat hangers in the attic or basement and the insulation has been worn off exposing the bare conductors.

MAINTENANCE AND UPKEEP

Replace knob and tubing wiring wherever practical because of its advancing age and archaic nature. Before continuing to use the system you should get advice from a qualified electrician or city building official.

5.5.6.4 CONDUIT

Conduit is tubing, (pipe) made of metal or plastic, used as channels or raceways to enclose wiring. Commercial buildings are often wired with conduit systems in which ridged conduit or lightweight tubing was run throughout the structure. Individual stranded conductors are inserted through the conduit to the various switches and devices. Conduit systems are rare in residential construction and are often confined to individual runs such as service entrance cable from the meter base to the main panel. PVC or plastic conduit is available.

MAINTENANCE AND UPKEEP

Not all pipes contain water. Ascertain what the pipe is and what it is for before you attempt to do any cutting, maintenance, or remodeling, etc. on the pipe. Sawing into a conduit containing electrical conductors can be a disaster. The conduit should be maintained properly anchored in the structure. Any evidence water is entering the conduit is cause to call a qualified electrician to examine this system and cure any problems it may have.

5.6 INTERIOR COMPONENTS

The interior components of the electrical system such as switches, lights, outlets etc. are the part of the system the owner lives with on a day to day basis. The modern electrical system is one of the great conveniences of this century, but there is a danger of electrocution.

MAINTENANCE AND UPKEEP

The interior components of the system should be kept in proper working order. Any cracked or damaged cover plates, switches, receptacles, etc. should be replaced as necessary by a qualified electrician. Any damaged light fixtures, etc. should be repaired or replaced promptly.

Maintain adequate lighting. Proper lighting is important to safety and comfort. Hallways and stairways should have bright, even lighting. There should be light switches at the top and bottom of steps and at both ends of halls. Switches should be convenient and usable without entering a dark room. The inspection takes place in daylight. Examine the house after dark and add lighting and switches for safety.

5.6.1 RECEPTACLES

Receptacles, commonly known as duplex receptacles or outlets, are the wall plugs allowing access to the wiring system. In other words, plugging a matching plug into a duplex receptacle connects some device (lamp, etc.) to the electrical system.

MAINTENANCE AND UPKEEP

Keep receptacles in proper working order. Repair or replace broken or damaged receptacles or cover plates promptly. There is a danger of electrocution and only qualified persons should attempt repairs. The outlets should be replaced with comparable outlets compatible with wiring in the system and capable of handling the amperage in that particular circuit. If you have aluminum wiring in the system, the outlets purchased as replacements must be compatible with aluminum wiring. Do not use outlets above ranges or stoves. Dangling cords may melt. Outlets above sinks or within six feet of plumbing fixtures should be on Ground Fault Current Interrupter protected circuits. (Read section 5.6.4 GFCI.)

5.6.2 SWITCHES

Switches control the flow of electricity within the system. The most common application is the wall switch, usually located beside the doors to the rooms. There are other types of switches and devices used to control the current such as breakers, switch boxes, etc.

MAINTENANCE AND UPKEEP

Keep switches in proper working order with cover plates in place. Repair or replace broken or damaged switches and cover plates promptly. Only qualified persons should attempt repairs. The replacement switches should be similar switches or devices capable of handling the current and compatible with the existing wiring. i.e. If you have aluminum wiring, the switches should be compatible with aluminum wiring.

Be sure switches are convenient for safety. If you must enter a darkened room to reach the switch, have additional switches installed nearer the door.

5.6.3 FIXTURES

Light fixtures are one of the most common attachments to the electrical system. The fixtures should be compatible with their usage. Maintain them in proper working order. Most common light fixtures are designed for dry locations such as bedrooms, dining rooms, and kitchens. Special water resistant or waterproof fixtures are sometimes used in bathrooms and are often required in showers, immediately above tubs, and other wet locations.

MAINTENANCE AND UPKEEP

Repair or replace any damaged fixtures preventing the possibility of shock or fire hazard. Replace with fixtures compatible with the wiring and the location. i.e. If you have aluminum wiring you must use fixtures and wire nuts compatible with aluminum wiring. Replace a specialized fixture with a similar type. Maintain adequate lighting. Only qualified electricians should make repairs.

5.6.4 GFCI

GFCI is a Ground Fault Current Interrupter. It is an electronic device located either in the panel box as a breaker or in a circuit as an outlet. These devices similar in function to a breaker or a fuse operate electronically to protect from a ground fault (a shock). A 15 amp breaker draws 16 to 20 amps of current for several seconds to trip. With a Ground Fault Current Interrupter the device trips on as little as five milli-amps and in a 40th of a second. Recently, these devices have been required for the outlets in bathrooms, outside outlets, garages, and kitchens. These are the most dangerous locations in the house and most likely to result in a shock.

MAINTENANCE AND UPKEEP

GFCI devices include a test button allowing you to exercise it. This is only a mechanical test, but you should trip these devices once a month to make sure they have not seized or frozen in the ON position. GFCI's can save your life.

Outlets can be wired together like a string of Christmas tree lights. The GFCI located in one bathroom can be protecting the outlets in another bathroom or the outside outlets. If you loose current in one bathroom outlet, you may have to look for the GFCI either in another outlet or in the panel and reset it. Often resetting a breaker GFCI requires manually turning the breaker off and turning it back on.

GFCI outlets allow the substitution of three prong outlets in a two wire service without the necessity of running the third wire. This may not provide the grounding required for good clean stereo sound or the proper operation of computers.

If you press the test button and find the device does not trip, replace it. Only qualified electricians should repair or replace them. Some devices, like fluorescent lights or microwave ovens, may generate false trips and you may not be able to plug these devices into a GFCI protected circuit.

5.6.5 SMOKE DETECTORS

Smoke detectors are economical and have wide spread acceptance and usage. They are required in new construction in many localities. Locate one or more per floor, on or near the ceiling, either battery powered or hard wired (wired directly into the wiring system of the house). Smoke detectors come in two varieties. One type is an ionization device and it detects the products of combustion. The other device is a photo electric type, with an electric eye looking for smoke.

MAINTENANCE AND UPKEEP

Most smoke detectors have a test button which you should press occasionally to be sure the device is operating. Keep your smoke detectors clean and dust free. The various types are subject to false tripping or false alarms. Dust or steam from the shower may set off the photo electric devices. Cooking fumes set off the ionization type. Experiment to find out which works best for you. It may be wise to have more than one type. In a power failure the hard wired devices cease to function. Use both battery powered and hard wired smoke detectors for the best protection.

Replace batteries as needed. Most smoke detectors include a sensor warning of a failing or weak battery. The warning is either a chirping noise as the battery weakens or a flag or other device. In the author's experience about half the smoke detectors in use do not work. Go test yours.

5.6.6 DEVICES

The type and number of electrical devices found in houses seems to be limited only by the imagination of the manufacturer's marketing. The inspection is limited to standard devices normally found in houses such as light fixtures and built-in appliances. Carefully inspect any other unusual or non standard devices included in your home not covered under the scope of the inspection. (Read your contract for the inspection and 5.1 Limitations.)

MAINTENANCE AND UPKEEP

Maintain electrical devices in safe working order. Check with the manufacturer of the devices for information on care and maintenance. Be aware of the danger of shock hazard. Only qualified electricians or service technicians should attempt to maintain electrical devices.

5.6.7 CLOSET LIGHTS

Closet lights are a popular feature and have gone through many changes in attitudes and building codes. They are of concern because closet lights are a source of residential fires.

A bare, exposed, incandescent bulb and a pull chain fixture were standard. These fixtures are hazardous if belongings on the closet shelves are too close to the bulb.

The next era in closet lights was the use of recessed lights. These often generated enough heat to either burn out or start fires. Another variation is to use fluorescent lights which generate less heat inside the closet. They do not have hot filaments.

MAINTENANCE AND UPKEEP
Closet lights are a convenience, but they should not be left on any longer than is necessary. This is particularly true of any incandescent bulb generating enough heat to cause a fire. Do not insulate over existing recessed lights. Never increase the bulb size beyond what is absolutely necessary to see in the closet. Most fixtures are labeled with a wattage size for the bulb and this should never be exceeded. Only qualified electricians should repair or replace damaged fixtures.

5.6.7.1 PULL CHAIN
Pull chain lights have fallen into disfavor because they have the potential to start fires. Many fabrics and packaging materials have low ignition temperatures and ignite from a light bulb left on in a confined space or from the filament of a broken light bulb. There are millions of pull chain lights in closets. Treat them with respect.

MAINTENANCE AND UPKEEP
Never install a higher wattage bulb than necessary. Never leave the light on longer than necessary or unattended. Should the fixture become broken or damaged have it properly repaired or replaced to eliminate the possibility of a shock hazard. Cap off and remove the fixtures in children's closets to prevent leaving them on. Only qualified electricians should repair or remove light fixtures.

5.6.7.2 RECESSED LIGHTS
As mentioned under section 5.6.7, recessed lights came in to use as an attempt to reduce the fire hazard associated with pull chain or bare bulb fixtures. Some recessed fixtures generated enough heat to serve as an ignition source. Most recessed light fixtures had to be installed without insulation over them. This leaves a hole in the insulation. There are some fixtures rated for direct burial in the insulation, but these are more expensive and rare.

MAINTENANCE AND UPKEEP
Do not cover recessed fixtures with insulation. This may cause heat build up in the fixture and serve as a source for fire. Never replace the bulbs with ones larger than the fixture's rating. Use bulbs as small as possible in wattage. Only qualified electricians should repair or replace the fixtures. Repair or replace damaged or broken fixtures immediately.

5.6.7.3 NONE
No closet lights. Read section 5.6.7 Closet Lights before installing closet lights.

5.7 EXTERIOR COMPONENTS

The exterior components of an electrical system can add greatly to the convenience, security, and safety of the home.

MAINTENANCE AND UPKEEP

Properly maintain exterior components of the system. They are subject to weather damage and physical abuse. Repair or replace damage promptly. Only qualified electricians should repair an electrical system. All materials and components should be rated for exterior use. Do not use interior fixtures or wiring. Install and maintain adequate lighting on walks, driveways, service walks, and entrances. Good exterior lighting discourages crime.

5.7.1 EXTERIOR RECEPTACLES

Exterior receptacles exposed to the weather must have a weatherproof cover. These covers have spring loaded doors which snap open to allow access to the receptacles and snap shut to seal against the weather. In newer construction exterior receptacles are protected by GFCI or Ground Fault Current Interrupter device. (Read section 5.6.4 GFCI.)

MAINTENANCE AND UPKEEP

Inspect exterior receptacles occasionally and repair or replace as necessary. Keep cover plates properly in place and sealed to prevent water entry into the system. Any physically damaged receptacles should be replaced promptly to prevent the hazard of electrical shock or electrocution. Only qualified electricians should repair the electrical system.

5.7.2 SWITCHES

Exterior switches must be rated for exterior use or enclosed and not subject to weather damage.

MAINTENANCE AND UPKEEP

Inspect exterior switches occasionally and keep them in good working order. Repair or replace any damaged, inoperable, or abused switches promptly. Only a qualified electrician should repair the electrical system.

5.7.3 FIXTURES

Only exterior type light fixtures should be exposed to the weather.

MAINTENANCE AND UPKEEP

Inspect the exterior light fixtures occasionally and protect them from physical abuse. Repair or replace any damaged or abused fixtures promptly to prevent the possibility of water entering the electrical system and the danger of shock or electrocution. Only qualified electricians should repair the electrical system.

5.7.4 DEVICES

As with interior devices the number and range of exterior electrical devices is limited only by the imagination of the manufacturers, marketers, and purchasers. The electrical inspection is limited to the standard electrical devices, outlets, and fixtures. Inspect your exterior electrical devices before closing. Bug zappers, motion detector switches, hot tubs, fish pond pumps, etc. are not inspected. See your contract for more details. Maintain these devices by following the manufacturer's recommendations and instructions.

MAINTENANCE AND UPKEEP

Inspect exterior electrical devices occasionally and keep them in proper working order. Only qualified electricians or service technicians should make repairs to the electrical devices. Maintain these devices by following the manufacturer's recommendations and instructions.

5.7.5 LIGHTNING RODS

Lightning rods and their associated cables and conductors are designed to shunt a lightning strike to the ground. Lightning rods are controversial.

MAINTENANCE AND UPKEEP

The inspector is not an expert on lightning rods. Get the manufacturer's or installer's instructions for the care and maintenance of the system. Only qualified service technicians should attempt to repair or maintain the system.

5.9 OBSERVATIONS

The inspector marks observations of conditions affecting the electrical system. More than one item can be marked as the electrical system may exhibit more than one symptom or problem. Some items are part of the normal aging process and do not require correction. Other items require either maintenance or repair if the electrical system is to reach the full potential or life expectancy. Read carefully each section applying to the system inspected.

Maintenance is the on going care required if a system or item is to reach the full potential including lubricating, painting, etc. Do maintenance as required by the manufacturer of the equipment or item. Repairs put items or systems back in good condition after damage or decay, etc. Repairs are caused by delayed maintenance, aging, normal wear and tear, or abuse. The workmanship and materials of the repairs should be equal to the quality of the system and have the same life expectancy. e.g. A limb plunges through an asphalt shingle roof. If the roofing otherwise has a life expectancy of ten years, the repair should also have a life expectancy of at least ten years. If the roofing only has a life expectancy of one year, then the repair should be capable of lasting one year or more. It is not prudent to put a one year patch on a ten year roof or to waste a ten year repair on a one year roof. All repairs should be by qualified competent professionals.

Repairs or additions to the electrical system should bring at least that section of the system into compliance with present Codes. Antiquated parts of the system should be upgraded and modernized as soon as practical. If you are remodeling, upgrade the electrical system at the same time. Where possible replace knob and tube wiring and older two wire systems with modern grounded wiring and include Ground fault protection, Smoke Detectors, etc. Do not attempt repairs yourself unless you are sure you are qualified and fully insured. Always work carefully and safely.

5.9.1 SOUND

The inspector thinks the item inspected is functioning at the moment of the inspection. This does not imply perfection, absence of minor defects, or absence of wear and tear.

5.9.2 TYPICAL

The inspector thinks the item, material, or aspect of construction is characteristic or similar to comparable products in similar houses. The electrical system has normal wear and tear.

5.9.3 OBSTRUCTIONS/DAMAGED/LOOSE/MISSING/LOW

These observations refer to the service entrance or incoming overhead power line:

OBSTRUCTION	A tree limb or structure touches or could touch the line.
DAMAGED	The line appears to be physically damaged.
LOOSE	The line appears to be inadequately anchored.
DAMAGED	The incoming overhead power line is damaged
MISSING	The incoming overhead power line is absent.
LOW	The incoming overhead power line is too low and presents the possibility of a contact or shock hazard.

Usually the local power company performs maintenance on this aspect of the system, but probably only at your request.

5.9.4 MAST DAMAGE

Sometimes overhead power lines enter through a pipe or mast rising above the level of the roof or sidewall. Mast damage ranges from the mast creating a roof leak to physical damage to the mast itself. e.g. A tree limb falling on the incoming power line applies enough force to bend the mast or dislocate it.

This portion of the system may be maintained by the local power company. They will probably perform maintenance only at your request.

5.9.5 WEATHERHEAD MISSING/ LOOSE/ DAMAGED

The weatherhead is the hooded device used to make the connection between the service entrance drop and the service entrance cable.

MISSING	The weatherhead is missing or absent from the system and there should be one present.

LOOSE   The weatherhead is not properly anchored and has pulled away from the structure.

DAMAGED   The weatherhead appears to be physically damaged and incapable of performing its function safely.

5.9.6 NOT SUPPORTED

The service drop is not supported. If the incoming power line or service drop is long enough, it must be supported by a cable. This is a weather resistant steel cable capable of spanning the distance between the pole and the house and physically supporting the service drop. The mechanical strain is born by the cable. This aspect of the system is most probably the responsibility of the local power company, however you have to request maintenance.

5.9.7 CONDUIT RUSTED OR DAMAGED

The conduit is rusted or physically damaged. The section of the service lateral rising from the ground to the meter base should be protected by a conduit.   Some localities use PVC or

plastic conduits. They are subject to damage by lawn mowers, rototillers, bush hogs, and other vehicles. This aspect of your system may be maintained by the local power company, but you may have to request maintenance.

5.9.8 a. Abandoned Equipment.
Some of this antiquated wiring was still energized.

5.9.8 ABANDONED EQUIPMENT OR WIRING

The inspector sees abandoned equipment or wiring. Be sure the equipment is not energized as a minimum. It may also be wise to remove the abandoned equipment or wiring from the property to prevent accidents.

5.9.9 CABINET LOOSE, RUSTED, OR DAMAGED

The meter base, main panel, or subpanel is LOOSE or pulled away from the structure, RUSTED or corroding, or physically DAMAGED. A damaged meter base may be repaired by the local power company at your request. If the damage is to a panel, a qualified competent electrician may be able to repair or replace it.

5.9.10 SEAL BROKEN

The seal on the cabinet is broken. Most power companies seal the meter base or cabinet to prevent current theft, tampering, and injury or electrocution. Contact the local power company before closing and have the meter base or cabinet inspected and the seal properly reinstalled.

5.9.12 INTERIOR PHYSICAL DAMAGE

Physical Damage on the inside of the main panel or subpanels. This ranges from broken fuse holders, to misaligned or damaged buss bars, etc. Any substantially damaged switch gear should be repaired or replaced to prevent the possibility of injury from short circuits, fire, or other hazards. Only qualified competent electricians should repair electrical equipment. Parts of this equipment remain energized always. There is real danger of electrocution.

5.9.13 CROWDED

This is a judgment call. Crowding may not be a defect, but indicates the system is fully extended and may be a candidate for upsizing or replacement.

5.9.14 DOUBLE TAP

Two wires connected to the same screw or lug in the panel. Most panel connectors are designed to accept only one wire. Double taps come in several varieties.

The simplest of double taps is two wires of similar amperage and similar metals (i.e. two twenty amp copper wires) connected to a twenty amp fuse or breaker. Another is two wires of dissimilar sizes (i.e. 15 amp wire and a 20 amp wire) connected to the same fuse or breaker. A third is two wires of dissimilar metals (i. e. a copper and aluminum wire) connected to the same fuse or breaker.

All double taps are technically unacceptable, however, two wires of a similar size and similar metal connected to a breaker appropriate for either wire, (i.e. two 20 amp copper wires connected to a 20 amp fuse) is the least objectionable of double taps. The circuit may be over taxed but either wire is capable of handling all the current available from the fuse and therefore the system is reasonably safe. It may blow fuses occasionally.

If the wires are of dissimilar sizes then the flaw should be corrected. If the double tap is two wires of similar metals but of dissimilar sizes, the smaller amperage wire dictates the amperage of the fuse or breaker. The fuse has no way of knowing which wire is getting which amp and the wires do not add up.

If the wires are of dissimilar metals, have the connections separated by a qualified electrician.

Double taps are an indication the panel is crowded and the system has been extended beyond its reasonable capacity. This may indicate the system should be upsized in both the number of available circuits and amperage. Double taps are common in fuse panels because of the limited number of available circuits.

5.9.14 a. Double Taps
Note the two wires connected together to the same breaker in the center of the picture.

5.9.15 MIXED METALS

Wires of different metals (i.e. copper and aluminum) joined improperly. There are problems resulting from this ranging from an overheating of the connection to a possible corrosion or displacement of some of the metal in the connection. Mixed metals must always join through proper connectors. Only qualified electricians should repair electrical systems.

5.9.16 OVERFUSING

Overfusing applies to both fuses and breakers and is an indication the overcurrent device is too large for the wire connected to it. Overfusing is dangerous, allowing more current flow than the wire is capable of handling. In simple cases correcting overfusing may be as easy as replacing the fuses with ones of proper size. In complex cases you will need the assistance of a qualified electrician. (See 5.9.17 Service undersized.)

5.9.17 SERVICE UNDERSIZED

The service entrance cable (i.e. the wire running from the meter base or weatherhead to the main interior panel) is undersized for the size of the panel. This is overfusing of the service entrance cable. The panel or system can ask for more current than the service entrance cable is capable of providing safely and is a fire hazard. Correcting an undersized service requires replacement of the inadequate parts of the system by a qualified competent electrician. (See also 5.4.4 Overfusing and 5.5.4.3 Compatibility.)

5.9.20 UNENCLOSED SPLICES

Splices not enclosed in proper boxes. Any splices in the wiring are to be made inside proper boxes accessible for repair and inspection. An exception is the knob and tubing wiring system. Air splices or unenclosed splices were legal and acceptable in that system. They should be regarded as potentially hazardous. Only qualified electricians should make repairs to electrical systems. (See 5.5.6.3 Knob and Tubing.)

5.9.20 a. Unenclosed Splice.
The box is supposed to anchor the wires and contain the flash if there is a short or arc. It also protects the owner and repairmen from accidentally contacting the wires. Have proper boxes installed.

5.9.21 LOOSE/DAMAGED/SPLICED GROUND

The ground connection is LOOSE or improperly connected, the wire physically DAMAGED, or the ground wires are SPLICED. The ground wire is a single unspliced conductor running from the main panel to a proper ground rod and properly clamped to the rod. If the wire is damaged or spliced it should be repaired or replaced. If the connections are loose, they should be properly secured. Only qualified electricians should make repairs to electrical systems.

5.9.22 NO GROUND OR NO BOND

No ground or no bond seen. Compliance with the National Electric Code requires the electrical system be properly grounded and properly bonded. Grounding is the connection of the system to either a proper ground rod or grounded metal water pipe. If the incoming water line is plastic or the water system has no ground of its own, it should be grounded through the electrical system. The water system should be bonded to the electrical system to assure a zero potential between the two systems. All electrical systems should be properly grounded and bonded. Only qualified electricians should make these repairs.

5.9.23 GROUNDED OR BONDED TO GAS PIPING

The electrical system is grounded through or bonded to the gas piping. Contact the local gas company for their working rules on this practice. If gas service is eliminated or converted to plastic pipe, have a qualified electrician ground the system.

5.9.24 UNBONDED SERVICE EQUIPMENT

The main panel and meter base should be bonded to one another by using bonding connectors or a bond wire. The service equipment is not properly bonded. The equipment should be properly bonded by a reputable electrician in accordance with local codes.

5.9.25 DAMAGED OR FRAYED WIRING

The wiring is physically damaged or the sheath or covering on the wire is frayed, potentially exposing the conductors. Repair or replace the damaged wiring immediately to reduce the potential for fire and shock hazards. Only qualified electricians should repair electrical systems.

5.9.26 EXPOSED WIRING

There is exposed wiring having a potential to create a shock hazard or fire hazard. Wiring should be concealed within the structure or protected by conduit or other protective enclosures. Have a qualified electrician move or properly enclose the wiring.

5.9.27 ALUMINUM WIRING IN 120 VOLT BRANCH CIRCUITS

Aluminum was used as a conductor in wiring in the 60's and 70's and is controversial. Fires were associated with the use of aluminum wire because of its tendency to generate heat at terminals. Aluminum wiring is "legal" under the National Electric Code. It must be properly connected to devices rated for use with aluminum wiring, such as switches and outlets marked CU-AL or CO/ALR. The question of the safety of aluminum wiring is a controversial one. Refer to other literature in the field.

5.9.28 METALLIC WIRING OR CABLE

Metallic wiring, known as BX cable, is the wire in which the conductor is wrapped with a spring like coil of metal serving as a ground protecting the wire. In some localities BX or metallic cable is still common, but in most parts of the country it has been supplanted by Romex or soft covered cables. (See 5.5.6.2 Metallic wiring.)

5.9.29 KNOB AND TUBING WIRING

Knob and tubing wiring was the first successful wiring system in this country and in many localities has not been installed for over 50 years. Conductors are strung from porcelain knobs or in tubes through framing members. The individual conductors are 10 to 12 inches apart. The system, though still legal, is old and not designed to meet modern day demands. It does not have a ground wire. Replace knob and tubing wiring wherever feasible. (Read 5.5.6.3 Knob and Tubing.)

5.9.32 LOOSE OR DAMAGED RECEPTACLES

Repair or replace loose, dangling, cracked or damaged receptacles. Keep cover plates properly in place. Only qualified electricians should make repairs to electrical systems.

5.9.33 IMPROPERLY WIRED RECEPTACLES

There are three wires connected to three terminals on each three prong receptacle. The wires can be incorrectly arranged. Reversed polarity or an open ground may be minor defects, but some combinations of wiring are hazardous. Correct improperly wired receptacles to prevent possible harm and shock hazards. The rewiring of receptacles should only be done by an electrician.

5.9.34 DAMAGED OR BROKEN SWITCHES

There are broken or damaged switches. Repair or replace damaged switches to operate properly and safely. Keep cover plates over the switches. Make repairs promptly and only by electricians.

5.9.35 DAMAGED OR MISSING FIXTURES

Damaged or missing light fixtures include fixtures with parts missing, exposed electrical components, dangling fixtures, or missing fixtures exposing the contents of the junction or hanger box. Replace or repair damaged or missing fixtures promptly to operate properly and safely. Only a qualified electrician should make repairs to electrical systems. Replacement fixtures should be proper for the locations.

5.9.36 IMPROPER FIXTURES

An interior type fixture used on the exterior is used improperly. Water could get into the fixture. A non-water resistant fixture in a shower or other wet location can be hazardous. Improper fixtures have the potential to be a shock or fire hazard. Replace improper fixtures promptly with correct ones. Only electricians should make repairs to the electrical system.

5.9.37 NO GFCI

A Ground Fault Current Interrupter device can protect the user of the electrical system from shock hazards. Some localities require GFCIs in certain locations. Commonly required locations are exterior outlets, bathroom outlets, garage outlets, and kitchen outlets. These devices can save your life. If your home does not have them, have an electrician install them. One GFCI device may protect several outlets.

5.9.38 GFCI BROKEN

The GFCI fails to trip and reset properly from either an induced ground fault condition, caused by the inspector's test device, or from pressing the test button, which trips the device mechanically. Repair or replace broken GFCI devices promptly. Only electricians should make repairs to the electrical system.

5.9.39 NO SMOKE DETECTOR

Many localities require smoke detectors in residential properties. Smoke detectors are inexpensive and are available in several versions. Some are battery operated and some "hard wired," or operating directly from the electrical current. Smoke detectors are recommended as warning devices for fire. Have one or more operating from the electrical system and one or more operating from batteries as a back up if the power fails. Some smoke detectors have rechargeable batteries allowing them to continue operating after the power fails.

5.9.40 SMOKE DETECTOR BROKEN

The smoke detector is not functioning properly, i.e. fails to respond either to its test button or to test conditions (spray or smoke). Repair or replace broken smoke detectors promptly. Some smoke detectors are hard wired or wired into the electrical system. Some are wired into alarm systems. Repairs should only be made by electricians or qualified technicians.

5.9.41 LACK OF COVER PLATES

There are missing cover plates for the switches or outlets. Cover plates over switches and outlets cover the openings into the electrical box and protect innocents and children from inserting objects or fingers into the boxes and getting shocked. Replace any missing cover plates promptly.

5.9.44 DAMAGED LIGHTNING ROD SYSTEM

The lightning system is damaged. Lightning systems are unusual and many have fallen into disrepair. Damage could include physical damage, the chains or cables disconnected from the ground rods, or parts missing. Lightning systems are not in the scope of a home inspection. Contact a knowledgeable local authority on lightning systems. Have the system inspected and repaired before closing.

5.9.45 CONTACT HAZARD

The inspector sees bare or an exposed wire(s). (i.e. Overhead conductors, frayed or damaged wiring.) Some part of the electrical system such as the cabinet of the main panel or the range or refrigerator etc. has become electrified. Eliminate contact hazards immediately. Turn off the power until repairs are complete. Only qualified electricians should make repairs.

5.9.46 INAPPROPRIATE WIRE

The inspector sees inappropriate wiring. An example would be the use of wiring designed for interior use, normally marked NM, underground or underwater. The wiring type required for use underground is UF. The use of inappropriate wire has the potential to be a shock or fire hazard. Repair or replace the wire as soon as possible. Only qualified electricians should make repairs.

5.9.46 a. Inappropriate Wire
The small single strand white wire is inappropriate in this location. It is unprotected by a conduit or sheath. This represents a possible amateur workmanship. The junction box needs a cover. This should be corrected by a qualified electrician.

CHAPTER SIX

HEATING/FIREPLACE

Central heating systems as we know them today have become the accepted norm, but not so long ago that was not true. Fireplaces have been in use a long time and are still a source of joy and danger. As with the electrical system, the heating system can add to your comfort and pleasure, but there is danger also. Someone dies of carbon monoxide poisoning nearly every month in this country. Any fired heating system or appliance and any fireplace can be a source of carbon monoxide. As we make our houses tighter and more energy efficient, the level of carbon monoxide and the likelihood of injury may increase.

Aging flues pose a threat. It is expensive to rebuild or reline older flues and many are in use without proper lining. Installing new high efficiency equipment into old, worn, unlined or damaged flues can be dangerous.

MAINTENANCE AND UPKEEP

Maintain your heating equipment and fireplaces in good working order. Yearly maintenance inspection contracts with reputable heating contractors is a good investment. Oil fired systems must be cleaned and tuned annually and gas systems at least every two years. Even heat pumps benefit. Some manufacturers claim that a properly maintained heat pump will operate 30% more efficiently and last 50% longer. The fee for the service is small and probably a good investment even if the claims are exaggerated. Don't ignore your flues. Have them cleaned and inspected regularly by a reputable chimney sweep and keep them in good repair. If the flue fails, you may fail to wake up.

6.1 LIMITATIONS ON THE INSPECTION

This section describes the aspects limiting the inspection of the heating system. Inspectors do the best inspection they can, but sometimes physical obstructions, weather conditions, or the condition of the heating system, prevent them from doing the whole job. Arrange for an inspection overcoming the limitations, if possible. An uninspected heating system or a severely limited inspection could be a total unknown. The inspector is a generalist with broad knowledge on many topics and does not represent he knows or can see everything about every system. A limited or restricted inspection may not give you the information you need. It is your responsibility to overcome the limitations. You should complete the inspection prior to closing even if you must hire others (service technicians, heating contractor's, etc.) or pay an additional fee to the inspector or industry specialist. Repairs can be expensive and at some point replacement is the best alternative. An uninspected system or one given a severely limited or restricted inspection could be a total unknown. The inspector cannot make representations about what was not inspected. If you close on the house with a Limited or Restricted inspection you are accepting the responsibility for the unknown items about the system. You may have to resort to service technicians who dismantle, test, and inspect the particular name brand and type of equipment.

6.1.1 TYPICAL

The inspector feels they have seen as much of the heating system as they normally see. Typically, the heating system is viewed from arm's length, but not dismantled. The inspection of every system is limited. Some parts of every system are hidden from view and can only be inspected indirectly or not at all. Heat exchangers and combustion chambers are good examples. Often less than 10% of either can be seen. We can't report on the 90% we can't see. Also a problem taking 4 hours to manifest itself cannot be found during a two to three hour inspection. Occasionally systems have no problem running satisfactorily for a test run but fail after a longer run or under more severe conditions. (Also read section 6.1 Limitations.)

6.1.2 RESTRICTED

The inspector feels they have seen less of the heating system than they typically see. (Also read section 6.1.1 Typical.)

6.1.2.1 NO FUEL OR HEAT OFF

The system cannot be operated without fuel or electricity. A shut down system is not lit or run. The inspector will not turn on the electricity or bring fuel or water to the site. It is often unsafe to start equipment "shut down" for a season. Repairs may be incomplete. Turning on the water to a boiler with a radiator removed or frozen can result in a flood. The system must be "up and running" for the inspection. The inspector will not make representations about items not inspected or operating at the time of the inspection. Arrange to turn ON the fuel or power, start the system, and inspect before closing. (Also read section 6.1.2 Restricted.)

6.1.2.2 PILOT LIGHT OUT

The pilot light is not lit. Light the pilot light before the inspector arrives. Inspectors do not light pilot lights or start systems. This is for the safety of the property and the inspector. Sometimes equipment is unsafe or damaged and may cause an accident if started.

The equipment was not run and the inspector has made no inspection of its operation. Arrange for a reinspection after the unit is lit. (Also read section 6.1.2 Restricted.)

6.1.2.3 FAILED TO RESPOND

The system failed to respond to its normal controls. Beyond checking the same switches and fuses the homeowner would ordinarily check, the inspector will make no attempt to override the controls or use any internal resets designed for use by service technicians. Make arrangements to have the system started by the owner or a service technician. Reinspect the heating system before closing. (Also read section 6.1.2 Restricted.)

6.1.2.4 HAZARDOUS

The system was not run because it was hazardous. The absence of some necessary safety device or the condition of the equipment make it unsafe. Oil fired equipment flooded with oil is unsafe to operate. Make arrangements to have the system repaired or replaced and inspected before closing. (Also read section 6.1.2 Restricted.)

6.1.2.5 NONINSPECTED ACCESSORIES OR UNDERGROUND TANK

Many accessory type items are not inspected or are indirectly inspected. An example of indirect inspection is a humidifier inspected only for the damage they may cause to the rest of the system. (e.g. Rusting heat exchangers, air handlers, ductwork, etc.) Humidifiers are not tested for operation or effectiveness of humidification. Clock thermostats (night time set back) are not tested through all their cycles. They are only checked as basic thermostats. The function of electronic air cleaners is not checked. Contact the manufacturer for service. (Read 6.3.2 Oil For Underground Tanks, also read section 6.1.2 Restricted.)

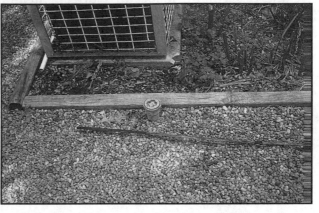

6.1.2.5 a. Underground Tank
The fill pipe indicates an underground oil tank. Such tanks remain in place long after they are abandoned. They may be leaking oil and expensive to remove.

6.1.2.6 EQUIPMENT OR FIREPLACE INACCESSIBLE

The inspection was physically limited or restricted more than typically. A boiler blocked by the owners' possessions, or a furnace in a crawl space or an attic too small to enter are inaccessible. Probably the most common example is an insert in the fireplace. A fire burning makes a fireplace flue inaccessible for inspection. (Read section 6.10.2 Stoves and Inserts.)

The inspector will not remove possessions or inserts to make the inspection. For his own safety, he will not enter confined or unsafe spaces. Arrange proper access and reinspect before closing. (Also read section 6.1.2 Restricted.)

6.1.2.7 NOT TESTED AS A HEAT PUMP

It is unsafe to run a heat pump, in the heat pump mode, when the outside temperature is above 75 degrees Fahrenheit at the time of the inspection. Under these conditions it could damage the equipment. The system will be tested in the back up mode for electric heating and as an air conditioner, if possible. The refrigerant may leak out from disuse causing poor performance. (Also read section 6.1.2 Restricted.)

6.1.2.8 SOLAR SYSTEM

No inspection is made of solar heating systems. These systems, specifically excluded from the inspection, will only be mentioned where they affect other systems (e.g. plumbing, roofing, and heating).

Learn about the system from the previous owners of the property and the seller/installer/maintenance people familiar with the system. Many solar systems carry high risks of freezing, high maintenance costs, and a danger of contaminating the domestic water system with antifreeze. Many are the products of inspired amateurs and many are being removed. (Also read section 6.1.2 Restricted.)

6.2 GENERAL

A quick reference and overview of the inspector's opinions or impressions. This section is subjective and relies on the inspector's judgement and experience in estimating the age, whether clues are important and if toxins are present, etc. (Read the heating chapter fully before forming any final opinion.)

6.2.1 SYSTEM INSPECTED (YES, RESTRICTED, OR NO)

The inspector marks whether the system was inspected. No information will be given about a system that was not inspected. If the inspector writes in or circles "R" for restricted, the system was partially inspected. Check 6.1 LIMITATIONS or discuss it with the inspector to learn the full extent of the restrictions. A severely limited inspection may not give you the information you need. You should do whatever is necessary to remove or overcome the restrictions and have the system fully inspected before you close on the house. (Read 6.1 Limitations.)

6.2.2 APPROXIMATE OR ESTIMATED AGE

The inspector's opinion of the estimated age of the heating system. It is impossible to tell the actual age of the heating equipment. Many things affect the aging process such as the original quality of the system, etc. The inspector is making the broadest of assumptions. Sometimes the dates are clearly imprinted on the equipment or are easy to decipher from the serial numbers. Often they are not. We do not carry cross reference indexes for manufacturers. If you wish to know the exact age, contact the manufacturer and give them the make, model and serial numbers. They may be able to help.

6.2.3 NUMBER OF ZONES OR SYSTEMS

This section points out the number of zones or separate systems. Multiple zones may give better control of comfort in different areas or levels.

6.2.4 ESTIMATED REMAINING LIFE

Remaining life is similar to estimated age and is a subjective judgment of the inspector and is the broadest of terms. It is the inspector's opinion of an estimation of remaining life in terms of years.

This always assumes proper maintenance and fuel. This is the broadest of assumptions and is for the system with the shortest life or on the major system.

6.2.5 ACTIVE FUEL LEAKS

Fuel is leaking from the system or its associated piping or tanks. It may also indicate exposed quantities of raw fuel (puddles of fuel or earth wet with raw fuel) or gas smelled or detected during the inspection. Cure leaks and clean up and remove raw or spilled fuel immediately to reduce the risk of explosion or fire. Leave this work to professionals. Fuel is also an ecological hazard.

6.2.6 AIR OR WATER LEAKS

There is damaged ductwork on air systems or leaking piping or boiler on water or steam systems. (Read Sections 6.8.4 Duct Work and 6.9.3 Distribution System.) These can range from minor repairs to system replacement. Corrections should be made immediately to prevent energy loses, system damage or damage to the structure.

6.2.7 ROOMS WITHOUT HEAT

The lack of either central heat or permanently installed space heating in a room or rooms. This limits the usefulness (value) of a space and can have serious consequences (pipes freezing, etc.).

6.2.8 CAPACITY

This is the rated input capacity (read from the label) of the heating system where it can be readily ascertained. This is in BTUH (British Thermal Units per hour) or tons (12,000 BTUH each). A BTU is the amount of heat required to warm one pound of water one degree Fahrenheit. The inspector does not do a heat loss/heat gain calculation and therefore makes no representation about the adequacy of the system.

6.2.9 TEMPERATURE RISE

The amount the air is heated each time it passes through the system. Forty-five to seventy-five degrees is appropriate for gas or oil furnaces and 14 to 20 degrees is acceptable for heat pumps.

6.2.10 FLAME COLOR

Flame color applies to gas and oil fired equipment. This is a subjective judgment and reflects whether the burner requires service and adjustment to burn properly. Gas burns with a blue flame and oil with a bright yellow flame. (Read section 6.3 Type of Fuel.)

6.2.11 NUMBER OF FIREPLACES

The number of fireplaces inspected. If split (1/3) it is one (1) inspected of three (3) fireplaces in the house. This does not imply any deficiencies observed by the inspector.

6.2.12 AMATEUR WORKMANSHIP (YES OR NO)

"YES"   The inspector notes workmanship of less than professional quality. Poor workmanship may constitute a major defect. Major defects cost $500.00 or more to repair or may affect the habitability of the house. The work may not serve the purpose intended and may require repair or replacement.

"NO"   No amateur workmanship noted. Some amateurs produce workmanship of equal or better quality than professionals.

6.2.13 SUBJECTIVE RATING
The inspector's grade for the heating system:

E   EXCELLENT, above average, new or like new. (e.g. A new heating system in an older house.)

A   AVERAGE, in typical condition for its age, showing normal wear and tear. (e.g. Five year old heating system looking 5 years old and a 5 year old house.)

C   BELOW AVERAGE, prematurely aged, showing heavy or excess wear and tear, or delayed maintenance. Perhaps showing minor (curable) defects. (e.g. A five year old heating system showing the wear and tear or age characteristics of a 10 year old heating system.)

F   SUBSTANDARD, failed, or reaching the end of its life expectancy. Any further service, even with repairs, should be considered a gift.

6.3 TYPES OF FUEL
This section reports the type of fuel or fuels in use. Read the section on your fuel carefully. Each type has different characteristics, advantages, disadvantages, and maintenance requirements. Although not interchangeable, some equipment is designed for different burner assemblies and different fuels. Most equipment is designed for one fuel type and suffers in performance if converted to another. The most common conversions are probably coal boilers converted to oil and their efficiency may be low.

6.3.1 GAS
Gas fired heating equipment is common in some areas. Natural gas is available from municipal or utility pipe lines in most major urban areas and has traditionally been an economical and clean source of heat.

Natural gas is largely methane with traces of propane, butane, isobutane, etc. and is lighter than air, colorless, and odorless. Both natural gas and propane are laced with a powerful odor to make even small leaks obvious. Natural gas contains about 1000 BTU's per cubic foot (a therm) and burns with a bright blue flame under proper conditions. Pressure in the lines varies but the gas pressure to your appliances is regulated to about 1/4 psi.

Propane (bottled gas) is propane and traces of methane, butane, and isopropane, etc., and is heavier than air, colorless, and odorless. It also burns with a bright blue flame when burned properly. It contains about 2 1/2 times as much heat energy per cubic foot as natural gas and operates at different pressures.

The tremendous differences in the heat energy content and pressures means the two are not readily interchangeable. Substantial changes must be made to convert a natural gas appliance (furnace, boiler, etc.) to propane or vice versa. Leave this work to professionals. Never connect a device to the wrong gas. Explosions and fire may result.

Gas or its fumes from properly burning appliances are not poisonous. The gas and fumes should be avoided because they displace the air (oxygen) and you could drown or suffocate. The fumes from a poorly adjusted device could be poisonous (carbon monoxide among others). Avoid the fumes and keep your equipment in good repair and properly adjusted. Obviously, raw (unburned) gas presents a fire and explosion hazard.

Unvented or improperly vented appliances can exhaust combustion fumes into the living space. (The vent is the chimney or flue.) These fumes can displace the oxygen, or replace it with carbon monoxide and cause drowsiness, brain damage, and death.

Flue gases also contain moisture vapor. One of the combustion by-products of burning oxygen and a hydrocarbon fuel is water, in the form of steam. If this vents inside the structure, it creates moisture as it condenses on cool walls and windows. Properly maintain any gas burners and venting to reduce harmful emissions and to carry the by-products and fumes outside.

Never sleep with an unvented gas appliance burning in the house. They compete for the available oxygen and you may die.

Gas may be piped to various appliances or devices. Natural gas is often piped in black (ungalvanized) iron pipe but may be in plastic, copper, or galvanized iron. Some utility companies object to the use of copper and some to plastic. Copper sometimes flakes off in the lines and clogs orifices or fuel filters. Propane can use any of them and often uses copper. Be careful doing plumbing repairs, some pipes are gas lines.

MAINTENANCE AND UPKEEP

Homeowner maintenance of any gas fired equipment consists of keeping the burner area clean and unobstructed. Have the local gas company or a service technician show you how to clean each piece of your equipment the first time. Learn how to light the pilot light. With the pilot off, clean the burner area of loose rust, scale, and dust using your vacuum cleaner and a soft brush. Have the technician show you how to remove and replace the "roll out" shield (a thin metal plate) for better access. This metal plate helps funnel the flame back inside the heat exchanger during ignition.

Once cleaned, examine it for holes or leaks in the heat exchanger. The clues to holes may be unusually heavy or large chunks of rust. Leaking boilers or water heaters may be more obvious. Relight the burner and start the piece of equipment (turn up the thermostat). The flame should be blue. If there is yellow or pink in the flame, call a service technician for an adjustment. Keep your face away from equipment about to ignite. It can puff or "wolf out" and burn you. Have this equipment adjusted.

Watch the flames in your gas furnace (warm air) as the fan runs. If the flames flicker and dance, or blow around, you may have a hole in the heat exchanger, allowing room air into the combustion chamber and flue gases into the house. Look for evidence of scorching on the cabinet and flue. Call for an inspection or service technician.

Inspect the flue pipes and chimneys for holes, rust, or blockages. Replace or repair any damaged equipment immediately. Have the flue cleaned (swept) and inspected at least every five years. People have died from loose bricks collapsing inward or other debris blocking the flue.

Properly maintained gas equipment is safe, economical, clean and pleasant to live with. Poorly maintained equipment can be deadly. If you smell gas, leave. Do not touch light switches or breakers. Do not use the phone. Leave the door open. Go somewhere else and call the gas company or fire department for help.

6.3.2 OIL

Oil fired heating equipment is common and includes furnaces, boilers, and units converted from coal or wood. Oil fired domestic hot water heaters are occasionally seen. The most common fuel in use is No. 2 fuel oil and is suitable for use in gun type (power) burner units. This fuel contains about 140,000 BTU's per gallon and is chemically similar to diesel fuel. (Do not try it in your Mercedes, it is too dirty and will ruin the engine.)

Most equipment pumps the fuel through a filter and a nozzle to atomize it. There is a blower mixing the spray with air and a high voltage electrode igniting the fuel/air mixture. This type of gun burner assembly has been retrofitted onto many old coal fired boilers, converting them to oil. The flame retention type do a better job of burning the fuel in a tightly contained shape in mid-air. These put less heat onto the surrounding walls of the combustion chamber, allowing more of it to pass through the heat exchanger and into the living space. These burners normally burn with a bright yellow flame when properly adjusted. There is a more sophisticated "blue flame" burner available. These efficient sealed units atomize the oil and burn at high temperatures with a blue flame. These units are rare.

Maintain the burner and equipment properly. Poorly adjusted, dirty, or sooted equipment is inefficient and can become dangerous and self destructive. The higher temperatures of today's burners are putting a strain on older equipment. Often combustion chambers must be relined or auxiliary liners installed. Burners must be adjusted to burn in mid-air, not blast the fuel/air mix against the walls and burn it. Once the refractory fails, the metal behind it may fail in minutes or hours.

"Pot" type equipment and space heaters do not have a power burner and must use No. 1 fuel oil or kerosene. Number one (No. 1) fuel oil has about 135,800 BTU's per gallon. These fuels are slightly more volatile than No. 2 fuel oil and are suitable for units where the oil flows into a pot and burns or for units relying on a wick. Always follow the manufacturer's directions for the type of fuel to buy. Using the wrong fuel can result in poor performance and can be dangerous.

MAINTENANCE AND UPKEEP

All manufacturers of oil fired heating equipment recommend annual service and cleaning of the equipment. This service should include cleaning the heat exchanger, changing oil filters and nozzles, testing and calibrating burner, etc. This service is essential if the equipment is to perform properly, safely and efficiently, and last its normal life expectancy.

Leave this work to competent professionals. They should be equipped to measure the performance of the burner and to adjust it properly. On any unfamiliar piece of equipment it would be best to have it serviced and tuned so you start with a "clean slate." Have service technicians explain to you what maintenance you can perform.

The homeowner should lubricate any circulating pumps or blower motors twice a season and inspect and change air filters every 30 days or as needed. You should keep the area around the unit clean and free of debris and be sure the unit has an adequate supply of combustion air. It needs one cubic foot per minute for each 3000 BTUH it is rated for.

Do not make your furnace room (or your house) so tight the burner sucks air back down the chimney. If you see soot around your registers or on the outside of flue pipe joints, you have a problem. It may be a hole in the heat exchanger, too little air returning in the duct system, restricted combustion air, etc. If you smell flue gases or fuel oil in the house, you have a problem. You should call an inspector or service technician to find the problem immediately. Some of these problems are not only dirty, they are hazardous. The equipment could be burning the air you breath and replacing it with dangerous fumes.

Have the flue for oil fired equipment swept and inspected every five years or as needed. Properly installed and maintained oil fired equipment is reasonably clean and efficient and pleasant to live with. Poorly maintained or damaged equipment can be dangerous and deadly.

Underground oil storage tanks are inaccessible by their nature and therefore never inspected. They appear to last 20 to 30 years depending on local soil and water and whether the tank is full. Information on the condition of an underground tank will be hard to acquire. Fill the tank at the end of the heating season and check to be sure the tank has not leaked down at the beginning of the following season. If it is leaking, contact an oil supply company or a service/maintenance company.

Leaking tanks should be emptied and replaced or if abandoned, filled with sand. Abandoned oil tanks can be dangerous sources of pollution and can collapse under the weight of vehicles. Do not park a moving van or a concrete truck on top of the tank. Empty tanks have been known to float out of the ground.

6.3.3 ELECTRIC

Electric refers to resistance type heaters and is differentiated from heat pumps. Passing an electric current through a resistance element produces heat. Heat radiates to the spaces from radiant ceilings or radiant heaters or convects to the air from most baseboard heaters. Radiant heat warms objects (people, furniture, etc.) and they in turn heat the air. Convection heaters warm the air and depend on it to heat the objects.

Both of these approaches heat individual rooms (spaces) and are not usually central systems, though they may heat the whole house. Controlled space by space, they are space heaters. Another approach is taken with the electric hot air furnace centrally located and controlled. (This is an electric heater in a box with a fan and ductwork.) One advantage to electric heating is no chimney or flue is required. There is no combustion, therefore no flue gases. The system is flexible and can be installed anywhere. Electric heat is clean and safe with proper care and maintenance.

Electric baseboard heaters have a normal life of 10 to 15 years. Do not allow curtains, drapes, or other inflammable objects to come close enough to the baseboard heater to ignite. Furniture, etc., should not block the air flow through the heaters.

Electric hot air furnaces have a normal life of 15 to 20 years, although at times the heating elements must be replaced. With radiant ceilings be careful not to damage the wires when installing plant hangers, etc. in the ceiling. You could get shocked and if a wire is severed a whole room or panel of heat could be lost.

MAINTENANCE AND UPKEEP

Care of electric heating systems consists largely of protecting the system from physical damage and keeping it clean. Keep dust and foreign objects out of baseboard convectors or radiators. Lubricate the blower motor on the electric furnace twice a season. Replace heating elements when they burn out. There is little or no professional maintenance until repairs are required.

6.3.4 HEAT PUMP

Heat pumps do not consume electricity as a fuel like other electric heat. Heat pumps are air conditioners running frontwards and backwards. They do not create heat but extract it from the atmosphere and pump it into the house. Freon (TM) is pumped by a compressor to a high pressure and temperature, then cooled and liquefied by a fan.

The liquid expands rapidly into the low pressure part of the system where it absorbs heat. Valves in the system control where the liquefication (heating) and expansion (cooling) occur. The system cools the atmosphere and warms the house or vice versa. Since the machine extracts heat from the environment, its efficiency is related to outside temperature and humidity. Heat pumps are often three times as efficient as electric furnaces on days above 47 degrees outside. A Coefficient of Performance of 3 or a COP of 3. Three dollars worth of heat for each dollar's worth of electricity compared to an electric furnace. As the temperature falls so does the COP. Most heat pumps have a built-in electric furnace. When the COP falls to about 1 the unit turns off the heat pump and turns on the furnace. There is no reason to strain the heat pump if there is no savings. This change occurs between 0 degrees and 23 degrees and is usually between 10 degrees and 17 degrees. The temperature set by the manufacturer may be adjusted locally. Most units do not change suddenly from one to the other. They sequence on the electric heat in small increments as the temperature falls. This auxiliary heat helps to maintain acceptable output temperatures as the efficiency drops. This is all automatic.

You can manually turn off the heat pump and switch to the electric back up (emergency heat). Most thermostats have a red warning light as a reminder to return to the heat pump mode. This is usually done if the heat pump fails. No harm is done by running the system on emergency heat. The light reminds you to have repairs made for sake of economy. The electric back up may cost 3 times more to run than the heat pump.

Heat pumps have been installed primarily for economy. It is an electrical form of heat competitive in some regions of the country with oil or gas heat. In the south, the systems are economical to install because air conditioning is almost always installed. The heat pump is an air conditioner operating frontwards and backwards. The additional equipment cost is slight. In colder climates, heat pumps are less economical. The unit's efficiency suffers as the average outdoor temperature lowers. A heat pump produces air 14 to 20 degrees warmer each time it passes through the system. (i.e. Its temperature rise is low.) The air coming out of the registers is warm, but feels drafty and cool to the occupants and often called "cold heat." Do not use night time set back. (i.e. Do not turn the thermostat down at night and back up in the morning.)

Setting back the thermostat at night allows the house to cool off. Turning it up in the early morning demands the heat pump extract heat from the atmosphere when the air is at the coldest and most hostile. The electric furnace also runs. Set the thermostat at an appropriate setting and forget it.

MAINTENANCE AND UPKEEP

Outside units have a normal life of 8 to 10 years. Heat pumps require service at least once a year. The air flow is more critical than with other forced air systems. Keep the filters clean. Change them every thirty days. It is not advisable to shut off supply grills to rooms except as required to balance heating and cooling. Undercut bedroom doors to allow air to return to the system. Keep leaves and debris away from the outside unit, it must move huge quantities of air.

The outside unit runs in both the heat pump and air conditioning modes. If the outside unit does not run, check the thermostat. Setting the thermostat to auxiliary or emergency heat turns off the heat pump and runs the system as an electric or back-up furnace. Set the thermostat to heat and wait up to fifteen minutes after raising the temperature setting enough to call for heat. The outside unit should run. If it does not run, the unit is not running as a heat pump. Check the fuses and breakers, including the ones in the service disconnect box near the outside unit. Mishandling the controls causes most heat pumps to shut off. They have a built-in safety lock-down feature that shuts the compressor off for up to seven minutes. It is dangerous to switch from heating to air conditioning and back quickly. If the fuses and wiring are good, the thermostat set correctly, and you have waited for the lock-down to clear, it should run when the temperature lever is raised. If not, call for help.

6.3.4 a. Heat Pump
In winter the outside unit will frost as the unit extracts heat from the air. It should automatically defrost itself. Frost occurs typically in cool, damp weather and may happen frequently.

6.3.5 WOOD

Wood is seldom seen as a fuel for central heating systems. There are a few wood fired boilers in existence and wood is seen as fuel for space heaters, woodstoves, fireplaces, and inserts. Wood is a controversial and high maintenance fuel. Wood fired equipment, whether it be a fireplace or woodstove, requires more attention from the homeowner than any other fuel. Keep the chimney clean, the flues swept, use safe burning techniques, guard against creosote build-up, and buy proper fuel (dry wood). Probably more fires result from improper use and maintenance of wood fired equipment than all others combined. Keep flues properly swept, at least annually. Keep equipment in sound condition according to manufacturer's instructions.

6.3.6 COAL

Coal and coal fired boilers once had a substantial percentage of the residential market. In the last 50 years, this has dwindled and represents roughly 1 percent of home heating. Coal is still used in fireplaces and in coal stoves. Coal burns hotter and different from wood and is not a substitute in a woodstove or fireplace. Do not use coal in any equipment not designed for its use.

6.4 EQUIPMENT LOCATIONS
The inspector writes the location of the heating equipment.

6.5 THERMOSTAT TYPE
Describes the type of thermostats.

6.5.1 MECHANICAL
Mechanical thermostats are the most common. They use a coiled strip of a special metal that alters shape with changes in temperature. A mercury switch turns the equipment "on" and "off" in response to temperature change. The thermostat can be set according to the homeowner's preference for temperature.

Several other settings are available on most thermostats. In many, but not all air systems, the fan may run constantly or in the automatic mode, with the fan running only when the system runs. The purpose of running the fan all the time could be two fold: 1. The noise level remains constant and does not change radically as the equipment cycles "on" and "off." Some people prefer to have the constant noise rather than the varying levels of noise. 2. Constant filtering, humidification, or dehumidification of the air. People particularly sensitive to dust, pollen, etc. might have sophisticated filters and run them 24 hours a day rather than only when the heat is operating.

6.5.2 ELECTRONIC
Electronic thermostats are beginning to be more prominent. They sense the temperature in a different manner than the mechanical thermostats. However, their function remains the same. They sense the temperature and turn the system "on" and "off." As they become more complex they are given other abilities, such as turning the equipment on and off at different settings and at different times of the day (i.e.night time set back). You could operate the equipment at a lower setting at night and allow the house to cool off slightly while you sleep. A clock in the thermostat could reset the temperature at the warmer setting early in the morning. These thermostats range from seventy-five to several hundred dollars. Do not use a night time set back thermostat for a heat pump unless it raises the temperature gradually in the morning and does not induce the back up heat to run.

6.5.3 MULTIPLE
There is more than one thermostat in the house indicating there is more than one zone or more than one type of heating system. Multiple thermostats could also refer to the possibility the heating system and air conditioning system have separate thermostats.

6.5.4 SIMULTANEOUS

Simultaneous implies it is possible for heating and cooling systems to operate at the same time. It is preferable to integrate them through a single set of controls to avoid simultaneous operation. This problem can easily exist with systems such as baseboard heat and central air conditioning. Be careful to turn off the air conditioning system completely before switching to the heating system and vice versa. Have the controls integrated where possible.

6.6 THERMOSTAT LOCATION

The inspector writes the location of the thermostat(s) in the house.

6.7 THERMOSTAT CONDITION

The inspector checks whether the thermostats are functioning, not functioning, loose, or damaged. We do not check accuracy of thermostats, the response time, delay mechanisms, or anticipators built into some thermostats. We check the thermostat function in a fundamental sense, (i.e. whether it will turn the equipment "on" and "off"). We do not check the timer, computer, or night time set back features of thermostats. Properly repair loose, damaged, or not functional thermostats. Loose implies the thermostat is not tightly secured to the wall. The thermostat must be secured to the wall to operate properly.

6.8 WARM AIR SYSTEMS

Warm air systems heat air and distribute it throughout the structure. Various methods of heating the air are used. There are oil and gas fired furnaces, heat pumps, fan coil units, etc. Air heat is common where air conditioning is popular. A single set of ductwork may serve both the air conditioning and heating. (Read section 6.3 Type of Fuel.)

6.8.1 FURNACE (HOT AIR)

A furnace heats air and distributes it to the house. There are various types, styles, designs, and life expectancies of furnaces. Most hot air furnaces last 15 to 25 years. There are many factors influencing the life expectancy of a furnace. Included are proper maintenance, location of the furnace, and its ancillary equipment such as humidifiers, air conditioners, etc. Furnaces enclosed in crawl spaces, attics, or outside storage sheds have a shorter life expectancy than furnaces within the living space. Moist air rusts heat exchangers roughly twice the rate of furnaces in the heated space. Crawl spaces are particularly hard on gas and oil furnaces. Some humidifiers mist moisture into the ductwork or furnace causing moisture to accumulate on the exterior surfaces of the heat exchanger, shortening equipment life. Condensation overflowing from an air conditioning coil above the heat exchanger may destroy the furnace. Proper maintenance and upkeep are essential. (Read section 6.3 Type of Fuel.)

6.8.1.1 UP FLOW

The air passes through the furnace in a vertical upward direction. The flame is in the bottom and the air passes from beneath upward through the heat exchanger and out the top of the furnace. The fan is blowing the air upward, the "natural" direction for heated air. Heat exchanger leaks in up flow furnaces are particularly difficult to find because the room air and combustion air pass through the system in the same direction. Therefore, minor leaks in the heat exchanger do not disturb the flame pattern, causing the flames to flicker and dance.

6.8.1.2 COUNTER FLOW

Counter flow furnaces are similar to the up flow furnaces. The flame is in the bottom but here the air passes through the furnace in a vertical downward direction. The returning room air is coming in from the top, down through the furnace, and out the bottom. An example of this would be a system with a high return in the ceiling and ductwork under the floor. The filters may be above the furnace and behind the flue pipe, making them difficult to remove and clean.

6.8.1.3 HORIZONTAL

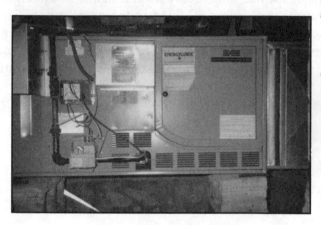

The internal components in horizontal furnaces are arranged so the furnace can be installed with the long axis parallel to the floor. They are used in crawl spaces and attics or where vertical space is limited. The shape and design of most horizontal furnaces makes their heat exchangers difficult to inspect. The filters are usually in the end of the furnace. Air passes through the furnace horizontally.

6.8.1.3 a. Horizontal Furnace.
This is a modern horizontal flow gas fired furnace. See 6.3.1 Gas.

6.8.1.4 GRAVITY

Gravity, in a furnace, implies there is no fan. The furnace is installed in a cellar or basement of the home. Large ductwork distributes heat without the help of a fan. The warm air from the furnace rises through the large diameter ducts into the living space. Cooler air from the living spaces returns through a low return to the furnace for reheating. Many of these systems have been modified with the addition of a blower or fan. Most gravity furnaces have been removed and replaced with furnaces including a blower.

6.8.1.4 a. Gravity Hot Air Furnace
Notice the large diameter ducts sloping upward away from the furnace. This was a 6.3.6 Coal Fired Furnace but has been converted to 6.3.2 Oil. See 6.12.21 System Aging.

6.8.2 HEAT PUMP

Many heat pumps were installed in the late 70's and early 80's because there was a 10 year moratorium on natural gas extensions. As discussed in section 6.3.4, heat pumps are air conditioners running frontwards and backwards. They extract heat from the air in the winter and pump it indoors. Heat pumps have certain idiosyncrasies making them difficult to inspect. A heat pump should not be run in the heat pump mode when it is above 75 degrees outside. It should not be run in the air conditioning mode when it has been below 60 degrees outside anytime in the past 24 hours. In the spring, we often find heat pumps not functioning properly because of the loss of Freon (TM) or mechanical problems. Heat pumps have built-in back up systems automatically taking over for any reason. Sometimes the homeowner does not know the unit failed until it is inspected.

6.8.2.1 ELECTRIC BACK UP

Most heat pumps have been installed with an electric furnace or electric strip-heaters as a back up system. Since heat pumps extract their heat from the atmosphere, an auxiliary or back up heating source is necessary if the atmosphere becomes very cold. Most original equipment heat pumps were installed with electric back-up. Fully integrated controls switch from heat pump to electric furnace, usually through a sequence of steps, until the outside temperature reaches a preset lower limit temperature. It turns the heat pump off in very cold weather and turns on the back up heat. This operation is fully automatic. When operating in the heat pump mode the air handler (inside unit) and the compressor unit (the outdoor unit) should both be operating. When the unit is operating in the electric furnace mode or emergency heat mode the outside unit will not be operating.

6.8.2.2 GAS OR OIL BACK UP

It is popular to install a heat pump as a back-up or an auxiliary system with an existing gas or oil furnace. As the furnace and the central air conditioning system ages or fails, a heat pump replaces the central air. This allows the furnace to last years longer than if used full time. The new heat pump can operate in mild weather and provide economic heat. The existing furnace can be used in colder weather to take advantage of its efficiency. This also provides central air conditioning from the heat pump.

The heat pump and oil or gas back up should be properly integrated through a single thermostat controlling both systems. If this is not done, simultaneous operation of the heat pump, the furnace, or air conditioning is possible.

6.8.2.3 WATER SOURCE

A Water Source heat pump is different from an air source heat pump. It extracts the heat from water as opposed to extracting it from the atmosphere. Some water source heat pumps are popular and efficient. A steady and reliable supply of water is needed as a heat source. Many of these systems are ground source systems using long loops of pipe buried 6 feet or deeper. Sometimes it is necessary to have two wells, one to pump the water from and one to dump the water back into. Sometimes the water is discharged into a local stream, pond, or storm sewer. This type of system demands a strong well.

Water source heat pumps do not usually have back-up or auxiliary heating systems because ground water does not vary widely in temperature. Water source heat pumps have been popular as additions to or parts of solar systems.

6.8.3 FAN COIL AND WATER HEATER

Fan coil systems are new and are also known by their brand names of Apollo or Hydro Heat. Hot water taken from the domestic hot water heater circulates through a fan coil (radiator) located in the ductwork. The heat is blown through the house by the fan used in the air conditioning system. The water heater is a high output gas water heater. It must be capable of providing enough heat for domestic hot water and the house. A gas water heater is economical to operate and install. You do not have a separate boiler or furnace. A single gas appliance (hot water heater) serves as both the boiler and the water heater. Get the operating manual from the present owner. Some systems have been known to vapor lock or air lock and cease to provide heat. Clearing the vapor lock is as simple as bleeding a radiator, but could result in a service call.

6.8.4 DUCTWORK

Ductwork is associated with hot air heat and air conditioning systems. Ducts for a gravity system must be large and sloping to encourage the proper distribution of the air. These systems are antiquated and most have been upgraded or replaced. Ductwork is often fabricated in metal. The metal should be galvanized or treated to prevent rusting. New forms of ductwork have been introduced such as ductboard. Ductboard, of high density fiberglass, is rolled or folded into the form of ductwork. The joints are taped. Most residential ductwork is not absolutely air tight. Its purpose is to distribute the heating and cooling throughout the house with reasonable reliability. Concealed ducts must be designed for permanent installation with minimum service and must be rodent, fire, and rust resistant, and large enough to handle the volume of air.

MAINTENANCE AND UPKEEP

Inspect any visible ductwork twice a year as you inspect the attic and crawl space. Check it with the system running. Look for damaged, dislocated, or disconnected ducts. Air escaping from or into the system may indicate problems. Keep the ducts properly connected, aligned, and supported. Avoid damaging the insulation and vapor barrier. Torn or damaged vapor barriers should be repaired.

6.8.4.1 INSULATED

Insulation is recommended for heating ducts installed in the attic or the crawl space. Uninsulated ductwork is acceptable within the living space. The attic temperature varies widely and ducts in the attic let the warmest air come into contact with the coldest environment of the house. Uninsulated ductwork is not recommended for air conditioning.

6.8.4.2 UNINSULATED

Uninsulated ductwork is commonly seen in older homes with gas heat or oil heat. As energy costs have risen, proper insulation has become more important. To insulate existing ductwork to today's standards can be expensive and elaborate, but is essential when used with air conditioning. Uninsulated attic ducts used in air conditioning can sweat, cause condensation to form, and drip onto the ceilings below, causing water damage. There are energy losses associated with uninsulated ductwork. Therefore, ductwork must be properly insulated for use with air conditioning to include a vapor barrier wrapped around the outside of any exterior fiberglass or fibrous insulation.

6.8.4.3 TRANSITE

Transite is a cement asbestos type material formed into many products. Ducts under slabs were often Transite. They contain asbestos and may have been contaminated by the drilling of termite companies. If you have transite ducts it may be wise to have an air test done for asbestos and insecticide contamination.

6.8.4.4 METAL

Metal ducts in the most common forms are light gauge galvanized metal. Main trunk ducts are rectangular and sized for the application. Branch ducts to individual supply registers are rolled metal pipe similar to stove pipe. Galvanizing gives it the ability to resist the corrosion from the moisture in the environment. Metal ducts should be mechanically fastened with screws in the joints or metal strips designed to clip or clamp the sections of ductwork together.

6.8.4.5 FLEXIBLE AND DUCTBOARD

In recent years manufacturers have provided us a wide variety of ducts manufactured from various products. One product previously mentioned is ductboard. This is a board of high density fiberglass which can be folded and cut on the site into rectangular sections. There are also hose ducts which are similar to dryer vent hoses, but insulated. They can be attached to the trunk ducts and to the floor or ceiling registers, completing the job. The insulation is already in place as is the exterior vapor barrier. Some types have been more successful than others.

Fiberglass ductboard is suspect when used in crawl spaces. The fastening systems holding ductboard together have not been successful in damp environments and main ducts are often waterlogged and collapsed in wet crawl spaces. The ducts in attics are sometimes damaged or crushed by homeowner storage or from people stepping on them. There is some question of fiberglass ductboard allowing the fibers to slough off inside and circulate into the air in the living space.

6.8.5 REGISTERS AND GRILLS

Supply registers and return grills are important parts of an air distribution system. Return grills may contain air filters. Air filters are important to the system. The veins in the supply registers disperse the air over a wide area and help achieve even heat distribution. Supply registers often contain dampers to allow the homeowner to balance the system.

Balancing the system is the idea of providing more or less air supply to individual spaces to accommodate the orientation of the house, the size of the rooms, wind angles, etc. which influence the room's temperature. These dampers and internal dampers in the system give the owner a chance to tune the system and balance it to his or her preference. You can have bedrooms cooler than the living room or vice versa.

Balancing is essential in two story houses and often must be adjusted seasonally. In the winter warm air rises so upstairs registers in two story houses may be tuned down or shut partially to restrict the air flow to the second floor. The registers on the first floor may be opened completely to allow heat to enter the first floor level. In summer the procedure can be reversed by closing the first floor registers and opening the second floor registers completely to force air conditioning to the second floor.

It is important the registers and grills properly distribute the air throughout the house and allow the owner to adjust or balance the system. In some systems the supply grills are in the ceiling or high in the side wall and return grills near the floor level. The problem is to force a wide and even distribution of air in the house. In other systems supply grills are at floor level and the return grills are near the ceiling. Occasionally duel duct systems are seen where there are supply and return grills in each room. Sometimes supplies are along the interior walls and the return grills on the outside walls. For comfort, it seems to be best to distribute the heat near the exterior and collect the returning air near the center of the house. All these systems have been devised to provide a comfortable environment.

It is important the flow of air from the grills not be totally restricted. In cases of heat pumps, they are designed so each register is an important part of the system and not more than two supply registers should be cut off. Full air flow is important to good operation of heat pumps. You should never close off returns in any system.

6.8.6 FILTERS

Air filters are important to any air system. Filters (1) protect the system and (2) protect the occupants and the house. Their primary purpose is to protect the mechanical equipment.

Filters can range from simple and inefficient paper or fiberglass types inserted in the ductwork or in a return air grill, to multiple stage paper filters or electronic filters capable of cleaning 99% of the matter from the air. Install a properly sized filter according to manufacturer's instructions so all air passes through the filter.

6.8.6.1 DISPOSABLE FILTERS

Disposable filters are designed to be used for a short time, thrown away, and replaced with another disposable filter. Change disposable filters every 30 to 60 days. Most standard size filters are available at hardware and similar stores. The cost can be up to several dollars each. They are beneficial to the equipment and occupants, and should be replaced regularly. Most are not efficient at filtering very small particles from the air.

6.8.6.2 WASHABLE FILTERS

Washable filters are similar in size to the disposable filters. They are made of fibrous mesh or shredded aluminum material with a metal frame. These filters are used for a brief period of time (30 to 60 days), washed, and replaced in the equipment. They have the advantage of not requiring constant purchasing of new filters. Some washable filters are designed to be sprayed with a tacky or sticky substance which aids in collecting the particles in the air. This spray material has a pleasant odor and is water soluble, making it easy to wash off. Some filters are designed to be washed with a hose and others may be washed in a dishwasher. Replace them as they weaken and soften with age. Old tired filters may be sucked into the equipment.

6.8.6.3 ELECTRONIC FILTERS

Electronic filters are more sophisticated and efficient than the disposable ones. The disposable filters do a good job of collecting large particles. Electronic filters have the advantage of being able to attract small particles from the air and therefore are beneficial for people with allergy or respiratory problems. Electronic filters are protected by disposable or washable filters collecting the large particles and allowing the electronic filter to filter only the small particles. Electronic filters require periodic maintenance and should be cleaned every 30 to 60 days. These filters are not tested under the scope of the inspection for their operation. You should have the seller show the cleaning procedure and maintenance to you. Many electronic filters are broken and abandoned in place. Be sure you have maintained a filter adequate to protect the equipment.

6.9 HYDRONIC SYSTEMS

Hydronic systems heat water and distribute the heat by circulating the water to the living spaces. Steam systems are also hydronic systems but are becoming rare. Hydronic systems are popular because they provide a pleasant, quiet, even, and comfortable heat. They are rare in new work because of the expense of installation. Air conditioning is becoming more popular and warm air systems are easier to integrate with air conditioning. The same ductwork can be used for both systems. When the hydronic system is used with air conditioning, two types of distribution systems must be installed.

MAINTENANCE AND UPKEEP

If you have a hydronic system you must be doubly careful to protect your house from freezing. Be sure to maintain proper and adequate fuel. When you leave on vacation, it is wise to have someone check your house occasionally to be sure the system is operating properly. If the house freezes, you may loose both the heating and plumbing systems. Read Section 6.3 for your type of fuel and the maintenance associated with it. Follow the advice of the manufacturer of your equipment. Have the system professionally serviced regularly.

6.9.1 BOILER

Any device heating water for use in heating the home is called a boiler. See the subsection below applying to your equipment.

6.9.1.1 BOILER (HOT WATER)

Most boilers do not boil the water but heat it to roughly 180 degrees Fahrenheit. Operating temperatures of these systems range from 160 to 200 degrees. The systems can be gas or oil fired, or heated by wood or coal. (See Section 6.3 Types of Fuel.) They can be economical to operate and pleasant, but require periodic maintenance. Some of this maintenance should be done by professionals. These systems include a series of important controls and safety devices (Low pressure filler valves, pressure relief valves, aquastats, etc.). Familiarize yourself with your equipment. Be present when the unit is serviced and have the technician instruct you. Take care to avoid freezing. Freezing may cause problems with the plumbing and heating systems which can damage the home.

6.9.1.2 STEAM BOILERS

Steam boilers are becoming so rare it would be wise to have the seller or a service technician fully describe its operation. Most cast iron boilers are old converted coal systems. Modern boilers can be set up to operate as steam systems, but because of so many conversions to hot water, their use has diminished. Steam systems can provide excellent heat but are temperamental and have idiosyncrasies such as venting the steam from the system, water noise, etc. The controls and safety devices on a steam boiler are somewhat different from those on a hot water system. Many steam systems require manual filling with water periodically. Be sure you know how to operate the system.

6.9.1.2 a. Steam Boiler.
This is a modern 6.9.2.1 Steel 6.3.2 Oil Fired boiler.

6.9.2 MATERIAL

Steel and cast iron are the traditional materials for boilers. The following sections give the advantages, disadvantages, characteristics, estimated life expectancy, and maintenance, etc. for each type. The material influences the performance and longevity of a heating system.

6.9.2.1 STEEL

Steel boilers have a life expectancy of 30 to 40 years. They are usually dry base boilers which means the firebox is below the level of the water in the system. The heat from the fire rises up through passages in the wet section of the boiler heating the water. These boilers sometimes include a domestic coil which heats the water used in washing and bathing. This water is separate from the water circulated in the boiler system.

6.9.2.2 CAST IRON

Cast iron boilers are often longer lived than steel boilers. They may last 40 to 50 years. They have been known to last 75 years or longer. Modern cast iron boilers are designed to operate as oil or gas fired boilers. Older boilers were wood or coal fired. Cast iron boilers sometimes include a domestic coil which is used to heat water for bathing and washing. This water is separate from the water circulated by the boiler.

6.9.2.3 CONVERSION BOILERS

Many older coal or wood fired boilers have been converted to operate with an oil burner. In these adaptations, an oil gun burner assembly is mounted through the door of the boiler and the oil flame fired into the cavity once containing the wood or coal fire. Due to the size and proportions of the boiler, these units are usually inefficient. These systems are old and replacement to a more modern system may be wise. Typical recovery of investment may be as little as 3 to 5 years. Some converted boilers operate with reasonable efficiency.

6.9.3 DISTRIBUTION SYSTEM

This section describes the type of distribution system used with the hydronic system. Each type of system has its own characteristic strong and weak points. Familiarize yourself with your system.

6.9.3.1 ONE PIPE

One pipe systems were used with steam boilers and free standing radiators. The large diameter pipes in the system slope slightly upward. The principle is the steam rises through the pipe into the radiators, condenses into water, trickles back through the bottom half of the same pipe to the boiler, is reheated and sent through the system again. A few of these systems remain in use but as time passes they become more rare and antiquated. A major disadvantage to the one pipe system is it cannot be easily converted to a hot water system. Hot water systems rely on a two pipe system to circulate the water to and from the radiators.

6.9.3.2 TWO PIPE

Two pipe systems were also used with radiators. Some gravity systems use large pipe three or more inches in diameter. Pipes in the system were sloped to let the hot water rise through natural convection, cool off, and settle back to the boiler to be heated again. Most gravity systems have been eliminated or modified to include circulators (pumps) which circulate the water mechanically. Mechanically circulated systems do not require the large diameter pipes. The pipes in mechanically circulated system are often 3/4 to one inch diameter. Both systems are capable of circulating water to free standing radiators, copper tube cabinet convectors, copper tube baseboard convectors, or cast iron baseboard radiators.

6.9.3.3 GRAVITY

Gravity distribution systems do not include circulators or pumps to circulate the water. They depend on large diameter piping. The piping is sloped so steam or hot water circulates through natural convection. The piping in the systems must be large to accommodate the sluggish flow of the water. A few gravity systems are still in use but most have been converted for use with circulators (pumps). Though the gravity systems were reliable, they were sluggish and slow to respond to changes in the weather.

6.9.3.4 CIRCULATED

There is a circulator (pump) included in the hydronic system. This pump induces the flow of the water in the system from the radiators to the boiler and back again.

This allows the system to respond faster and circulate the water more efficiently. Circulator pumps appear to have a life expectancy of roughly 10 or 15 years. Most pumps should be lubricated twice a year. Have the service company show you how.

6.9.3.5 RADIANT SLAB

Radiant slabs have been used in houses for a long time. They consist of pipes buried in the slab either directly in or under the concrete. Hot water circulates through the piping warming the slab and therefore warms the house. The system can be quiet, produce warm floors, and almost invisible requiring no radiators, ducts, registers, grills, etc. The disadvantages to the system are it can be sluggish and unresponsive to the weather. It may require outdoor thermostats to anticipate changes in the weather and is difficult to repair.

6.9.3.6 RADIANT CEILING

Radiant ceiling systems are made by burying small tubing in the plaster or just above the ceiling. Hot water circulates through the tubing warming the plaster, thus warming the space. The system can be pleasant, quiet, and invisible (i.e. no radiators, grills, registers, and ducts). The heat enters at the highest point in the living space. If the insulation is not adequate, heat loss can be substantial. The expansion and contraction of the piping in the ceiling often causes characteristic cracks in patterns in the ceiling. You must be careful not to puncture the piping when installing light fixtures, plant hangers, etc. This can create a leak.

6.9.4 RADIATORS OR CONVECTORS

Radiators are devices in the living space through which hot water or steam circulates. The heat radiates into the living space. Radiant heat travels through the air and warms the objects in the rooms as opposed to warming the air in the room.

Convectors also rely on hot water or steam for heat, but warm the air and it carries (convects) the heat into the room. Some heat radiates from a convector also.

6.9.4.1 CAST IRON RADIATORS

The house has the free standing radiators of cast iron. These radiators can be used with hot water or steam. The efficiency and capacity relates to the number of elements (sections) in each radiator, size and surface area of the elements, etc. The number of coats of paint on the radiator may influence the efficiency.

Protect the radiators from freezing. Cast iron radiators can be hazardous if allowed to freeze because it is possible for the cast iron to rupture violently. It can throw pieces of metal across the room with great force. You must maintain the radiators properly, bleed them, and give attention to the valves and piping associated with the radiators to avoid leaking. A dripping valve or pipe on a radiator can damage the floor structure if the leak continues. When a radiator is warm at the bottom and cold at the top, it usually has air in it and must be bled.

6.9.4.2 CAST IRON BASEBOARD

Cast iron baseboard is a modern variation of the old cast iron radiator. It is a system installed around the outside perimeter walls. It can be long lived, pleasant, and less obvious than the free standing radiators.

6.9.4.3 COPPER TUBE BASEBOARD

Copper tube baseboards are sheet metal baseboard with aluminum fins enclosing the copper pipe. This system is a convector circulating hot water through the pipe. Room air passes through the fins, picks up heat from the pipe, and rises or convects into the living space. These systems may require bleeding from time to time if they fail to heat.

6.9.4.4 COPPER TUBE CABINETS

Copper tube cabinets are similar to copper tube baseboard convectors except for their cabinet shape. They are often used in areas where wall space is limited and proper amount of convection cannot be included with copper tube baseboards. These systems may require bleeding from time to time if they fail to heat.

6.10 SPACE HEATING

Space heating is differentiated from central heating. Central systems heat the entire structure or zones of the structure from a central location. Space heating warms the structure space by space or room by room.

6.10.1 FLOOR FURNACES

Gas and oil fired floor furnaces have been in use for many years, but have fallen into disfavor. Several problems have arisen with the furnaces leading to this lack of popularity. The central grate becomes very hot and can be hazardous for young people, barefooted people, and those who have trouble walking. Grates may become hot enough to melt rubber soles on shoes. Another problem is all doors must be open so warm air can circulate. Mold and mildew may occur behind furniture and in other remote locations away from the furnace.

6.10.2 STOVES AND INSERTS

Stoves and fireplace inserts are not inspected because they are personal property. Many house fires occur because of the improper maintenance of wood stoves and inserts. The stove or insert should be carefully examined before using it. Fireplace inserts leave fireplaces sooted and creosoted when removed. Creosote and soot is an invitation for a chimney fire. Have the insert removed and the flues cleaned and inspected by a reputable chimney sweep before closing. Expect to find a damaged flue. It is also possible to have an odor problem after removing an insert and cleaning the chimney. The sweep may be able to help with the odor. Check with the local fire marshal for more information on the safety of the installation and local burning ordinances.

6.10.3 WALL FURNACES

Wall furnaces come in several forms and can be gas or oil fired. Wall furnaces should be used with extreme care because they "rust out" and "hole" the heat exchangers more often and rapidly than central furnaces. They can be hard to light because of back drafting through their flues. They are often prone to extinguish the pilot light because of the back drafting. You should have the seller carefully explain the operation of the wall furnace to you. If possible, learn to light and manipulate the furnaces while the seller can help you.

6.10.4 SPACE HEATERS

Space heaters are personal property and not examined under the scope of this inspection. If not properly maintained and operated, they can be hazardous to the occupants. Do not operate them in enclosed spaces, they compete with the occupants for the available oxygen. Never sleep with an unvented fuel burning appliance in the room with you. Space heaters must use the exact fuel the manufacturer recommends, proper wicks and igniters. Heaters using the incorrect fuel or mixed fuel may explode.

6.10.5 DUCTLESS FURNACES

Ductless furnaces are similar to floor furnaces because they too are centrally located. They may be in a hall closet or central space behind a louvered door. The furnace depends on a small fan to circulate air across the outside of the furnace's heat exchanger and blow the air into the hall or other central location. Such furnaces often rely upon a pot type burner which requires the use of kerosene or No. 1 fuel oil. These furnaces are somewhat rare and only suitable in smaller homes. They have the same drawbacks as other centrally located furnaces. They do not have a distribution system. The heat distribution from the furnace will be poor and the outlying spaces may be cold and unregulated. As with floor furnaces you will need to have the interior doors open so the heat can circulate. Mold and mildew may occur behind furniture and in other remote locations.

6.10.6 ELECTRIC BASEBOARD

Electric baseboard is probably the most common and popular of the space heating systems in use. It is often installed throughout the house, but qualifies as space heating because the heat is controlled room by room. Electric baseboard heaters have a normal life of 10 to 15 years. It is not wise to allow curtains, drapes, or other inflammable objects to come in contact with the baseboard heater or to come close enough to ignite. Furniture, etc. should not block the air flow through the heaters.

6.10.7 THROUGH THE WALL HEAT PUMPS

"Through the wall heat pumps" are occasionally seen as space heaters. They are installed like window air conditioners. Motel rooms sometimes use "through the wall heat pumps" because they both cool and heat the room with the same system. They are often in additions or in remote sections to boost the performance of a central system weak in that area of the house. (Read sections 6.3 Type of Fuel and 6.8.2 Heat Pump.)

6.10.8 RADIANT CEILING

Two types of electric radiant ceilings are: (1) heating cables attached to the ceiling and plastered in place or (2) drywall panels with radiant cables built-in. The cables heat from electric resistance and are controlled room by room. They provide a pleasant form of heat, are quiet and almost invisible. They sometimes leave lines or characteristic cracks in the ceilings. The homeowner must be careful not to damage the ceiling panels. (i.e. Installing light fixtures, hooks, etc.)   Cutting one of the cables could possibly give you an electric shock and cause the loss of heating in that space. Poor ceiling insulation can make this an expensive way to heat.

6.11 FIREPLACE AND FLUES

Fireplaces have been a source of pleasure and pride for homeowners for many years. Years ago a coal or wood burning fireplace was a principal source of heat. Necessity for heat and regional climate have influenced the design and style of fireplaces. In the north (colder climates) the fireplace is central in the house so the mass of the masonry heats and radiates into the house. In the deep south (warmer climate) fireplaces are generally on the end of the house and sometimes the flues were spaced several inches away from the house. The mass of the fireplace is on the outside of the house so over heating would not occur in mild weather. Some fireplaces are unlined and still in use today. These fireplaces can be a source of chimney fires.

MAINTENANCE AND UPKEEP

Maintenance and upkeep of a fireplace depends on the frequency of use, its age, condition, and construction. Keep the joints pointed between the firebricks, flues and flue tiles pointed and sound, and periodically clean or sweep the flue. Cleaning of a fireplace should be done according to the use. If you burn green or poorly seasoned wood on a regular basis, have the fireplace swept annually or more. If you burn it occasionally, (a few times a year) you may only need to have it swept every five years.

If you use an air tight wood burning stove and burn poor quality wood, it is wise to have it swept twice a year. Wood burning stoves are prone to leave the flues, etc. sooted and dirty because they burn with little air. They exhaust so little heat up the chimney the combustion products condense in the form of creosote.

Check the mortar joints in the firebrick periodically to be sure they are sound. It may be necessary to chisel away crumbling mortar between the firebrick and replace it with proper mortar or stove or fireplace mortar available in caulking tubes. (Do one or two joints at a time so the bricks don't fall out.)

The flues for gas furnaces should be swept at least every five years. The flues for oil furnaces should be checked at least every two years. Flues have become damaged with age and heat and have collapsed inward stopping the flow of fumes out of the house. This has been a source of injury or death to the occupants. Keep the connector between the furnace or appliance and the flue (flue pipe) free of holes and defects. Venting gas fired devices into unlined flues is not recommended. Moisture in the combustion by-products condenses on the walls of the flue and soaks into the brick and mortar. The condensate attacks the mortar chemically and may accelerate freeze thaw damage to the chimney. Check with the local Fire Marshal or a reputable chimney sweep for advice on lining the flue.

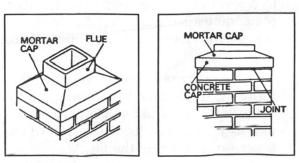

6.11 d. Flues.
Note the slope on the cap.

The exterior of flues and fireplaces should be inspected annually and maintained as necessary. The cap or coping (wash) on top of masonry chimneys may need replacement every five to ten years. (Read section 1.6 Flashing and Joint Material.)

6.11.1 MASONRY

Masonry fireplaces have been traditional in American homes since colonial times. Today they are built with firebrick lining a firebox. This brick is made of a refractory material and the flues are lined with terra-cotta or fired clay tile flue lining. Older fireplaces were built with unlined fireboxes and flues. Do not use fireplaces with unlined flues for solid fuels. There is a danger of flue gas escaping into the structure or a chimney fire igniting the structure. Consult with the local Fire Marshall or a reputable chimney sweep before using an unlined fireplace. The unlined flue your grandfather used safely 50 years ago is now 50 years older, and he knew more about burning wood than you know.

6.11.1.1 WOOD BURNING FIREPLACES

Modern wood burning fireplaces are characterized by a large square opening and are generally 18 to 24 inches deep. It is wise to have a damper to simplify operation. The flues should be lined and sound. Most wood burning fireplaces are inefficient and viewed as a source of pleasure, not heat. Many fireplaces have negative performance. They draw more heat out of the house than they produce. Have a hearth in front of the firebox a minimum of 16 to 20 inches wide and at least 1 foot wider than the firebox on each side. Without this incombustible material in front of the firebox, embers, logs, and sparks could fall out of the fireplace, damage the floor, or possibly set fire to the house.

6.11.1.2 COAL BURNING FIREPLACES

At one time coal burning fireplaces were popular in urban areas. These fireplaces were shallow and small. The grates were usually built into the fireplaces. These fireplaces sometimes had ornate cast iron front panels closing them off in the warm months. They can be beautiful and decorative. Most were built without dampers. Today it is felt the flues should be lined and surrounded with 8 inches of masonry to be safe for coal or wood burning fire.

6.11.2 MANUFACTURED FIREPLACES

Manufactured fireplaces are available in many styles, sizes, and applications. Many are designed to be built-in and come in a sheet metal cabinet enclosing a conventional looking firebox. A metal flue is run through a flue enclosure through or up the outside of the structure to a level above the roof. The front of the fireplace is then covered or surrounded with a noncombustible material. In many cases slate, stone, or brick is used. The exterior of a manufactured fireplace can appear similar to a masonry fireplace.

There are other versions of the manufactured fireplace. Some are the contemporary, free standing, metal cone variety hanging from the ceiling or standing in the middle of the floor. Some versions are like a built-in stove. A few of these fireplaces are 30 to 40% more efficient than masonry fireplaces. (i.e. 30 to 40% of the heat available from the wood radiates into the living space rather than up the flue.)

MAINTENANCE AND UPKEEP

Care and Maintenance is similar to masonry fireplaces. They must be kept clean and free of soot and creosote to avoid chimney fires. Rusted or damaged interior panels must be replaced to protect the surrounding area from exposure to the heat. Interior panels are easy to remove and can be replaced. This can be less expensive than repairing the firebox of an aging masonry fireplace. Be sure the metal flue does not become disconnected or dislodged during cleaning. The chimney chase is built of combustible materials.

6.11.2.1 BUILT-IN FIREPLACES

Built-in manufactured fireplaces can be incorporated into almost any structure and mimic the appearance of a masonry fireplace. They may have a traditional appearance and be acceptable in a traditional form of architecture. They are also available in contemporary styles and designs. One advantage of the built-in manufactured fireplaces is they have been tested and are known to draw well.

6.11.2.2 FREE STANDING MANUFACTURED FIREPLACES

There are many styles of free standing manufactured fireplaces. One is the "cone type" which has a circular pan lined with a refractory material and a funnel shaped flue inlet above it. These are often in the center of a large room. There is a version of the free standing fireplace designed to fit into the corner of a room. A free standing fireplace takes up a lot a room. A free standing fireplace should have a hearth on all sides.

6.11.3 FLUES

These are the flues used by furnaces, boilers, and other interior heating devices. The flues for these devices must be kept sound and in good condition. Flues blocked either by crumbling debris, bird nests, or similar material are hazardous. The blocked flue will force combustion fumes or flue gases to exhaust into the living space.

MAINTENANCE AND UPKEEP

Flues for a gas furnace should be inspected at least every 5 years and kept clean and free of obstructions. Flues for an oil furnace should be inspected at least every two years, swept, cleaned of debris, and obstructions. (Read 1.6 Flashing and Joint Material.)

6.11.3.1 MASONRY FLUES

Masonry flues have been in use for hundreds of years. Gas appliance flues should be lined. Moisture condensing from the combustion fumes attacks the masonry chemically and accelerates freeze/thaw damage to the chimney. Unlined flues should be checked and inspected twice as often as lined flues. Get advice on lining flues from reputable chimney sweeps or the Fire Marshall.

6.11.3.2 METAL FLUES

Metal flues come in several varieties including single wall stove pipe. It must be spaced nine to eighteen inches from a wall to prevent the possibility of the flue igniting a fire. Properly insulated pipes can be placed 1 to 2 inches from the surrounding materials with little danger from the flue. There are flues for gas furnaces designed to be run inside a 3 1/2 inch thick stud wall. As with all flues, metal flues should be inspected and swept periodically. It is necessary for the flues to remain free of rust and holes. Keep sections properly connected. If allowed to slip apart and become misaligned, they let flue gases escape into the structure and may start fires.

6.11.3.3 TRANSITE

Transite (TM) is a cement asbestos pipe often used for municipal water lines. It is occasionally found as flue pipe or flue liner. It has proven unsuccessful, especially on gas fired devices. The fumes are corrosive and contain water in the form of steam. The inner surface of the pipe sloughs or flakes off in sheets and has been known to clog itself. Have it replaced with a better material. At least have it inspected by a reputable chimney sweep or the local fire marshal.

6.11.3.4 CONNECTOR

"Connector" is the connection between the vented appliance (i.e.the furnace or boiler) and the flue. The connector is usually a piece of single wall stove pipe of galvanized or blue iron. These connectors should be mechanically fastened to one another, the appliance, and the flue according to the manufacturer's directions. The connectors should run upward from the appliance to the flue. Horizontal runs should be kept to a minimum length and the slope on horizontal runs should be at least 1/4" to the foot. Flue pipes should be free of holes and rust. Joints in the connectors should be kept aligned and inserted into one another and mechanically fastened where possible. "Mechanically fastened" means they should be screwed together so they cannot slip apart.

There is a draft vent or hood associated with gas appliances which appears to be a large funnel located above the water heater or gas furnace. The location and design of the draft hood is specified by the manufacturer of the equipment and should not be altered at the site. The flue for oil fired devices often includes a barometric damper which appears to be a "T" in the flue pipe with a flap in it. The flap usually has a small weight on it and often opens and closes with changes in wind direction or speed. These devices allow the flue to draw in a certain amount of room air, equalize the pressure, and draw properly without back drafting. Do not block their operation.

6.12 OBSERVATIONS

The inspector marks observations of conditions affecting the heating system. More than one item can be marked as the heating system may exhibit more than one symptom or problem. Some items are part of the normal aging process and do not require correction. Other items require either maintenance or repair if the heating system is to reach the full potential or life expectancy. Read carefully each section applying to the system inspected.

Maintenance is the on going care required if a system or item is to reach the full potential including lubricating, painting, etc. Do maintenance as required by the manufacturer of the equipment or item. Repairs put items or systems back in good condition after damage or decay, etc. Repairs are caused by delayed maintenance, aging, normal wear and tear, or abuse. The workmanship and materials of the repairs should be equal to the quality of the system and have the same life expectancy. e.g. A limb plunges through an asphalt shingle roof. If the roofing otherwise has a life expectancy of ten years, the repair should also have a life expectancy of at least ten years. If the roofing only has a life expectancy of one year, then the repair should be capable of lasting one year or more. It is not prudent to put a one year patch on a ten year roof or to waste a ten year repair on a one year roof. All repairs should be by qualified competent professionals.

6.12.1 SOUND

The inspector thinks the item inspected is functioning at the moment of the inspection. This does not imply perfection, absence of minor defects, or absence of wear and tear.

6.12.2 TYPICAL

The inspector thinks the item, material, or aspect of construction is characteristic or similar to comparable products in similar houses. The heating system has normal wear and tear.

6.12.3 CLEAN

The inspector feels the oil or gas fired equipment is clean enough to operate in its present condition and does not indicate the need for immediate cleaning or service. For a heat pump or air conditioner, clean indicates the coil inside the air handler was found to be reasonably clean and free from impacted dirt, dust and debris.

6.12.4 SOOTED AND DIRTY

The equipment is sooty and dirty enough to warrant cleaning and annual service, maintenance, and inspection by a local service contractor immediately.

6.12.5 HEAT EXCHANGER DAMAGE

The inspector sees evidence of damage to the heat exchanger. As many as three tests determine whether the heat exchanger is sound. The tests used are:(1) visual inspection of the heat exchanger with a flash light and mirror, (2) observation of the burner during operation in which the color and the nature of the flame is observed, and the reaction of the flame while the fan is on. If the flames in the unit flicker and dance it indicates a hole in the heat exchanger. (3) The use of a portable gas detector which is capable of picking up traces of fuel or combustion gases in the air distributed to the living spaces. (Read section 6.8.1 Furnace / Hot Air.)

6.12.6 VIEW OF HEAT EXCHANGER/COMBUSTION CHAMBER RESTRICTED

The view of the heat exchanger is restricted because of the design or location of the equipment or the owner's possessions block access to the furnace. Also internal damaged to the furnace can restrict the view. Have the heat exchanger or combustion chamber inspected before closing. (Read section 6.8.1 Furnace (Hot Air) and 6.9.1 Boiler.)

6.12.7 DIRTY COIL

The coil in the heat pump or air conditioner is coated with dust and debris from the air stream. This indicates the system has been operated with dirty or damaged filter or with no filter. This can be hazardous to the equipment because it forces it to operate at improper temperatures and pressures and can shorten the compressor's life dramatically. Have the coil properly cleaned. (Read section 6.8.2 Heat Pump.)

6.12.7 a. Dirty Coil
Have coil cleaned and proper filter
installed before system is damaged.

6.12.8 FAN VIBRATES

The fan in the air handler or outdoor unit vibrates abnormally. This vibration is noisy and shortens the life of the fan or the equipment. Have the fan repaired or replaced promptly.

6.12.9 FAN BELT AGING

The fan belt is cracked, frayed, worn, or aging. Aging fan belts should be replaced to avoid the loss of the fan and thus the heat when the belt breaks.

6.12.10 NO FILTER

There is no filter present in the air handler or system. Filters are essential for the protection of the equipment. They are especially important to heat pumps and air conditioning systems. The absence of a filter will shorten the life of a heat pump or air conditioning system substantially. It will also degrade the performance of other heating systems. Replace or install a proper filter immediately. (Read section 6.8 Warm Air Systems.)

6.12.11 DIRTY FILTER

The filter is dirty and should be cleaned or replaced immediately. Dirty air filters can cause the air flow through the system to be restricted (slowed) to the point the temperature readings taken on the system are false or altered. (Read section 6.8 Warm Air Systems.)

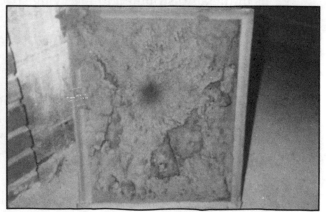

6.12.11 a. Dirty Filter.
This filter is extremely dirty and would restrict
or choke the air flow through the system.
This causes the system to work at artificially
high temperatures and may shorten its life.

6.12.12 NO HEAT SOURCE IN EACH ROOM

There was no heat source in each room of the living space. The absence of a heating source in a living space can reduce the usefulness of the space, make it unpleasant and prone to freeze, or have mold, mildew, and condensation on the walls.

6.12.13 DOORS NOT UNDERCUT

The normally closed doors, such as bedroom doors, are not properly undercut allowing the heat and air conditioning to return to the central air return. It is important, especially with heat pumps, to allow the air to circulate freely. The doors should be cut a minimum of 3/4 of an inch above the level of the carpet. If this is not done the system will be difficult to balance and it will be hard to maintain proper temperatures within the rooms with the doors shut. (i.e. too hot or cold for comfort.)

6.12.14 DUCTWORK DAMAGED

Physical damage found to the ductwork. This may be crushed, disconnected, wet, or rusted ductwork. It can also indicate ductwork has collapsed, fallen loose, shifted, and leaks heated air into the crawl space or attic. (Read section 6.8.4 Ductwork.)

6.12.15 INSULATION DAMAGED

The insulation on the ductwork has substantial damage influencing the system's performance or economy. (Read section 6.8.4 Ductwork.)

6.12.16 UNDERSIZED DUCTWORK

The inspector feels the ductwork is undersized for its present application or undersized for the addition of future air conditioning. (Read section 6.8.4 Ductwork.)

6.12.17 POSSIBLE ASBESTOS

The inspector sees materials he believes may possibly contain asbestos. Asbestos, wherever it's found, is of concern to all homeowners. If it breaks down into small fibers (becomes friable) and is inhaled or ingested, it can have serious and far reaching health effects. Only proper laboratory tests can confirm or deny its presence and only then can an appropriate response be suggested. The treatment and removal of asbestos is dangerous and expensive and should be left to experts. Contact a qualified asbestos testing laboratory to test and identify the material and advise on removal.

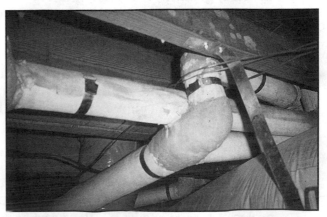

6.12.17 a. Possible Asbestos
The pipe insulation is most probably asbestos.

6.12.18 CABINET DAMAGE

There is damage to the cabinet or shell of the furnace or heating system. This can range from physical damage such as bent doors, damaged panels, to rusted cabinets. Rust can form on the equipment by periodic flooding of the basement or crawl space. Air conditioning coils whose drains have become blocked can overflow and flood the cabinet. Humidifiers spraying water into the system can be harmful. Cabinet damage affecting performance must be repaired.

6.12.18 a. Cabinet Damage.
The rust around the base of this boiler indicates the basement has flooded. This is a clue or tell tale sign of a wet basement. Chronic or severe damage of this type may eventually destroy the boiler.

6.12.19 TOO SMALL

The inspector feels the heating equipment is too small for the residence. We do not do a heat loss/heat gain survey of the property. This is a subjective judgment. Have experts perform heat loss/heat gain calculations and determine whether the equipment is adequate.

6.12.20 NOT FUNCTIONAL

The system does not operate. The inspector makes a cursory inspection of the system to be sure it is safe to operate using the same controls and devices the homeowner uses. The inspector will not attempt to override the system's internal controls or use any reset devices or manipulate the system to force it to operate. Have the system repaired to operate properly and inspected before closing.

6.12.21 SYSTEM AGING

In the inspector's opinion, the equipment has reached the end of its useful life and is old, antiquated, geriatric, worn out, and beyond repair. Any additional life or use from equipment at this stage should be considered a "gift" even with repairs.

6.12.22 PRESENTMENT

Soot, creosote, flue gas, or other effluent is "presenting" itself. i.e. Noxious substances are leaking out of cracks or joints and may indicate a failed flue, connector, or severely damaged equipment. Have a chimney sweep or qualified service technicians do further inspection on your equipment.

6.12.24 BOILER LEAKING

The boiler is leaking water. Do not confuse this with boilers left shut down in a cool, damp, basement environment where condensation forms on or in the boiler. Have the boiler repaired or replaced to cure the leak. (Read section 6.9.1 Boiler.)

6.12.25 COMBUSTION CHAMBER DAMAGE

There is damage within the firepot or the combustion chamber of the boiler. This may be a cracked refractory lining, collapsed internal parts, damaged firepot, or any interior damage noted to the boiler. Have the boiler repaired immediately to prevent further damage or fire. (Read section 6.9.1 Boiler.)

6.12.26 ABSENCE OF PARTS OR CONTROLS

Every hydronic heating system must have certain parts and controls to operate economically and safely. Some of these parts or controls are missing. Have the system repaired or completed to operate safely, before closing. (Read section 6.9 Hydronic Systems.)

6.12.27 HEAT DAMAGE TO CABINET

There is damage on the outside of the cabinet from heat. Heat damage such as scorching or buckling of cabinet panels indicates the firepot and associated lining or the heat exchanger of the boiler or furnace has failed or has overheated. Have the equipment repaired or replaced to operate safely.

6.12.28 PIPING LEAKS

There are leaks on the piping system of the boiler. These leaks can be on the distribution piping or on the radiators or convectors of the system. Have the leaks repaired promptly to prevent damage to the system or structure.

6.12.29 PIPING UNSUPPORTED

The piping system is not properly supported and is subject to being damaged by collapsing under its own weight. Have the piping properly supported.

6.12.30 POOR LAYOUT

The system is poorly "laid out" and will not or cannot function economically, safely, or properly. If the system cannot perform satisfactorily, repair or replace it.

6.12.31 FREEZE DAMAGE

The inspector notes freeze damage or apparent freeze damage. This can range from cracked radiators to bulged or cracked piping. Repair the system to operate properly and call for a reinspection before closing. Severe freeze damage can completely destroy a system, including the boiler.

6.12.32 LEAKING VALVES

Valves in the system are leaking. Radiator valves can leak onto the floors damaging them and the structure. Repair the valves, curing the leaks and repair the structure and floors as necessary.

6.12.33 DAMAGED CONVECTORS

Convectors have cabinet damage or damage to the convection fins which can restrict the air flow through the system. This may also indicate the convectors are dirty or contaminated to the point they cannot function properly.

6.12.34 SPILLAGE\BACKDRAFTING

Spillage is the __momentary__ escape of flue gases into the living space as the equipment ignites and before the draft is established. Backdrafting is the drafting of fresh combustion air back through the flue and the dumping of flue gases into the living space. Potentially hazardous to the occupants, equipment and structure. Have the flue and equipment checked and repaired by qualified professionals __immediately__. This can be caused by whole house fans, down draft ranges, dryers, or any fan taking the air from the house. There must be adequate combustion air.

6.12.36 FAN FAILED

The fan in the system failed to respond and distribute air through or across the heat exchanger into the living space. Have the fan repaired or replaced.

6.12.37 RUSTED

The equipment is rusted or shows water damage.

6.12.38 CLEARANCE

The clearance around the heating equipment is not adequate and safe. Various types and pieces of equipment have distinct distances required by the local fire marshal and manufacturer of the equipment. These distances vary widely with the different types of equipment and different wall surfaces. It appears the clearance around the equipment is not adequate. Have the equipment moved or proper heat shielding installed to reduce the danger of fire.

6.12.39 UNVENTED

Most appliances must be vented to the exterior. An unvented device is present (i.e. no flue). Have a proper flue or vent installed.

6.12.42 SOOTED OR CREOSOTE

The piece of equipment appears to be dirty with soot or creosote. Have the equipment cleaned or swept before using again. Soot or creosote may conceal other damage. (Read section 6.11 Fireplaces and Flues.)

6.12.43 DAMAGED MORTAR

Damaged mortar was found in the mortar joints in the firebrick lining of a masonry fireplace or in any other visible section of the fireplace. Generally the mortar is damaged from heat and age in the fireplace or from a possible chimney fire. Such mortar should be repaired or replaced before using the fireplace. (Read section 6.11 Fireplaces and Flues.)

6.12.44 FLUE FIRE

There has been a flue or chimney fire. The evidence may be cracked flue tiles, and is sometimes visible on the outside as cracked brick work. Such cracks may bleed creosote and soot from inside the flue, called "presenting." Damaged flues are a fire hazard and should be repaired before use. Seek the advice of the local Fire Marshal or a reputable chimney sweep. (Read section 6.11 Fireplaces and Flues.)

6.12.45 MISSING OR DAMAGED DAMPER

Either the fireplace never had one, or part of the damper is rusted, broken, missing, or misaligned. Fireplaces without dampers can be used but are difficult to control and may operate unsatisfactorily. Without a damper it is difficult to regulate the draw of the fireplace. Heat is lost up a chimney after the fire dies. Several possibilities exist: (1) repair the existing damper, (2) install a hood damper in the fireplace, (3) use glass doors, or (4) install a flue top damper on the chimney using a chain hanging through the flue into the firebox to control the damper. Properly reinstall or repair any misaligned or damaged damper. (Read section 6.11 Fireplaces and Flues.)

6.12.46 UNLINED

Either the firebox or the flue for an appliance is unlined. Masonry fireplace chimneys are required to have a terra cotta flue liner with eight inches of masonry surrounding each flue in order to be safe and to conform with most building codes.

During a visual inspection it is common to be unable to detect the absence of a flue liner either because of a stoppage at the firebox, a defective damper, or lack of access from the roof. (Read section 6.11 Fireplaces and Flues.)

6.12.47 FAILED OR RUSTED

The manufactured fireplace has failed refractory panels or rusted and damaged metal parts. Have the unit properly repaired or replaced before using it. Contact the manufacturer for parts and help. (Read section 6.11.2 Manufactured.)

6.12.48 LEAKING AT THE FLASHING

Water is leaking around the flashing at the chimney or flue vents. The flashing or vents are failing. Make repairs promptly to protect the structure from water damage. A qualified roofer may be able to help. (Read section 1.6 Flashing and Joint Material.)

6.12.49 CRACKED

The masonry of the flue was cracked. Often caused by chimney fires or excess heat. (Read section 6.11 Fireplaces and Flues.)

6.12.50 INTERIOR UNINSPECTED

The interior of the flue was not inspected. No information about the condition is given. Damaged flues can be deadly. Repairs are expensive. Have all flues swept and inspected by a reputable chimney sweep or local Fire Marshal before closing. (Read section 6.11 Fireplaces and Flues.)

NOTES

CHAPTER SEVEN

AIR CONDITIONING

Air conditioning makes our homes, schools, and offices pleasant during hot weather. Air conditioning has become the norm. Many people cannot remember not having some type of air conditioning whether a wall unit, window unit, or central air.

Before World War II, buildings were cooled with fans. The ceiling fan was used as it is today. The fan is the best method to move air through a structure. Depending on the climatic conditions, air conditioning units can be simple fans or the elaborate units using Freon™ as a refrigerant.

7.1 LIMITATIONS

This section describes the aspects limiting the inspection of the air conditioning system. Inspectors do the best inspection they can, but sometimes physical obstructions, weather conditions, or the condition of the air conditioning, prevent them from doing the whole job. When it has been below 60 degrees within the last 24 hours it is not safe to operate air conditioning systems. Arrange for an inspection overcoming the limitations, if possible (i.e. come back when outside temperatures are above 60 degrees for 24 hours, even if it's in the spring). An uninspected air conditioning system or a severely limited or restricted inspection could be a total unknown. The inspector cannot make representations about what was not inspected. Realize every inspection is limited in some fashion. The inspector is a generalist with broad knowledge on many topics and does not represent they know or can see everything about every system. It is your responsibility to overcome the limitations. You should complete the inspection prior to closing even if you must hire others (service technician, AC contractors, etc.) or pay an additional fee to the inspector or Air conditioning specialist. Repairs can be expensive and at some point replacement is the best alternative. An uninspected air conditioning or one given a severely limited or restricted inspection could be a total unknown. The inspector cannot make representations about what was not inspected. If you close on the house with a Limited or Restricted inspection you are accepting the responsibility for the unknown items about the system. You may have to resort to service technicians who can dismantle and test and inspect this name brand of equipment.

7.1.1 TYPICAL

The inspector feels they have seen as much of the air conditioning system as they normally see. The air conditioning is inspected from arms length. The inspection of every system is limited in some fashion. Some parts of every system are hidden from view and can only be inspected indirectly or not at all. An example is an air conditioning coil installed with no access to inspect the return side of the coil without dismantling the system. We cannot find a problem taking four or more hours to manifest during a 2 or 3 hour inspection. Occasionally systems run satisfactorily for a test run but fail after a longer run or under severe conditions. (Read section 7.1 Limitations.)

7.1.2 RESTRICTED

The inspector feels they have seen less of the air conditioning system than they typically see. (Also read section 7.1.1 Typical.)

7.1.2.1 ELECTRICITY OFF/24 HOURS

The inspector cannot operate a system when the electricity is off during the inspection. The electricity must have been on 24 hours before the central cooling system can be tested. Some systems, especially heat pumps, contain small heaters keeping the oil in the compressor warm and prevent the refrigerant from condensing and damaging the compressor. (Read section 7.1.2 Restricted.)

7.1.2.2 WEATHER TOO COOL

The outside temperature must have been at least 60 degrees Fahrenheit for at least 24 hours before the inspection to operate the equipment safely. There is a danger of drawing liquid Freon™ into the compressor, probably destroying it, by operating it when the temperature has been too cool. Replacement of compressors is expensive. (Read section 7.1.2 Restricted.)

7.1.2.3 FAILED TO RESPOND

The inspector made a cursory safety inspection of the unit and judged it safe to operate. It failed to respond to its normal controls. (Read section 7.1.2 Restricted.)

Beyond checking the same switches and fuses the homeowner would ordinarily check, the inspector will make no attempt to override the system's controls or use any internal resets designed for use by service technicians. You should make arrangements to have the system started by the owner or a service technician and inspected. (Read 7.1.2 Restricted.)

7.1.2.4 HAZARDOUS

The system was not run because it was hazardous either to itself or to the inspector to do so. This could mean the absence of some necessary safety device or the equipment was in such poor condition it was unsafe. Air conditioning systems with exposed wiring or physical damage are examples. (Read section 7.1.2.2 Weather Too Cool.)

7.1.2.5 NONINSPECTED ACCESSORIES

Many accessory type items are not inspected or are indirectly inspected. Humidifiers are only inspected for the damage they may cause to the rest of the system. (Rusting heat exchangers, air handlers, ductwork, etc.) Humidifiers are not tested for operation or effectiveness of humidification. Clock thermostats (night time set back) are not tested through all their cycles. They are only checked as basic thermostats. The function of electronic air cleaners is not checked. If you desire to have these and other similar items inspected, make arrangements with proper service companies.

7.1.2.6 EQUIPMENT INACCESSIBLE

The inspection was physically limited or restricted more than typically. An example would be an air conditioner blocked by the owner's possessions, or an air handler in a crawl space or an attic too small to enter. (Read section 7.1.1 Typical.)

The inspector will not remove possessions to make the inspection. For their safety they will not enter confined or unsafe spaces. It is your responsibility to arrange for proper access and for a full inspection. (Read section 7.1.2 Restricted.)

7.1.2.7 NOT TESTED AS AN AIR CONDITIONER

It is not safe to run a heat pump in the air conditioning mode when it has been below 60 degrees Fahrenheit outside within the last 24 hours. (Read 7.1.2.2 Weather Too Cool.) Under these conditions it could damage the equipment and therefore the system will be tested in its back up mode for heating and as a heat pump if possible. This provides a reasonably good inspection of the system. The system may lose refrigerant and perform poorly simply from disuse. Be careful to monitor the condensate drain from the system after starting it as an air conditioner. No condensation is produced by the indoor unit in the heat pump mode, but switching to air conditioning could produce 20 gallons or more a day. Be certain the drain is functional. (Read 7.1.2 Restricted.)

7.1.2.8 CRAWL SPACE INACCESSIBLE

The crawl space was not entered. It is less than two feet high, the access hole was too small, or it is too wet to enter safely. This leaves much of the air conditioning system uninspected and a total unknown. (Read section 7.1.2 Restricted.)

7.2 GENERAL

A quick reference and overview of the inspector's opinions or impressions. This section is subjective and relies on the inspector's judgement and experience in estimating the age, whether clues are important and if toxins are present, etc. (Read the Air Conditioning chapter fully before forming any final opinion.)

7.2.1 SYSTEM INSPECTED (YES, RESTRICTED, OR NO)

The inspector marks whether the system was inspected. No information will be given about a system that was not inspected. If the inspector writes in or circles "R" for restricted, the system was partially inspected. Check 7.1 LIMITATIONS or discuss it with the inspector to learn the full extent of the restrictions. A severely limited inspection may not give you the information you need. You should do whatever is necessary to remove or overcome the restrictions and have the system fully inspected before you close on the house. (Read 7.1 Limitations.)

7.2.2 ESTIMATED AGE

The inspector's opinion of the estimated age of the air conditioning equipment. It is impossible to tell the actual age of the air conditioning. Many things affect the aging process such as the original quality of the equipment, etc. The inspector is making the broadest of assumptions. Sometimes the dates are clearly imprinted on the equipment or are easy to decipher from the serial numbers, etc. Often they are not. We do not carry cross reference indexes for all manufacturers. If you wish to know the exact age, you should contact the manufacturer and give them the make, model, and serial numbers. They may be able to help, but sometimes even they don't know.

7.2.3 NUMBER OF ZONES OR SYSTEMS

The number of zones or separate systems seen in the house. Multiple zones may give better control of comfort in different areas or levels.

7.2.4 ESTIMATED REMAINING LIFE

Remaining life is similar to estimated age. It is a totally subjective judgment and can only be given in the broadest of terms. It is the inspector's opinion of an estimation of remaining life in terms of years. This always assumes proper maintenance and proper air filters will be used. This is the broadest of assumptions and for the system with the shortest life or on the major system.

7.2.5 CONDENSATE LEAKS (YES OR NO)

"YES"   Condensate was leaking from the system or the associated piping. May also indicate the system has leaked condensation or water in the past. Leaks have the potential to damage the system or associated equipment such as furnaces. They may damage the house if the equipment is in the attic or living space, and contribute to a wet crawl space if the equipment is under the house. Condensate leaks should be cured immediately. Leave this work to professionals. Stagnant condensation in air conditioning systems has been known to harbor algae and Legionnaires disease.

"NO"   No evidence of condensate leaks was seen. The system only produces condensate when it is running as an air conditioner. In winter, heat pumps produce condensation and frost on the coil of the outdoor unit, but not in the air handler. If your system is a heat pump, check the condensate drain during the air conditioning season.

7.2.6 AIR LEAKS (YES OR NO)

"YES" The inspector has seen damaged ductwork on the air conditioning system allowing cool air to escape. This can range from minor repairs to system replacement. Corrections should be made immediately to prevent energy loses and system damage.

"NO"   No air leaks seen.

7.2.7 ROOMS WITHOUT AIR CONDITIONING

"Yes"   There are spaces lacking either central air conditioning or permanently installed space air conditioning. This limits the usefulness or value of a space.

"No"   All rooms appear to have Air Conditioning.

7.2.8 CAPACITY

This is the rated input capacity (read from the label) of the air conditioning system where it can be readily ascertained. This is in BTUH (British Thermal Units per hour) or tons (12,000 BTUH each). A BTU is the amount of heat required to warm one pound of water one degree Fahrenheit. The inspector does not do a heat loss/heat gain calculation and makes no representation about the adequacy or size of the system.

7.2.9 TEMPERATURE DROP

Temperature drop is the amount the air is cooled on each pass through the system. It should be between 14 degrees to 20 degrees. Too little temperature drop often reflects low refrigerant. Too much temperature drop often indicates dirty filters, a dirty coil, or restricted air flow. Service the system immediately. The inspector writes the temperature drop in the space.

7.2.10 OUTDOOR TEMPERATURE

The inspector writes the outdoor temperature on the morning of the inspection. This is important for the safe operation of an air conditioning system. (Read section 7.1.2.2 Weather Too Cool.)

7.2.11 AMATEUR WORKMANSHIP (YES OR NO)

"YES"   The inspector notes workmanship of less than professional quality. Poor workmanship may constitute a major defect. Major defects cost $500.00 or more to repair or may affect the habitability of the house. The work may not serve the purpose intended and may require repair or replacement.

"NO"   No amateur workmanship noted. Some amateurs produce workmanship of equal or better quality than professionals.

7.2.12 SUBJECTIVE RATING

The inspectors grade for the air conditioning system.

E   EXCELLENT, above average, new or like new, (e.g. a new air conditioning system in an older house).

A   AVERAGE, in typical condition for its age, showing normal wear and tear and proper maintenance, (e.g. a five year old air conditioning system looking 5 years old in a 5 year old house).

C   BELOW AVERAGE, prematurely aged, showing heavy or excess wear and tear, or delayed maintenance.

F   SUBSTANDARD, failed, or reaching the end of its normal life expectancy. Any further service, even with repairs, should be considered a gift.

7.3 EQUIPMENT LOCATION

The inspector writes the location of the air conditioning equipment.

7.4 THERMOSTAT TYPE

Describes the type of thermostats. (Read section 6.5 Thermostat Type.)

7.4.1 MECHANICAL

Mechanical thermostats are the most common. They use a coiled strip of a special metal altering shape with changes in temperature. A mercury switch turns the equipment "on" and "off" in response to temperature change. The thermostat can be set according to the homeowner's preference for temperature.

Several other settings are available on most thermostats. In an air system the fan may run constantly or in the automatic mode with the fan running only when the system runs. The purpose of running the fan all the time could be two fold: 1. The noise level remains constant and does not change radically as the equipment cycles "on" and "off." Some people prefer to have the constant noise rather than the varying levels of noise. 2. Constant filtering, humidification or dehumidification of the air. People particularly sensitive to dust, pollen, etc. might have sophisticated filters and run them twenty-four hours a day rather than only when the air conditioning is operating.

7.4.2 ELECTRONIC

Electronic thermostats are beginning to be more prominent. They sense the temperature in a different manner than mechanical thermostats. However, their function remains the same. They sense the temperature and turn the system "on" and "off." As they become more complex they are given more abilities such as turning the equipment on and off at different settings at different times of the day (i.e. night time set back). You could operate the equipment at a higher setting while you're away from home and allow the house to warm up slightly. A clock in the thermostat could reset the temperature at the cooler setting before you return home. These thermostats are falling in price and range from seventy-five to several hundred dollars. Only the most sophisticated thermostats are suitable to use with heat pumps as set back thermostats.

7.4.3 MULTIPLE

There is more than one thermostat in the house indicating there is more than one zone or more than one type of cooling system. Multiple thermostats could also refer to the possibility the heating system and air conditioning system have separate thermostats.

7.4.4 SIMULTANEOUS

Simultaneous implies it is possible for the heating and cooling systems to operate at the same time. It is preferable to integrate them through a single set of controls to avoid simultaneous operation. This problem can easily exist with systems such as baseboard heat and central air conditioning. Be careful to turn off the air conditioning system completely before switching to the heating system and vice versa. Have the controls integrated where possible.

7.5 THERMOSTAT CONDITION:

The inspector checks whether the thermostats are Functioning, Not Functioning, Loose, or Damaged. We do not check accuracy of thermostats, the response time, the delay mechanisms or anticipators built into some thermostats. We check the thermostat function in a fundamental sense (i.e. whether it will turn the equipment "on" and "off"). We do not check the timer, computer, or night time set back features of thermostats. Loose implies the thermostat is not tightly secured to the wall. The thermostat must be tightly secured to the wall and level to operate properly. Repair loose, damaged, or non functional thermostats properly.

7.6 THERMOSTAT LOCATION:
The inspector writes in the location of the thermostat(s).

7.7 EQUIPMENT TYPE
The inspector identifies the air conditioning equipment by type. Read it carefully. Each type has different characteristics, advantages, disadvantages, and maintenance requirements. Some types are not inspected at all.

7.7.1 CENTRAL ELECTRIC
Electric air conditioners are the most common type. They cool the house by extracting heat and moisture from the indoor air and "pumping" the heat outside. The process uses a compressor, a refrigerant (a fluorocarbon commonly known as Freon™), two coils and two fans. The compressor compresses the Freon™ into the high pressure side of the system. Compressing the Freon makes it hot. A fan in the outdoor unit (the condenser) blows the heat into the atmosphere and the Freon liquefies. The liquid Freon then flows to the indoor air handler (the evaporator). Suction from the compressor keeps this coil at low pressure. The Freon expands rapidly through a metering valve and chills the coil. The fan in the air handler blows room air through the coil, cooling the air. The coil is so cold it "sweats." This condensation is moisture extracted from the room air.

Both cooling and dehumidification are important for comfort. Air conditioners too large do not do a thorough job of dehumidification and produce cold clammy air. Properly sized equipment does a better job and is more economical to operate.

Filters are essential because coils get wet as they dehumidify. The coil has many closely spaced fins of aluminum or copper (like the radiator in an automobile). The coil is a good filter. If dusty air is drawn through the coil while wet, it soon becomes clogged. Even a thin coating of dirt can reduce the efficiency of the coil and cause the compressor to strain unnecessarily. Ironically, a dirty coil slows down the air's velocity and it lingers in the coil, picks up more "cool" than it should and comes out colder than normal. This fools the occupants into thinking the unit is working efficiently, when it is struggling.

MAINTENANCE AND UPKEEP
An air conditioning compressor has a normal life of 10 to 14 years. Change air filters every 30 to 60 days to provide proper air circulation throughout the house and to protect the coil. All central air conditioning systems have their idiosyncrasies. Place a service contract on the unit with a reputable air conditioning contractor to clean and service regularly. With regular professional monitoring, you should receive good performance for the life expectancy of the unit.

7.7.1 a. Central Electric
Do not allow leaves, pine straw, other debris to clog the outside unit. Keep plantings cut back several feet. The unit needs a tremendous amount of air to operate properly.

7.7.2 HEAT PUMPS

Many heat pumps were installed in the late 70's and early 80's because there was a 10 year moratorium on natural gas extensions. As discussed in Section 6.3.4, heat pumps are air conditioners that run frontwards and backwards. They extract heat from the house in the summer and pump it outdoors. They can extract heat from the air in the winter and pump it indoors. Heat pumps have certain idiosyncrasies making them difficult to inspect. A heat pump should not be run in the air conditioning mode when it has been below 60 degrees outside anytime in the past 24 hours. In the spring, we often find heat pumps not functioning properly because of the loss of refrigerant or mechanical problems. Heat pumps have built-in back up systems automatically taking over for any reason. Sometimes, the homeowner often does not know the unit failed until it is inspected.

7.7.2 a. Heat Pump
The junk stored around the heat pump will severely restrict the air available to the unit. The compressor had already been replaced once. Do not allow shrubbery, fencing or personal possessions to block the air flow.

7.7.3 THROUGH THE WALL

Through the wall units work on the same principal as central units. (Read section 7.7.1 Central Electric.) These are the equivalent of space heaters. They usually cool one or two rooms and lack central distribution. If permanent, these units are checked for basic function (cooling) only.

7.7.4 WINDOW UNITS

Window units are identified but are not inspected. They are personal property. If you are purchasing them with the house, have the seller demonstrate the operation and acquire any papers, warranties etc.

7.7.5 GAS CHILLERS

Gas chillers function on a principal entirely different from central electric air conditioning. They use a chemical (often lithium bromide) with a violent affinity for water. It absorbs water vapor in a closed system, so aggressively the water boils at a very low temperature. This low temperature cools the air in the house. Heat from a gas flame dries the lithium bromide allowing the process to continue. This is a simplistic explanation of the process. The water is absorbed creating the cooling effect so the systems are absorption chillers. These systems are rare in homes and not inspected. Get all the information you can from the sellers, installer, maintenance company, and local gas utility.

7.7.6 WATER SOURCE

Water Source heat pumps are fundamentally different from air source heat pumps. They deposit their heat into water as opposed to exhausting it into the atmosphere. The obvious problem with this type of heat pump is it requires a steady and reliable source of water. Many of these systems are ground source systems using long loops of pipe buried at a depth 6 feet or deeper. Sometimes it is necessary to have two wells, one to pump the water from and one to dump the water back into. Sometimes the water is discharged into a local stream, pond, or storm sewer. This type of system demands a strong well.

7.8 DUCTWORK TYPE

Ductwork is used with hot air systems and air conditioning systems. Ductwork for a gravity system must be large and sloping to encourage the proper distribution of the air. These systems are antiquated and most have often been upgraded or replaced. Ductwork is often fabricated in metal. The metal in the ductwork should be galvanized or treated to prevent rusting. In recent years new forms of ductwork have been introduced such as ductboard.

Ductboard, of high density fiberglass, is rolled or folded into the form of ductwork. The joints are taped. Most residential ductwork is not absolutely air tight. Its purpose is to distribute the heating and cooling throughout the house with reasonable reliability. Concealed ducts must be designed for permanent installation with a minimum of service and must be rodent, fire, rust resistant, and large enough to handle the volume of air.

Many old gas or oil heating systems used small (4" or 5" diameter) ductwork. Much of it was uninsulated or poorly insulated and did not include a vapor barrier. Air conditioning systems move higher volumes of air than heating systems. Gas and oil furnaces deliver air 45 degrees to 75 degrees above room temperature and air conditioning only cools the air 14 to 20 degrees. Undersized ductwork may restrict air flow to the point air conditioning will not function properly and the ducts must be replaced and properly insulated.

MAINTENANCE AND UPKEEP
(Read section 6.8.4 Ductwork.)

7.8.1 INSULATED

Insulation is essential for air conditioning ducts installed in the attic or the crawl space. Ductwork installed within the living space need not be insulated. The attic temperature varies widely and ducts in the attic let the coldest air come in contact with the hottest environment in the house. Air conditioning ductwork also requires a proper vapor barrier to prevent condensation.

7.8.1 a. Insulated Ductwork
The insulation on this 7.8.3 Transite Duct is 7.11.13 Insulation Damaged. The insulation had fallen off the duct. Transite ductwork is unusual in this application. Transite or cement asbestos board may contain asbestos.

7.8.2 UNINSULATED

Uninsulated ductwork is commonly seen in older homes with gas or oil heat. As energy costs rise, insulation becomes more important. To insulate existing ductwork to today's standards can be expensive and elaborate, but insulation is essential when used with air conditioning. Uninsulated attic ducts can sweat, cause condensation to form, and drip to the ceilings below causing water damage. There are energy losses associated with uninsulated ductwork. Therefore, ductwork must be properly insulated for use with air conditioning, to include a vapor barrier wrapped around the outside of any exterior fiberglass or fibrous insulation.

7.8.3 TRANSITE

Transite is a cement asbestos type material formed into many products. Ducts under slabs were often transite. They contain asbestos and may have been contaminated by the drilling of termite companies. If you have transite ducts it may be wise to have an air test done for asbestos and insecticide contamination.

7.8.4 METAL

Metal ducts are of light gauge metal. Main trunk ducts are rectangular and sized for the application. Branch ducts to individual supply registers are rolled metal pipe similar to stove pipe. Galvanizing gives it the ability to resist the corrosion from the moisture in the environment.

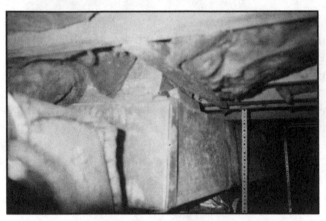

Metal ducts should be mechanically fastened with screws in the joints or metal strips designed to clip or clamp the sections of ductwork together.

7.8.4 a. Metal Duct.
The metal main or trunk duct appears to be 7.8.2 Uninsulated. Unless it is insulated on the interior, it must be wrapped with insulation and a vapor barrier to avoid condensation.

7.8.5 FLEXIBLE DUCTS

In recent years manufacturers have provided us with a wide variety of ducts manufactured from various products. There are hose ducts similar to dryer vent hoses, but insulated. They can be attached to the trunk ducts and to the floor or the ceiling registers, completing the job. The insulation and vapor barrier are already in place. Some have been more successful than others.

7.8.6 DUCTBOARD

This is a board of high density fiberglass which can be folded and cut on the site into rectangular sections. Fiberglass ductboard is suspect when used in crawl spaces. The fastening systems holding the ductboard together have not always been successful in damp environments and main ducts are often waterlogged and collapsed in wet crawl spaces. The ducts in attics are sometimes damaged or crushed by homeowner storage or from people stepping on them. There is some question of fiberglass ductboard allowing the fibers to slough off inside and circulate in the air of the living space.

7.9 REGISTERS AND GRILLS

Supply registers and return grills are important parts of an air distribution system. Return grills may contain air filters. Air filters are essential to air conditioning systems. Supply registers often contain dampers to allow the homeowner to balance the system.

Balancing the system is the idea of providing more or less air supply to individual spaces to accommodate the orientation of the house, the size of the rooms, wind angles, etc. which influence the room's temperature. These dampers and internal dampers in the system give the owner a chance to tune the system and balance it. You can have bedrooms cooler than the living room or vice versa.

Balancing is essential in two story houses and often must be adjusted seasonally. In the summer, cold air settles, so open upstairs registers completely to allow air conditioning to enter and close or restrict first floor registers to force air upstairs. In winter the procedure can be reversed by closing the second floor registers and opening the first floor registers completely to force heat to the first floor.

The veins in the supply registers disperse the air over a wide area to achieve even distribution of cool air from the system. It is important the registers and grills properly distribute the air throughout the house and allow the owner to adjust or balance the system. In some systems the supply grills are in the ceiling or high in the side wall and return grills near the floor level. The problem is to force a wide and even distribution of air in the house. In other systems supply grills are at floor level and the return grills are near the ceiling. Occasionally duel duct systems are seen where there are supply and return grills in each room. With these the supplies can be along the outside wall and the returns in the center of the room or vice versa. For comfort it seems best to distribute the supply around the outer perimeter and collect the returning air near the center.

All these systems have been devised to provide a comfortable environment. It is important the flow of air from the grills not be totally restricted. With heat pumps, they are designed so each register is an important part of the system and not more than two supply registers should be cut off. Full air flow is important to good operation of heat pumps.

You should not close returns in any system. Return grills can be used to contain air filters. Air filters are essential to the system.

7.10 FILTERS

Air filters are essential to any air conditioning system. Filters are (1) to protect the system and (2) to protect the occupants of the house. Their primary purpose is to protect the mechanical equipment.

Filters can range from simple and inefficient fiberglass types inserted in the ductwork or return air grill, to multiple stage paper filters or electronic filters capable of cleaning 99% of the matter from the air.

7.10.1 DISPOSABLE FILTERS

Disposable filters are designed to be used for a short time, thrown away, and replaced with another disposable filter. Change disposable filters every 30 to 60 days. Most standard size filters are available at hardware and similar stores. The cost can be up to several dollars each. They are beneficial to the occupants and essential to the equipment and should be replaced regularly. Most are not efficient at filtering small particles from the air.

7.10.2 WASHABLE FILTERS

Washable filters are similar in size to the disposable filters. They are a fibrous mesh or shredded aluminum material with a metal frame. These filters are used for a brief period of time (30 to 60 days), washed, and replaced in the equipment. Some washable filters are sprayed with a tacky or sticky substance which aids in collecting the particles in the air. This spray material has a pleasant odor and is water soluble, making the filter easy to wash. Some filters are designed to be washed off with a hose and others may be washed in a dishwasher. Replace them as they weaken and soften with age. Old tired filters may be sucked into the equipment.

7.10.3 ELECTRONIC FILTERS

Electronic filters are more sophisticated and efficient than the disposable ones. The disposable filters do a good job of collecting large particles from the air. Electronic filters have the advantage of being able to attract small particles from the air and therefore are beneficial for people with allergy or respiratory problems. Electronic filters are protected by disposable or washable filters collecting the large particles allowing the electronic filter to collect only the small particles. Electronic filters require periodic maintenance and should be cleaned every 30 to 60 days. These filters are not tested under the scope of the inspection for their operation. You should have the seller demonstrate the cleaning procedure and maintenance to you. Many electronic filters are broken and abandoned in place. Be sure you have maintained a filter adequate to protect the equipment. Running an air conditioning system without a proper filter can destroy the compressor in a single season.

7.11 OBSERVATIONS

The inspector marks observations of conditions affecting the air conditioning system. More than one item can be marked as the system may exhibit more than one symptom or problem. Some items are part of the normal aging process and do not require correction. Other items require either maintenance or repair if the system is to reach the full potential or life expectancy. Read carefully each section applying to the system inspected.

Maintenance is the on going care required if a system or item is to reach the full potential including lubricating, painting, etc. Do maintenance as required by the manufacturer of the equipment or item. Repairs put items or systems back in good condition after damage or decay, etc. Repairs are caused by delayed maintenance, aging, normal wear and tear, or abuse. The workmanship and materials of the repairs should be equal to the quality of the system and have the same life expectancy. e.g. A limb plunges through an asphalt shingle roof. If the roofing otherwise has a life expectancy of ten years, the repair should also have a life expectancy of at least ten years. If the roofing only has a life expectancy of one year, then the repair should be capable of lasting one year or more. It is not prudent to put a one year patch on a ten year roof or to waste a ten year repair on a one year roof. All repairs should be by qualified competent professionals.

7.11.1 SOUND
The inspector thinks the item inspected is functioning at the moment of the inspection. This does not imply perfection, absence of minor defects, or absence of wear and tear.

7.11.2 TYPICAL
The inspector thinks the item, material, or aspect of construction is characteristic or similar to comparable products in similar houses. The system has normal wear and tear.

7.11.3 COIL CLEAN
The coil in the air handler is substantially free of dirt, dust, and debris. It does not need immediate cleaning.

7.11.4 COIL DIRTY
The coil in the air handler is coated with dust and debris. This indicates the system has operated with a poor filter or with no filter. This can be hazardous to the compressor because it forces it to operate at improper temperatures and pressures and may shorten the compressor life dramatically. The coil is dirty enough to warrant cleaning. Have a qualified service technician properly clean the coil and operate the system with the service gauges in place to assure proper performance. If the coil can be cleaned in place it may cost $50.00 - $75.00, but if it must be removed and chemically cleaned and high pressure washed it may cost $250.00 - $300.00. If the compressor has been damaged it may cost an additional $750.00 - $1250.00. (See 6.12.7.a. Dirty Coil.)

7.11.5 COIL NOT SEEN
The inspector cannot gain access to see the side where the air enters the coil. (This would be the dirty side.) Therefore the system performance is judged indirectly and may seem normal when it is not. (Low Freon™ and a dirty coil are common problems and have off setting effects on performance.) Have a service company install an inspection port and check the coil.

7.11.6 FAN VIBRATES
The fan in the air handler or outdoor unit vibrates abnormally. This vibration is noisy and can shorten the life of the fan or the equipment. Have the fan repaired or replaced promptly.

7.11.7 FAN BELT AGING
The fan belt is cracked, frayed, worn, or aging. Aging fan belts should be replaced to avoid the loss of the fan and thus the air conditioning when the belt breaks.

7.11.8 NO FILTER
There is no filter present in the air handler or system. As previously explained filters are essential for the protection of the equipment. They are especially important to heat pumps and air conditioning systems. The absence of a filter will shorten the life of a heat pump or air conditioning system substantially. It will also degrade the performance of other heating systems. Replace or install a proper filter immediately.

7.11.9 DIRTY FILTER

The filter is dirty and should be cleaned or replaced immediately. Dirty air filters cause the air flow through the system to be restricted (slowed) to the point the temperature readings taken on the system are false or altered. Clean or replace the filter immediately.

7.11.10 LOOSE FILTER

The system's filter was not properly installed or was too small for the opening. If the filter is loosely mounted and "floats" around or so small air by passes it, the coil may become blocked by debris in the unfiltered air. Install a proper filter immediately.

7.11.11 DOORS NOT UNDERCUT

The doors left closed for long periods of time, such as bedroom doors, are not properly undercut to allow the heat and air conditioning to return to the central air return. It is important, especially with heat pumps, to allow the air to circulate freely. Cut the doors a minimum of 3/4 of an inch above the level of the carpet. If this is not done the system will be difficult to balance and difficult to maintain proper temperatures within the rooms with the doors shut. (i.e. too hot or cold for comfort.)

7.11.12 DUCTWORK DAMAGED

Physical damage found to the ductwork. This may be crushed, disconnected, or wet and rusted ductwork. It can also indicate ductwork has collapsed, fallen loose, shifted, and leaks air in the crawl space or attic. (Read section 7.8 Ductwork.)

7.11.12 a. Ductwork Damaged
Notice the crack where the round duct joins the "boot" or floor register adapter. The black spot is also a hole in the boot. Such damage allows conditioned air to blow into the crawl space. Have the damage repaired to save energy.

7.11.13 INSULATION DAMAGED

The insulation on the ductwork has substantial damage influencing the system's performance or economy. (Read section 7.8.1 Insulated.)

7.11.14 NO VAPOR BARRIER

Air conditioning ductwork must be insulated in attics and crawl spaces not only to conserve energy, but also to prevent condensate forming on the ductwork. A vapor barrier is essential to prevent warm moist air from saturating the insulation. The condensation can rust and damage the ductwork, and drip onto the ceiling below, ruining it.

7.11.15 UNDERSIZED DUCTWORK

The inspector feels the ductwork is undersized for its present application or undersized for the addition of future air conditioning. (Read section 7.8 Ductwork.)

7.11.16 POOR LAYOUT

The inspector feels the system is poorly "laid out" to the extent designed. It will not or cannot function economically, safely, or properly. If the system cannot perform satisfactorily, repair or replace.

7.11.17 POSSIBLE ASBESTOS

The inspector sees materials he believes may possibly contain asbestos. Asbestos, wherever it's found, is of concern to all homeowners. If it breaks down into small fibers (becomes friable) and is inhaled or ingested, it can have serious and far reaching health effects. Only proper laboratory tests can confirm or deny its presence and only then can an appropriate response be suggested. The treatment and removal of asbestos is dangerous and expensive and should be left to experts. Contact a qualified asbestos testing laboratory to test and identify the material and advise on removal.

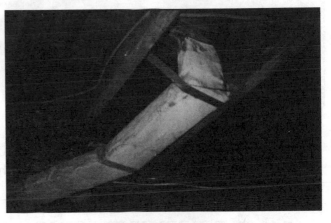

7.11.17 a. Possible Asbestos
The white material wrapped around the duct may contain asbestos.

7.11.18 CABINET DAMAGE

There is damage to the cabinet or shell of the air conditioner or associated equipment. This can range from physical damage such as bent doors or damaged panels, to rusted cabinets. Rust can form on the equipment by periodic flooding of the basements or crawl spaces. Air conditioning coils whose drains have become blocked can overflow and flood the cabinet. Humidifiers spraying too much water into the system can be harmful. Cabinet damage influencing performance must be repaired.

7.11.19 TOO SMALL

The inspector feels the air conditioning equipment is too small for the size of the residence. We do not do a heat loss/heat gain survey of the property. This is a subjective judgment. Have experts perform heat loss/heat gain calculations and determine whether the equipment is adequate.

7.11.20 DRIP PAN ABSENT

There is no drip pan. The absence of a drain pan allows water overflowing from an attic air handler to damage the house. Condensation drain pans placed under the air handler of central air conditioning units are there to remove excess condensate water from the house.

They drain to the exterior of the house through plastic pipe or hose. Either from lack of maintenance or in an emergency, these pans could fill and overflow causing water damage to whatever is underneath. Keep the pans free of debris, insulation, etc., to enhance the drain's function.

7.11.21 WATER IN THE DRIP PAN

There is water in the drip pan. The presence of water in the drain pan indicates a problem with the unit. A qualified service company should be contacted. Condensate has been known to harbor Legionnaires Disease and algae.

7.11.21 Water In The Drip Pan.
The rust (dark stain) in the condensate drip pan or tray under the air conditioner indicates the condensate drain has failed. If the pan overflows, the house below will be damaged. Notice the duct has shifted away from the air conditioner and the vertical crack leaks conditioned air into the attic. Have the drain cleared and the duct properly reattached.

7.11.22 CONDENSATION DRAIN NOT FUNCTIONAL

The condensation drain is clogged or physically damaged and is not functioning. Have the drain repaired immediately.

7.11.23 EQUIPMENT AGING

The system is aging, antiquated, and reaching the end of its useful life. Any additional life or service from such systems should be considered a "gift." The system can be replaced with modern equipment of higher efficiency. The pay back period may be relatively short due to the increased efficiency of the new equipment.

7.11.24 EQUIPMENT OLD/WORN OUT

The equipment has reached the end of its useful life and is old, antiquated, geriatric, worn out, or beyond repair. Any additional life or use from equipment at this stage should be considered a "gift" even with repairs.

7.11.25 NOT FUNCTIONAL

The system does not operate. The inspector will make a cursory inspection of the system to be sure it is safe to operate using the same controls and devices the homeowner would use. The inspector will not override the system's internal controls, use any reset devices intended for service technicians, or manipulate the system to force it to run.

CHAPTER EIGHT

INSULATION

Insulation is any material used to reduce the transmission of heat or to reduce fire hazard. Heat and moisture flow through buildings is complex and poorly understood. Fiber type insulations combat convection or the movement of air. Air is a good insulator and insulation holds the air still, resisting the air currents carrying the heat away. Insulation soaked with water is not a good insulator. Warm moist air infiltrates the walls allowing condensation to soak the insulation. Mold, mildew, or rot may result. The structure must be kept dry and allowed to dry as quickly as it wets.

Organic products such as grass, animal hair, and sawdust tried as insulation were found to rot or attract insects or vermin. Inorganic mineral wool production (derived from iron ore slag) started in the late 1800's and fiberglass production began in the 1920's. Blowing these products into wall cavities and attics or installing them in batt form produced houses for the first time pleasant to occupy. Until then people roasted on one side and froze on the other.

Insulation has two primary purposes: fuel economy and comfort. It may also reduce sound transmission and help to prevent the spread of fire. Insulation is good in most climates.

Since the 1930's houses have been insulated, but not regularly until after World War II. Other changes in construction techniques affected energy and moisture flow. Using plywood, storm siding, weatherstripping, storm windows, etc. reduced infiltration. Increased insulation has reduced heat loss. Many changes occurred reducing construction costs or energy loss but not controlling moisture. The latest shift is from using "active chimneys." Traditional gas and oil fired heating systems drew combustion air from the house as they burned. This ventilated the house and drew in fresh air. Heat pumps, electric heat, and modern "Decoupled" furnaces do not draw air from the house. When houses were leaky, drafty, and the heating equipment forced ventilation, moisture was not a big issue. A damp crawl space did not have much influence if all the air in the house exchanged with outdoor air every hour.

Draftiness or infiltration into and out of the house has little to do with insulation. Insulation cannot be effective if air leaks through or around it. Refreshing the air in the house is important. Older houses may have air changes as often as once an hour. This is too high, wasting energy and producing an indoor environment often too dry for comfort. Air changes at the rate of 3 to 5 per 24 hours seem to produce a good balance between energy conservation, proper interior moisture, and controlling odor, disease, and contaminants.

MAINTENANCE AND UPKEEP

The insulation should be close around the heated space. Retain the heat in the living space. Insulate the ceiling, not the rafters in the attic. Insulate knee walls between heated spaces and storage areas. Insulate floors above garages and crawl spaces. Be careful to insulate on the cold side of pipes. If the insulation is between the pipe and the heat source, the pipe may freeze. If in doubt, insulate the pipe itself.

Keep the insulation in good condition and properly distributed. Don't move it around and not replace it. Don't allow the wind to blow it around and uncover ceilings. If loose insulation is blowing around, replace it with batts. Don't crush or compress insulation more than a little. Thirteen inches of loose attic insulation compressed to twelve inches by installing a floor may still have nearly an R-30 and may benefit from being covered with plywood. (The cover cuts infiltration.) But thirteen inches crushed down to six inches may have less than an R-19. You need both optimum density and depth to maintain the desired R factor.

Vapor barriers (usually plastic or aluminum foil), now called vapor retarders, should be installed on the warm side of the insulation. The change in the name from barrier to retarder comes from the fact they are seldom perfect and true "barriers," so "retarder" describes them better. They are difficult to retrofit unless remodeling. Enamel or vapor barrier type paints may help on the interior of exterior walls and on ceilings. It is also important to seal cracks to prevent warm moist air seeping into the wall spaces or attic. Seal around electrical outlets, switches, and ceiling fixtures.

Vapor or moisture barriers on the grade in the crawl space also suppress water rising into the crawl space through capillary action. Moisture from humid air can attack the structure above. By preventing the vapor from wetting the air in the crawl space, the vapor retarder on grade keeps the air in the crawl space dryer and protects not only the lumber in the crawl space, but the structure above. By keeping the insulation dryer, vapor retarders help maintain the insulation's effectiveness.

8 a. Insulation
Sometimes dew evaporating or snow melting from the roof reveals whether insulation is effective and evenly distributed. The insulation should not touch the underside of the roof.

How much insulation is enough? Check with the local gas or electric utility or building official. Genuinely concerned with energy conservation, they may provide energy audits or information. The E-7 program adopted by some utilities recommend comprehensive guidelines for various climates. In Virginia, it requires R-30 attic insulations, R-19 floors insulation, and R-13 batts wall insulation. It also requires thermopane windows or storm windows, high efficiency heating/cooling equipment, and sealing against infiltration.

R-Value is resistance to heat flow. (The higher the R-Value the better the insulation.) Every material and component has a R-Value including air spaces. The R-Value of the individual materials and components adds up to the total R-Value of the wall or floor. If installed properly 3-5/8 inch fiberglass batts have a R-Value of 13. 3-5/8 inches of wood has a R-Value of roughly 4.5, 3-5/8 inches of brick has a R-Value of approximately 0.4, and aluminum foil has almost no R-Value per se but is useful in reflecting radiant heat.

Analyze the cost verses the benefit of any insulation/weatherization project. The following suggestions may help.

PROJECT	POTENTIAL SAVINGS
Weatherstripping doors and windows	3 to 5%
Storm windows and doors (all openings)	10 to 20%
Attic or ceiling insulation	5 to 20%
Wall insulation	5 to 15%
Floor insulation	5 to 10%

Weatherstripping might cost $50 if done by the homeowner and save 4% annually. Insulating ceilings may cost $300 and save 10% annually. Insulating walls may cost $2000 and save 10%. (i.e. Annual energy cost is $2400, Project cost is $350 for weatherstripping and ceiling insulation, saving $336 the first year. Spending $2000 insulating walls only saves $240 the first year. It will take 8.33 years to pay back.) It is often not cost effective to insulate outside walls unless extensively remodeling.

Recent studies indicate not as much heat escapes around windows and doors as once thought. Unless you are in a constantly windy area, much of your heat loss may be from the warm air inside the house rising and escaping through the ceiling. This vertical heat loss is called the "stack effect" and causes heated air to escape through the ceiling, drawing in cold air through the floor. Without wind pushing on them, there is little force to make air leak through windows. You may do well to seal the ceiling against air leakage by caulking light fixtures or installing gaskets and stuffing or caulking holes in the top of the walls and ceiling from the attic and through the floor from the crawl space.

8 a. Insulation
Dirt around the edge of the carpet indicates air leakage, not bad housekeeping.

8.1 LIMITATIONS

This section describes the aspects limiting the inspection of the insulation. Inspectors do the best inspection they can, but sometimes physical obstructions, weather conditions, or the condition of the insulation, prevent them from doing the whole job. Arrange for an inspection overcoming the limitations, if possible. It is your responsibility to overcome the limitations. You should complete the inspection prior to closing even if you must hire others (insulation contractor's etc.) or pay an additional fee to the inspector or industry specialist. Repairs can be expensive and at some point replacement is the best alternative. An uninspected system or one given a severely limited or restricted inspection could be a total unknown. The inspector cannot make representations about what was not inspected. If you close on the house with a Limited or Restricted inspection you are accepting the responsibility for the unknown items about the system.

You should also be aware insulation limits the inspection of other components and systems. Inspectors are not required to remove insulation to inspect the materials of construction or systems it conceals.

8.1.1 TYPICAL

The inspector feels they have seen as much of the insulation as they normally see. The visible insulation is inspected from the crawl space and attic, while walking around the house, and from arms length. A typical inspection does not include removing wall covering or cover plates to expose the insulation for inspection. The inspection is not a heat loss/heat gain calculation or an energy audit. The inspection does not address the adequacy of the insulation. Concealed insulation (in walls, under attic floors) is not inspected. Areas concealed by insulation are not inspected and are often not as well insulated as visible areas. (Also read section 8.1 Limitations.)

8.1.2 RESTRICTED

The inspector feels they have seen less of the insulation than they typically see. (Also read section 8.1.1 Typical.)

8.1.2.1 CRAWL SPACE INACCESSIBLE

The crawl space is not entered. It is less than two feet high, the access hole was too small, or is too wet to enter safely. This leaves much of the insulation uninspected and a total unknown. (Read section 8.1.2 Restricted.)

8.1.2.1 a. Crawl space Inaccessible.
The hole is too small for the inspector to pass through safely. They cannot inspect what they cannot see.

8.1.2.2 ATTIC INACCESSIBLE

Personal possessions, lack of an access hole, or the size of the attic can make access to the attic impossible. The inspector will not remove personal possessions or do damage to gain access to the attic. There may be insulation left uninspected. Eliminate this restriction, so the attic can be inspected. (Read section 8.1.2 Restricted.)

8.2 GENERAL

A quick reference and overview of the inspector's opinions or impressions. This section is subjective and relies on the inspector's judgment and experience in estimating the age, whether clues are important and if toxins are present, etc. (Read the Insulation chapter fully before forming any final opinion.)

8.2.1 SYSTEM INSPECTED (YES, RESTRICTED, OR NO)

The inspector marks whether the system was inspected. No information will be given about a system that was not inspected. If the inspector writes in or circles "R" for restricted, the system was partially inspected. Check 8.1 LIMITATIONS or discuss it with the inspector to learn the full extent of the restrictions. A severely limited inspection may not give you the information you need. You should do whatever is necessary to remove or overcome the restrictions and have the system fully inspected before you close on the house. (Read 8.1 Limitations.)

8.2.2 SUBJECTIVE RATING

The inspector's grade for the insulation system:

E   EXCELLENT, above average, new or like new, (e.g. a new insulation on an older house.)

A   AVERAGE, in typical condition for its age, showing normal wear and tear. (e.g. five year old insulation looking 5 years old and a 5 year old house.)

C   BELOW AVERAGE, prematurely aged, showing heavy or excess wear and tear, or delayed maintenance. Perhaps showing minor (curable) defects. (e.g. five year old insulation showing the wear and tear or age characteristics of 10 year old insulation.)

F   SUBSTANDARD,   failed, or reaching the end of its life expectancy. Any further service, even with repairs, should be considered a gift.

8.3 TYPE

The material of the insulation is identified. Each material has characteristics differing from the others. Insulation must be able to resist the passage of heat from the living spaces. It should be decay, vermin, and fire resistant.

8.3.1 FIBERGLASS

Fiberglass insulation is millions of hair like glass fibers. It is available in a chopped or shredded version poured or blown into attics or wall cavities. Batts or fluffy blankets are another form. Batts come in several thicknesses and used in walls, ceilings, and floors. Blankets are used in commercial buildings and on ductwork and water heaters.

Loose fill or blown fiberglass has a R-value of about 2.3 per inch. Batt types have a R-value of about 3.1 per inch. Proper installation, density, moisture, and air infiltration influence its performance dramatically. Fiberglass does not burn, support fire, produce toxic smoke, decay, or attract vermin. Mice like to nest in it. It is a skin irritant and makes you itch. Avoid contact with it and do not store clothing or personal possessions in contact with it.

8.3.2 CELLULOSE

Cellulose insulation is finely shredded paper or wood pulp treated to be fire and vermin resistant. It is loose fill insulation and poured or blown into ceilings and wall cavities. It is blown in a wet form (like papiermache) into the stud cavities of new houses and allowed to dry.

The treatment process is suspect and the fire and vermin resistance of some older versions may degrade with age.

Cellulose loose fill has a R-value of about 3.1 to 3.7 per inch. Proper installation, density, moisture, and air infiltration influence its performance dramatically. Poorly treated products may burn and attract insects. It absorbs water readily and may conceal or disguise roof, plumbing, and equipment leaks indefinitely. The water eventually destroys the insulation. The dust from the product may cause an allergic reaction or irritate eyes and respiratory systems. If dust continues to bother you, try misting the surface of the insulation with a fine spray of water. A garden sprayer works well. The damp insulation forms a crust and may stop spreading dust.

8.3.3 ROCKWOOL OR MINERAL WOOL

These products are similar to fiberglass except they are of slag or mineral products. (Read section 8.3.1 Fiberglass.) R-value ranges from about 2.75 to 3.2.

8.3.3 a. Rockwool
The insulation is a blown in type of rock wool or mineral fiber. Notice the drip marks of water stains on the framing.

1.10.45 a. Condensation
Water condenses on the cold nails on the underside of the roof sheeting in the attic and drips on the framing and insulation. Notice the elongated rust stains around the nails. Condensation in the attic is a clue or tell tale sign the crawl space or basement is wet. See also 1.10.45 Condensation.

8.3.4 FOAM

Many foam insulation products exist including glass foams and volcanic products. Foam in residential applications is usually a plastic or organic product. Although foams offer high R-Values per inch, many are controversial because they produce toxic fumes and carcinogens when they burn. They should never be left exposed in the living space. Production of some foams may also use fluorocarbon gases accused of depleting the ozone layer.

8.3.4.1 EPS

EPS is Expanded Polystyrene. Polystyrene graduals are heated in a mold. They expand many times their original volume filling the mold. Large blocks are sliced into sheets for insulation with hot wires or saws. This is the foam used in inexpensive coolers and packing materials. It looks like popcorn molded together.

EPS has a R-value of about 3.75 per inch. It is usually white and may become saturated if used underground or under water. It may be one of the least toxic of foams when burned but should not be exposed. This foam is fragile compared to most others.

8.3.4.2 POLYSTYRENE

Extruded polystyrene is of the same plastic as Expanded Polystyrene, but the manufacturing process forces it through a die (extrudes it into a sheet) and eliminates the beads. The end product is often colored blue or pink. It is somewhat sturdier than EPS and does not absorb water readily. Its R-value is about 4 to 5 per inch. It should not be exposed on the interior.

8.3.4.3 UREA FORMALDEHYDE

Urea Formaldehyde was injected as a liquid foam into the wall cavities of homes and buildings. It was a soap like foaming agent mixed with a urea formaldehyde product. The combination allowed the foam to dry and harden into a stable mass. It is fine textured, delicate to the touch, and white or cream colored. Controversy arose because the foam had a tendency to "out gas" formaldehyde fumes as it cured. Formaldehyde is an irritant and a carcinogen.

The controversy over the foam was so intense, the demand for the foam ceased, and the industry died in this country. Installation of the product may have been banned but a clear case against the foam was never established and the ban was quietly lifted. As far as the author knows, there is little health risk associated with the foam once it has cured. You are more likely to expose yourself to formaldehyde from particle board, plywood, cabinets or any of dozens of other products.

8.3.4.4 ISO CYANURATE

Iso Cyanurate foam is most often used in sheet form for storm siding over the framing and under the siding. The foam is usually fiberglass reinforced and foil faced. The aluminum foil facing has caused controversy. It is a vapor barrier and is on the wrong side of the wall. (Vapor barriers must be on the warm side of the wall to operate properly.) The foil also appears to reflect the sun's heat back onto the back of the siding, cooking it. This appears to cause the knots to fall out of wood siding and shorten the life of composition siding. Moisture and heat flow through structures is a complex process and this application of foil and foam may have far reaching effects and has not been fully sorted out. Local climate also influences the process. A version of the foam with paper or moisture permeable faces is also in use.

The foam has an initial R-value as high as 7.2 per inch, but may degrade with age to 6 or less. Claims that the foil face gives a 1/2 inch sheet a R-value of about 4 are doubtful. This foam may "out gas" toxic fumes in a fire and should never be left exposed.

8.3.4.5 URETHANE

Urethane foam can be installed in sheets of cured foam cut from large blocks, or sprayed in as a liquid. The sheets have one of the highest R-values initially (up to 8), but also generate toxic fumes when burned. The R-value degrades to as little as 6 an inch with age. Do not leave it exposed.

Liquid urethane is sometimes sprayed into the stud cavities in new construction in a thin layer to seal against infiltration and to add to the R-value of the wall. It is also injected into cracks and crevices around windows, wires, pipes and other penetrations to cut infiltrations. In its liquid form it is sticky and is an excellent sealant. It expands or grows as it cures. This can be a problem if the expansion crushes a window or bulges a wall.

8.3.5 ALUMINUM FOIL

Foil is used in many building products and is an excellent vapor barrier and insulation. As insulation it functions entirely differently than foam or fiber insulations. Foil's shiny surface reflects the radiant component of the heat. The foam and fiber types hold a layer of air still and work to reduce convective loses. Foil has no R-value per se, but each shiny surface appears to equal about a R-3.

Foil is used on the back of drywall, on the face of foam, as a building paper, and in a batt form. As a batt it is fabricated in multiple layers that "accordion" apart or fluff up when stretched into position and stapled. Some types have up to five layers of foil. The foil must face an air space. If it touches anything, it becomes a conductor instead of a reflector. Installation is more critical than with fiber and foam types. A tear or hole can allow air to circulate around an entire piece, negating its value. If the foil is not properly stretched and "inflated," the reflectiveness of the layers will be lost.

In some applications the combination of a vapor barrier and insulation is excellent. In many places the foil must be perforated with thousands of tiny holes to allow it to "breath" and let the moisture to escape properly. In the deep south and other climates where air conditioning

is the dominant use of energy, foil is proving successful at reflecting the sun's heat and reducing the cost of air conditioning.

8.3.5 a. Aluminum Foil Insulation
This foil insulation above a crawl space is 8.5.5 Water Damaged. There was a plumbing leak dripping into the insulation. Insulation is a restriction on an inspection because it conceals damage and blocks the inspectors view.

8.3.6 CONCEALED

Part of the insulation is out of sight or hidden from inspection. In most houses wall insulation is concealed. Often an attic floor prohibits inspection of all or part of the ceiling insulation. The inspector does not speculate on what is concealed. Do not assume the concealed areas are insulated as well as the visible areas. Often they are not insulated at all.

8.3.7 VAPOR BARRIER OR RETARDER

Once known as Vapor Barriers they are now called Vapor Retarders. Their function is to stop or retard moisture in the form of vapor from migrating into cold areas of the building and condensing on cold surfaces. They are important, misunderstood, and controversial. Most often they are sheets or films of materials that are impermeable or highly resistant to the passage of moisture vapor. They stop the movement of most of the moisture before it gets into the wall cavity, attic, etc. and condenses, wetting the insulation and the wood. Often they are installed as sheets of plastic film (usually polyethylene) or aluminum foil.

The film may cover the wall and occasionally the ceiling surface before the interior wall covering is installed. Often the batts of insulation have a vapor barrier facing on them. Some have foil faces and some have craft paper faces. The paper is not a vapor retarder, but the tar used as an adhesive to attach the fiberglass to the paper is a retarde. Another vapor retarder can be created with enamel or vapor barrier paint. Several coats of proper paint on interior walls and ceilings can create an effective vapor retarder.

As we build tighter houses, vapor retarders become more important. When houses were loose and drafty, the moisture readily and harmlessly escaped along with the air and the energy. The tighter the house becomes, the more likely water is to condense unseen inside the walls, attic, and the crawl space, wetting the structure. The wetness may dramatically reduce the effectiveness of insulation. Fiberglass insulation that is wet enough to "feel" wet may have lost 80% of it's R-Value.

Vapor retarders are difficult to install or retrofit into older houses. Blowing insulation into side wall may cause moisture to accumulate there and eventually rot the framing unless a way is found to reduce the amount of vapor entering the wall. Adding ceiling insulation may retain heat in the house and cool the attic enough to allow condensation to form, wetting and delaminating the roof sheeting. Increasing attic ventilation may help, but it may have to be tremendously effective to carry out all the moisture before it has a chance to condense.

The colder the climate the more important vapor barrier become. In the northern half of the US and Canada they are important and necessary to prevent damage. The further south we go the less important they become. If the weather outside stays above thirty five degrees (F) the moisture vapor will seldom freeze and will generally migrate out harmlessly. If the weather stays below freezing for more than a few days and stays cold enough to cause condensation for weeks at a time, problems may result from the lack of or improperly installed vapor retarders.

MAINTENANCE AND UPKEEP

The average home owner should do at least three things to control moisture flow through the house. Reduce excessive moisture at its source, reduce air flow from conditioned spaces into cavities, and reduce vapor flow from conditioned spaces.

Every house has the traditional sources of moisture such as cooking, bathing, and the breathing of the occupants. Unless you have activities that produce excessive moisture, a large number of aquariums or house plants or drying clothes indoors, this is unlikely to cause a problem. Typical activities generally produce a few pounds of moisture vapor a day. A wet crawl space or basement can add ten times as much to the air of the house and is often the cause of mold and mildew and condensation in the walls and the attic. Dry the wet crawl space or basement. Read Chapter Three carefully for suggestions and discuss it with your inspector. A vapor barrier on grade even in a slightly damp crawl space can dramatically reduce water vapor entering the structure above.

Seal any penetrations into the wall cavities or through the floor and ceiling. As air leaks through these holes, it takes its moisture and heat with it. You can stuff large holes with fiberglass batts, compressed tightly enough to cut of the air flow or cover them with plywood or other materials. Smaller holes can be sealed with foam or caulk. Light fixtures and outlet cover plates can have gaskets added. Ready made gaskets are available at well equipped Home Centers. By reducing the movement of air, you also reduce the movement of moisture and heat.

You can paint interior wall and ceiling surfaces with one or two coats of vapor retarder paint or enamel.

Remember to tighten the interior surfaces only. Do not wrap the outside or cold side of walls with a vapor barrier. If moisture finds its way into the cavities it must have an escape route. Don't trap it. Do not cover the bottom of the floor joists with a vapor barrier or the tops of the ceiling joists. For the limited scope of a home inspection, the proper locations for vapor retarders are, the surface of the soil in the crawl space, and the warm or living side of the wall, ceiling, and floor. For more information contact a reputable insulation contractor, and manufacturer of insulation, or a local university.

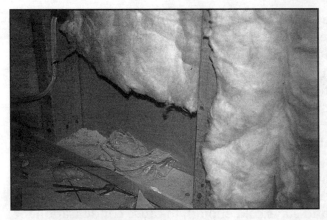

8.4 a. Percentage Insulated.
The Inspector will note the percentage of insulation present. Note the piece missing in the picture.

8.4 INSULATION CHART

The inspector will fill in the chart for the visible parts of the ceilings, roof, floors, and walls only. The scope of this inspection does not include concealed areas and the inspector will not remove attic floors or make access holes to inspect insulation. **Type** refers to section 8.3 Type and **Rating** is from 8.2.2 Subjective Rating. **Thickness** estimated in inches and **R-value** is noted in the broadest of terms. The **Percentage Inspected** is an estimation of how much of the area the inspector was able to see. The **Percentage Insulated** is an estimation of how much of the visible area is insulated as opposed how much is uninsulated. i.e. If one half of the under-floor has R-11 batts and one half has no insulation, it is 50 percent insulated. If a ceiling has R-7 insulation over 100 percent of the visible area, it is recorded as 100 percent even if local climate and standards of practice demand R-30 ceilings. **Vapor Retarder or Barrier** will be marked as **Y** for Yes, **NS** for None Seen, and **N** for None. Be aware vapor barriers are usually concealed behind wall and ceiling coverings and the insulation. Most often the inspector will not be able to judge the extent of coverage or its effectiveness. Sometime indirect evidence such as condensation (See also 1.10.45 Condensation and 1.10.46 Mold and Mildew) in the attic will indicate the lack of an effective vapor retarder. For clarity the inspector may also include the numbers of observations from Section 8.5 Observations in the **Rating/Observation** section of the chart. e.g. Insulation found to be wet and falling out in a crawl space might be recorded as C, 3,4. (C from section 8.2.2 Subjective Rating and 3 and 4 from Section 8.5 Observations indicating 8.5.3 Falling or Collapsed and 8.5.4 Water Damaged.) The falling insulation should be properly reinstalled and the water damaged insulation dried or replaced.

8.5 OBSERVATIONS

The inspector marks observations of conditions affecting the insulation. More than one item can be marked as the insulation may exhibit more than one symptom or problem. Some items are part of the normal aging process and do not require correction. Other items require either maintenance or repair if the insulation is to reach the full potential or life expectancy. Read carefully each section applying to the system inspected. Examine the chart in section 8.4. The inspector may mark observations from section 8.5 Observations in the Rating column of the chart. A "6" in the column would indicate 8.5.6 Physical Damage.

Maintenance is the on going care required if a system or item is to reach the full potential including lubricating, painting, etc. Do maintenance as required by the manufacturer of the equipment or item. Repairs put items or systems back in good condition after damage or decay, etc. Repairs are caused by delayed maintenance, aging, normal wear and tear, or abuse. The workmanship and materials of the repairs should be equal to the quality of the system and have the same life expectancy. e.g. A limb plunges through an asphalt shingle roof. If the roofing otherwise has a life expectancy of ten years, the repair should also have a life expectancy of at least ten years. If the roofing only has a life expectancy of one year, then the repair should be capable of lasting one year or more. It is not prudent to put a one year patch on a ten year roof or to waste a ten year repair on a one year roof. All repairs should be by qualified competent professionals.

8.5.1 SOUND

The inspector thinks the item inspected is functioning at the moment of the inspection. This does not imply perfection, absence of minor defects, or absence of wear and tear.

8.5.2 TYPICAL

The inspector thinks the item, material, or aspect of construction is characteristic or similar to comparable products in similar houses. The insulation has normal wear and tear.

8.5.3 FALLING OR COLLAPSED

The insulation is falling or collapsing from its proper position. Properly reinstall the insulation and support it to prevent falling again. Insulation cannot function if it is out of place.

8.5.3 Falling or Collapsed Insulation
This 8.3.1 Fiberglass Insulation has fallen out of the floor framing. This is often a clue or tell tale sign the crawl space is wet.

8.5.4 WATER DAMAGED

The insulation is damaged by water. Find the source of the water and eliminate it. Plumbing and roof leaks often damage insulation, but wet crawl spaces also contribute to this problem. Most fiberglass insulation will dry and not be significantly damaged from being wet. Wet fiberglass is a poor insulator and is heavy. Repair or replace any damaged insulation.

8.5.5 WIND DAMAGED

The insulation is out of position as if blown around by wind. Restore the insulation to its proper position. It may be necessary to install air baffles or reduce the air velocity to prevent a reoccurrence. Batt insulation may stay in place better than loose fill.

8.5.6 PHYSICAL DAMAGE

The insulation is physically damaged. Aluminum foil type insulations suffer from physical damage. A tear or hole defeats the value by allowing air to circulate around it. Other types of insulation suffer from being moved around and disturbed. Repair the damage.

8.5.7 UNSUPPORTED

The insulation lacks proper supports. Insulation in crawl spaces or above other unfinished spaces must be supported well enough to stay in place. Fiberglass batts friction fit between joists, but must be supported by arched wires (insulation supports) for permanence. Unsupported insulation should be properly supported.

8.5.8 NONE SEEN

No insulation was seen in the space.

8.5.9 EXPOSED

Insulation is exposed in the living spaces or in other commonly occupied areas such as garages. The fiber type insulations are skin and eye irritants and should be covered to protect you from regular contact and to protect it from wear and tear. Foam products are often a source of irritating and potentially toxic fumes. Some foams out gas slowly as they age and many produce smoke, lethal fumes, and carcinogens when burned. Most manufacturers and codes require covering them with a fire resistant covering to give the occupants time to escape. Cover insulation products properly to protect yourself from exposure.

CHAPTER NINE

INTERIOR

The inspector looks for telltale signs of structural distress, plumbing leaks, roof leaks, and other major defects. (Read section 2.2.4 Major Defects.) The inspector will not comment on the cosmetics or esthetics of the interior. They are not concerned with attractiveness of wall finishes or cleanliness of the house. These are items of personal taste and outside the scope of the inspection.

9.1 LIMITATIONS

This section describes the aspects limiting the inspection of the interior. Inspectors do the best inspection they can, but sometimes physical obstructions, weather conditions, or the condition of the interior, prevent them from doing the whole job. Arrange for an inspection overcoming the limitations, if possible. An uninspected interior or a severely limited or restricted inspection could be a total unknown. The inspector cannot make representations about what was not inspected. The responsibility for the concealed or limited aspects of the property is yours.

9.1.1 TYPICAL

The inspector feels they have seen as much of the interior as they normally see. There are always some limitations because the owner's possessions block the view of many wall areas, carpets cover floor areas, etc. In addition, all inspections are limited because the walls, floors, and ceilings, etc. conceal the underlying plumbing, structure, wiring, etc. A typical inspection does not include moving carpet, pictures, or other possessions or cutting holes to gain access. (Also read Section 9.1 Limitations.)

9.1.2 RESTRICTED

The inspector feels they have seen less of the interior than they typically see. The owner's possessions cover a large area of the walls or floors. Another example is a locked room. Arrange to overcome any restrictions. (Also read section 9.1 Limitations and 9.1.1 Typical.)

9.1.2.1 INTERIOR FRESHLY PAINTED/REMODELED

The interior painting/remodeling may be for the purpose of freshening the house for sale, but it also covers any cracks or stains. This may be done to conceal these clues and tell tale signs from you and the inspector.

9.2 GENERAL

A quick reference and overview of the inspector's opinions or impressions. This section is subjective and relies on the inspector's judgment and experience in estimating the age, whether clues are important and if toxins are present, etc. (Read the Interior chapter fully before forming any final opinion.)

9.2.1 SYSTEM INSPECTED (YES, RESTRICTED, OR NO)

The inspector marks whether the system was inspected. No information will be given about a system that was not inspected. If the inspector writes in or circles "R" for restricted, the system was partially inspected. Check 9.1 LIMITATIONS or discuss it with the inspector to learn the full extent of the restrictions. A severely limited inspection may not give you the information you need. You should do whatever is necessary to remove or overcome the restrictions and have the system fully inspected before you close on the house. (Read 9.1 Limitations.)

9.2.2 CLUES OR TELL TALES (YES OR NO)

"YES" The inspector observes evidence suggesting an underlying problem. (i.e. Stained ceilings may indicate failed and leaking plumbing above.)

"NO" The inspector does not see evidence suggesting hidden defects. (Fresh paint and wall paper may obscure clues and telltales.)

9.2.3 INDICATIONS OF CONTAMINANTS (YES OR NO)

"YES" The inspector sees material that may be asbestos, lead based paint, or urea formaldehyde foam, etc. (i.e. Most houses built before 1979 probably were painted with lead based paint.)

"NO" The inspector does not see a hazardous substance. A home inspection is a visual inspection not designed to reveal every possible hazard or dangerous chemical around the home. Experts can perform extensive tests to identify the presence of such matter or gas, if desired. (Read the contract and other sections in this report referring to toxic chemicals.)

9.2.4 AMATEUR WORKMANSHIP (YES OR NO)

"YES" The inspector notes workmanship of less than professional quality. Poor workmanship may constitute a major defect. Major defects cost $500.00 or more to repair or may affect the habitability of the house. The work may not serve the purpose intended and may require repair or replacement.

"NO" No amateur workmanship noted. Some amateurs produce workmanship of equal or better quality than professionals.

9.2.5 SUBJECTIVE RATING
The inspector's grade for the interior:

E   **EXCELLENT**, above average, new or like new. (e.g. a newly remodeled interior in an older house.)

A   **AVERAGE**, in typical condition for its age, showing normal wear and tear. (e.g. five year old interior looking 5 years old and a 5 year old house.)

C   **BELOW AVERAGE**, prematurely aged, showing heavy or excess wear and tear, or delayed maintenance. Perhaps showing minor (curable) defects. (e.g. a five year old interior showing the wear and tear or age characteristics of a 10 year old interior.)

F   **SUBSTANDARD**, failed, or reaching the end of its life expectancy. Any further service, even with repairs, should be considered a gift.

9.3 WALLS AND CEILINGS MATERIAL
The inspector identifies the material covering the interior walls, ceilings, and floors. Advantages, disadvantages, and maintenance are discussed below.

9.3.1 PLASTER
Plaster and similar wall coverings, used for centuries to coat interior walls, make them smooth and esthetically pleasing. They range from crude, rough work to smooth wall finishes known to include elaborate decorative forms and moldings.

9.3.1.1 PLASTER ON WOOD LATH
Until forty or fifty years ago plaster was often over wooden laths. Laths are thin wooden strips roughly 1/4 to 3/8 inch thick and 1 to 1 1/2 inches wide, nailed side by side over the interior wall and ceiling surfaces. They were approximately 1/4 inch apart and plastered. The plaster was three or four coats. The initial coat is a ground coat and applied so it squeezes through the laths and curls behind them. These fingers or "keys" gripped the laths. The plaster does not adhere to the wood but hangs on to it physically.

9.3.1.1 a. Plaster on Wooden Laths
Notice the "keys" are breaking and failing.

At one time the wooden laths were rived or hand split from logs selected for their straight grain. Old houses had hand rived wooden laths. Later the laths were sawed and usually left rough, with the saw marks. The keys break, the plaster loses its grip, cracks, and falls. It falls from small areas or entire ceilings. This problem is aggravated by sagging or settling, roof leaks, vibration, etc.

MAINTENANCE AND UPKEEP

Repairs range from replacement to patching. An area can be replastered using classic techniques or a patch of drywall can be cut to fit the missing area and patched. This technique is considered cheating by purists. Another alternative is to install drywall directly over the plaster. "Blue board" has fiberglass reinforcement giving it strength to support the plaster above or behind. The technique uses long drywall screws reaching through the drywall, through the plaster, and into the laths or framing. One undesirable aspect of drywall over plaster is the increase in weight. Covering the interior with drywall can add thousands of pounds of load to the structure and cause sagging or settling. It may be better to remove the plaster before drywalling to trade "weight for weight." Another repair possibility for a small area sagging or settling but not fallen is to lift the plaster back into place against the laths and use the drywall or plaster screws to hold it. Repair or patch over the screw heads so they don't show. (Read section 9.3.1 Plaster.)

9.3.1.2 PLASTER ON ROCK LATHS

The process of installing wood laths was labor intensive and brought about the use of plaster installed on rock laths. Rock laths are like drywall and come in many shapes and thicknesses. One version has pieces approximately 16 inches by 4 feet. All the interior walls and surfaces covered with this product are plastered with an additional two or more coats. A base coat approximately 1/4 to 3/8 inch thick is applied and topped with an 1/8 inch finish coat. A slightly different version is imperial coat plaster similar to drywall. Large sheets are installed and topped with an 1/8 inch thick plaster coat over the entire surface. (Read section 9.3.1 Plaster.)

9.3.1.2 Plaster on Rock Laths.
This decorative ceiling finish has been applied over plaster on rock laths. The same finish could be installed over drywall.

9.3.1.3 PLASTER ON WIRE LATHS

Plaster installed over wire lath or wire mesh. Here, expanded metal mesh, a screen like product, is nailed over the walls and ceilings and plastered with a heavy coat of plaster. Additional coats give it the finished appearance. Wire laths have the advantage of reinforcing the plaster and making it stronger than either of the other two types of laths. One of the most common applications in homes is as a base coat or wall finish for the installation of ceramic tile in bathrooms, particularly in tub surrounds. This is mud set tile. (Read section 9.3.1 Plaster.)

9.3.1.4 PLASTER ON BLUEBOARD

Blueboard is a plaster base gypsum product cast between two sheets of paper, like drywall. However, blueboard is intended to receive a thin veneer of plaster over the entire board. (Read 9.3.1.2 Plaster on Rock Laths.)

9.3.2 DRYWALL

Drywall is a gypsum product cast between two sheets of paper. (i.e. It has paper faces reinforcing the sheets giving them the strength to serve as wall and ceiling coverings.) The product is common and has generally replaced plaster. The product comes in many varieties and forms. Drywall used for walls and ceilings ranges from 3/8 to 5/8 inch thick.   Other versions are moisture resistant, often coated with light green paper, and recommended for use in bathrooms, carports, and areas with high humidity. Another type is a fire resistant version similar to the standard type except it has fiberglass reinforcing the gypsum. This product stays in place and does not collapse after the paper face has burned. The gypsum contains chemically bonded moisture and when heated the moisture releases. This process makes drywall fire resistant. Blue coated drywall is also fiberglass reinforced and intended to be installed over plaster. The fiberglass reinforcement gives it the strength to hold the old plaster on the wall.

Often, it is best to remove the old plaster before installing drywall because of the increase in weight. If you remove the plaster, you have probably replaced weight with weight. If you install drywall over the plaster you have dramatically increased the weight on the structure. If the structure was settling and sagging with age, this increase in weight may be more than it can tolerate.

MAINTENANCE AND UPKEEP

Repair and maintenance of drywall is fairly easy and within the range of skills of many home owners. It is best to avoid damaging the drywall where possible. Keep door bumpers in good repair and avoid allowing furniture to bump or rub against walls.

Most lumber yards, hardwares, and home centers will have books and even video tapes on repair and installation techniques. Small holes can be covered with fiberglass drywall tape and coated with drywall compound often called "mud." You will need a container for the compound and a knife or spatula to spread it with. A small cake pan will work as a container. Buy a 4" or 6" putty knife. If the repairs are large and elaborate, you may end up buying a set of knives with the larger ones 10 or 12 inches wide. Buy the compound ready mixed rather than the powdered form.

The techniques are too detailed to discuss here, but basically consist of filling the holes and covering the joints and cracks with successively thin and wider layers of compound and allowing them to dry in between applications. The best advice is to plan on four or five coats and to make them thinner rather than thicker. Have patience and build up slowly. Thick layers tend to crack. It is easier to install numerous thin layers than to sand off a few thick ones and start over.

It is probably not wise to try to use plaster of Paris or spackling. They set chemically and too quickly to be smoothed out. Spackling can be useful for nail holes.

9.3.3 PANELING

Wood paneling used to cover interior wall surfaces. It ranges from crude board paneling to carved panels and lately to plywood paneling.

MAINTENANCE AND UPKEEP

Care for the finish on the paneling. Clean and coat the finish with products compatible with the finish. Before attempting to clean the paneling or to apply a finish rejuvenator, test the cleaner or finish product to be sure it does not damage the paneling or the finish. Apply a small amount in an inconspicuous area and wait several days.

9.3.3.1 SOLID WOOD

Board paneling comes in a wide variety of shapes, sizes, and styles. Individually applied tongued and grooved boards nailed either vertically, horizontally, or at an angle. Wood shrinks and swells with changes in moisture content causing a variety of strategies to accommodate the movement. Tongue and groove joints, ship laps, raised panels, etc. are all techniques used to accommodate the seasonal changes. Keep this in mind any time you choose to stain or paint wood paneling and remember to allow the wood freedom to move. Stain or paint it when the wood is dry. If painted when swelled, as the wood shrinks, the areas newly exposed will not be painted or stained. (For Maintenance and Upkeep, see 9.3.3 Paneling.)

9.3.3.2 PLYWOOD PANELING

Plywood paneling comes in many forms from ¼", 4 x 8 Vee grooved paneling to elaborate veneered panels made of exotic wood with highly unusual grain patterns. The grain can be "book matched" or sequenced around the room. Some "plywood" paneling is particle board. Inexpensive paneling has paper faces printed to resemble wood or other wall coverings. (For Maintenance and Upkeep, see 9.3.3 Paneling.)

9.3.4 ACOUSTIC CEILING

Wood fiber and cement are used to manufacture acoustic tile. Before 1980 asbestos was sometimes included for strength and fire resistance. The material is "Acoustic" because it absorbs part of the sound striking it. It is popular with "do it yourselfers" because it is inexpensive and easy to install.

MAINTENANCE AND UPKEEP

Protect the tile from physical abuse. It is "tender" and easily damaged by pool cues, etc. It also watermarks or stains easily when wet. Protect it from roof and plumbing leaks. Stains must be sealed with white shellac or a product like "Kilz," made for the purpose, and available at paint stores. Once sealed, you may paint the tile with interior paint. The paint may seal the holes and texture and reduce the sound absorbing properties.

Treat all tile as if it contains asbestos unless tested by an asbestos laboratory. Removing old tile may expose you to asbestos and can injure your health. Contact local experts or your health department for advice.

9.3.4.1 TILE (BLOCK)

Block ceiling tile is manufactured in one foot square and one foot by two foot versions. The installer staples or glues the tile to the ceiling or to furring strips. The installation is permanent, not removable. (For Maintenance and Upkeep see 9.3.4 Acoustic Tile.)

9.3.4.2 DROPPED GRID

Popular in commercial buildings, dropped grid systems include tracks and hangers to support the acoustic tile. The grid system also supports lighting and heating vents. The grid design allows the tile panels to be removed for easy access to the plumbing, wiring, etc.

This system may lack residential appeal because of the "commercial" appearance, increased cost over block tile, and difficulty of the installation. (For Maintenance and Upkeep see 9.3.4 Acoustic Tile.)

9.3.5 CERAMIC TILE

As a wall covering, ceramic tile is usually in bathrooms and tub surrounds and showers. The tile is usually glazed and impervious to water. The joints are porous and often crack. As mentioned in section 9.4.4.1 Ceramic Tile (floor), this tile is heavy and brittle. Cracked tiles are the result of a combination of brittleness, weight, aging, and sagging of the structure.

MAINTENANCE AND UPKEEP

Bathroom tile installed in a plaster bed is excellent. Keep the joints between the tile and the tub or shower caulked or sealed preventing water leaking through and damaging whatever is below. Ceramic tile is often installed in mastic. Keep the tile caulked or water will seep behind the tile causing deterioration under the leak. Pay special attention to the area around faucets and other tile penetrations. Use high quality bathroom caulk containing a fungicide to avoid mold and mildew.

9.3.5.1 THIN SET

Ceramic tile glued to drywall is "thin set." (See also Mud Set 9.3.5.2.) Water resistant "green board" or MR (moisture resistant) board is for this application. (Wonder Board TM or Duro Board TM is waterproof.) Thin set tile is only as good as the wall behind. (For Maintenance and Upkeep see 9.3.5 Ceramic Tile.)

9.3.5.2 MUD SET

"Mud set" tile is over a plaster (mud) base built-up in place by the tile mechanic. Usually, three coats of plaster are applied over metal lathing and the ceramic tile is cemented to it. This is the "classic" method of installing tile and recognized by the thickness of the tile. The plaster is built-up and special rounded or "bull nose" tiles are used for edges.

Sometimes, two layers of drywall are installed only under the ceramic tile and bull nose edges are used to imitate a mud set tile installation. This is not detectable during a home inspection unless the inspector cuts the wall apart. Inspectors do not cut walls or damage the property to decipher the type of installation.

If metal lathing is not lapped for strength, we often see a horizontal crack in the tiles over the underlying joint. Sagging or settlement strains the wall and the weakness of the lath joint shows in the tile. (See 9.3.5. Ceramic Tile for Maintenance and Upkeep.)

9.3.6 BRICK AND STONE

Brick and stone are occasionally used as interior wall finishes, such as the mantle or front facing of fireplaces. Keeping them clean involves brushing and vacuuming the surface, etc. Stains or soot damage can be removed but the process can be elaborate. Masonry products can be cleaned with muriatic acid, but this is impractical indoors. It involves scrubbing and flooding the walls and therefore the floors with the acid product. This may damage the floor covering. It is not recommended homeowners use acid type cleaning products inside the home. There are some non acidic products available. Try a wire brush on the masonry. Start with a soft wire brush and then perhaps a stiffer one. If you clean one portion of a brick or masonry wall you may have to clean the entire wall, whether it was dirty or not, to maintain a consistent appearance. For soot or fire damage, sand blasting may be necessary. Sandblasting the wall will clean it but will also alter its appearance.

9.4 FINISHED FLOORS

The finished floors are not inspected for cosmetic or esthetic defects. The inspector looks for clues or tell tales of defects such as settlement, plumbing leaks, etc. Form your own opinion of the appearance and wear and tear. If the floor covering has been recently replaced, refinished or cleaned, the clues may be obscured.

9.4.1 WOOD FLOORS

Wide boards shrink more than narrow boards. Wood shrinks and swells as much as 10% in its width with extreme changes in moisture content. A 10 inch wide board has the potential to shrink as much as an inch. Typically wood in the interior of the house will shrink and swell 1% to 2%. If a room is 100 inches wide, 1% of 100 inches is 1 inch. Therefore, with wide boards each shrinks and swells a noticeable amount. With narrow boards, each board shrinks and swells, but the amount is not as noticeable. Many have come to think of the wider boards as being elegant. In earlier times the narrow boards were considered elegant.

MAINTENANCE AND UPKEEP

Keep the floors clean, avoid damage and scratches to the finish. Different types of finishes require different maintenance. Most wood floors can be damp mopped or vacuumed. Some finishes require wax or acrylic over them. Other finishes, such as urethane, do not require any additional finishes. Find out from the previous owner what care was given to the floors and continue if it was successful. When refinishing, investigate the finishes available and install the one suiting your housekeeping. In general, gloss finishes are more durable than semi-gloss or flat finishes and require less care.

9.4.1.1 PLANK OR STRIP

Wood floors made of individual boards or planks. Species include oak, pine, maple, cherry, beech, etc. The harder the wood, the more resistant the floor is to impact damage, but some plantation homes had pine floors. With proper care, any reasonably hard wood will suffice. (For Maintenance and Upkeep see 9.4.1 Wood Floors.)

9.4.1.2 PARQUET FLOORS

Parquet floors range from individual pieces of wood crafted at the site to a more modern factory type of plywood parquet available at the lumber yard. (For Maintenance and Upkeep see 9.4.1 Wood Floors.)

9.4.2 CARPET

Carpet is not inspected, but is an inspection limitation. The inspector cannot see what is under the carpet. Carpets often conceal damaged floors. Sometimes, when wall to wall carpet is removed the floor below can be successfully refinished, but often water and pet stains are difficult to remove from many types of wood floors.

MAINTENANCE AND UPKEEP

Keep carpets clean. Dirt and grit cause the demise of the carpet. The carpet should be vacuumed frequently and steam cleaned or professionally cleaned as necessary.

9.4.2.1 WALL TO WALL

Carpet covering 100% of the floor area in a room is glued or attached by tack strips around the perimeter. The inspector will not remove the carpet and will not determine the type or quality of floor below. Some wall to wall carpet is installed over finished floor such as hardwood or tile that could be restored if the carpet is removed, but often the floor below is only plywood or other common materials not suitable to be left exposed. Some finished floors covered by carpet are so damaged they can not be restored and must be replaced or covered. (Read section 9.4.2 Carpet.)

9.4.2.2 LOOSE LAID

Carpet not attached and not usually covering 100% of the floor area. For the purpose of the inspection loose laid carpet is personal property and not inspected. The inspector will not remove carpet to inspect the floor below. Be aware that carpet often covers worn or stained floors. (Read item 4 in the contract and Read section 9.4.2 Carpet.)

9.4.3 SOFT TILE

Soft tile is vinyl, linoleum, and block tile.

MAINTENANCE AND UPKEEP

Keep it clean and properly dressed or waxed if necessary. The individual brand or type of vinyl will determine whether it is necessary to wax or dress the floor.

Caution! Many older soft tile floor coverings contained asbestos. The asbestos in vinyl asbestos tile is fixed in the tile and is reasonably safe as long as the tile remains intact. The same is true for the asbestos used in the backing of sheet goods. Do not crumble, chip, scrape or try to grind the tile from the floor. It is probably best left in place and covered with a thin layer of plywood and new floor covering. Asbestos can have serious and far reaching health effects. You should contact a service representative or other expert before removing any soft tile.

9.4.3.1 SHEET VINYL

Linoleum has fallen into disuse and has been replaced by vinyl and similar products. As with carpet these products are not inspected per se except as they may reflect damage caused by other systems in the house (i.e. plumbing leaks, etc.). Properly installing vinyl requires a solid, smooth subfloor. The best subfloor material is an underlayment grade of plywood manufactured specifically for the purpose. The upper surface of the plywood must be solid and smooth and the interior plies must not contain any voids a chair leg or high heel shoe might puncture. The underlayment must be securely fastened to the floor with either ring shank nails or screws and the seams in the plywood should be sanded smooth and properly treated before installing the vinyl. Particle board products are generally not acceptable as an underlayment for vinyl.

The vinyl industry has several vinyls called "loose lay" products. They are not glued to the entire surface, but are only fastened or glued around the perimeter. These work as replacement products because they span across slight imperfections in the floor disguising the texture of the underlying floor. It may not be necessary to cover the old floor with a layer of plywood before installing new vinyl. (Read section 9.4.3 Soft Tile.)

9.4.3.2 BLOCK TILE

Block tile is a vinyl like product in two sizes (9 in. x 9 in. and 12 in. x 12 in.). The product ranges from asphalt tile through vinyl asbestos tile to the modern vinyl block tiles. A word of caution about block tile; it is not an impervious surface. The cracks between the squares of tile seem to provide an ideal opportunity for water to penetrate the flooring, get under the tile, and do damage. Take extra precautions to keep the floor dry. (For Maintenance and Upkeep and a caution on Asbestos, see 9.4.3 Soft Tile.)

9.4.4 HARD TILE

Hard tile is slate, marble, ceramic tile, and stone floor coverings. These products are inspected to note whether they have been damaged by other systems or settlement in the house and whether they have contributed to settlement in the house.

MAINTENANCE AND UPKEEP

The joints between the tile are not impervious to water. Keep the floors dry to prevent water from attacking the underlying structure. Secondly, ceramic tile is often over a base of sand cement recessed between the floor joists. The sand cement is up to three inches thick and contributes much weight to the structure. The combination of the sand cement, the floor tile, the tile on the walls, and the weight of the plumbing fixtures is the reason settlement and cracking occurs around bathrooms. This may be combined with and aggravated by damage to the structure by water and the installation of the plumbing system. (Plumbers have done more damage to houses than termites ever have.) Ceramic tile is hard and any bottles or fragile objects dropped on the tile will probably break or break the tile. In some bathrooms the floor tile does not have a non-skid surface. Avoid household accidents on these slippery surfaces. Use proper mats or appliques. Textured "non-skid" floor tiles are available.

9.4.4.1 CERAMIC TILE

Ceramic tile is a pottery or vitreous china product commonly used as a bathroom floor covering and sometimes in other areas such as laundry rooms, foyer, etc. The tiles come in many shapes and styles and are usually fired in a kiln to produce a glazed surface. (See 9.4.4 Hard Tile for Maintenance and Upkeep.)

9.4.4.2 QUARRY TILE

Quarry tile is a hard tile similar to ceramic tile. Quarry tile is red or gray clay and usually sold unglazed in its classic "terra cotta" color. Glazed versions are available as types with "non-skid" surfaces. Quarry tile is almost impervious to water and can be used on exterior surfaces. (See 9.4.4 Hard Tile for Maintenance and Upkeep.)

9.4.4.3 SLATE AND MARBLE

Slate has cleft face. It will naturally cleave into thin sheets and is often used for floor tiles. Marble is sliced into thin sheets and used for floor tile. These products are often in entry ways and foyers. Keep these hard type tile floors clean. They are often coated with a dressing or coating specially designed for the marble or slate making the care and upkeep as easy as vinyl. Because of the textured surface, slate is more difficult to clean than the smoother marble surfaces. As the surface wears, new coatings can be applied. Check with a tile or marble company for types of finishes available and applicable to your floors. (See also 9.4.4 Hard Tile 9.4.3.1 Sheet Vinyl for Maintenance and Upkeep.)

9.5 CABINETS AND COUNTERTOPS

Only the exterior of the cabinets and the countertops are inspected. Inspectors do not open doors and drawers to check for function. No representation is made about the adequacy, lay out, or amount of cabinets.

9.6 INTERIOR DOORS AND HARDWARE

Interior doors are inspected for function and as indicators of sagging or settlement. Misaligned doors may be a clue or tell tale of other problems. Hardware is checked for basic function only.

MAINTENANCE AND UPKEEP

Some bedroom and bathroom doors have privacy locks. Check these locks occasionally and be sure you keep a "key" handy outside the rooms for emergencies. Learn how to unlock the doors.

Interior doors in houses with air conditioning or warm air heat should be undercut to clear the floor covering 3/4 inch or more to allow for air circulation.

9.7 INTERIOR OF WINDOWS

The inspection of the windows is completed from the interior. One window per room and exposure is checked. They are opened to test function. Window locks are checked for function. The glass and glazing or putty is examined.

MAINTENANCE AND UPKEEP

Keep windows functional for emergency egress (escape). Keep them properly puttied and painted to protect them from the weather. Do not allow storm windows to cause water to pond in the sill. Drill drain holes if necessary. Replace sash cords as necessary. The library has "how to" books explaining and illustrating the steps in replacing the cords and spring balances in newer windows. Lubricate metal windows with silicon or graphite. Grease and oil attract dirt. The cure for fogged insulated glass is to replace it.

9.8 RAILS AND STAIRS

Many accidents happen on stairs. Stairs and railings are inspected for sturdiness and compliance with reasonable safety standards.

MAINTENANCE AND UPKEEP

Inspect your stairs and railings carefully. The spaces between the rails or pickets should be small enough to prevent an infant from slipping through. Current standards call for six inch or smaller spaces. It is possible for a child to slip through a smaller space. Future standards will be three and a half inches. If your railings are more than three and a half inches apart, change or screen them for safety. Children will use railings or screen to climb and fall over the railing.

Choose the screen or rail design carefully.

Stairs should be evenly spaced and comfortable to walk. No step (Riser) should vary more than three eighths of an inch from any other. Doors leading to stairs should open onto landings, not swing out over the steps. Head room should be at least eighty inches. There should be light switches top and bottom and the lighting should be bright and even. Repair or replace worn or torn carpet runners. Poor lighting, low head room, and treacherous footing are dangerous. Home inspections occur in daylight and poor nighttime lighting may not be apparent until living in the house. Improve your lighting and stairs as necessary for safety. Stairways should be a minimum of three feet wide for safe passage and to allow for moving furniture.

9.8.1 HANDRAILS

Handrails should be 30 to 34 inches above the nosing of the stairs. They should be sturdy and attached well enough to support 200 pounds. The shape and size of the rail should fit the hand comfortably and allow for a firm grasp. They should protrude into the space 3 ½ inches or less and extend the entire length of the stairway. Keep rails securely mounted.

9.8.2 SAFETY RAILS

Safety rails should be 36 to 42 inches high and should enclose any platform or floor more than one step above surrounding areas. Rails or pickets should be 3 ½ inches apart or less. A child can slip through a wider spacing and get hung or fall. Railings should be sturdy and capable of supporting a person falling against them. Keep the rails secure and screen them if necessary for safety.

9.8.3 STEPS

Steps must be evenly spaced and comfortable to walk. They should be about seven inches high (riser) and ten inches wide (run). Interior steps should not rise over 8 ¼ inches or run less than 9 inches. Two risers and one run should total between 24 and 26 inches. The run does not include the overhanging or nosing part of the tread. The treads should be about 11 inches wide for comfort. Keep stairs in good condition. Secure any loose treads. Replace or repair any broken ones. Keep carpet or runners in good condition. Secure any loose treads. Replace or repair any broken ones. Keep carpet or runners in good repair. Loose and torn carpet causes accidents. Check for proper and adequate lighting.

Spiral stairs are seldom satisfactory as primary staircases. It is difficult to move furniture up and down them. To be acceptable the treads must be a minimum of six inches wide and at least nine inches wide, twelve inches from the narrower side. Spiral stairs are treacherous and difficult, especially coming down. Proper lighting is difficult. The stairs cast confusing shadows on themselves.

Winders, the triangular steps in corners, must be at least four inches wide and average nine inches or more. If you have winders, it is better if they are at the bottom. You are going to fall down them. Have good lighting and insurance.

9.8.4 BALCONIES

Balconies and catwalks must be sturdy and capable of supporting people and other loads. Enclose them with adequate safety rails.

9.9 APPLIANCES

"YES"   There is an appliance of the type listed.

"NO"   There is no appliance of the type listed.

"UNINSPECTED"   The appliance seen was not inspected.

"#"   The inspector writes the number of each seen.

"F"   The item or appliance seen was functional.

"NF"   The appliance seen was not functional.

9.9.1 BUILT-IN DISHWASHERS

are run through a normal wash cycle to check for leaks around the door gasket, leaks from the tub or plumbing, and to see if the controls properly sequence them through the wash cycle. Only one cycle is checked. Portable dishwashers are personal property and are not inspected.

9.9.2 RANGE BURNERS

are turned to a random setting and allowed to heat momentarily. Electric burners are not heated red hot because this occasionally damages them. The flame color of gas burners is checked. It should be bright blue. (With gas it is wise to have vent fans carry the combustion fumes outside the house rather than recirculating the fumes through a filter.)

9.9.3 OVEN ELEMENTS

are turned to a random setting and allowed to heat momentarily. The flame color and pattern is inspected if the flame is visible. It should be bright blue and evenly distributed. Oven controls are not checked for temperature accuracy or calibrated. Some ovens vent through one of the range elements. Check the manufacturer's directions for information on using the burner while using the oven.

9.9.4 INDOOR GRILLS

are checked in the same way as range burners. Jenn Air grill ranges have grease drains emptying into a bottle under the counter or in the range. Empty the bottle as necessary. It is not sealed and makes a mess when it overflows. In newer ranges the grease trap is a plastic box.

9.9.5 HOOD FANS

and other kitchen vents are run briefly. The duct to these vents is usually concealed from inspection. The duct or piping should be metal pipe like flue pipe. Grease builds up in them over the years and may burn like a chimney fire. Sometimes they are improperly vented into wall cavities or cabinet boxing. If you discover improper venting, improve it to local safety standards immediately. It is wise to keep a fire extinguisher handy. Buy one meant for kitchens. Recirculating vents filtering the air through charcoal or other filters, rapidly lose their effectiveness and should only be used in kitchens with a window or other natural ventilation. The filter cartridges are usually clogged and overwhelmed with grease and dirt.

9.9.6 MICROWAVE OVENS

are run briefly on a basic cycle at a random power setting with a cup of water or other target in the oven. It is not safe for the oven to run it without a target. While running, ovens are checked for microwave leakage with a simple microwave detector. Any significant leakage can be injurious and a cause for repair or replacement. Portable microwaves are personal property and not tested. Only built-in microwaves are inspected.

9.9.7 GARBAGE DISPOSERS

or waste grinders are run briefly and visually checked to determine if the drum turns or the unit is seized. The grinder teeth or hammers are checked for freedom of motion. Units with "frozen hammers" or grinders rusted fast don't operate satisfactorily. No test is made of the unit's ability to grind anything. Seized units may be freed with a broom stick. With the power off at the breaker, push against a hammer or grinder inside the drum and twist or turn the drum. Disposers seize after a period of disuse. Older units in unoccupied houses often sieze from disuse.

9.9.8 BUILT-IN TRASH COMPACTORS

are checked through one cycle. Follow the manufacturer's directions for bags and deodorizing spray. Clean the unit as necessary to keep sanitary.

9.9.10 BATH VENTS

are run briefly and only for apparent function. They are often largely concealed inside walls and other construction cavities. They should extend to the exterior and deliver their moisture and odor laden air outside the structure. In the past they often terminated in the attic or crawl space. They are now often extended into the soffit near exterior vents. Observe these areas over time and if moisture condenses there they should be extended out through vents of their own.

9.9.11 DRYER VENTS

are visually inspected only, but they are often concealed. Failure is noted through effects such as condensation or moisture damage, and accumulation of lent. Dryers produce large amounts of warm moist air and should not be purposefully or accidentally vented into the attic or crawl space. The moisture and warmth contribute to or cause mold, mildew, and rot.

The dryer should be vented through smooth wall metal tubing of ducting, to a vent outside the building. The vent should have a flap or other device to prevent air leaking into the building when the dryer is not in use. The vent should be as large or larger than the vent outlet on the dryer and it should slope downward to the vent to drain out any condensation in the tube. There should be no screws or other fasteners protruding into the tube to catch lent.

The dryer should not be vented upward through the ceiling. Venting upward may cause lent to accumulate in the vent and possibly catch fire. If you must vent upward the vent should include a side inlet tee with the bottom leg of the tee used as a "drip" to catch lent. You can remove the bottom cap occasionally to remove the lent.

9.10 INTERIOR OBSERVATIONS

The inspector marks observations of conditions affecting the Interior. More than one item can be marked as the interior may exhibit more than one symptom or problem. Some items are part of the normal aging process and do not require correction. Other items require either maintenance or repair if the interior is to reach the full potential or life expectancy. Read carefully each section applying to the system inspected.

Maintenance is the on going care required if a system or item is to reach the full potential including lubricating, painting, etc. Do maintenance as required by the manufacturer of the equipment or item. Repairs put items or systems back in good condition after damage or decay, etc. Repairs are caused by delayed maintenance, aging, normal wear and tear, or abuse. The workmanship and materials of the repairs should be equal to the quality of the system and have the same life expectancy. e.g. A limb plunges through an asphalt shingle roof. If the roofing otherwise has a life expectancy of ten years, the repair should also have a life expectancy of at least ten years. If the roofing only has a life expectancy of one year, then the repair should be capable of lasting one year or more. It is not prudent to put a one year patch on a ten year roof or to waste a ten year repair on a one year roof. All repairs should be by qualified competent professionals.

9.10.1 SOUND

The inspector thinks the item inspected is functioning at the moment of the inspection. This does not imply perfection, absence of minor defects, or absence of wear and tear.

9.10.2 TYPICAL

The inspector thinks the item, material, or aspect of construction is characteristic or similar to comparable products in similar houses. The interior has normal wear and tear.

9.10.3 FUNCTIONAL

The item, material, or aspect of construction operates. It does not imply easy, safe, or perfect operation and does not address Energy efficiency, security, or durability.

9.10.4 STAINED

The item, material, or aspect of construction is discolored. This may be a clue or tell tale of a plumbing or roof leak. Some stains such as those in hardwood floors may ruin the appearance and value and are extremely difficult to remove. Stains to drywall or plaster may require sealing with shellac or similar products before painting with water base paint. It's important the source of the stain is cured or eliminated.

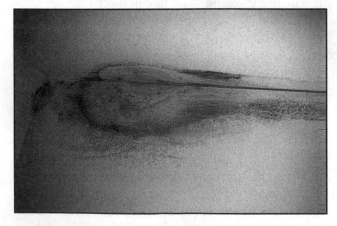

9.10.4 a. Stained
This is a view from the floor looking up at the corner of the room. This stain was caused by a leaking air conditioning condensate line. Mildew is present. This will need to be sealed before painting.

9.10.5 CRACKED

An observation usually regarding interior walls and ceilings of the structure and potentially a clue or tell tale sign of a structural or settlement problem. Cracks are a cause of concern for all homeowners. When we look at a crack, we are looking at one frame of a motion picture often 10, 20, 30, or more years long. Based on the physical evidence presented at the inspection, the structural significance of the crack (if any) will be addressed in the Foundation/Basement/Structure section (Chapter 3).

9.10.5 a. Cracked
The drywall above the corner or the door is
cracked. This is in the foyer at the foot of the steps
in a two story house. The joists are 9.10.7 Sagging,
causing "star burst" cracks above several doors
and causing them to be 9.10.19 Misaligned.

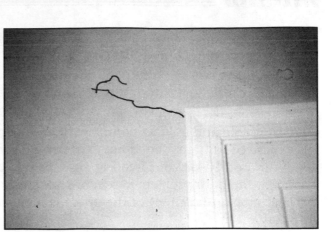

9.10.6 NAIL POPS

A "nail pop" is a bulge caused by a nail backing out. The phenomenon is noticeable in drywall and vinyl floors. Changes in moisture content causes the lumber to shrink and swell and "squirt" the nails out. The nail lifts the drywall compound or vinyl over the nail. In drywall, the cure is to drive a proper ring shank drywall nail beside the offending nail "capturing" it under the head of the new nail. Repair the dimple with three or four coats of drywall compound, sand, and repaint.

Vinyl complicates the solution. You must remove the vinyl and the offending nails and refasten the underlayment with proper ring shank nails or screws. It may be cheaper to install a new layer of underlayment. Reinstall the (new) vinyl. The expense of the repair makes it worthwhile to follow the manufacturer's installation instructions. Use proper nails, underlayment, and glue.

9.10.7 SETTLEMENT OR SAGGING

Some portion of the structure has apparently settled or sagged. Almost all floors and ceilings sag eventually. If they sag slightly and evenly it may go unnoticed. If they sag dramatically (i.e. more alarming than charming), it sometimes requires repairs. It is necessary to know the history of the problem to make a diagnosis of whether repairs are necessary. More investigation and monitoring may be necessary. Sagging implies beams or joists have bent more than expected or the framing members have compressed or shrunk under the load. Settlement implies one part of the structure has sunk into the earth more than the rest. Settlement is addressed in Chapter 3. The Inspector looks for clues or tell tales of settlement or sagging during the inspection of the interior.

9.10.8 BUCKLING

The item, material, or aspect of construction is bent, warped, or crumpled. Buckled items may require replacement.

9.10.9 HOLES

The item, material, or aspect of construction has holes in it. Repair the holes or replace the damaged items.

9.10.10 MOLD OR MILDEW

Mold and mildew will grow on any surface and can survive on little more than moisture.

Modern paints (without lead) are only mildew resistant, not mildew proof. It must be removed before repainting. Try a solution of water and chlorine bleach on an inconspicuous area. Mildew remover is also available at hardware, paint stores, and super markets. Unless carefully removed, mildew will float through new paint and reestablish.

Mold and mildew flourishes at a temperature above 50 degrees and in a moist environment. These conditions sometimes exist behind furniture, in closets, or in corners. Poor air circulation from poorly laid out heating systems can contribute to the problem. Mold and mildew can create an odor problem in severe cases and some people are allergic to them. They are a warning the moisture content of the space is higher than it should be. If the space remains damp, rot may set in.

The cure for mold and mildew is to reduce the moisture content below the minimum 12 or 13 percent in lumber necessary to sustain it. Lumber appears to acquire a moisture content roughly 1/5 of the relative humidity of the surrounding air. It is possible to have the desirable 30 to 50% relative humidity indoors and have framing lumber at the 12% for the elimination of mold and mildew. Look for the source of the moisture and eliminate it. Often plastic vapor barriers are effective in reducing the viability of mold and mildew in the crawl space.

Improving air circulation may be as simple as moving furniture several inches from walls and away from corners. Cold damp closets may require louvered doors or a heat source. Sometimes leaving the light on in a closet is enough. Be careful. Light bulbs can start fires. (Read section 1.8 Ventilation and 3.5 Ventilation.)

9.10.11 MISSING OR DAMAGED
The item, material, or aspect of construction is missing or broken.

9.10.12 UNLEVEL
The floors are not level. Interior floors are usually level. Exterior floors and decks should slope to drain away from the structure. Floors unlevel may be a clue or telltale of 9.10.7 Settlement or Sagging or other problems noted in Chapter 3.   (Read Chapter 3 Foundations/Basements/Structures.)

9.10.13 WOOD ROT
The item, material, or aspect of construction has rotted. Rot occurs in moist wood at temperatures above 40 degrees and is the result of fungi or other wood destroying organisms attacking the wood. Rotted wood has no structural value and no strength.

Significantly damaged structural elements or safety rails, steps, etc. should be promptly repaired. The conditions causing the rot must be remedied to prevent a reoccurrence or increase of the problem. Repairs should be made with treated wood or decay resistant species.

9.10.14 LOST SEALS INSULATED GLASS
The seal around the edge of the insulated glass has failed. Moisture vapor infiltrates the air space, condenses, and is acidic enough to etch and "frost" the glass if the unit remains fogged more than a few days. Replacing the glass or sash is the cure. Expect other panes to fog soon.

They fog in cold weather and clear in warm weather until the desiccant is saturated and the glass etches.   (Read section 2.5.3.2 Insulated Glass.)

9.10.14 Lost Seal on Insulated Glass. The "fogged" pane has been ruined. Look closely. One side is fogged and one is not. Eventually the glass will "frost" as if painted white.

9.10.15 STUCK OR CLOSED TIGHT

The windows or doors are stuck or closed tight and will not open with normal effort. They may be stuck in the paint, swollen by moisture, jammed by settlement, or permanently fastened shut. Free the windows and doors immediately to permit emergency egress (escape). Do not use locks requiring tools or keys to operate. If you must have keyed locks, keep a key near the floor beside each window and door so you can crawl to it in event of a fire.

9.10.16 CRACKED OR BROKEN PANES

The inspector observes damaged, cracked, or missing glass. Missing glass allows rain and snow to enter and heat to escape. Cracked glass may allow water to seep in and rot the frame. Repair immediately.

9.10.17 MISSING LOCKS

Security locks are missing from the windows or exterior doors. Install proper locks immediately. This inspection is not a security check. The quality of your locks and level of home security is up to you. Consult with experts in the field.

9.10.18 WATER SEEPING

Water is seeping into the interior. Water that seeps into wooden parts of the house can cause rot in a surprisingly short time, especially if it is under vinyl or other tile or behind paint or wallpaper that retards.drying.   Find the source of the problem and cure it.

9.10.19 MISALIGNED

The doors or windows have sagged, shifted or settled enough so the hardware is out of alignment and perhaps not functional. Misalignment indicates wear and tear of the individual unit or may be a clue or telltale of settling or sagging of the structure. Review the report carefully, checking the balance of the Interior section for other reports of settlement or sagging, or unlevel floors and check Chapter 3 for reports of under sized framing, rot damage, settled foundation, etc.

Discuss these clues with your inspector and monitor them carefully. If these clues accumulate, you may wish to consult with others such as Professional Engineers, soils experts, etc.

9.10.20 FAILING PUTTY OR GROUT

The inspector observes cracked or crumbling glazing (putty) around the glass (lights) in windows or doors. Checking the window glazing for signs of cracking when repainting is important. Water seeping into these cracks will ultimately rot the window. Repair when repainting.

9.10.21 MISSING OR BROKEN TRIM

Interior trim is missing or broken.

9.10.22 WEAR AND TEAR

The item, material, or aspect of construction shows evidence of wear and tear. Wear and tear is part of aging and reflects the use and abuse the building has received. One function of maintenance and upkeep is to offset the effects of wear and tear.

9.10.23 BURNED OR DAMAGED

The item, material, or aspect of construction is burned or physically damaged.

9.10.24 BROKEN OR LOOSE RAILS

The rails are physically damaged, broken, or loose and improperly secured. Safety items should be repaired immediately.

9.10.25 PEELING PAINT

The paint is too thin, peeling, blistering, chipping, flaking, etc. Interior paint should be capable of protecting the structure from normal wear and tear and may improve its appearance. Paint fails for many reasons. It may die of old age, too many coats, or fail to "Breath." It can lose the flexibility, crack, and flake off. Eventually, it must be properly removed and the surface prepared for new paint. Treat all paint as if it were "lead based" and poisonous unless you know better. Local paint stores or government authorities may be able to help.

9.10.26 SASH CORD OR SPRING BALANCE

The sash cords or spring balances are broken or damaged. Replacement spring balances are sometimes available from window manufacturers or lumber yards. Replacing sash cords is a handyman chore. Books are available at the library or book store diagraming the procedure step by step. Replacing the cords will damage the trim paint, requiring repainting.

9.10.27 LOOSE PLASTER

Plaster is loose, sagging, or falling. Failing plaster can be repaired several ways. (See Maintenance and Upkeep under 9.3.1 Plaster.)

9.10.28 LOOSE CARPET
Loose carpet, particularly in halls and doorways or on steps is a tripping hazard. Properly fasten the carpet or vinyl immediately.

9.10.29 TRUSS LIFT
Truss lift is a seasonal change in the shape of trusses causing them to lift the ceilings from the interior walls from time to time. The phenomenon is not thoroughly understood. Two suggested remedies. One, attach crown molding around the affected rooms, fastened to the ceiling only. It slides up and down, disguising the problem. Two, install separate ceiling joists beside each truss, but not attached to them. Fasten the ceiling to new joists and detach it from the trusses. The trusses can now move independently of the ceiling unnoticed. Neither of these solutions is ideal. Another possibility is to attach the drywall of the ceiling to the top of the wall and detach it from the truss for about two feet. This will allow the ceiling to bend yet remain attached to the wall if the trusses only move slightly. Check with a reputable local truss manufacturer for alternatives. Trusses are manufactured under the auspices of an engineer. They may be able to help.   (Read section 3.4.2.1.7 Trusses.)

9.11 INTERIOR CHART

ITEM
The area or item inspected.

GENERAL RATING
The inspector's grade for the interior:

E   EXCELLENT, above average, new or like new. (i.e. New windows in an older house.)

A   AVERAGE, in typical condition for its age, showing normal wear and tear. (e.g. five year old windows looking 5 years old and a 5 year old house.)

C   BELOW AVERAGE, prematurely aged, showing heavy or excess wear and tear, or delayed maintenance. Perhaps showing minor (curable) defects. (e.g. five year old windows showing the wear and tear or age characteristics of 10 year old windows.)

F   SUBSTANDARD, failed, or reaching the end of its life expectancy. Any further service, even with repairs, should be considered a gift.

OBSERVATIONS
The inspector writes observations of conditions affecting the Interior. More than one item can be marked as the interior may exhibit more than one symptom or problem. Some items are part of the normal aging process and do not require correction. Other items require either maintenance or repair if the interior is to reach the full potential or life expectancy. Read the observation reference written beside each item. The inspector may use the observations in 9.10 to note the conditions seen. e.g. 4, 5 in the Observations column of the Walls line indicate the walls are stained and cracked. (See 9.10.4 Stained and 9.10.5 Cracked.)

SUGGESTIONS

The inspector may write suggestions or explanations about each item listed in the chart.

APPROXIMATE COST:

The cost estimates quoted are estimates based upon the inspector's judgment or a range of prices available in the area. Individual bids from contractors can vary substantially from these ranges depending on the quality of the work, the circumstances, and the contractors submitting bids.

GLOSSARY

Alligatoring	Extensive surface cracking in a pattern looking like an alligator hide.
Amateur Workmanship	The inspector notes workmanship of less than professional quality. Poor workmanship may constitute a major defect. The work may not serve the purpose intended and may require repair or replacement.
Approximately	(See Estimated)
Areaway	An open subsurface space around a basement doorway. Provides light, ventilation, and access.
Cement	A substance made of powdered lime and clay mixed with water and used to fasten stones and sand together to form concrete.
Comments	Additional information provided by the inspector.
Concrete	A mixture of stones, sand, cement, and water.
Coping	The upper surface of a wall or chimney. Seals against water penetration and shaped to shed water.
Efflorescence	A white powdery substance appearing on masonry wall surfaces. It is composed of soluble salts brought to the surface by water or moisture movement.
Estimated	Roughly, broadly from experience, not from calculations. Not to be taken as exact.
Estimated Annual Maintenance	A rough assumption of the cost of keeping the item or system in good repair on a yearly basis. Varies from owner to owner and house to house depending on your personal skills and contribution and the quality of the system or item. You should also budget for replacement. Read the **Preface** for more details.
Estimated Cost of Repairs	A rough assumption of the cost of returning or upgrading an item or system to proper condition. Repair costs vary widely with the quality of the repairs and from contractor to contractor. The estimated amount is only a guideline figure and may be correct only in "order of magnitude." If the estimate is $500.00 then neither $50.00 nor $5000.00 repair bids seem reasonable, but $250.00 to $1000.00 bids might be correct. Get actual bids from several reputable contractors before proceeding.

Fascia	A horizontal board nailed vertically to the ends of roof rafters; sometimes supports the gutter.
General	Widely, popularly extensively, or in a general way without reference to details, not specifically.
Grade	The surface of the earth.
Gray water	Waste water not containing sewage or fecal matter or food wastes. Waste water from bathing and laundry is gray water. Wastes from garbage disposers and toilets are not.
Limitations	Factors limiting the inspection. Read each section about limitations.
Mortar	A mixture of sand, water, and a binder used between courses of masonry. The binder is either lime or cement or both.
Natural	Behavior, operation, etc. conforming with the nature or innate character of the item or system.
Normal	Conforming with an accepted standard or model, corresponding to the median or average for type, appearance or function. i.e. Natural standard or regular.
Observations	These are conditions observed by the inspector affecting the system or material. Some are part of normal aging and others require immediate repair.
Operational	Bringing about the desired or appropriate action or response.
Parapet Wall	The part of the wall extending above the roof line.
Physical Damage	Harm or injury to an item or system. May influence function or life expectancy. May reflect abuse.
Pitch (Roof Pitch)	The slope of the roof stated as the amount the roof rises in the 12 feet. 4 in 12 roofs rise 4 feet for 12 feet horizontally.
Pointing	Mortar between courses of masonry.
Primary windows	The most numerous or dominant type.
Proper	Specially adapted or suitable to a specific purpose or specific condition, (appropriate) or conforming to an accepted standard or of good usage (correct) of good or fine quality.
Properly	In a proper manner.

Roof	The top of the house. Used broadly to include the roofing, flashing, sheeting, substructure, gutters, and roof attachments.
Roofing	The covering of the roof. The part intended to keep the water from damaging the rest.
Satisfactory	Fulfilling the requirements for the system or item.
Sheathing or sheeting	The structural covering, usually wood boards or plywood, over a building's exterior studs or rafters. Nonstructural sheeting may be wood fiber composition materials or foam.
Soffit	The visible underside of a roof overhang or eave.
Tell Tale	A hint or clue. A visible trace or evidence of a hidden or disguised condition or problem.
Tuck pointing	Inserting mortar between courses of masonry.
Typical	The inspector feels they have seen as much of the system as they normally see.
Wear and Tear	Loss or damage resulting from use.

IMPROVEMENT COST AND REPAIRS

ROOF

Add gutters (aluminum or galvanized)	$200 min or $2.00 - 3.00 linear feet
Install asphalt shingles (nail-over)	$60.00 - 100.00/square
Install asphalt shingles (tear-off)	$90.00 - 130.00/square
Install four ply built-up roof	$250.00 - 400.00/square
Install single membrane roof	$400.00 - 600.00/square
Add a skylight	$300.00 - 600.00
Repair a slate roof or tile roof	$35.00/slate
Repair flashing leak	$50.00 and up

ADD VENTILATION

Vent ridge	$15.00 - 20.00 linear ft.
Soffit Vents	$20.00 - 30.00 each
Replace vent collar	$35.00 - 50.00
Foundation vents	$35.00 - 65.00 each

EXTERIOR

Repaint exterior wood siding	$50.00 - 75.00/sq. ft.
Repoint mortar	$2.50 - 5.00/sq. ft.
Remove and replace concrete slab	$5.00/sq. ft.
Replace a window	$200.00 - 400.00
Replace single pane glass	$10.00 - 15.00/pane + trip charge
Replace fogged thermal pane glass up to replacement of door or window	$50.00 or $10.00 - 15.00/sq. ft.
Replace fogged door panel (may be wise to replace complete door system)	$200.00 - 300.00 each
Replace rotting bandboard between the house and deck	$25.00 - 50.00 linear foot
Repair masonry steps	$25.00 - 50.00 per tread

FOUNDATION/BASEMENT/STRUCTURE

Replace rotted wood deck	$12.00 - 15.00/sq. ft. and up
Replace rotted or damaged joist	$50.00 - 75.00 each
Repair water damaged floor	$10.00 - 20.00 per sq. foot
Underpin sagging joist	$100.00/pier + 25.00 per ft. of beam
Install vapor barrier on the grade of the crawl space	$100.00 - 200.00
Regrade exterior to promote positive drainage	$400.00 and up
Install swale	$3.00 - 5.00 per linear foot

Install drainage leaders for downspouts	$2.50 - 5.00 per linear foot
Install interior subslab drainage	$3000.00 up

PLUMBING

Install 40 gal. hot water heater	$350.00 - 450.00
Reinstall commode to cure wax ring failure	$50.00 - 75.00
Repair/Replace trap or drain assembly	$35.00 - 75.00
Repair/Replace leaking faucet	$35.00 replacement of faucet
Cure simple leak	$50.00 - 75.00 (Service call)
Replace a commode	$200.00 and up
Replace water heater pressure relief valve	$40.00 - 75.00
Replace thermostat or element in hot water heater	$50.00 - 75.00

ELECTRICAL

Replace fuses	$5.00 each + service call
Upgrade from fuses to breakers	$750.00 - 1500.00
Upsize electrical service	$750.00 - 1500.00
Replace GFCI Breaker or outlet	$75.00 - 100.00
Add GFCI Branch	$75.00 - 300.00
Replace smoke detector	$75.00 - 100.00
Install Hardwired smoke detector	$100.00 - 200.00

Replace/Repair damaged switch or receptacle	$35.00 - 50.00
Upgrade system to eliminate knob & tubing wiring (considered unsafe)	$2.00 - 3.00/sq.ft. of house
Add circuit for appliances (dryer, etc.)	$100.00 and up
Correct reversed polarity	$35.00 min. + 7.50 each

HEATING

Add Freon™ to heat pump or A.C.	$50.00 - 75.00 + 5.00/lb. of Freon™
Clean and service, gas or oil furnace/boiler	$75.00 - 150.00
Repair/Replace burner assembly	$250.00 - 400.00
Replace circulator	$200.00 - 400.00
Replace filler valve or control	$75.00 and up
Replace gas or oil furnace	$1500.00 - 2500.00
Replace boiler	$1750.00 - 3000.00
Remove asbestos	$15.00 - 20.00/linear foot, $1000.00 minimal
Replace heat pump compressor	$750.00 - 1250.00
Sweep fireplace or flue	$75.00 - 150.00
Repair chimney coping or cap	$75.00 - 150.00
Install rain cap	$50.00 - 75.00
Line an unlined flue	$1000.00 - 2000.00
Repoint firebrick lining in fireplace	$100.00 - 300.00

AIR CONDITIONING

Add Freon	$50.00 - 75.00 + 5.00/lb. of Freon™
Clean coil	$75.00 - 300.00
Replace compressor	$750.00 - 1250.00
Clear condensate drain	$50.00 - 75.00
Replace existing system	$1500.00 - 2500.00
Install proper insulation/ vapor barrier to duct work	$300 and up

INSULATION

Reinstall fallen insulation	$50.00 plus 35.00/hr.

INTERIOR & APPLIANCES

Repair/Replace range burner or oven element	$50.00 - 100.00
Replace disposer	$150.00 - 200.00
Replace cooktop	$250.00 - 400.00 and up
Replace dishwasher	$400.00 - 600.00 and up
Replace sheet vinyl	$12.50 and up/sq. yard
Repair cracked or damaged drywall	$100.00 plus 5.00/linear or sq. foot
Refinish damaged wood floors	$ .60 sq. ft. and up

ACKNOWLEDGEMENTS

Diagram 1.10.15 d & 1.6 d

New Life For Old Dwellings,
(U.S. Department of Agriculture,
1975 rpt.) p. 43 & 73.

Diagram 1.7.5 d, 6.11 d & 2.11.26 d

Simple Home Repairs... Outside,
(U.S. Department of Agriculture,
1978 rpt.) p. 13, 23, & 27.

Diagram 3.6.1 d

Moisture & Home Energy
Conservation, (U.S. Department
of Energy, 1983) p. 24.

Diagram 3.7 d

Drainage Around Your Home,
(U.S. Department of Agriculture, 1975).

Diagram 2.3.1 d & 2.3.25 d

Preservation Briefs: 2
Repointing Mortar Joints In
Historic Brick Building, (U.S.
Department of the Interior,
1980) p. 4 & 5.

Diagram 1.4

Carpenter, (U.S. Department
of the Army, 1960) p. 8-1.

NOTES

NOTES

NOTES